D0504156

Jutland 1916:
Twelve hours to win the War

Jutland 1916: Twelve hours to win the War

Angus Konstam

Aurum
Press

Quarto is the authority on a wide range of topics.
Quarto educates, entertains and enriches the lives of
our readers—enthusiasts and lovers of hands-on living.
www.QuartoKnows.com

First published in Great Britain in 2016 by Aurum Press Limited
74–77 White Lion Street
Islington
London
N1 9PF
www.aurumpress.co.uk

Copyright © Angus Konstam

Maps by Nick Buxey

Angus Konstam has asserted his moral right to be identified as the Author of this
Work in accordance with the Copyright Designs and Patents Act 1988.

All rights reserved. No part of this book may be reproduced or utilised in any
form or by any means, electronic or mechanical, including photocopying,
recording or by any information storage and retrieval system,
without permission in writing from Aurum Press.

Every effort has been made to trace the copyright holders of material quoted in
this book. If application is made in writing to the publisher, any omissions
will be included in future editions.

A catalogue record for this book is available from the British Library.

ISBN 9781781312889

eBook ISBN 9781781316160

2016 2018 2020 2019 2017

1 3 5 7 9 10 8 6 4 2

Typeset in Dante by SX Composing DTP, Rayleigh, Essex
Printed and bound by CPI Group (UK) Ltd, Croydon, CR0 4YY

© (c) Erich Lessing / lessingimages.com 5 (top); © National Maritime Museum, Greenwich,
London 3 (top), 4 (bottom); © Stratford Archive 1 (top), 2, 3 (bottom), 4 (top), 5 (bottom),
6, 7, 8 (bottom); © Sueddeutsche Zeitung Photo / Alamy Stock Photo 1 (bottom); ©
ullstein bild via Getty Images 8 (top).

Front Cover: German dreadnoughts at sea.
Back Cover: "Boy" Cornwell,standing at his post on board HMS Chester.

Contents

Preface

Jutland is an enigma. It was a battle that both sides claimed to win – but one in which there was no easy way to tell the victor from the vanquished. It is almost as if the mist which cloaked the North Sea that day also obscured the truth of what actually happened there. A century later, things have become a little clearer. While none of the sailors who took part are still around to tell us their story, many of them wrote about their experiences, and so there is no shortage of first-hand accounts. In fact, there are probably too many – a lot of the accounts contradict each other, or clearly get things wrong. That is hardly surprising – the battle was a long and complex one and no one eyewitness could have seen everything. We also have a wealth of other more official records, and recently the wrecks of many of the warships that were sunk at Jutland have been found and examined. The mist has begun to lift.

I first heard of the battle as a child. Growing up in Orkney, within sight of the Grand Fleet's great wartime anchorage, you couldn't help being fascinated by the notion that Scapa Flow was once filled with warships – and that in May 1916 they steamed out of this vast and remote anchorage to do battle. I read about the battle as a youngster, and I was enthralled by the tales of lines of dreadnoughts locked in combat, or of swarms of destroyers racing into the attack. To me there was no doubt Britain had won. After all, tangible evidence of Germany's defeat lay within view of my bedroom window. It overlooked the spot where the German High Seas Fleet was interned after its surrender, and where, a year later, the German sailors scuttled the whole fleet rather than let it fall into Allied hands. Later, I even dived on the three German dread-noughts which still lie there – a rusting underwater monument to Germany's bid to wrest control of the seas from Britain. All three fought at Jutland.

Thanks to my Orkney roots I was also more painfully aware of two other Jutland veterans which lie in Scapa Flow. In 1917, the dreadnought *Vanguard* blew up at her moorings, the victim of an accidental magazine explosion. Her remains still lie scattered across the seabed. Then there was the *Royal Oak*, sunk almost within sight of my bedroom window, taking 834 of her crew down with her. She survived Jutland, only to fall prey to a German U-Boat while anchored in Scapa Flow in 1939, at the start of another war. Later I joined the Royal Navy, which paid me through university, and allowed me to indulge my growing passion for naval history. My few years in the Navy gave me a little insight into what life might have been like for the sailors who fought at Jutland, although their navy was very different from mine. The memory of these five shipwrecks never left me, though, nor my thoughts about what they represented.

Today, the era of the dreadnought seems almost a long-forgotten memory. The Royal Navy is scarcely a shadow of what it was a century ago, at the height of Britain's naval power. The summit of imperial power, too, as navy and empire were inextricably linked. What bound them together was 'seapower' – and Jutland was all about that all-important asset. Britain relied on control of the seas, and without the fleet her imperial power would have crumbled like a pile of dead leaves. The real arbiter of seapower was the battle fleet – the nation's force of dreadnoughts. Today, these great steel leviathans might look like something from some turn-of-the-century 'Steampunk' fantasy, but they represented the industrial and technological might of their age. Whether British or German, these ships combined a majestic elegance with a destructive power greater than any warship that had come before.

My fascination with these great ships never waned – quite the reverse. The more I read about them, and their one great test – the more I became fascinated by Jutland. Whole libraries of books have been written about the battle – some favouring one side, some the other, while further volumes have analysed the fighting in rivet-counting detail. Ever since the fleets returned home arguments have raged over just about every aspect of the battle, from the design of the ships, the way they were employed and the tactics used, to the finer technical aspects of the rival fire-control systems. Both Jellicoe and Scheer have had their share of criticism, as have Hipper and Beatty. The more I studied all this, the more I felt my own views changing. I began to feel a growing respect for Jellicoe and Scheer, who had to deal with new factors like torpedoes, submarines, aircraft and radio, while fighting a battle with untried ships and guns. I tip my hat to them.

Above all, I felt that Jutland was a battle that is as poorly understood now as it was a century ago. Many see it as indecisive – a battle that achieved absolutely nothing and decided even less. Others view it as a British victory, as her naval dominance remained absolute, the Germans had scuttled back into port, and after Jutland they seemed reluctant to emerge from it again. A few even claim the Germans won, citing the comparative losses of ships and men. The casualties of course, paled into insignificance when the bloodletting at the Somme began a month later. The Somme though, was indecisive – despite over 1,000000 casualties, the carnage did nothing to end the war. By contrast Jutland, where casualties were less than one per cent of this, ultimately did more to ensure German defeat than any amount of deaths on the Western Front. Jutland, after all, was less about winning than losing – the laurels of victory were sweet, but defeat at sea was tantamount to losing the war. That is why Jutland was arguably one of the most decisive battles of the First World War, and why, a century later, it deserves to be better understood.

Angus Konstam
Edinburgh 2016

Prologue

It was just after 4 p.m. on the afternoon of 31 May 1916, and British and German battlecruisers were locked in battle. This was not their baptism of fire – they had met before – but this clash was different. The fight was on a larger scale, it was more frenetic, and it was certainly more deadly. Nobody is alive today who was there that afternoon, but the drama, the excitement and the fear of the moment is still palpable – captured in the writing of those who were present. Many felt a surge of pride watching these great warships steam into action. Others were too busy doing their job; loading the guns, calculating trajectories and checking the ever-shortening ranges. Others were gripped by the very rational fear that the next enemy shell was heading directly towards them. All though, would have understood that they were experiencing the most important few moments of their lives. For all too many those moments would also be their last.

A battlecruiser was a new kind of warship – one that combined the deadly firepower of a battleship with the speed and elegance of a cruiser. For naval architects, the balance between the 'holy trinity' of firepower, speed and protection was all important. In battlecruisers though, especially British ones, armour had been sacrificed to make the ships as fast and deadly as possible. Jutland would be the ultimate test of this radical and lopsided design. Eleven of these great, powerful but vulnerable warships were now ranged against each other, spitting great bursts of flame as their guns hurled huge shells at the enemy. Six British battlecruisers were pitted against five German ones in a deadly duel.

A single hit by a shell from any one of these could spell disaster for a ship and her crew. In a few moments, a shell would do exactly that.

On their respective flagships *Lion* and *Lützow*, Vice-Admiral Sir David Beatty and Vice-Admiral Franz Hipper watched the battle with a studied air of detachment. They'd fought this duel before, and this time both men thought they had the measure of their opponent. They also felt that they had a secret advantage. They each knew that somewhere behind them a fleet of dreadnoughts was racing up to support them. Neither though, was aware that the enemy dreadnoughts were at sea. This would be no mere skirmish. It was merely the start of the long-awaited day of reckoning, the one the Germans simply called *Der Tag* ('The Day'). The war at sea could be won – or lost – that very afternoon. For nearly two years the two great fleets had either stayed in port, or tried in vain to lure their foes into battle. Now though, all this waiting was over. First, the rival battlecruisers would fight their duel to the death. Then the battle fleet would arrive and overwhelm what remained of the enemy.

The battle had been raging for twelve minutes by now, and both sides had found their range, and were starting to pound the enemy. Firing big 12-inch guns at battlecruisers has been likened to hitting walnuts with hammers. In the case of the British, the walnuts had particularly thin shells. Already hits had been scored, but none of them had proved a telling blow. Five minutes before, at 3.55 p.m., on the British battlecruiser *Tiger* a main gun turret had been knocked out, but casualties were light, and within a few minutes the guns would be back in action. Far more serious was the hit to the German battlecruiser *Seydlitz*. Her 'C' turret was destroyed, and most of its crew were killed – incinerated in the explosion. At 4 p.m. a German shell had done the same to 'Q' turret on Beatty's flagship *Lion*. The turret was ripped open, its crew were killed or wounded, and only luck had stopped the flash fire from the explosion reaching the magazines. That would have been the end for the *Lion*, and for Beatty.

The British and German battlecruisers were on parallel courses, about seven miles apart. While the ships ahead of them were exchanging salvos, the two ships at the end of each line, the British *Indefatigable* and the German *Von der Tann*, had been fighting their own private duel, trading salvos with each other. Neither had scored a hit – until now. A little after 4 p.m. *Indefatigable* was straddled by a salvo of 11-inch shells, the shell splashes falling all around her. On the *Von der Tann* the Gunnery Officer Commander Marholz peered through his binoculars, and saw that he had scored a hit on the British ship's stern. High up on the *Indefatigable*'s foremast, Leading Signalman Charlie Falmer was busy untangling some signal flags, and so he had a grandstand view of the battle, and of the enemy's first hit. He was still there two minutes later when the *Von der Tann*'s shells struck again.

This fresh salvo from the *Von der Tann* descended around the *Indefatigable*, and two shells struck the ship. They fell behind Falmer's perch on the foremast, landing between the mainmast and 'X' turret. Just ahead of the *Indefatigable* was the battlecruiser *New Zealand*, and on her bridge Lieutenant Commander Lovett-Cameron looked astern in time to see the explosion. Then he noticed the ship was veering off to port; 'We were altering course at the time, and it seemed as if her steering was damaged, as she didn't follow round in our wake.' It was clear that something was wrong. Standing next to Lovett-Cameron, Rear-Admiral William Pakenham also saw the hit; 'Two or three shells falling together hit the *Indefatigable* about the outer edge of the upper deck, in line with 'X' turret. A small explosion followed and she swung out of the line, sinking by the stern.' To him, it looked like a mortal wound. As he watched, the *Indefatigable* was struck again.

This time the German salvo landed around the battlecruiser's bows, and two shells struck 'A' turret. A mile away, on the German destroyer *B-98*, observers remember an explosion, and then a huge column of flame shot skyward. On the *Von der Tann*, Marholtz also saw smoke and flames rise up as high as the *Indefatigable*'s foremast. On the mast itself, Falmer watched as his own ship was torn apart beneath him. 'There was a terrific explosion aboard the ship – the magazines went. I saw the guns go up in the air just like matchsticks – 12-inch guns they were – bodies and everything.' The ship then began rolling over. On the *New Zealand*, a horrified Lovett-Campbell watched the ship blow up; 'The main explosion started with sheets of flame, followed immediately by a dense, dark cloud of smoke which obscured the ship from view. All sorts of stuff was blown into the air, a 50-foot picket boat being blown up about 200 feet, apparently intact although upside down.'

Indefatigable's crew never stood a chance. That morning 1,019 men and boys had sailed into action on board the ship. There were only two survivors. One of them was Charles Falmer. He was thrown clear of the ship, and so avoided being sucked under as she sank. He was badly dazed though, but somehow he survived, floating in the freezing oil-covered water for almost five hours before he was rescued by a German destroyer. The only other survivor, an Able Seaman, had also been in the foremast when the ship sank. Everyone else perished.

An entire ship's company had been wiped out in an instant, blown apart if they were lucky, or else trapped deep in the sinking wreckage as the cold sea flooded in. The duel between the battlecruisers had been raging for just fifteen minutes, and already more than a thousand men were dead. The great sea battle though, would rage on intermittently for another twelve hours. The ripping apart of the *Indefatigable* merely heralded the start of the great clash of steel-clad leviathans that we now call the Battle of Jutland.

PART I

The Inevitable Showdown

I

The First Dreadnought

The path that led to Jutland began at a great oak desk in the British Admiralty. It stood on a patterned burgundy carpet, dominating the office of the First Sea Lord, Admiral of the Fleet Sir John Fisher. The room's high windows overlooked Whitehall, the very heart of imperial government, while the other walls bore paintings of former great admirals, and an oil painting of Trafalgar, the greatest victory of Britain's greatest naval hero, Horatio Nelson. It was from this desk, covered in neatly stacked bundles of reports and letters, that Fisher imposed his will upon Britain's Senior Service, dragging it into the modern age of steam, steel and firepower. Some serving officers opposed what amounted to a revolution in naval thought and substance, and a few crusty retired admirals wrote disapproving letters to *The Times*. Most though, realised that change was vital if Great Britain was to retain its edge over potential rivals, the naval supremacy which had been won at Trafalgar in 1805. A century later, John Fisher was fighting just as hard to keep it.

'Jacky'

To his contemporaries, John Arbuthnot Fisher (1841–1920) was more a force of nature than a human being. For his entire naval life – his service spanning more than half a century – he had been a staunch advocate of reform, modernisation and the embracement of new technology. He rejected a navy where spit and polish were deemed more important than fighting efficiency, and instead he wanted a fleet which was not just ready and able to fight, but would do so better, faster and at a greater range than its enemies. Naturally, this provoked conflict with the more reactionary elements in the service, but as Fisher rose to prominence he was able to ride roughshod over his opponents. On 21st October 1904, the ninety-ninth anniversary of Trafalgar, Fisher became First Sea Lord, the professional head of the Royal Navy. From that moment on, he set about dragging the service into the modern age.

Fisher was a man with many facets. He disliked organised sports, loved to dance, and was extremely accomplished at it. At sea, when no women were available, he still organised dances on board ship. He was a religious man, who, when ashore, was apt to attend several sermons every Sunday. In fact, the Dean of Westminster once warned him against 'spiritual indigestion'. Fisher never suffered fools, and could ruin the careers of officers he thought were unprofessional. He developed a reputation as something of a tyrant. The rest of the world called him 'Jacky', although never to his face – it infuriated him – and he ruled his naval world with a rod of iron.

However Fisher could also be extremely charming; first Queen Victoria and then Edward VII thought the world of him, as did many leading politicians and the more progressive among Britain's naval officers. More conventional officers were shocked by the breadth of his reforms, his blunt language and his ruthless trampling of anyone who stood in his way. Now, as the new professional head of the Navy, his control was virtually absolute, save for the largely benign governing forces of Parliament and the Treasury. Fisher was free to shape the Navy as he liked.

Most of his life had been building up to the moment, and the challenge. He was born in Ceylon (now Sri Lanka), the first-born son of a pretty Englishwoman and a young love-struck captain in the 78th Highlanders. His father left the army to become a coffee planter, and when that failed he became a poorly paid colonial policeman. At the age of six, 'little Jack' was sent home to live with his equally penniless grandfather in London, and at thirteen he joined the Royal Navy. In July 1854, Fisher proved his suitability for naval service by writing out the Lord's Prayer, drinking a glass of sherry and jumping naked over a chair. He became a cadet, and that summer he joined his first seagoing ship.

HMS *Calcutta* was a wooden-hulled sail-powered ship-of-the-line, a vessel rendered obsolete by the coming of steam. Fisher later recalled;

'The day I joined as a little boy I saw eight men flogged, and I fainted at the sight.' Fisher thrived though, although he was prone to seasickness, a trait he shared with Nelson. In the summer of 1855 the *Calcutta* sailed off to fight the foe. Britain was at war with Russia, and so *Calcutta* was sent to the Baltic to reinforce Admiral Dundas's squadron there. Unfortunately, Napier regarded the sailing man-of-war as a liability, and sent her home.

In July 1856, Fisher became a midshipman, and joined the steam-powered gunboat *Highflyer*, which was bound for Chinese waters. So began the five years that would be the making of him. By the time *Highflyer* arrived, Britain was at war with the Chinese emperor. Despite its name, the Second Opium War (1856–60) was fought to confirm Europe's trading monopoly with China; the drug the British exported from India to China was merely an important trading commodity. It was here, during this unnecessary little war, that Fisher would first see action. A small skirmish against pirates off Canton, though, did little to prepare him for his real baptism of fire.

In June 1859, *Highflyer* joined a British squadron which was lying off the mouth of the Pei-ho (now the Hai) River, which led to Peking (now Beijing). The river mouth was guarded by the Taku Forts, a sprawling series of well-defended earthworks, and Fisher joined the assault on them. The British landing parties soon became pinned down in the mud flats in front of the defences. Sailors were killed or maimed all around Fisher as he crouched in the mud. Then the Chinese launched fire-bombs – naphtha – which burned men alive in front of their shipmates. Fisher later wrote; 'I never smelt such a horrid smell in my life.' The assault was abandoned, and the sailors withdrew under cover of darkness.

One of those injured at the Taku Forts was Captain Charles Shadwell of the *Highflyer*. He had been something of a father figure to the teenager, and when his wounds caused him to be sent back to England, Fisher was sorry to see him go. Before they parted, Shadwell gave Fisher his cufflinks, a keepsake Fisher still wore and treasured more than half a century later. He also spoke well of his young protégé, and so the following spring Fisher was given an acting promotion to lieutenant, and sent to another gunboat in Chinese waters, HMS *Furious*. Fisher later described this paddle-wheeler as 'a horrid old tub', and her commander as 'Satanic', but Captain Jones approved of his new young officer. When the ship paid off in Portsmouth the following year, Jones said of Fisher; 'As a sailor, an officer, a navigator and a gentleman I cannot praise him too highly.' To a young mariner it is hard to imagine a greater accolade.

Having easily passed his exams to confirm his lieutenancy, Fisher was assigned to the Navy's gunnery school, HMS *Excellent*. She might have been a mere wooden hulk moored in Portsmouth Harbour, but in 1861 *Excellent* was the hub of naval research into gunnery, the arbiter of victory at sea. It was here that Fisher really began to make his mark. This was an exciting time for a progressive naval officer. The last few decades had seen the supremacy of steam-power over sail confirmed, and the emergence of the ironclad, with its superior protection of iron or steel plates. Young officers like Fisher read about the latest technological developments, and followed the naval clashes of the American Civil War, the Prusso–Danish War and the Italian War of Independence. Fisher embraced technological change with fervour, becoming a passionate advocate of gunnery and then a staunch promoter of the torpedo. From now on, Fisher would be closely associated with reform, innovation and fighting efficiency.

A Force for Change

Fisher's posting on *Excellent* was followed by a spell as gunnery officer of HMS *Warrior* – the navy's first ironclad, then another posting to the gunnery school, this time as an instructor, and then as a professional evaluator of a new naval weapon – the torpedo. In between his duties he also found time to court and marry Frances Katherine Delves Broughton, a clergyman's daughter, beginning a happy union that served as a bedrock for Fisher during his high-flying career. In fact, the marriage was so loving that a subsequent spell at sea as First Lieutenant of HMS *Ocean* in Hong Kong was an enforced separation which Fisher found hard to bear. He applied himself though; thanks to Fisher the ironclad was fitted with an electrical system allowing all her guns to be fired at once, the first ship in the fleet to adopt this innovation.

Fisher returned to *Excellent* in 1872, and one of the first things he did was to hive off the torpedo school, establishing it in another floating hulk, HMS *Vernon*. Under Fisher, these two technical schools would produce a series of enterprising and gifted officers, including John

Jellicoe, and Percy Scott, who would become the navy's leading advocate of gunnery. Fisher became a captain in 1874, and was given command of increasingly prestigious ships, culminating in HMS *Inflexible* – the most powerful warship in the fleet. She looked ungainly, but with four enormous muzzle-loading guns *Inflexible* packed a real punch. In 1881, Fisher became her first captain, and in July 1882 he and his ship took part in the bombardment of Alexandria – the navy's largest action since the Crimean War. The eyes of the country were watching, and Captain Fisher became a naval celebrity.

Afterwards, once British landing parties secured the port, Fisher had a train armoured, and used this to defend the city. His spell ashore won him acclaim in the British press, but it almost killed him. He contracted malaria and dysentery, and was invalided home. At one stage it was felt he would die before he reached the naval hospital in Malta, but Fisher survived, and on his return home was invited by no less than Queen Victoria to convalesce at her summer residence, Osborne House. It was clear that Captain Fisher's star was in the ascendant. Some of his critics – a growing band – ascribed the resulting yellow tinge of his skin to Oriental ancestry, and the German Kaiser would later describe him as 'half-Asiatic'. The rising star of the navy paid no heed.

Fisher was fit for duty again in April 1883, when he returned to *Excellent*, this time as its commanding officer. Other important duties followed – as the Director of Naval Ordnance, supervising the design of the navy's guns, then after his promotion to flag rank in 1890, Rear-Admiral Fisher became the new Superintendant of Portsmouth Dockyard. It was a key appointment. During his brief tenure there he supervised the building of a new battleship, the *Royal Sovereign*, which was completed in record time. This experience served as a blueprint for his own fast-tracked building programme fourteen years later. Two years later Fisher became the Third Sea Lord, responsible for the design and building of British warships. He became a Vice-Admiral in 1896, and the following year he returned to sea as commander of the North Atlantic and West Indies Station. Under Fisher, what was once considered a backwater station soon became the bustling epicentre of fleet training.

Success there was rewarded with a plum appointment, the command of the Mediterranean Fleet. What he began in American waters he brought to fruition in those around Malta. Fisher believed that the fleet should be permanently ready for war, and he brooked no slackness or resistance in his drive for efficiency. Training exercises became commonplace, along with gunnery competitions and professional lectures. He maintained this frenzied level of activity until the summer of 1902, when he returned to London as a full Admiral to serve as the Second Sea Lord, in charge of personnel and training. His time in the Mediterranean was not forgotten.

The civil service mandarin Lord Hankey, then a Royal Marine officer, described the Fisher whirlwind; 'It is difficult for anyone who had not lived under the previous regime to realize what a change Fisher brought about in the Mediterranean Fleet. Before his arrival, the topics and arguments of the officers' messes were mainly confined to such matters as the cleaning of paint and brass work . . . These were forgotten and replaced by incessant controversies on tactics, strategy, gunnery, torpedo warfare, blockade, etc. It was a veritable renaissance and affected every officer in the Navy.'

As Second Sea Lord, Fisher continued to shake things up, giving engineering officers an equal status to seamen ones, and even trying to merge the two groups into one. This proved a step too far, but he managed to overhaul officer selection and training; jumping naked over chairs was replaced by interviews, and he also founded the Britannia Royal Naval College at Dartmouth, where aspiring midshipmen still go to learn their trade. The following year Fisher completed that last stepping stone to the naval throne as Commander-in-Chief, Portsmouth, the very heart of the seagoing fleet. By now it was inevitable that Fisher would become the new First Sea Lord, and so in May 1904 the politician Lord Selbourne, First Lord of the Admiralty, travelled to Portsmouth to offer him the position. So it was that on Trafalgar Day 1904 'Jacky' Fisher became the autocratic head of the Royal Navy.

Fisher held the office from October 1904 until January 1910, just over six years that proved vital to Britain and the Royal Navy, and which set in motion a train of events that, with the benefit of hindsight, led directly to the Battle of Jutland. His reforms during this period transformed the Navy. Despite vociferous opposition, he scrapped the most obsolete ships in the fleet, particularly the Victorian gunboats he deemed 'too weak to fight, too slow to run'. The money saved and the thousands of crew freed for other duties were soon used to man the new battleships which would become the core of Fisher's navy. He reorganised the fleet reserve so it was permanently ready for active service, he encouraged thorough training and proficiency, and he and Admiral Percy Scott set about improving the generally poor standards of naval gunnery. Above all though, he created the first modern battleship.

The Big Gun Battleship

During previous decades, considerable advances had been made in naval gunnery and warship design. Steam propulsion, armoured hulls, breech-loading guns and armour-piercing shells had all transformed the appearance and fighting abilities of capital ships (as the Navy's battleships were known). At the time Fisher became First Sea Lord, most sea-going battleships in the world's navies were designed in a similar way – the differences between them were relatively minor ones of scale or weaponry. Almost all of them carried a main armament of four heavy guns mounted in two twin turrets. In the Royal Navy, the most modern of these were the eight battleships of the King Edward VII class, all of which were still being built when Fisher assumed control of the Navy.

There was no doubt that the *King Edward VII* and her sisters were majestic-looking warships. They had a grace and symmetry to them, as was expected of battleships designed by Sir William White, the Director of Naval Construction. They also had an impressive armament by the standards of their day – four 12-inch, four 9.2-inch and ten 6-inch guns apiece. In theory this made them some of the most powerful battleships afloat. Unfortunately, by the time *King Edward VII* entered service in early 1905, she was already obsolete. This obsolescence was the work of Fisher, who was now free to pursue his dream of a 'big gun battleship'. That meant that instead of one with a polyglot assortment of guns of various calibres, their firepower consisted of main guns of a single calibre – and preferably as large as possible. This was the basic idea behind a ship that would turn the naval world on its head.

Fisher was lucky enough to have an ally who shared his enthusiasm for a big gun battleship. In 1902, Sir Philip Watts (1846–1926) succeeded Sir William White as the Director of Naval Construction. His first job was to oversee the eight King Edwards and nine other battleships designed by his predecessor which were still under construction. He also had to supervise the completion of two others built for the Chilean navy, but bought and commissioned by the Admiralty. Before Fisher's arrival, Watts had argued for the development of a big gun battleship, but encountered considerable resistance in the Admiralty. This was understandable, as there was little appetite for rendering the existing battle fleet prematurely obsolete. In other words, the ability to build a modern battleship was there, but the political will was not. Fisher would change all that.

In the meantime, Watts designed a pair of battleships of the Lord Nelson class, which reduced the number of main gun calibres down to just two. The result was a powerful hybrid and the last of the old type of battleships. After October 1904, Watts found a supporter in Fisher, and the two men set about designing a battleship which would be dramatically faster and better armed than anything that had gone before. Although Fisher formed a committee of highly experienced officers to determine the design of this new battleship, he and Watts were able to steer their deliberations along a path they had already determined. It was Fisher and Watts who were the true architects of the battleship design that would transform naval warfare.

Fisher and Watts favoured a battleship capable of carrying multiple turrets of big guns, with armour that was proof against other capital ships, and whose modern turbine-powered engines meant that she was faster and mechanically more reliable than her rivals. The two men were spurred on by developments in America and Japan, where naval designers were already working on similar ambitious projects such as the South Carolina and Satsuma classes of battleship. It was clear to Fisher that unless action was taken, the Royal Navy would lose its numerical and technological edge over its naval rivals. Reluctantly; the Admiralty agreed to commission the building of a new battleship designed by Watts. The result was HMS *Dreadnought*, a warship which would utterly break the mould.

What spurred the two men on were naval developments taking place on the far side of the world. In early 1905, the Japanese laid down the first of their two Satsuma class of battleships, which were planned as all big-gun battleships, mounting twelve 12-inch guns. Shortages of suitable barrels led these to be modified to a mix of four 12-inch and twelve 10-inch guns, but even this made them more powerful than Watt's two battleships of the Lord Nelson class. Then news reached the Admiralty that the United States Navy was about to commission the building of two big-gun battleships of their own – the South Carolina class – the first of which was to be laid down in late 1906. These would carry eight 12-inch guns in four turrets, two on the forecastle and two aft, with the rear turret raised up (or 'superimposed') over the front one. Britain was about to be left behind.

It was clear that any desire to maintain the naval status quo would soon become irrelevant. If the Royal Navy wanted to maintain its naval supremacy, then it had to compete with these two foreign powers. That meant it needed a big gun battleship of its own. It was exactly the spur Fisher and Watts needed. Armed with intelligence reports from America and Japan, they were able to force through their own plans, or rather those developed by Fisher's closely supervised design committee. The result was a battleship design which, while revolutionary in its concept, was the result of a broader evolution in warship design. The day of the big gun battleship had arrived – it was only that Fisher made sure it arrived in Britain first.

When it came to building this battleship, Fisher remembered his time in Portsmouth Dockyard and the way he had masterminded the building of the *Royal Sovereign* in record time. He would do the same again. The new battleship, which Fisher decided to call *Dreadnought*, was laid down in Portsmouth on 2 October 1905. The First Sea Lord was no slouch when it came to organisation. He had already stockpiled steel plates and other vital components, and made sure that *Dreadnought* received first priority when it came to materials, labour and resources. As a result, the battleship was ready for launching in just over four months. So, at noon on 10 February 1906, with Fisher standing beside him, after a first botched attempt, King Edward VII broke a bottle of Australian wine over the bows of the battleship, and cried; 'I christen you *Dreadnought*'. With that, as the Royal Marine band played the national anthem, the great ship glided down the slipway and into the cold waters of Portsmouth harbour.

Of course the launching of *Dreadnought* was only the start. She was brought alongside the dockyard again, and swarms of workmen returned on board to begin the process of fitting her out. Over 1,000 men worked almost twelve hours a day to finish the ship. The great steel plates of her armoured belt were bolted in place, her great Babcock and

Wilcox boilers were fitted, and then in May her turbines arrived. *Dreadnought*'s propulsion system was almost as revolutionary as her armament. All previous battleships used reciprocating steam engines to drive their propellers. Not *Dreadnought*. She used turbines – multiple steel disc-like blades mounted on a spindle which spun when high-pressure steam was blown over them. There was far less to go wrong than with a reciprocal engine, which involved many more moving parts and put a great strain on bearings and cylinders. Turbines were the future of marine propulsion, and both Fisher and Watts knew it.

The trouble was, turbines had never been fitted to large warships before, just to small torpedo boats. However, the great Cunard liners *Lusitania* and *Mauritania* were designed to use turbines, and Fisher saw no reason they could not be used in *Dreadnought*. The four immense turbines were manufactured by the Parson Marine Turbine Company of Tyneside, and were delivered to Portsmouth in May. Three months later, in August, they and the rest of her propulsion system was tested as *Dreadnought* lay in the dry dock. They worked perfectly. *Dreadnought* was therefore powered by a combination of coal-fired boilers and steam turbines, driving four great propellers that gave her a top speed of 21 knots – three knots faster than the *King Edward VII*. While this didn't seem like much, it made her the fastest battleship in the world.

In June, *Dreadnought*'s armament arrived. Fisher had cut corners and diverted the eight 12-inch guns and their turrets due to be mounted in the two Lord Nelson class battleships designed by Watts. This speeded up the completion of the more important *Dreadnought*. As a result, the new battleship was ready for her sea trials by October 1906 – a year and a day after she was laid down. It was a stupendous achievement, and the result was an even more incredible ship. Just over a fortnight later, she tested her main guns – eight of them being fired in a single broadside. Once more everything went smoothly, and the final fitting out was completed. So, on 11 December 1906, fourteen months after being laid down, HMS *Dreadnought* was commissioned into service with the Royal Navy. Incidentally, the two Japanese Satsuma class battleships took between four and five years to build, while *South Carolina* took over three.

Everything about *Dreadnought* was impressive. She was longer than previous battleships, and much more strongly constructed. She had to be, to accommodate her much larger armament, and to withstand the shock of her guns being fired. Instead of the four 12-inch guns carried on previous battleships, *Dreadnought* carried ten 12-inch guns in five twin turrets; one in her bow, one in her stern, one amidships and one each on either side of her forward superstructure. This meant she could fire eight guns to either side, and up to six guns ahead of her. Unlike earlier battleships though, the fire of these guns was directed centrally, using a fairly complex fire control system, which allowed the firing of coordinated and closely grouped salvos at the enemy. On paper she carried two and a half times the heavy armament of earlier battleships. In reality, her firepower was exponentially better, thanks to the quantity and potential accuracy of her salvos.

Put simply, after the arrival of *Dreadnought*, all previous battleship designs were rendered obsolete. These antediluvian battleships even included ones which were still being completed when *Dreadnought* entered service. However, they were soon given the collective and somewhat derisory name of 'pre-dreadnoughts'. In fact, the new battleship was so revolutionary that her very name gave rise to an entirely new kind of warship, 'the dreadnought'. A new naval age had dawned. The future of naval warfare clearly lay in the *Dreadnought*, and in great powerful naval titans like her.

2

Racing towards Armageddon

The *Dreadnought* may have been the most powerful warship in the world, but it was not without its critics. Future British Prime Minister David Lloyd George called her 'a piece of wanton and profligate ostentation'. From one perspective he was right – the coming of the dreadnought would cost Britain dear. By rendering Britain's enormous existing fleet obsolete, Fisher had virtually forced the country on a course of increased naval expenditure. Much has been made of the savings Fisher achieved during his time as First Sea Lord by cutting the costs of old obsolete ships and making sure money was well spent. This though, was mere small change in comparison to the expense of building a new fleet from scratch.

The coming of the dreadnought also levelled the playing field. All of a sudden Britain's powerful battle fleet now counted for naught, and her unquestioned control of the seas was no longer guaranteed. A single dreadnought could wreak havoc amongst her enemies, and a fleet of them would give their owners unquestioned naval domination. While Britain had 'stolen a march' on her rivals by building the first dreadnought, unless the country embarked on an immediate and costly shipbuilding programme, then one of her leading maritime rivals could build their own dreadnought fleet, and use it to wrest the mantle of seapower from the Royal Navy.

Fisher was well aware of this, and argued that the naval budget be modified to allow for the building of more dreadnoughts. While *Dreadnought* was still being completed, three similar vessels were approved, ships whose specifications would be virtually identical to the original. The first of these Bellerophon class dreadnoughts was laid down in Portsmouth on 3 December 1906, a week before *Dreadnought* herself was commissioned into service. In fact, she was built on the same slip. She would be the first of many, as Britain sought to keep ahead of the game. The danger posed by Britain's rivals embarking on their own dreadnought programme was clear. While Fisher had built *Dreadnought* as secretly as he could, other rival powers were well aware of her. After all, protocol demanded that Rear-Admiral Coerper, the German naval attaché in Britain was invited to the launching ceremony. His detailed report was on its way to Berlin in the next diplomatic bag.

The Kaiser's Navy

For decades, Britain had viewed France as her most likely opponent in any future war. The French navy was no match for its British counterpart, and a lack of political commitment in Paris and any coherence in naval strategy did little to help. This meant that French naval development was fitful at best, and a lack of resources meant that it could take ten years to build a new warship. That made it impossible for the French navy to keep up with technological changes, and so its ships were outdated and outclassed even before they entered service. One school of French naval thinking was to ignore battleships, and concentrate France's resources on building a fleet of torpedo boats and commerce raiders. Even that policy, though, suffered from a lack of commitment.

By 1900, though, there was a new kid on the block. Since its political emergence in the late seventeenth century, Prussia had developed into a state whose power centred around a powerful army. It had few naval pretentions. Even its military aspirations were relatively modest. The Prussian army had played its part in the defeat of the French at Leipzig and Waterloo, but the pan-European peace accord established in 1815 meant that it was not needed to fight external wars. Prussia's 'Iron Chancellor' Otto von Bismarck changed all that. He saw warfare as a vital extension of diplomacy, and so the highly proficient Prussian army was committed to three European conflicts; against the Danes in 1864; the Austrians in 1866; and the French in 1870–71. Not only did Prussia win these wars with comparative ease, but they also helped the unification of Germany into a single state.

In January 1871, the patchwork of little German states coalesced into a new German nation, with Wilhelm I of Prussia as its emperor (or 'Kaiser'). Bismarck became its chancellor, and he spent the next two decades using diplomacy rather than the army to safeguard this newly unified German state. He did this by forming alliances with neighbouring powers, a diplomatic game which largely involved preventing France and Russia from joining forces. During this period Germany also became an industrial and economic powerhouse. Although the country's industrial capacity would not match that of Britain, steelworks, gun foundries and engineering works meant that Germany now had the wherewithal to build a fleet if it wanted to.

In 1888 the German emperor died, and his son Friedrich succeeded him. He too was dead within a few months, the victim of throat cancer. So, in June 1888, his impetuous twenty nine-year-old son became the Emperor Wilhelm II. Relations between the new Kaiser and his chancellor deteriorated, as Wilhelm was more bullish than his grandfather and sought to pursue a more aggressive foreign policy. Above all, he wanted 'a place in the sun', a colonial empire similar to those of Britain or France.

Bismarck resigned in 1890, and from that point on the Kaiser was free to pursue his own diplomatic and military course. A *Punch* cartoon of the time captioned 'Dropping the Pilot' showed Bismarck being put ashore, leaving the Kaiser free to steer his own ship of state. It was a particularly apt metaphor, as, against Bismarck's advice, Wilhelm was determined to turn Germany into a maritime power.

Kaiser Wilhelm had close ties with the British royal family. His mother was Queen Victoria's eldest daughter, and Edward, Prince of Wales, the future King Edward VII, was her younger brother – and so Wilhelm's 'Uncle Bertie'. He visited his British relatives, and his enthusiasm for the sea was kindled by watching Royal Naval fleet reviews off Portsmouth, and attending regattas at Cowes. In 1894, he read Alfred Mahan's *The Influence of Sea Power upon History* (1890), and the American naval strategist's arguments in favour of seapower chimed with the Kaiser's vision of a Germany with both naval and colonial pretensions. With the help of Bismarck, his grandfather had moulded Germany into a leading European power. Now he, through the development of a navy, would turn it into a *Weltmacht* (world power).

Germany already had a navy of sorts. Prussia had maintained a small force for coastal protection, and it played its part in the brief German–Danish War of 1864. However, Austria-Hungary provided the largest contingent to the pan-German naval alliance created for the duration of the conflict. During the subsequent wars with Austria and France, the largely toothless Prussian fleet formed part of the *Norddeutsche Bundesmarine* (North German Confederation Navy), before emerging as the core of the new *Kaiserliche Marine* (Imperial Navy) in 1871. In 1869, a naval base had been established on the Jade Estuary, named Wilhelmshaven after the Prussian ruler. It and Kiel on the Baltic coast would become the main ports of his grandson's Imperial German Navy.

At the time of Wilhelm's accession in 1888, the German navy boasted a sizeable force of twelve ageing ironclads, all of which were of little fighting value. Still, the previous year the digging of the Kaiser Wilhelm (now the Kiel) Canal had begun, providing a secure link between Germany's two naval bases, Kiel and Wilhelmshaven. Wilhelm immediately began augmenting his small fleet. Within months of his coronation, a class of eight coastal defence battleships were ordered, based on plans first approved by Wilhelm's grandfather. The first of them, the *Siegfried*, was laid down in Kiel's Germaniawerft shipyard, but it would be five years before funds were set aside to build all eight vessels. In July 1888, Wilhelm appointed Vice-Admiral Alexander von Monts as head of the German Admiralty, and ordered him to draw up plans for a class of proper sea-going battleships.

Before he died in early 1889, Monts spent the winter persuading the reluctant politicians that the new battleships would replace the entire fleet of ageing ironclads. So, that spring, a very reluctant Reichstag approved the setting aside of sixty four million marks to build four of these new ships. The plans were finished that year, and in early 1890 all four of them – now designated the Brandenburg class – were laid down in shipyards in Kiel, Wilhelmshaven and Stettin, and would be commissioned three or four years later. This marked the real start of the modern German navy. By then the Kaiser Wilhelm Canal was open, an event viewed with consternation in the French press. For their part the British barely seemed to notice. That attitude, though, was about to change.

On the death of Monts, the Kaiser divided the German Admiralty into three departments. The *Reichsmarineamt* (Imperial Navy Office) was responsible for administration and funding, as well as providing a link between the Navy and the rest of the German government. A separate body, the *Marinekabinett* (Navy Cabinet), supervised naval staff, a task that had previously been undertaken by the Military Cabinet, which oversaw personnel in the German army. Finally, the *Kaiserliches Oberkommando der Marine* (Imperial Naval High Command) became the operational arm of the fleet. The Kaiser kept a close eye on his two administrative departments, and used the Navy Office to approve his increasingly ambitious plans. However, he left actual command of the fleet to the professionals. Following the death of Monts, Vice-Admiral Max von der Goltz was appointed Chief of the High Command, a new title, which in theory embraced all three departments. In more practical terms, though, he was the de-facto Commander-in-Chief of the Imperial Navy.

The next big tranche of naval funding came in 1895, when the Reichstag approved the setting aside of funds to build a new class of battleships, even larger than the Brandenburg class, which had just entered service. The four new battleships of the Kaiser class were better laid out than the Brandenburgs, but they still compared unfavourably to the latest more powerful capital ships in British, Russian or even French service. The trouble was, it almost seemed as if Germany's battleships had been designed by committee. This was understandable, as not only did the Navy's small design department lack experience, but they also had to cope with interference from the Kaiser, who adopted a 'hands-on' approach to battleship design. What the Navy needed was a coherent plan for the future, and a commander willing to implement it. Fortunately, Germany's naval saviour was waiting in the wings.

Tirpitz

Alfred von Tirpitz has been called the father of the Germany navy, and for good reason. In the summer of 1897, he arrived in Berlin to take up a new appointment as Secretary of the Navy Office. His previous job had been the command of Germany's East Asia Squadron, a small group of cruisers which were stationed in the Far East more for diplomatic reasons than anything else. During his long trip back from China to Germany, he drafted a document which would go a long way to setting Germany on a collision course with Britain. It established that, in naval terms, Britain posed the greatest threat to Germany. Any future naval war would be fought against the Royal Navy, and the battleground would be the North Sea. There should be no more piecemeal shipbuilding. Instead, Germany would concentrate its resources on building up a powerful battle fleet, capable of holding its own against the British. The Kaiser read the document, and approved its bold vision and its assumptions.

The architect of Germany's new aggressive naval policy had first entered the Prussian navy in 1865, the year after Prussia's victory over the Danes. During the Austro–Prussian War of 1866 and the Franco–Prussian War of 1870–71, Tirpitz served on a sail-powered gunboat, but saw no action. He frequently put in to British ports, and Tirpitz became an Anglophile, claiming once that he felt more at home in Portsmouth than he did in Kiel. He rose slowly through the ranks, and in 1878 he was placed in charge of the Torpedo Inspectorate, where, like Fisher, his task was to evaluate the new weapon. From there, he went on to develop torpedo boats to launch these weapons, which in turn led to his involvement in the re-evaluation of German naval tactics. Tirpitz was beginning to make his mark.

In 1888, Tirpitz, now a captain, was given command of a cruiser – a necessary step for further promotion. From there he went on to become Chief of Staff of the key Baltic Fleet, which he brought to a high state of efficiency by conducting frequent exercises, drills and mock battles. It was during an Imperial visit to Kiel that Tirpitz impressed the Kaiser with his belief in a powerful battle fleet. Tirpitz was asked to develop these ideas, and in early 1892 he presented Wilhelm with a detailed planning document, outlining the way he thought the fleet should develop. This dovetailed precisely with the Kaiser's own beliefs, and within months Tirpitz was promoted to Chief of the Naval Staff. Still, the hands of both men were tied, as a parsimonious Reichstag was unwilling to increase the naval budget.

In 1895, Tirpitz, now a Rear-Admiral, produced a plan to build a battleship squadron, as both he and the Kaiser were frustrated by the ad hoc approach to shipbuilding forced by a lack of resources. The following year the Reichstag slashed the naval budget by 17 per cent, and a frustrated Kaiser lost patience with both his parliament and his Navy Office. By that time Tirpitz was away in the Far East, commanding the

East Asia Squadron, but Wilhelm was in no doubt as to who he needed to fight the Navy's corner. Tirpitz was recalled.

As Secretary of the Navy Office, Rear-Admiral Tirpitz had to control both the Reichstag and the Kaiser. It was no easy task, but the admiral who had never heard a gun fired in anger proved a natural when it came to warfare in the political arena. He set out to win over the likes of the retired and ageing Bismarck, who still wielded considerable influence, as well as the leaders of political parties of every hue. He did the same with other German figures, from the minor kings of Bavaria and Saxony to the council leaders of Germany's ports, who were growing rich through a rise in German maritime trade. He slowly turned things around, creating broad support for a stronger navy for the defence of German trade and of German ports. As a result, in March 1898, the Reichstag passed Tirpitz's Navy Bill with a handsome majority.

The Kaiser and the admiral now had the money they needed. Two of the four Kaiser Friedrich III class battleships had already been built, but work on the remaining two had been postponed due to lack of funds. This was no longer a problem, and work began on them in Kiel and Elbing before the end of the summer. Next, Tirpitz approved the final plans for the first of his new battleships – the Wittelsbach class, and in 1899 these were laid down in Wilhelmshaven, Kiel and Elbing. As battleships went, these were unremarkable ships; like the Kaisers they carried a main armament of four 24 cm (9.6 in) guns, no match for the 12-inch gun battleships being produced in Britain at the same time. This was intentional; Tirpitz had no wish to antagonise the British deliberately. Still, the Wittelsbachs represented a major step forward in terms of the creation of a battle fleet.

This though, was not enough. In late 1899, war erupted between the British and the Boers of South Africa, a people whom many Germans saw as kindred spirits. When three German merchant ships were stopped by British cruisers, there was a national outcry. The fact they were filled with arms and supplies for the Boers was considered an irrelevance by the German press. The same newspapers cried out for better naval protection, and Tirpitz, now a Vice-Admiral, seized the moment to propose a Second Naval Bill. This called for a dramatic expansion of the fleet and a rolling programme of shipbuilding over the next two decades. It was everything both Tirpitz and the Kaiser could have wished for, and in June 1900 it was passed by the Reichstag amid a tide of patriotic fervour.

This move set alarm bells ringing in London. Why would Germany want to double the size of its battle fleet, if not to challenge the might of the Royal Navy? Although the bill made no direct reference to Britain, it frequently mentioned a larger naval power. There was little doubt to whom Tirpitz was referring. The bill also mentioned his 'Risk Theory'. In a nutshell, this argued that this larger naval power was a global force, and would have to deploy its ships accordingly. Although the German battle fleet was much smaller, it was concentrated in home waters, and in the event of a war it could inflict considerable damage on the enemy before the bigger power could concentrate its ships. This would undermine the global position of the large naval power, something it could not risk. In other words, by maintaining a powerful German fleet, Tirpitz was arguing that Britain would shy away from fighting it.

For an admitted Anglophile like Tirpitz, this showed a remarkable lack of understanding of British resolve. The British expected their navy to win, regardless of the odds, and in the event of a war it would actively seek battle. It also ignored Britain's ability to out-build Germany, or to concentrate its vast naval resources where it mattered. When Fisher became First Sea Lord in 1902, he laid plans to do just that – concentrate his fleet in the North Sea and English Channel and give the Navy the ships it needed to destroy the German fleet. He even drew up plans for a pre-emptive strike, just as Nelson had done against the Danes in 1801, although for diplomatic reasons this notion was quietly abandoned.

Meanwhile, German shipyards were kept busy by the burst of ship-building that followed in the wake of the two naval bills. In 1901, Tirpitz approved plans for a class of five Braunschweig class battleships that would be the equal of Britain's latest capital ships. These German battleships were armed with 28 cm (11.1 in) guns, which were slightly lighter but every bit as good as the 12-inch guns favoured by the British. A second group of five battleships – the Deutschland class – would follow two years later, as soon as the Braunschweigs were launched and off the stocks. In all, since 1895 the Imperial German Navy had commissioned the building of nineteen new battleships, to augment the four older Brandenburg-class vessels laid down in 1890. The German battle fleet was fast becoming a force to be reckoned with.

For his part the Kaiser was amazed that the British appeared so suspicious of Germany's new battle fleet. In fact, it was not just the warships that were causing concern. Germany's merchant fleet was growing rapidly; the two largest international ocean liner companies were now German, rather than British. German industrial capacity was rising steadily, just as British production was contracting. Germany was also on the verge of overtaking Britain in terms of steel production, while thanks to the house of Krupp its armaments industry was all-powerful. However, it was the rise of German naval power that worried the British most. By 1902, Lord Selbourne, the First Lord of the Admiralty warned the British cabinet of the growing threat posed by Germany; 'The more the composition of the new German fleet is examined, the clearer it becomes that it is designed for a possible conflict with the British fleet.'

The German *Dreadnought*

This was the atmosphere of growing suspicion in which Admiral Fisher pushed through his plans for the *Dreadnought*. It was at this crucial juncture, when the German fleet was fast becoming the second greatest naval power, that the whole naval world was turned on its head. The secrecy surrounding the building of *Dreadnought* had perplexed German naval intelligence, but in late 1904, the German naval attaché Rear-Admiral Coerper reported to Berlin that the new ship would be armed with ten or twelve 12-inch guns. This was verified a few weeks later when the 1905 edition of *Jane's Fighting Ships* said she would be an 'all big-gun battleship', and would be powered by turbines. The Kaiser was impressed, but both he and Tirpitz realised that for the moment they would be unable to match her.

The problem was the Kaiser Wilhelm Canal. When the 98-kilometre (60 mile) canal was opened in 1895, it was large enough to accommodate the biggest warships of the day. A decade later it was proving a liability, as it was too shallow to accommodate anything as large as a dreadnought. So, either Germany had to limit the size of its warships, or spend a small fortune dredging the canal. Tirpitz was in no doubt how to solve this dilemma. In 1907 work began on the widening of the canal. In the meantime, large German warships would simply have to move between the North and Baltic seas by sailing around Denmark. This demonstrates that Tirpitz had not predicted the building of the *Dreadnought*. Certainly, he was aware of the arguments in favour of a big-gun battleship; he just had not imagined one would be built so quickly, and before Germany had developed plans for one of her own.

As *Dreadnought* was being built, Tirpitz was forging ahead with his own battleship programme, the building of a new battle fleet of what would soon be termed pre-dreadnoughts. The argument that the construction of *Dreadnought* levelled the playing field of naval construction is a sound one, but Tirpitz was still playing on the old pitch. Despite knowing that a big-gun battleship was being built in Britain, he went ahead and completed the building of the last three Braunschweig class battleships, and the building of the Deutschland class. It was almost as if he didn't know how to respond, so he went about building his fleet, even though he was aware the unfinished ships were already obsolete. However, on hearing Coerper's report, he secretly ordered his naval architects to begin designing a big-gun battleship of their own.

This would be the SMS *Nassau*, the lead ship of four dreadnoughts in her class. The problem facing the German designers though, was that they had no clear idea of *Dreadnought*'s capabilities. They knew her size – the able Carl von Coerper had told them that – and they knew she would carry ten 12-inch guns, and would use turbine propulsion. Beyond that, the designers were in the dark.

The ship they created was unremarkable, save for her armament. *Nassau* would be shorter than *Dreadnought*, but would be better armoured, and therefore the two ships had similar displacements. Instead of ten 12-inch guns *Nassau* was originally designed to mount eight 28 cm (11.1 in) ones (later increased to twelve), the same weapons fitted to the latest German pre-dreadnoughts. *Nassau* would carry a turret fore and aft, and one on either side of her forward superstructure, meaning that six could fire to either side, two fewer than *Dreadnought*. However, *Nassau* would also carry a powerful battery of secondary guns, a type of weapon Fisher decided weren't needed in *Dreadnought*. The German ship would still use conventional propulsion, giving her a top speed of 19½ knots – a little less than its turbine-powered British rival. *Nassau* was designed quickly, and it showed. Still, it was a start.

Funding for these new ships was provided through an emergency amendment to the Naval Bill, won by some skilful and pragmatic lobbying by Tirpitz. He would have to scale back his plans to build a squadron of armoured cruisers, but in May 1906 he was granted enough funds to build Germany's first four dreadnoughts. The order to begin work on *Nassau* was given in July 1906, by which time *Dreadnought* was nearing completion. Suddenly though, Tirpitz ordered the work to be halted, so he could modify her design in light of the first hard information on *Dreadnought*. The result was the addition of a second twin 11.1-inch turret on either side of the superstructure, giving her a broadside equal to that of her British counterpart. The secondary gun battery would consist of twelve 15 cm (6 in) guns, fitted in armoured casemates, six on either side of her hull. This done, work resumed on *Nassau* in July 1907.

The Race Begins

That lost year would cost Tirpitz dearly. *Dreadnought* was only the start, and Fisher was determined to out-build the Germans. For the moment he was in favour with the Liberal Government, having actually cut the naval budget. So, funding for six new dreadnoughts was set aside, and to save time Fisher made sure that the first batch of three ships – the Bellerophon class – were virtually exact copies of the original dreadnought. This was something of a gamble, as *Dreadnought* was not even commissioned, let alone tried and tested. For Fisher, speed was more important than perfection.

Still, minor improvements were made before the three new dreadnoughts were completed. For instance, in *Dreadnought* the foremast was placed behind the funnel, and the spotters found the smoke often obscured their view. So, on the Bellerophons the foremast was moved forward. A torpedo bulkhead was also added, a second skin just inside the hull, designed to protect the ship from torpedo hits. These little tweaks fitted Fisher's new dictum; 'Build First, Built Fast – Each Better than the Last'. He realised better than most that any delay would give Britain's naval rivals a chance to catch up or even overtake her. They were certainly keen to try. It was not just Germany that was busy designing its own version of the *Dreadnought*. The United States, Japan, France, Russia and even Austro-Hungary were all keen to follow Britain's lead.

So began a naval arms race between Britain and Germany, while other maritime powers struggled to catch up. In Britain, Fisher embarked on a large-scale public relations campaign, extolling the virtues of the dreadnought, and the need to maintain Britain's control of the seas. The Liberals were committed to defence cuts, but in 1908 the Fisher-inspired slogan 'we want eight and we won't wait' – a reference to eight new dreadnoughts – proved impossible to ignore. So in 1909, the Chancellor of the Exchequer Lloyd George was forced to raise taxes in order to push through Fisher's dreadnought-building programme. Fisher had his money and his ships, but his campaign won him few favours in Parliament. By then three more dreadnoughts of the St Vincent class had been launched, and the budget had been approved for three more – *Neptune* and her two near sisters of the Colossus class.

In Germany a second amendment to the Naval Bill was passed in 1908, and new commercial shipyards sprang up to cope with the increasing demand for warships. By the time work began on the two Colossus class dreadnoughts, the Germans had already launched four Nassau class dreadnoughts, and three similar vessels of the Helgoland class were under construction. Unlike their predecessors though, these ships carried 30.5 cm (12 in) guns. The press of both countries were filled with articles defaming the perfidy of their naval rivals, circulating rumours that foreign dreadnoughts were being built in secret, that invasion plans were being hatched or pre-emptive strikes planned. The newspapers also took delight in publicising the growth of their potential enemy's fleet. While this helped sell newspapers and inflame public opinion, it also created an atmosphere where success in the naval arms race was now a matter of national pride.

Other dreadnoughts would follow. Armed with his new funding Tirpitz ordered the construction of a new generation of dreadnoughts, equipped with 12-inch guns. The five ships of the Kaiser class were the largest and most powerful German warships yet, with their five turrets mounted along the centreline, allowing them to be fired to either side. They were laid down between December 1909 and January 1911, and entered service between December 1912 and December 1913. One of them, the *Friedrich der Grosse*, would become the German flagship at Jutland. These were powerful, well-built ships, and they were followed by four more. This new four ship batch – the König class – were largely similar to the Kaisers, but their turrets were more sensibly laid out. Both of these classes of German dreadnoughts had superimposed turrets; one turret was raised up above the deck so it could be fired over the turret in front. Eight of these nine powerful dreadnoughts would form the core of the German fleet at Jutland.

Effectively they were a second generation of dreadnought, built in response to a similar new batch of ships appearing in British shipyards. The design of the original *Dreadnought* and her successors was not particularly efficient, as not all of their guns could fire at the same target. *Neptune* and the two ship Colossus class were an attempt to remedy this, by placing turrets so that they could fire between blocks of superstructure. The design was not that efficient, and so designers came up with a new arrangement, where all the guns were mounted on the ship's centreline. This was achieved by having one turret mounted amidships, and two turrets fore and aft, with one superimposed behind the other. This design proved a great success, and became a standard layout for the new generation of British dreadnoughts.

The first of these were the four ships of the Orion class, launched in 1910–11 and commissioned in 1912. Unlike all their predecessors, they carried 13.5-inch guns, which earned them the title 'super dreadnoughts'. These were magnificent ships, and the design was largely copied in a new batch – the King George V class. These four 'super dreadnoughts' were laid down in 1911, and entered service in 1912–13. The last batch of four 'super dreadnoughts' were dubbed the Iron Duke class, and at Jutland the namesake of the class would serve as the flagship of the British Grand Fleet.

A brief look at when these dreadnoughts entered service is particularly revealing. It clearly shows just how much of a head start Britain enjoyed, and how Germany gradually got left behind. So, by the time the war began Britain enjoyed a seven dreadnought lead over her opponent. Later in 1914 and early 1915, her shipbuilding totals were boosted by three dreadnoughts, vessels which had been built in British yards for foreign navies, but which were now compulsorily purchased by the Royal Navy. By the time of Jutland, the gap had widened even further, and counting the new 'fast battleships' which joined the fleet, the British enjoyed an overwhelming lead of 33 to 17, almost two ships to one.

	Royal Navy		Imperial German Navy	
	Dreadnoughts commissioned that year	Dreadnoughts Total	Dreadnoughts commissioned that year	Dreadnoughts Total
1906	1	1	–	–
1907	0	1	–	–
1908	0	1	–	–
1909	4	5	–	–
1910	2	7	4	4
1911	3	10	3	7
1912	5	15	2	9
1913	3	18	4	13
1914 (1)	2/4	20/21*	-/1	13/14
1915	4	25*	3	17
1916 (2)	5	3w0	–	17

(1) Before/After outbreak of war (August 1914)

(2) Before Jutland (May 1916)

* One dreadnought (*Audacious*) lost in November 1914

In this two-horse race, Germany got off to a late start, and Britain started edging away well before the final furlong. Tirpitz realised the growing disparity was not just a matter of numbers. His first generation of dreadnoughts were outgunned by the British. By the time the second generation, with their 12-inch guns began entering service in December 1912, the British had already commissioned five dreadnoughts armed with 13.5-inch guns. The real advantage these German dreadnoughts enjoyed lay in their protection. As well as having a thicker armoured belt made from marginally better steel, they also boasted better internal protection in the form of torpedo bulkheads, watertight compartments and heavily protected magazines. This, though, was not enough to compensate for Britain's sheer weight of numbers. By 1912, it was clear that Britain had won the naval arms race, and had done so by a handsome margin.

3

Fisher's Follies

While the dreadnought race was under way, Fisher embarked on another pet project, one that would have disastrous consequences at Jutland. While battleships – now in the shape of dreadnoughts – formed the core of the battle fleet, the sea lanes were protected by fast but lightly armed cruisers. These were the steam-powered descendants of the sailing frigates of Nelson's navy, and their duties were equally varied. They could protect convoys, patrol the sea lanes, hunt down enemy cruisers or commerce raiders, and also scout ahead of the battle fleet. During the last decades of the nineteenth century, these ubiquitous little ships grew steadily in size and firepower. So, during the 1890s a new type of warship was developed, called the armoured cruiser, and designed specifically to hunt them down.

This new breed of ship was better armed and protected than other cruisers. Inevitably, each new class of armoured cruiser was larger and more powerful than the last. In the Royal Navy, these vessels reached their peak with the Minotaur class, laid down in 1905. With 9.2-inch guns, a powerful secondary armament and a speed of 23 knots, they were the best-armed cruisers afloat. Despite their name though, these armoured cruisers only carried enough protective steel to defend themselves against 6-inch shells. In effect they were fast, well-armed, but relatively poorly protected. Now Fisher planned to take these ships to a whole new level. By designing an armoured cruiser with a homogenous armament of big guns, he hoped to do for them what he had just done for the battleship.

The Coming of the Battlecruiser

Fisher's new armoured cruiser would have only a 6-inch armoured belt, but it would be powered by steam turbines, making it faster than any cruiser or battleship afloat. Above all, it was to carry a powerful all-big gun armament of eight 12-inch guns. Due to the space taken up by the propulsion system and the guns, these ships were longer and heavier than other armoured cruisers, but the design Fisher's committee finally approved carried a similar size of broadside to *Dreadnought* herself. Three of the new ships were ordered, and construction began during the spring of 1906. They were all launched a little over a year later, and entered service in 1908–9. In the event of a war, these big-gun armoured cruisers were designed to sweep all other enemy cruisers from the seas. After all they had the speed and the firepower to do just that. Unfortunately, that was not their only task.

Before the advent of naval airpower, the task of scouting ahead of a steam-powered battle fleet was the preserve of the light cruiser – sometimes called the protected cruiser. While scouting they were expected to fight enemy cruiser patrols, but were meant to keep clear of larger warships. The idea of the armoured cruiser was that not only could it scout, but it had the firepower needed to drive off smaller enemy cruisers. This concept would work perfectly if only one side had armoured cruisers in their fleet. If both did, then they would most likely be drawn into a gunnery duel with their enemy counterparts. With their relatively big guns and light armour this was a singularly dangerous undertaking. It was of course also the big flaw in the concept of the big-gun armoured cruiser, a ship type that was soon dubbed the battlecruiser.

Fisher's original idea was for a fictitious ship he called 'HMS *Unapproachable*'. It would be able to outfight any armoured cruiser afloat, while having the speed to keep clear of other heavier warships. There were two flaws here. The first was the same as before; if the enemy had similar ships, then they would be drawn into a fight for which they were ill equipped. The second was that their armament made them too useful to keep out of the fight when it came to a major sea battle. Instead, they were expected to lurk around the edges of the engagement, and use their firepower to support their own dreadnoughts, while using their speed to keep their distance from the enemy. Their armour though, was designed to protect them from other cruisers, not from the fire of dreadnoughts or even other battlecruisers. At Jutland, this woolly thinking led directly to the deaths of more than 3,000 British sailors.

The first big-gun armoured cruisers were the three ships of the Invincible Class, which were launched between March and June 1907. They carried the 12-inch guns Fisher wanted, and their turbines gave them an impressive top speed of 25 knots. The public loved the combination of firepower and speed, and it was the press rather than Fisher who first coined the term 'battlecruiser'. In 1909–10 a virtual repeat of these first battlecruisers was laid down. The two Indefatigable class battlecruisers were slightly longer than the Invincibles, but were otherwise very similar to them. Incidentally, one of them, the *New Zealand*, was paid for by that dominion, while a third identical vessel, the *Australia,* was built for service with the Australian navy.

Word of these developments reached Germany in 1907. The Germans had already been building armoured cruisers, and the construction of the latest, the *Blücher,* was far too advanced to cancel. So Tirpitz had a new ship designed, the *Von der Tann* – Germany's answer to the *Invincible*. She was a much better-designed ship. Despite carrying 28 cm. (11.1 in) guns, she could match her British counterpart for speed thanks to imported Parsons turbines, but was larger, and she carried a more powerful secondary armament. More importantly the *Von Der Tann* was much better protected; her 10-inch thick armoured belt was backed up by an impressive network of watertight bulkheads. This meant that a hit on her was less likely to penetrate, and if it did the hit was less likely to be fatal.

Inevitably, the development of the battlecruiser spurred on an arms race in miniature. While the *Von der Tann* was still being built, the *Moltke* was laid down in Hamburg. The following year, work began on her sister ship *Goeben*. By then it was 1909, and the naval arms race was at its height. Refusing to be outdone, the British response was the building of 'The Splendid Cats'. These were the battlecruisers *Lion, Queen Mary* and *Princess Royal,* all of which were longer than any dreadnought, and carried a powerful armament of eight 13.5-inch guns. They were soon followed by a similar battlecruiser, the *Tiger*. These were not ships designed to patrol the sea lanes; they greedily burned almost a hundred tons of coal an hour, but were the fastest battlecruisers afloat. These large, elegant ships were built for no better reason than to win this miniature naval arms race. This set a very dangerous precedent, as it meant the ships had no real function apart from fighting enemy battlecruisers, a job for which they were dangerously unsuited.

Inevitably, the Germans responded with a second generation of battlecruisers. The one-off *Seydlitz* was merely an improved version of the Moltke class, but throughout 1911 naval architects worked on plans for a large German battlecruiser, designed to carry 30.5 cm (12 in) guns. The result was the *Derfflinger* and *Lützow*, arguably the best all-round battlecruisers of the war. The two ships of the Derfflinger class to enter service before Jutland were of a similar size to Fisher's 'Splendid Cats', but their design was far more sophisticated. The most obvious difference was that unlike the latest British battlecruisers, the four twin turrets of these German ships were placed fore and aft, with one turret super-imposed over the other. Less obviously, they were protected by 12-inch thickness of armoured belt, making them as well protected as most contemporary dreadnoughts. This, though, came at a price.

The cost of these ships was escalating fast. The bill for building the *Von der Tann* was 36.5 million marks. Four years later, the *Derfflinger* cost the German taxpayer 56 million marks. This tendency to make each successive group of ships bigger and better meant that costs escalated, making a mockery of Germany's naval budget. The same was happening with dreadnoughts; the *Nassau* cost 38 million marks, while the *Helgoland* cost 45 million. Worse, in the 1909–10 fiscal year Tirpitz ordered five powerful Kaiser class dreadnoughts, and four more König-class ships would follow in 1911–12. The British were building ships at an even greater rate, but they were better able to afford them. Already burdened by a huge military budget, and by the cost of widening the Kaiser Wilhelm Canal, this burgeoning naval budget was proving almost too much for the German state to bear.

In 1901, before the coming of the *Dreadnought*, Germany's naval budget of 201 million marks was more than enough to cope with Tirpitz's ambitious shipbuilding plans. In 1908, this had risen to 348 million marks, a quarter of the national budget. The army already soaked up half, leaving little else to go round. While Germany's economy was growing, the naval budget was doing so even faster. This inevitably meant that Tirpitz encountered growing opposition in the Reichstag after the latest supplement to the Naval Bill was passed in 1908. It was put to him that if he tried to keep up his naval arms race, Germany would become bankrupt. Still, the latest tranche of funding ensured he could keep building three or four capital ships a year until 1911. After that, the pace would inevitably have to slow. Germany had tried its best, but it was fast becoming clear that this was a race the country could not win.

This funding problem had little impact on the way German naval expansion was viewed in Britain. The launch of the *Nassau* and an aggressive programme of building dreadnoughts and battlecruisers could only be viewed as a potential threat to British naval supremacy. This led to a dramatic sea change in British public opinion. Before 1900, German naval expansion was viewed with some degree of condescension, and the German people were seen as Britain's cousins on the continent. By 1907, when Germany began building the *Nassau*, this had changed, thanks to mounting pressure in the press and in parliament. Germany's actions were viewed with deep suspicion. In Erskine Childers' novel *The Riddle of the Sands* the plot centred around a secret German invasion plan, and to the British public real events seemed to be unfolding in a similar way. While the naval arms race and the suspicion it engendered may not have led directly to the outbreak of the war, they certainly laid the groundwork for it by breaking a long-held bond of trust and friendship between the two countries.

Fisher's Legacy

It was a rift that Fisher exploited to the benefit of the fleet. The spectre of a German invasion was used to justify the expansion of the dreadnought programme and the creation of a powerful force of battlecruisers. The growth of the German merchant fleet was also used as an excuse to build more cruisers, designed to destroy these merchant ships on the high seas. At the time, Germany's passenger liners were some of the biggest and best in the world and had the speed to escape from most warships in the British fleet. Fisher argued that these great German liners could be turned into auxiliary cruisers, and used this as yet another rationale for building battlecruisers with a greater turn of speed than them. By the time Fisher stood down as First Sea Lord in January 1910, he had transformed the British navy, but for all his triumphs – the creation of *Dreadnought*, the development of the destroyer, improvements to naval gunnery and training – it was his concept of the battlecruiser which was the most controversial, although at the time this was more about their expense than their questionable capabilities. To this day the, battlecruiser remains the Achilles' Heel of Fisher's immense legacy.

The problem was that Fisher's battlecruisers were impressive ships, but they had no clear purpose. Certainly they were admirable for hunting enemy cruisers on the high seas, the role they were originally designed for. However, their combination of big guns and weak armour made them an expensive liability in any other role. The Germans realised this, and so gave their own battlecruisers a reasonable level of armoured protection – almost as much as their own dreadnoughts. The British didn't, and when the time came they would pay the price. As Britain's battlecruiser fleet grew, they collectively became too much of an asset to leave out of a full-scale battle. So the notion that they would add their weight of firepower to a fight became enshrined in policy. Anyone who questioned this dangerous policy was ignored by the Admiralty, as by then these fast, elegant warships had become the public relations pin-ups of the British fleet. To criticise them would have been seen as unpatriotic.

Admiral Sir John Fisher officially retired on 25 January 1911, his seventieth birthday. When he accepted the job in 1904, he had expected to retire in January 1906, his sixty-fifth birthday. His promotion to Admiral of the Fleet brought with it another five years of service before retirement. His successors as First Sea Lord, first Sir Arthur Wilson and then Sir Francis Bridgeman, both lasted just a year in post. Neither could match Fisher's drive and enthusiasm, in fact quite the reverse. Wilson was a supporter of Fisher, but resigned a year later over plans to establish a permanent Naval Staff of the kind used by the Germans. Bridgeman was equally ineffectual, and resigned following a clash with the First Lord of the Admiralty, Winston Churchill. The next First Sea Lord was Prince Louis of Battenberg, an amiable but ineffective figurehead who proved unable to stand up to Churchill, even though the First Lord was a mere civilian. It was Prince Louis who was still in post when war was declared in August 1914.

Interestingly, these three largely ineffective First Sea Lords did little to change Fisher's policies. The warships laid down during Fisher's time were all launched and commissioned into service, including the eight dreadnoughts he talked a reluctant government into approving in

1909–10. These ensured Germany was completely left behind in the naval arms race. In 1912, Germany realised this, and abandoned its aggressive shipbuilding programme. In what was possibly history's most expensive competition until the Space Race, Fisher had left Tirpitz standing. Of course, it was not just dreadnoughts and battlecruisers that Fisher built. His expansion of Britain's cruiser fleet was almost as ambitious, and his time in office saw the development of the numerous and highly successful family of Town-class light cruisers, ships that would be the 'eyes and ears' of the wartime Grand Fleet.

Fisher had also virtually invented the destroyer. Existing torpedo boats were small, with limited armament and a restrictive range of operations. Fisher called for fast, well-armed 'torpedo boat destroyers' with a top speed of 33 knots, and which could remain at sea for a week, a feature which in turn allowed them to accompany the battle fleet during its operations. The first of these small craft were launched in 1906, and by the time the war began over a hundred were in service. By then, their name had been abbreviated to just 'destroyer' and the torpedo boat had been rendered an irrelevance, as these new craft carried torpedoes as well. Like all of Fisher's innovations, though, the destroyer was copied by the Germans and built by them in similarly large numbers.

While Fisher was an advocate of both the torpedo and the submarine, and submersibles were built in reasonable quantities during his tenure at the Admiralty, this was an area where the Germans excelled. It was true both in the capabilities of these boats and the way they were used. At first Fisher envisioned them in a defensive role; it was only in 1906 that he approved the design of a truly seagoing boat. Even then, its main wartime use was seen as one of reconnaissance rather than the sinking of enemy ships. The Germans were faster to appreciate the offensive capabilities of submarines, and by 1912 had begun producing highly effective ocean-going boats. During the war these boats caused considerable damage to the British war effort, even though arguments over the ethics of their employment led to the resignation of Admiral Tirpitz, the man who approved their development in the first place.

One of Fisher's greatest achievements during the years before the outbreak of war was in the strategic redeployment of the British fleet. When he took over as First Sea Lord, the battle fleet was divided between the Home Fleet, the Channel Fleet, the Mediterranean Fleet and the

China Station. Fisher realised that Britain's most likely adversary was now Germany, and so he decided to concentrate his battleships closer to home. He recalled all of them from the Far East, and reduced the size of the Mediterranean Fleet. He then rebranded the Home Fleet as the Channel Fleet, while the former Channel Fleet became the Atlantic Fleet and was based in Gibraltar. This meant that in the event of a war, the Atlantic Fleet could be sent to reinforce the Channel or the Mediterranean fleets with equal ease. This was an elegant and flexible solution to the growing German threat and meant that the bulk of the battle fleet was now concentrated in or near home waters.

Fisher's Grand Strategy

Fisher also did what his successors as First Sea Lord failed to do, he devised Britain's strategy for pursuing a naval war against Germany. Much has been made of his 'Copenhagen' solution to the German naval threat. This reference was to Britain's pre-emptive attack on the Danish Fleet in Copenhagen in 1801, and more than once Fisher proposed launching a similar attack on Germany. On examination though, this was mere rhetoric; no plans were drawn up, and instead Fisher developed a cohesive strategy based on geography, resources and a pragmatic disregard for neutrality.

Fisher realised that Germany was vulnerable to a naval blockade. The country was reliant on the import of a quarter of its food and up to half of its copper, nitrates and other vital war materials such as oil and rubber. Starving Germans of these crucial imports and the cash generated by exports would have a serious impact on Germany's economy. It would also sabotage the country's ability to wage war, or even to feed its own people. This would place an intolerable burden on the German state and would inevitably bring about its collapse.

By 1908, Fisher had begun laying the naval groundwork for the imposition of just such a blockade. This was in spite of Britain being a signatory in the Declaration of London (1909), an agreement which limited the use of blockades and which safeguarded the rights of neutrals. Fisher though, was well aware that if a war came, Britain would have to stop goods entering neutral countries too, or risk ports like Antwerp, Rotterdam or Copenhagen becoming a back door to Germany. The solution was to determine the final destination of the cargo as the key, rather than the port it was being shipped to. This way Britain might earn the wrath of neutral countries, but the blockade would be rendered watertight.

Strangely, Fisher never seemed to have put much thought into the way the blockade might be implemented. Certainly he realised that a 'close blockade' of German ports was impractical. This had worked during the Age of Sail, but was no longer viable in an era of mechanical reliability, submarines, mines and torpedo boats. While he argued for aggressive patrolling inside the Helgoland Bight – within reach of the German base at Wilhelmshaven – Fisher's blockade would be established well away from enemy ports. He understood that Britain's greatest asset here was geography. The only way ships could reach German ports from outside Europe was by passing through the North Sea. All the navy had to do to blockade Germany was to seal off this virtually landlocked sea.

Fisher planned to use cruisers to seal the English Channel, where they could stop and search all shipping heading through it, but neither he nor his successor Sir Arthur Wilson laid plans for establishing a similar force at the northern end of the sea, between Orkney and the Norwegian coast. It would be 1914 before plans for a Northern Patrol were put in place. Still, once this concept of a 'distant blockade' was established by Fisher, he set about reorganising the way the fleet could enforce it. This meant the Channel Fleet, including the bulk of the British battle fleet, needed to be able to react to any sortie by the German High Seas Fleet. Britain's traditional naval bases, Portsmouth, Plymouth and even Chatham, were poorly placed for this. So Fisher advocated the enlargement of the small naval base at Rosyth in the Firth of Forth, the establishment of another fleet base in the Cromarty Firth, and a large, secure wartime base in Scapa Flow, the great natural harbour in Orkney.

The basis of Fisher's plan was to use a combination of patrols by light forces and submarines to warn the fleet of any foray by the Germans. A fleet of older pre-dreadnoughts, cruisers and destroyers would protect the entrance to the English Channel, leaving the faster units of the fleet to form the main battle fleet. This would be ready to intercept the Germans, preceded by its own screen of cruisers and destroyers. The battlecruisers would also join in the operation and, thanks to their high speed, it was expected that they would make contact with the enemy before the rest of the fleet caught up. In these circumstances, they would either pin the Germans or shadow them from a safe distance until the dreadnoughts arrived to bring the enemy to battle. This whole plan required two things; good intelligence and a speedy response to this information. With those, Fisher was confident his new dreadnought fleet would utterly demolish its weaker German foe.

Similar conclusions had been reached in Germany. First, there was little the Germans could do to counter a distant blockade, apart from sinking the British cruisers and auxiliaries that carried out the job. That was a task best left to U-Boats and minelayers. While no clear role had been devised for the High Seas Fleet, Tirpitz and his subordinates were well aware that its greatest asset was its very existence. By simply existing as a 'fleet in being', it forced the Royal Navy to concentrate its naval strength in home waters, which in turn reduced its presence in other places, such as the sea lanes of the North Atlantic. This in turn made a U-Boat campaign particularly appealing. While Germany was dependent on imports, Britain's reliance was even greater. This meant that even a limited U-Boat campaign against British merchant shipping would have a serious effect on the British war effort. In other words, while the British sought to bring Germany to its knees through their blockade, the Germans would increasingly try to do the same through the use of U-Boats.

Just as importantly, if Germany was to win a future war at sea, then it needed to whittle down the strength of Britain's dreadnought fleet. This could be achieved two ways; through inflicting losses from U-boat attacks and the use of mines, and through luring small portions of the British Fleet into battle with superior numbers of Germans. A few successes of either kind would reduce Britain's numerical superiority in dreadnoughts. Once that happened, the Germans could bring the British to battle on reasonably favourable terms. To help achieve this, they needed to entice elements of the British battle fleet away from the rest, and then pounce on them. This desire to entrap the enemy lay behind the planning of hit-and-run raids against the British coast in 1914, and in the German willingness to use their own battlecruisers as a decoy, one the British would be unable to ignore.

To give the High Seas Fleet room to manoeuvre, and to keep British intelligence guessing, the Germans needed to control the waters bordering their own coastline, from Frisia to the coast of the Danish peninsula near the Danish-German border. This was achieved by laying mines. An initial minefield belt guarded the outer fringes of the Helgoland Bight, the area of sea between the island of Helgoland and the estuaries of the Jade and the Elbe. Once this was done and the channels through the minefield were protected by regular naval patrols, then the German battle fleet had a secure area in which to operate, safe from prying eyes or enemy torpedoes. During the war, this safe cordon was extended outwards, particularly in the north, where it reached beyond Sylt. This meant that once it put to sea, the German fleet could strike through gaps in the minefield to the west, or continue north to emerge near Horns Reef. This defensive cordon would play an important part in the great naval clash of May 1916.

So, as the war clouds gathered, both Britain and Germany struggled to come up with a coherent strategic plan for conducting a naval war. While no doubt the opening shots of any naval campaign would take place in far-flung corners of the globe, as Germany's scattered warships were destroyed, the real battleground remained the North Sea. When war came, everyone expected a decisive naval battle to be fought within the first weeks or months of the war. When this didn't happen, and as the death toll in the trenches mounted, public pressure for decisive action increased steadily. After all, what was the point of having a fleet of expensive dreadnoughts and battlecruisers if they weren't being used? When that clash of titans eventually came, not only would it reveal the true horror of modern naval warfare, but it would also expose the folly of designing ships as vulnerable as the battlecruiser, and then sending them into the epicentre of a naval maelstrom.

4

The First Clashes

Every year the German battle fleet, now dubbed the *Hochseeflotte* (High Seas Fleet), conducted fleet exercises off the coast of Norway. Kaiser Wilhelm also spent part of the summer in the Norwegian fjords on board his royal yacht. The assassination of the Archduke Franz Ferdinand, heir to the Austro-Hungarian throne on 28 June, barely registered in the Navy, as the crews busied themselves preparing their ships for sea. The Kaiser set sail for Norway's Sogne Fjord on 7 July, and three days later the naval exercises got under way. In Britain, a similar scene was unfolding, as the Home Fleet, known as the Channel Fleet until its rebranding in 1909 prepared for its own annual exercise. This was preceded by a royal review off Spithead. So, on 20 July the bulk of the Royal Navy steamed past King George V, watching from the quarterdeck of his royal yacht. It took six hours for all the ships to pass.

Afterwards the fleet headed into the English Channel for its exercise. It was a great success, and on Thursday 23rd July the ships returned to port, and their crews flooded the pubs and brothels of Portsmouth and Weymouth. That same day though, Austria sent an ultimatum to Serbia, the nation they blamed for the assassination. On Friday the Serbs responded favourably, but as a precaution they mobilised their army. This was too much for the Austrians, who on 28th July declared war on Serbia. By then the Kaiser was back in Berlin, and the High Seas Fleet had returned to Kiel. It refuelled, and then sailed through the canal to Wilhelmshaven, where it waited on a war footing. For its part, the British Home Fleet remained fully mobilised, and steamed north to Scapa Flow, where it would be safe from any pre-emptive attack. While the public prayed for peace, the fleets were preparing for war.

War between Austro-Hungary and Serbia prompted a chain reaction that would sweep across Europe, and then fan out around the world. Thanks to a network of alliances, what should have been a largely irrelevant war in the Balkans became a global conflict. Russia began mobilising her army in support of the Serbs, prompting Germany to invoke her treaty with Austria, and to declare war on Russia on 1 August. France was bound by treaty to the Russians, and so war between France and Germany began on 2 August. According to the war plan created by Count von Schlieffen, German troops entered Luxembourg and began marching through Belgium, hoping to outflank the French army that was massing in Alsace. Until now, Britain had remained neutral, but she was bound by treaty to both France and Belgium. So at 11 p.m. on 4 August – midnight in Berlin – Britain and Germany found themselves at war with each other.

The coming of war came as a shock to most people in both countries, not least to the Kaiser, who seemed surprised that the diplomatic game he had been playing had ended so badly. He was reported to have said that if his grandmother Queen Victoria were still alive, she would never have allowed it. He could just as easily have said the same about Otto von Bismarck. The naval arms race has been blamed for forcing Britain and Germany apart and for encouraging Britain to forge a defensive alliance with France, which in turn bound her indirectly to Russia. This was exactly the situation Bismarck had spent his life trying to avoid. If Wilhelm had heeded the Iron Chancellor's advice, then this utterly needless war might never have happened and the lives of tens of millions could have been spared. Instead, a combination of rash diplomacy and the Kaiser's bullishness had tipped Europe over the edge of a terrifying abyss.

The North Sea

On 1 August, the British Home Fleet entered its assigned wartime anchorage of Scapa Flow. This great natural anchorage was fringed by the islands of Orkney; its mainland to the north, Hoy to the south, and a string of smaller islands to the east. There were only six entrances, four of which were too shallow for large warships. The remaining two, Hoy

Sound in the east and Hoxa Sound in the south, could be secured by shore batteries, minefields, anti-submarine nets and acoustic warning cables. The trouble was that when the fleet arrived none of these were in place. Scapa's only defence was its remoteness from the German coast. Strategically though, its location was ideal. If the Germans wanted to break the blockade, then they would have to come out and fight. A British fleet based in Scapa Flow was well placed to intercept them.

The peacetime Home Fleet was commanded by Admiral Sir George Callaghan. The day after he dropped anchor in Scapa, Vice-Admiral Sir John Jellicoe arrived with orders to relieve him of his command. This was a bitter blow to Callaghan, who had worked hard to prepare the fleet for war. However, his health was poor, and the Admiralty felt he lacked the stamina needed to lead this great armada into battle. When Jellicoe arrived, the fleet was already preparing for sea. As soon as Callaghan departed, Jellicoe raised his flag in the *Iron Duke*, and led his ships out into the Pentland Firth. The fleet was conducting fleet manoeuvres in the North Sea, and so it was at sea when war was declared. On the same day, 4 August, the name of the force was changed. It would no longer be the Home Fleet. From now on, this great armada would be called the 'Grand Fleet'. At the same time, Jellicoe was promoted to the rank of admiral, as befitted the commander of such a prestigious force.

There was little chance that the sweep would encounter any Germans. In Wilhelmshaven, Jellicoe's counterpart, Admiral Friedrich von Ingenohl, knew that his High Seas Fleet was outnumbered and that Britain was building more new dreadnoughts than Germany. So his plan was to seek a quick and decisive battle before these British reinforcements could enter service, a battle to be fought on his own terms. Instead, though, the Kaiser, Tirpitz and the Naval High Command were more cautious, and so he was ordered to keep his fleet within reach of the German coast, going no further into the North Sea than an imaginary line linking the Dutch Frisian island of Terschelling with the Horn Reef, off the western coast of Denmark. The exception was if a favourable opportunity suddenly presented itself to destroy part of the British fleet. With Jellicoe keeping his fleet in Scapa Flow, it seemed unlikely that there would be any such opportunity for some time.

So, after the first tense days of the war slipped by, and as the German army marched through Belgium and France, the two great dreadnought fleets remained in their respective ports of Scapa Flow and Wilhelmshaven at opposite ends of the North Sea. There, both sides watched and waited for their opponents to make the first move. So, the focus of the naval drama shifted to other parts of the world, as isolated German warships tried their best to return home, or to fight to the death if they could not. In the Far East, the German East Asia Squadron was so far from Germany that it was highly unlikely it would ever make it back to Europe. Meanwhile, in the Mediterranean the battlecruiser *Goeben* had been on a goodwill tour to the Adriatic. British and French ships now blocked her way home. For the next few months the fate of these isolated German forces would dominate the world's headlines.

The Homeless Squadron

As part of the Kaiser's 'place in the sun' policy, Germany had acquired the Chinese port of Tsingtao (now Qingdao). It was here that Vice-Admiral Maximilian von Spee's East Asia Squadron had its base. His force consisted of six warships; the armoured cruisers *Scharnhorst* and *Gneisenau*, and the four light cruisers *Dresden, Emden, Leipzig* and *Nürnberg*. Von Spee realised that the coming of war spelt disaster for him and his men. He summed up his situation when he told a German civilian; 'I am quite homeless. I cannot reach Germany. We possess no other secure harbour. I must plough the seas of the world doing as much mischief as I can, until my ammunition is exhausted, or a foe far superior in power succeeds in catching me.' This, of course, is exactly what he planned to do

Staying in Tsingtao was not an option. Japan was expected to enter the war at any time, and British and Australian warships, including the new battlecruiser *Australia*, would be sent north to corner him. When war was declared, *Dresden* and *Leipzig* were on the east and west coasts of Mexico respectively, *Emden* was in Tsingtao and *Nürnberg* was in mid-Pacific on her way to relieve the *Leipzig*. *Scharnhorst* and *Gneisenau* were on their annual cruise, and on 6 August *Nürnberg* joined them off Ponape, having been recalled when she reached Honolulu. *Emden* and several supply ships were ordered to sail from Tsingtao to join them, and on 12 August the fleet made rendezvous off Pagan in the Marianas. *Emden* was detached to go to act as a raider in the East Indies, and the following day the rest of the squadron headed into the vastness of the Pacific.

Off the Marshall Islands *Nürnberg* was detached to put in to neutral Honolulu to send word to Berlin of von Spee's plan and to make sure the German consul there arranged for coal to be available for the squadron. The cruiser rejoined the rest of the squadron two weeks later. On 15 September, von Spee reached Samoa, a German colony which had just been seized by the Allies. Finding no enemy ships there, he continued on to the east, lingering only to shell French-owned Tahiti. By mid-October, the German squadron had reached Easter Island, where it was joined by *Leipzig* and *Dresden*, the latter having sailed there from the Caribbean. They replenished their coal stocks in the Juan Fernandez Islands, and by the end of the month they arrived off the Chilean coast. Word reached them that a British squadron was hunting for them in the same waters. At little after 4 p.m. on 1 November, the two forces spotted each other off the Chilean port of Coronel, and battle was joined.

Rear-Admiral Sir Christopher Cradock flew his flag in the armoured cruiser *Good Hope*. His force included another armoured cruiser, the *Monmouth*, as well as the light cruiser *Glasgow* and the armed merchant ship *Otranto*. With four ships against five, Cradock was outnumbered, and the *Otranto* was no match for any of the German ships. Still, he decided to fight. The lumbering *Otranto* was ordered to avoid battle, but Cradock led his remaining three ships northwards to close the range with the enemy. The British ships were silhouetted against the setting sun, and Spee's flagship *Scharnhorst* soon found the range. She began hitting *Good Hope*, while *Gneisenau* pummelled *Monmouth*.

While the British ships didn't score any hits on von Spee's armoured cruisers, *Good Hope* and *Monmouth* were struck repeatedly, until they were little more than floating hulks. At 7.50 p.m. *Good Hope* exploded and began to sink, drifting off into the night to die alone, and taking Cradock down with her. The *Monmouth* sank a little under an hour later, having been pounded to pieces by the German guns. Both *Glasgow* and *Otranto* managed to escape in the darkness.

An officer from the *Glasgow* described the destruction of the squadron; 'By 1945 [7.45 p.m.], when it was quite dark, *Good Hope* and *Monmouth* were obviously in distress. *Monmouth* yawed off to starboard, burning furiously, and heeling slightly. *Good Hope* was firing only a few of her guns, with the fires onboard increasing their brilliance. At 1950 there was a terrible explosion between her mainmast and her after funnel, the flames reaching a height of over 200 feet, after which she lay between the lines, a black hull lighted only by a dull glow.'

Spee put in to Valparaiso, where his ships replenished their coal bunkers, and his crews were feted by the locals. There too, von Spee received a telegram, ordering him to 'break through for home'. So the squadron put to sea again, and rounded Cape Horn during the first few days of December. By 6 December, they were in the South Atlantic, and von Spee set a course for the Falkland Islands. Two days later, he arrived off Port Stanley, only to find another squadron had reached there before him. These were the ships commanded by Vice-Admiral Doveton Sturdee, which had been sent from Britain specifically to hunt down and destroy the German squadron. At Sturdee's disposal were three armoured cruisers, two light cruisers, an armed merchantman and two Invincible class battlecruisers – *Invincible* and *Inflexible*. If Coronel had been a one-sided contest in favour of von Spee, the presence of the battlecruisers made what followed an even greater turkey shoot.

Von Spee turned away and the British ships gave chase. It took three hours for the faster British battlecruisers to come within range of the German squadron, at which point von Spee sought battle with his two armoured cruisers, buying time for his lighter ships to get away. Poor British gunnery let Sturdee down at first, but eventually the battlecruisers found the range and began scoring hits. When *Scharnhorst* was badly hit, the German admiral turned his flagship towards the enemy, trying to cover the escape of her sister ship. It was no good. First *Scharnhorst*, then *Gneisenau* was pounded heavily until they sank, at 4.17 and 6.02 p.m. respectively. Sturdee described the last moments of his opponent's flagship; 'At 16.04 the *Scharnhorst*, whose flag remained flying to the last, suddenly listed heavily to port, and it became clear that she was doomed. The list increased very rapidly until she was on her beam ends. At 16.17 she disappeared. She sank with all hands, including von Spee.

A general pursuit followed, and by nightfall *Nürnberg* and *Leipzig* had been sunk too. The *Leipzig* described her final moments; 'Many men sought shelter behind the gun shields, but they were mown down in heaps by shell splinters that ricocheted from the conning tower. Others decided to jump overboard and swim towards the enemy, but the cold water numbed them. The survivors stood with the Captain on the forecastle as darkness fell.' When the order was finally given to abandon ship, the British sent boats to pick what few survivors remained. In the end, only the *Dresden* and a German supply ship managed to escape the debacle which claimed the lives of 1,871 German sailors. This decisive victory was down to Sturdee's battlecruisers, which had done precisely the job they had been designed to do.

The Great Chase

Apart from the Far East Squadron, the only other German force outside home waters when the war began was made up of the battlecruiser *Goeben* and her smaller consort, the light cruiser *Breslau*. The two ships formed the German navy's 'Mediterranean Division', a grand-sounding name for such a small force. When the Archduke Franz Josef was assassinated the two ships were in the Austro-Hungarian port of Pola. Rear-Admiral Wilhelm Souchon, who flew his flag in *Goeben*, realised that a crisis was looming, and he had no desire to be trapped in the confined waters of the Adriatic. On 2 August, he was in the Strait of Messina, between Sicily and the Italian 'toe'. There he learned that Italy had declared her neutrality, but that war with France was imminent. Souchon decided to cruise off the coast of Algeria, hoping to intercept French troop convoys. However, on the night of 3–4 August he received new orders. He was to run the gauntlet of the Mediterranean, and head for Constantinople.

It really was a gauntlet, as to reach the Turkish capital, Souchon had to pass close to Malta, the bustling headquarters of the British Mediterranean Fleet. The German admiral bombarded the French Tunisian ports of Bône and Phillipeville that night, then headed back to Messina to take on coal. Shortly before noon on 4 August, the two German ships encountered the British battlecruisers *Indefatigable* and *Indomitable*. However, war had not yet been declared, and the British were unable to open fire. Gradually, Souchon's faster ships pulled away, and slipped over the horizon. Admiral Sir Berkeley Milne, commander of the Mediterranean Fleet, had orders to respect Italian neutrality, so he could not pursue Souchon into Messina. Instead, he posted ships to guard the exits from the Strait of Messina, and waited for the German commander to make his move.

Later, in the afternoon of 6 August, Souchon left Messina, and headed south. He hoped to slip past the British under cover of darkness, but while *Goeben* made it through unchecked, *Breslau* had to fight her way past the British light cruiser *Gloucester* before reaching the open waters of the Mediterranean. The British cruiser did her best to shadow the German ships, and used her radio to call for support. To complicate matters, Milne had been ordered to protect the French convoys, so he posted his battlecruisers off the coast of Sicily to prevent the Germans from doubling back to the west. In the Adriatic, Rear-Admiral Troubridge was waiting with four armoured cruisers in case Souchon tried to reach an Austro-Hungarian port. Still, the Germans were at sea, and both Milne and Troubridge were determined to find them, and then bring them to battle.

That night, Troubridge tried to catch the Germans, but his ships were too slow, and by dawn he had given up the chase. It was down to Milne now, and his battlecruisers raced eastwards in pursuit. By 9 August, Souchon had reached the Aegean, where he took on coal before steaming on towards the Dardanelles. Turkey was still a neutral country, but her sympathies lay with the Central Powers. Both Souchon and the German ambassador in Constantinople hoped that the arrival of two powerful German warships would encourage Turkey to ally with them. Souchon spent several fraught hours waiting for permission to enter Turkish waters, and when it came it was not a moment too soon. The funnel smoke of Milne's battlecruisers could be seen from the *Goeben*'s masthead. By nightfall, though, the two ships were safely at anchor off Constantinople, and Milne had lost the race.

Six days later, as a result of some frenzied diplomatic activity, *Goeben* and *Breslau* were handed over to the Turkish navy, and were renamed the *Yavus Sultan Selim* and the *Midilli*. Souchon and his men still continued to crew the two ships, though; all that changed was the flag flying from their mastheads. In fact, on 23 September, Souchon became the commander-in-chief of the Turkish navy. In late October, the two ships joined a Turkish squadron that bombarded the Russian ports of Odessa and Sevastopol, a deliberate move to force Russia's hand. Russia obliged by declaring war on Turkey on 2 November. So the failure of Milne at Troubridge to catch the *Goeben* led directly to Turkey joining the war as a German ally. For the Kaiser, this was well worth the loss of two German warships. However, the *Goeben* would also have been invaluable had she stayed in home waters.

Helgoland

These opening actions were important in setting the agenda of the naval war. The isolated German squadrons had no real hope of reaching home again, but they were commanded with courage and consummate professionalism. Less impressive was the British performance. In the Pacific it resulted in a small outgunned squadron being annihilated at Coronel before the naval status quo was restored off the Falkland Islands. In the Mediterranean, contradictory orders from the Admiralty and poor decisions made at sea led to two valuable German ships evading capture. This caused the disgrace of two British admirals, Milne and Troubridge. The incident also gave rise to a dramatic widening of the scope of the war when Turkey became a German ally. However gripping these campaigns were, though, and however avidly followed they were by the world's media, they did nothing to alter the naval balance in the real theatre of war.

In the North Sea, armchair admirals who predicted a decisive clash during the war's opening weeks were confounded by a surprising lack of activity. Meanwhile, the German armies drove through Belgium, investing the fortified city of Liège before marching on towards the French border. Brussels fell on 20 August, and four days later the stronghold of Namur surrendered. On 23 August, the British entered the fray near Mons, but the following day they joined the French in a general retreat towards the south. In other words, by the fourth week in August the German army was advancing steadily on all fronts. During these heady weeks, Jellicoe moved the Grand Fleet from Scapa Flow to Loch Ewe, on Scotland's west coast, until his anchorage in Orkney could be properly defended. Meanwhile, the British newspapers demanded action.

They got it on 28 August. Since the war began, Commodore Reginald Tyrwhitt's Harwich Force, a collection of light cruisers and destroyers, had been busy patrolling the southern part of the North Sea, reaching as far east as the island of Helgoland. This small fortified island marked the edge of Germany's defensive belt of minefields. A particularly large operation was planned for the last week in August, supported by a string of British submarines and a squadron of battlecruisers commanded by Vice-Admiral Sir David Beatty. When Jellicoe withdrew to Loch Ewe, Beatty moved his battlecruisers down to Rosyth near Edinburgh, where he was better placed to intercept the Germans if they made a sortie.

The plan was to ambush the daily patrol of the area by German destroyers, hitting them with an overwhelming number of British destroyers, supported by light cruisers. Beatty's battlecruisers and a second light cruiser force under Commodore William Goodenough would take up position well to the west of Helgoland, in case they were needed.

At 7 a.m. on 28 August, the cruiser *Arethusa* spotted the leading German destroyer and promptly opened fire. Behind the British cruiser, the destroyers deployed for the attack. Visibility was poor – just three nautical miles – and neither Tyrwhitt, Beatty or Goodenough really knew what to expect. The same was true of the German destroyer commander, Rear-Admiral Leberecht Maass, or his direct superior Vice-Admiral Franz Hipper, commander of the German battlecruiser group. The British destroyers sped past Tyrwhitt's flagship *Arethusa*, and soon a swirling destroyer melee began. The Germans were outnumbered, though, and pulled back to Helgoland. Tyrwhitt's destroyers gave chase, until, just after 8 a.m., they came upon a supporting force of German light cruisers. These had been sent forward by Hipper as soon as Maass had reported he was being attacked. For a moment, it seemed that the ambushers had become the ambushed.

The British destroyers were recalled, and *Arethusa* covered their withdrawal by exchanging fire with the leading German cruiser, the *Frauenlob*. Both ships were battered by enemy fire, but at 8.25 a.m. *Frauenlob* broke off the fight and limped back into Wilhelmshaven. The other German cruisers covered her retreat, then returned to the battle at 11 a.m. At this stage, Tyrwhitt radioed for help. It would take Beatty's battlecruisers a little over an hour to reach him, but Goodenough was a little closer. Tyrwhitt's two cruisers held on until they arrived, as German cruisers flitted in and out of the thickening mist. Half an hour later, the first of Goodenough's cruisers appeared from the north-west, taking the German cruiser *Mainz* by surprise. Within minutes, she was a floating wreck, although it would be another hour before she sank.

Then Beatty arrived, his ships powering out of the mist three miles to the north of the German cruisers. The Germans turned away at full speed, but before they could escape two of them, the *Köln* and the *Ariadne*, were reduced to burning hulks. Both cruisers sank during the afternoon. Meanwhile, the rest of the German vessels fled into the mist. At 2 p.m., Hipper's battlecruisers had finally raised enough steam to put to sea, but by then the British had withdrawn. The scrappy engagement known as the Battle of Helgoland was a clear British victory. The Germans had lost three light cruisers and three destroyers or torpedo boats, while several other warships had been damaged. By contrast, the only serious British casualty was Tyrwhitt's *Arethusa*, which had been badly damaged in her fight with the *Frauenlob*.

An officer on the *Ariadne* described the death of his ship; 'The *Lion* and another English battlecruiser fired at us for about half an hour at ranges from 6,000 down to 3,000 metres, scoring many hits that started numerous fires, which could not be extinguished because the fire mains were destroyed. Towards 13.30 the enemy turned away to the west. I assume that he could no longer make out the *Ariadne* through the smoke from the fires. It was impossible to remain on board because of the smoke and heat, and because the ready-use ammunition began to explode. So, the crew assembled on the forecastle, and three cheers were given for the Kaiser, after which *Deutschland über Alles* was sung. Then, shortly before 14.00, the *Danzig* approached and sent boats for the wounded. The rest of the crew jumped overboard, and swam to the *Danzig* and *Stralsund*.' Just over an hour later, the blazing cruiser capsized and sank, taking fifty-nine crewmen down with her.

In Britain, the Battle of Helgoland was dubbed a great victory. In fact, it was little more than a skirmish, albeit one that cost the Germans dear. The most significant outcome was the knee-jerk reaction of the Kaiser, who decreed that the fleet should avoid action that might lead to more losses, Worse, he added that from now on, his permission would be needed before the fleet could engage in any major operation. That meant that every time he wanted to sail further than Helgoland, Admiral von Ingenohl had to ask the Chief of the Naval Staff Admiral von Pohl, who would then seek the Kaiser's permission.

Tirpitz protested to the Kaiser, but Wilhelm was adamant. In fact, as Tirpitz put it; 'There sprang up from that day forth an estrangement between the Emperor and myself which steadily increased.' It was almost as if the Kaiser, who had always wanted a large and powerful fleet, now had no clear idea how it should be used. So it fell to the likes of Admiral Tirpitz, the Chief of Naval Staff Admiral Hugo von Pohl and Commander-in-Chief of the High Seas Fleet Admiral von Ingenohl to invent a coherent naval strategy on his behalf. It was certainly needed. So far, the Navy's handful of small U-Boats had achieved more than the rest of the fleet put together. It was now up to these admirals to establish a proper role for the High Seas Fleet. They also needed to find a low-risk way of tipping the balance – one the Kaiser could agree to. They knew that a shift of power would not come through remaining on the defensive.

5

Baiting the British

Thanks to the Kaiser, after Helgoland Admiral von Ingenohl had to wage a naval campaign with one hand tied behind his back. Still, he had little intention of ceding the initiative to the British. The Navy had lost face by letting the enemy attack them off Helgoland, just over an hour's sailing from Wilhelmshaven. He needed to restore the German public's faith in the fleet. What better way than to conduct a similar lightning raid against Britain? So, throughout October, von Ingenohl and his staff developed a plan they hoped was relatively risk-free, but which would humiliate the British. The scheme was duly given the Kaiser's blessing, and so on the afternoon of 2 November, Vice-Admiral Hipper's Scouting Group put to sea. His force consisted of three battlecruisers, an armoured cruiser and four light cruisers, one of which was laden with one hundred mines. Their objective was the small Norfolk seaside town of Great Yarmouth

At dawn the next day they arrived off the port. As the cruiser *Stralsund* laid its mines offshore, the rest of the German force engaged a local patrol – a minesweeper and two old destroyers. The British ships laid a smoke-screen and withdrew, leaving Hipper free to carry out a bombardment of the town. In fact, most of the shells fell harmlessly on the seafront. After just a few salvos, though, Hipper led his ships back out to sea, and the raid came to an end. Three British submarines were based in Yarmouth, and they put to sea during the attack, even though they had no real chance of catching the Germans. One of them, the *D-5*, ran straight into one of *Stralsund*'s mines, and she sank within minutes, taking all but five of her crew down with her. These submariners were the only casualties of the raid. It could have been different though; Beatty's battlecruisers were at sea, but failed to intercept Hipper as he returned home.

In fact, the Germans suffered a substantial loss of their own the following day. The armoured cruiser *Yorck* had formed part of a covering force for Hipper, and with the rest of her squadron she returned to Wilhelmshaven. Amid thick fog that morning she missed the swept channel into the port and ran into a minefield. She struck two mines almost simultaneously, and quickly capsized and sank with the loss of 336 men. It was an expensive end to such an unprofitable operation. This was the reason that Hipper refused a medal for his part in the action. Unlike the Kaiser, he and his men knew that the raid was not worthy of the honour. Despite achieving absolutely nothing, the raid was dubbed a huge success in the German newspapers. The Kaiser was delighted, and so von Ingenohl suggested another, even more ambitious sortie.

The Hartlepool Raid

This time von Ingenohl decided to attack the Yorkshire coast, bombarding the coastal towns of Hartlepool, Whitby and Scarborough. The first of these was defended by coastal batteries and harboured a small destroyer flotilla, but otherwise the towns were of no military or naval importance. However, the British knew the raid was coming. In late August, the German light cruiser *Magdeburg* ran aground off the coast of Estonia, and was captured. The Germans had thrown her top-secret fleet code books overboard, but unknown to them these were recovered, and were eventually passed on to the British Admiralty. Another code book was recovered by British fishermen the following month, after the sinking of a German destroyer off the Texel, while a third was taken from a German merchant ship impounded in Australia. The code-breakers in the Admiralty's 'Room 40' could now read German naval signals.

This meant that from early December on, the British were able to decrypt German radio traffic. As a result, they knew another raid was about to take place, they just didn't know where the Germans would strike. Strangely, the Germans failed to realise their 'SKM battle fleet code' had been broken until after the end of the war. That meant that until they introduced a new code system, 'FKK', in the spring of 1917, the

British could decrypt all of their naval signals. This was a coup almost as great as the celebrated breaking of the German Enigma codes in the Second World War. Another advantage enjoyed by the British was in direction finding. A chain of wireless receiving stations along Britain's North Sea coast intercepted German radio signals, and by comparing signal strengths at different points in their chain they could work out what direction the signals were coming from. This meant the British not only knew when the Germans would strike, but where their ships were. The Germans had a similar system, but the geography of their coastline limited its effectiveness.

For this new raid, von Ingenohl decided to use Hipper's battlecruisers again. This time Hipper commanded two Scouting Groups (SGs); the 1st SG consisted of four battlecruisers; his flagship *Seydlitz* plus *Moltke*, *Derfflinger* and *Von der Tann*. They were accompanied by the armoured cruiser *Blücher*. The 2nd SG was made up of four light cruisers, accompanied by a flotilla of destroyers. Hipper put to sea well before dawn on 15 December, and headed northwards towards the top of the belt of protective mines that now screened the waters west of Helgoland. By nightfall, he was heading westwards through the darkness towards the British coast.

Von Ingenohl was wisely taking no chances. During the Yarmouth attack he had sent out a small force to linger in the middle of the North Sea, to help extricate Hipper if anything went wrong. This time, as though he had a premonition of trouble, von Ingenohl led the bulk of the High Seas Fleet to sea as a covering force. It would wait near the Dogger Bank, the great submerged sandbank that dominated the centre of the North Sea. It was a sensible precaution, as Hartlepool was much closer to Beatty's base at Rosyth than Yarmouth had been – 136 nautical miles away rather than 200. This meant an encounter with Beatty's battlecruisers was much more likely than it had been a month before.

Thanks to their code-breakers in 'Room 40', the British Admiralty were well aware that something was afoot. So, during the morning of 15 December, Beatty sailed from Rosyth with four battlecruisers. From the Cromarty Firth, Vice-Admiral Sir George Warrender's 2nd Battle Squadron of six dreadnoughts headed southwards too, both groups driving through the heart of a winter gale. The two squadrons made a rendezvous at noon, and two hours later they were joined by a third squadron of four armoured cruisers. Many of the attendant destroyers were forced home by the bad weather, but a few persevered, and screened this powerful force as it sped south. By nightfall, Beatty had taken up station a little to the south of Dogger Bank, where he waited for Hipper. So, unbeknown to each other, during the night of 15–16 December, two forces of dreadnoughts were lurking within thirty miles of each other, with just the shallows of the Dogger Bank lying between them.

In fact, Hipper was already well to the west of the Dogger Bank, heading through the gale towards the British coast. They passed through the known gap in the minefield belt opposite Whitby before dawn, and then *Von der Tann* and *Derfflinger* plus a minelayer headed south to the seaside resort of Scarborough, while the rest of Hipper's force moved northwards towards Hartlepool. At 8 a.m. the southern group opened fire, the first shells landing near the town's Grand Hotel. Guests and staff alike hid in the hotel cellar as explosions rocked the building. The bombardment lasted for half an hour, demolishing buildings and churches, and even pounding the ruins of Scarborough Castle. By the end of it, seventeen people were dead and almost a hundred wounded. As the minelaying cruiser unloaded her deadly cargo off Flamborough Head, the two German battlecruisers steamed north towards their next target, the little fishing town of Whitby.

Whitby is best known through its association with its most famous son, Captain James Cook, the great eighteenth-century mariner who put Australia, New Zealand and half of the Pacific on the map. This time the port itself was largely spared, and most of the shells landed around the coastguard station, perched on top of the cliff overlooking the town. Still, the ruined abbey behind it was damaged, and by the time the ten-minute bombardment was over two townspeople were dead. Their job done, *Von der Tann* and *Derfflinger* and the minelaying cruiser headed north to rejoin Hipper, who was busy causing even more mayhem in Hartlepool. This town was an altogether more impressive target. It boasted a sizeable harbour, a shipyard and several engineering works, factories and foundries. It also warranted its own defences – a gun battery on a headland by the lighthouse, and a small naval force of two obsolete cruisers, four destroyers and a submarine.

Hipper began his bombardment at 8.10 a.m. A thick mist hung over the offshore side of Tees Bay, reducing visibility to less than three nautical miles. Lookouts on the shore saw the ships appear out of the mist, and wondered what nationality they were. The answer came moments later, when a ripple of flashes erupted from them, and shells began landing around the battery. Simultaneously, three destroyers from Hartlepool's naval contingent were returning home from a routine patrol, when the same line of ships appeared through the mist in front of them. The German gunners were ready, though, and within moments the secondary guns of the battlecruisers began firing at the destroyers. The destroyers turned away, but not before one of their crew was killed. In Hartlepool itself, the old cruiser *Patrol* tried to put to sea, but was stopped short by two shells fired from the *Blücher*. Meanwhile, the battlecruisers kept pounding the town.

The shooting was not all one way, though; the three 6-inch guns of Hartlepool's Lighthouse Battery fired back and even scored hits on *Blücher* and *Moltke*. Hipper's three ships had been steaming slowly northwards, firing as they went. Then, at 8.40 a.m., *Blücher*, the rearmost ship, turned away towards the open sea, while *Seydlitz* and *Moltke* reversed course and fired one last salvo before following the armoured cruiser into the mist. Within thirty-five minutes of the first salvo, the Germans had gone, while behind them a pall of smoke hung over the battered town. Both a steelworks and the town gasworks had been set ablaze, and over a hundred buildings had been damaged. As soon as the shells began falling, terrified and bewildered civilians fled inland, either heading towards the railway station or flooding down the roads leading out of town.

When the smoke cleared, the true extent of the damage was revealed. A total of ninety-two people had been killed, and hundreds more injured, most of them civilians. Hartlepool looked like a battle had raged through its streets, with rubble and bodies choking the streets. Further casualties were inflicted in Scarborough and Whitby, but there the damage had been less extensive. However, one of the key sites in both towns, the wireless and signal stations which formed part of Britain's direction-finding chain, had been utterly destroyed. With hindsight, the raid was a public relations disaster for Germany. The killing of innocent civilians, especially women and children, never looks good in the world's newspapers, and the British made the most of this. In Britain itself, 'Remember Scarborough' became a rallying cry for the enlistment offices. There was also criticism that the raid could have been allowed to happen by the Navy, whose job it was to defend Britain's coasts.

After they ceased fire Hipper's battlecruisers slipped back through the 'Whitby Gap' in the minefields, leaving their mine-carrying cruiser to sow more mines astern of them. The force steamed east throughout the morning, preceded by a screen of destroyers. The winter weather was atrocious, but Hipper made steady progress. Still, he was wary, as the Germans now knew that a sizeable British force lay somewhere out there, waiting to intercept him. A little after 7 a.m., a screen of destroyers despatched by von Ingenohl ran into their British counterparts, sent out by Beatty. A running fight followed, as the outnumbered Germans withdrew to the north and the British chased them. The German flotilla commander radioed the news to the flagship; the message was picked up by Hipper, who was just about to begin his bombardment. A British destroyer screen meant British capital ships were probably close by. While this was a serious threat, at least both von Ingenohl and Hipper now knew about it.

As dawn broke, von Ingenohl reached a decision. It was too risky to steam west to join forces with Hipper. The British now knew he was at sea, and his standing orders to avoid any major losses forced him to adopt a more cautious approach than he might have wished. So, Hipper would have to look after himself, trusting in the speed of his Scouting Group to stay out of trouble. The rest of the High Seas Fleet set a course for home. A little before 11.30 a.m., the light cruiser *Southampton* sighted a German cruiser to the west. This was the *Stralsund*, one of Hipper's 2nd Scouting Group. *Southampton* was part of Goodenough's squadron, and the commodore radioed Beatty, asking for orders. The reply came to disengage. Beatty thought *Southampton* had spotted a lone enemy cruiser, while his really quarry was the enemy battlecruiser squadron. Finding them was his top priority. So, Goodenough pulled away, not knowing that the German cruiser was the lead ship of Hipper's whole force.

An hour later, *Stralsund* spotted *Orion*, one of Warrender's dreadnoughts, but once again the order was given not to open fire. So *Stralsund* slipped from sight and continued on her way. The rest of the two Scouting Groups followed astern of her, hidden from the British by the swirling mist. The result was that Hipper escaped, and by mid afternoon he was well out of range of the British and heading back to Wilhelmshaven.

This was a real missed opportunity for Beatty. With his force of dreadnoughts and battlecruisers he could have annihilated Hipper's Scouting Group. Instead, he let them slip through his fingers. Of course, von Ingenohl had also missed a great opportunity, possibly the best chance the High Seas Fleet had during the war of overwhelming a major part of the Grand Fleet. With his superiority in dreadnoughts, victory would almost certainly have been his.

Rather hypocritically, the Kaiser reprimanded von Ingenohl for his caution when he read the report. His caution, of course, was the result of Wilhelm's standing orders about not putting the fleet at risk. So, caution on the German side and poor communications between Beatty and his subordinates meant that the chance of a decisive battle had been lost. If anything, though, this increased the likelihood of a clash the next time the fleets met, as the Germans were less willing to be cautious, while the British tried to improve the way they reported sightings. Christmas was coming, the first of the war, and while many sailors were able to snatch a few days of leave, Jellicoe, von Ingenohl and their chiefs of staff were already planning a new operation. This time, no opportunities would be missed in the quest to bring the enemy to battle.

Dogger Bank

The close-run thing that was the Hartlepool operation didn't deter von Ingenohl from planning a fresh enterprise after the New Year. The Kaiser authorised a series of short sweeps into the North Sea, largely to show the British that German naval forces were not just hiding behind their defensive minefields. This time, the secondary aim of luring of Beatty into a trap seems not to have been uppermost in von Ingenohl's mind. Instead his objective was very limited. For a while, German Naval High Command had suspected that British spy trawlers had been operating from the fishing grounds of the Dogger Bank. Hipper was ordered to sink or drive them off, together with the British light forces that usually protected the British fishing fleet when it was in the area. This was to be a quick raid, entirely in keeping with the Kaiser's directives. Few could have guessed that it would end in disaster.

At 5.45 p.m. on 24 January 1915, Hipper's two Scouting Groups left the Jade Estuary, and set a course through the belt of minefields to the west of Helgoland. The 1st Scouting Group was the same force that had taken part in the Hartlepool operation a month before, with one important exception: the battlecruiser *Von der Tann* was undergoing a refit in Wilhelmshaven, and so Hipper's flagship *Seydlitz* was accompanied by *Derfflinger*, *Moltke* and the *Blücher*. Hipper knew he might encounter Beatty, but he felt his Scouting Groups could handle themselves in any fight if the British should appear. He was forgetting his Achilles' Heel – the armoured cruiser *Blücher* lacked the armour and firepower of her larger consorts.

Thanks to wireless intercepts the British already knew that Hipper was putting to sea, and that his destination was the fishing grounds off the Dogger Bank. Jellicoe acted fast; men on leave were hurriedly recalled, and the ships raised steam. While this was happening, Jellicoe came up with a plan involving the Battlecruiser Fleet, the Harwich Force and the Grand Fleet. On the evening of 23 January, Beatty left Rosyth and steamed towards the Dogger Bank. A week before his Battlecruiser Force had been divided into two squadrons: the 1st comprising the 'Splendid Cats' *Lion, Tiger* and *Princess Royal*; and the 2nd under Rear-Admiral Sir Archibald Moore with *New Zealand* and *Indomitable*. Beatty flew his flag in the *Lion*. Accompanying him was Goodenough's 1st Light Cruiser Squadron. Meanwhile, Commodore Tyrwhitt's Harwich Force was heading north to rendezvous with Beatty off the Dogger Bank at 7 a.m. the following morning. Tyrwhitt's force comprised three flotillas of destroyers, each with a light cruiser acting as flotilla leader.

Jellicoe also put to sea with the bulk of the Grand Fleet and steamed towards the south-east. He would take up position 150 nautical miles to the north of the fishing grounds, in case Beatty needed his support. Finally, four submarines were sent from Harwich to take up position off the western edge of the German minefields. They were stationed there in case the High Seas Fleet should leave port, or in the hope they would be able to intercept Hipper's ships heading home. So, while Jellicoe, Beatty and Tyrwhitt knew the German Scouting Groups were steaming towards the Dogger Bank, neither Hipper nor von Ingenohl were aware the British were heading towards the fishing grounds from two different directions. Hipper was sailing into a trap, and without the support of the dreadnoughts his battlecruisers would be on their own.

Hipper reached the north-eastern corner of Dogger Bank just before dawn and ordered his four light cruisers to search for the British fishing fleet. When dawn broke, it revealed a clear, crisp day, with near perfect visibility. At 7.15 a.m., the German screen spotted British light cruisers approaching from the north-west. This suggested that a substantial British force was in the area. The two sides opened fire, and both the British *Aurora* and the German *Kolberg* were hit in the brief exchange. The 2nd Scouting Group commander was Vice-Admiral Georg Hebbinghaus, who flew his flag in the cruiser *Graudenz*. He ordered his ships to turn away to the south-east, and radioed the news to Hipper. Although the British cruisers belonged to Tyrwhitt, Hipper suspected they formed part of Beatty's Battlecruiser Fleet. He was right of course; Beatty and Tyrwhitt had joined company shortly before the rival fleets made contact.

Hipper must have sensed he was heading into danger. His orders were also clear about avoiding unnecessary risk. So, at 8.30 a.m., he turned his battlecruisers about, and within minutes the 1st Scouting Group began racing out of the jaws of Beatty's trap. This done, he sent a radio message to Wilhelmshaven, reporting the sighting to von Ingenohl, and relaying his suspicions that Beatty was pursuing him. The order was given and the dreadnoughts of the High Seas Fleet began raising steam. By 10.30 a.m. they began filing out of Wilhelmshaven, as von Ingenohl laid his own plans to ambush Beatty after Hipper had lured him eastwards towards the High Seas Fleet. It was an interesting situation, with both battlecruiser forces and both main battle fleets at sea. This could well have developed into the great clash everyone had been waiting for.

By now, Beatty was just a dozen miles to the north-west of Hipper, and soon the two lines of battlecruisers spotted each other. Both groups were on the same south-easterly heading, with the Germans ahead of the British. With their superior speed, Beatty's faster 'Splendid Cats' were gradually closing the range. Like Hipper, Beatty's ships were steaming in line astern, with the flagship in the lead. At 8.52 a.m., *Lion* opened fire with her forward guns, even though technically the Germans were out of effective range. Her target was the *Blücher*, the last ship in the German line. Within seventeen minutes, the gap between the ships had dropped to 9½ miles (19,000 yards) and despite this extreme range *Lion* scored her first hit. This was something of a milestone in naval gunnery – the longest distance at which one ship had successfully fired at another.

It was a harbinger of naval warfare to come, and a justification for Fisher's emphasis on the importance of long-range gunnery.

In fact, the two lines of battlecruisers were not following each other, they were on parallel courses, with the Germans 3½ miles (7,000 yards) to the east of Beatty. This meant that as the faster British ships began to overhaul the Germans, the ships in both lines drew in range of each other. The British ships trained their bow guns as far forward as the ship in front of them would allow, while the Germans trained their stern guns aft in the same way. Soon all five British and four German ships were blazing away, their guns elevated to almost maximum range. The range was shortening though, with Hipper's ships managing just 24 knots to the 29 knots logged by the British. Beatty enjoyed another advantage, too. The wind was from the north-east, and so it blew the funnel smoke away from his ships. The opposite was true for Hipper's battlecruisers, where the billowing smoke made the job of range finding especially difficult.

The faster 'Splendid Cats' began to edge away from the two slower battlecruisers at the end of the British line, but this didn't matter – everything centred around the chase. On board *Lion*, Lieutenant Young was climbing the foremast when 'a terrific blow and a shake proclaimed that *Lion* had been hit'. A shell from *Blücher* had hit *Lion*'s 'A' turret, and put it out of action. It would be the first of many hits on both sides as the great guns found the range. To avoid confusion, Beatty ordered that each of his ships should fire at the equivalent ship in the enemy line: *Lion* at *Seydlitz*, *Tiger* at *Moltke*, *Princess Royal* at *Derfflinger* and then *New Zealand* and *Indomitable* at *Blücher*. On board *Tiger*, the message was misunderstood, and it kept firing at Hipper's flagship *Seydlitz*. This meant that nobody was firing at *Moltke*.

A young British officer was watching the scene unfold from the light cruiser *Aurora*; 'It was wonderful to see our battlecruisers steaming at top speed with spurts of flame and brown smoke issuing every minute or so from their bows and sides – and in the far distance the enemy's guns flashing in reply. From shots falling in the water there were tall columns of white spray. From others, there were, more ominously, no splash, as they scored a hit, which caused black smoke and bright flashes from the injured craft.' He added, with the enthusiasm of youth; 'It was all very exciting!'

At 9.45 a.m., a shell from *Lion* pierced the after turret of *Seydlitz* and it exploded in the hoist. This ignited a powder charge being brought up from the magazine, and a flash fire incinerated almost everyone inside the gun turret. The flash also travelled down the hoist to the magazines, where men tried to escape the rushing flames by jumping into an adjacent compartment. This didn't work. Instead, the fireball swept through the protective door, and roared into the handling room of 'C' turret. The result was an explosion and a second fireball which rose up the shaft into 'C' turret. Only quick thinking saved the ship – at the cost of yet more lives. The after magazines were flooded, drowning the men trapped inside. However, a greater disaster was averted. That one shell hit had claimed the lives of 159 men, all immolated within a few horrifying seconds, or consigned to a slower death by drowning as cold sea water slowly filled the sealed magazine compartments.

Still, *Seydlitz* was still afloat, and hitting back. This, though, prompted Hipper to contact von Ingenohl again, signalling 'need assistance badly'. His superior sent back the message 'main fleet and flotillas will come as soon as possible'. For Hipper, at that moment, it looked like that might not be soon enough. Beatty had slowed his speed to 24 knots now, so that the two forces were keeping at a constant range. This made gunnery easier, but the Germans were now concentrating on *Lion*, and she began taking hits. At 10.01 a.m., a shell from *Moltke* pierced her below the waterline, and she began listing to port. Shells kept striking her, and then at 10.18 a.m. she took a real body blow. Lieutenant Filson Young in the foretop spotting tower thought that they must have been torpedoed. In fact, the battlecruiser had been hit twice below the waterline, and was flooding fast. She also lost steam power to one of her boilers and her electrical systems failed. As her speed dropped dramatically, the British flagship pulled out of the fight.

Now *Tiger* was in the lead, and the German battlecruisers began concentrating on her. A shell from *Derfflinger* struck the roof of 'Q' turret but didn't penetrate its armour. Still, the turret was jammed and the guns silenced through lack of hydraulic power. Other shells struck the boat deck below her funnels, and a raging fire began. Amazingly it did little real damage; after setting the boats ablaze it died back, and the ship's damage control teams managed to get the blaze under control. It was at that moment that Beatty made a blunder that would spare

Hipper, and seal the fate of the *Blücher*. Imagining he had seen the wake of a periscope to starboard, he ordered an immediate turn to port, and the rest of the British force followed. This meant he was now steaming at right angles to Hipper's fleeing ships. There was no U-boat, but the false sighting allowed Hipper to slip away.

With the rest of the German fleet pulling out of range, the British concentrated their fire on the hapless *Blücher*. Again, this was down to Beatty, who hoisted the signal 'engage the rear of the enemy', but dallied over the second part of his order – 'course north-east' – a course that would have resumed the chase of Hipper's ships. So the five British ships began pounding the *Blücher* as the rest of Hipper's Scouting Group sped to safety. A little after 11 a.m. a shell from *Princess Royal* hit the armoured cruiser, and her speed dropped off. Soon, she was being struck repeatedly as the other battlecruisers found the range. A German survivor recalled that they were hit so many times it was like one continuous explosion. Fireballs raced through her lower decks, and steam scalded men in the engine room. Her coal ignited in her bunkers, and bodies were scattered like dead leaves by the great blasts of air pressure caused by so many shells hitting such a small confined space. *Blücher* was fast became a floating charnel house.

At 11.45 a.m., the British guns stopped firing and the battlecruisers sped by the fire-ravaged ship, their crews watching as German sailors jumped into the sea to avoid being burned alive. At 12.07 p.m., *Blücher* capsized and sank, and the cruiser *Arethusa* and several destroyers moved in to pick up survivors. Of her 1,200-man crew, only 234 men lived long enough to be rescued.

Watching the tragedy unfold 1,300 feet above the North Sea was Lieutenant Commander Heinrich Mathy, in the zeppelin *L-5*. Later, he wrote; 'The four English battlecruisers fired at her [*Blücher*] together. She replied for as long as she could, until she was completely shrouded in smoke and apparently on fire. At 1207 she heeled over and capsized.' The former destroyer captain was obviously frustrated by his inability to intervene. He added; 'You can imagine how distressing it was to watch the *Blücher* capsize, and be helpless to do anything but to observe and report.'

By then, Hipper's battlecruisers had disappeared. He had watched the *Blücher* tragedy unfold, but was unable to do anything about it. To turn back would mean losing the rest of his squadron. The crew of the *Seydlitz* were fighting to keep their ship afloat, so Hipper was hopelessly out-numbered. The battle was over. That afternoon Hipper managed to rendezvous with von Ingenohl, and the lurking British submarines failed to make contact. By evening the German fleet was safely back in port. On the other side of the North Sea, Beatty transferred into a destroyer, and then boarded *Tiger*. His priority was to make sure the crippled *Lion* reached port without sinking; the crew's success was no mean feat considering the damage she had suffered. At 5.30 p.m. Jellicoe's Grand Fleet arrived to escort the battlecruisers into Rosyth. *Lion* survived – as did *Seydlitz* – and both ships would clash again at Jutland.

Meanwhile, the recriminations began. Jellicoe was criticised for not moving the Grand Fleet south in time to join in the fight, while of course Beatty had numerous charges levelled at him by the British press, the most serious of which was the mishandling of his squadron. In fact, he led it reasonably well, right up until he spotted his imaginary periscope. That course change and the signalling problems that followed allowed Hipper to get away, and saved the *Seydlitz* from following *Blücher* to the bottom. Hipper was castigated for taking *Blücher* with him on the operation and also for abandoning her to her fate. These though, were not viable charges, and he had done the best he could in the circumstances.

The most serious condemnation was reserved for von Ingenohl. Why, Tirpitz argued, had he kept the fleet in port, when it should have been covering Hipper? Because of that, he missed a great opportunity to ambush Beatty. Captain von Egidy of the *Seydlitz* commented; 'The plan for the operation didn't take into account the likelihood of English warships being in the North Sea. The 24th demonstrated how precarious a situation battlecruisers can find themselves in when sent into battle without the battle fleet's support. If we had known that our main body was behind us, Hipper would not have been forced to abandon the *Blücher*. We would have saved this ship, just as the English saved the *Lion*.' The whole operation had been badly planned, and Hipper's battlecruisers had been left to their own devices. The Kaiser agreed, and a week after the battle he sacked his fleet commander.

Von Ingenohl was replaced by Admiral Hugo von Pohl, the Chief of the Admiralty Staff. The decision was made by the Kaiser, but it surprised Tirpitz, who felt von Pohl was not up to the job. In fact, the decision was in keeping with Wilhelm's desire not to risk the battle fleet. Von Pohl was an overly cautious commander, and under his wardship there would be no repeat of the rash sorties indulged in by his predecessor. Instead, he placed a greater emphasis on the U-Boat campaign, a course that would bring the new fleet commander into conflict with Tirpitz. Meanwhile, the two great fleets repaired their ships, and settled down to wait for the next clash. Few would have guessed they would have to wait a full year before the fleets would meet again.

Part II

The Clash of the Titans

6

The Spring Sorties

Soon after the New Year of 1916, Admiral Hugo von Pohl began to feel ill, and went to see a naval doctor. On 8 January, he was transferred to a hospital ship, where he was given a thorough examination by specialists. They confirmed what he already suspected; he was suffering from liver cancer, and the disease was already in its advanced stages. That afternoon he was taken by train to Berlin, for a last-minute attempt to cut out the cancer. The surgery failed and the admiral's condition continued to worsen. He died on 23 February, just six weeks after falling ill. At the time, von Pohl's second-in-command was Vice-Admiral Reinhard Scheer, commander of the III Battle Squadron. He immediately took over command of the fleet on a temporary basis. On 18 January, when it was clear the Admiral was dying, the Kaiser confirmed Scheer as the new permanent commander of the High Seas Fleet.

Scheer takes Command

The two commanders could hardly have been more different. Von Pohl was autocratic and dour. A pre-war British naval attaché described him as a man who looked like he had lost half a crown and found sixpence. He was also imbued with the Kaiser's sense of caution, preferring to wage the naval campaign through the U-Boat fleet rather than risk his dreadnoughts in another ill-advised sortie. By contrast, Scheer was a middle-class Saxon rather than an aristocratic Prussian, and he was popular with his men, despite his reputation as a strict disciplinarian. Scheer's career had been one of slow and steady advancement, but his proficiency in his specialist field of torpedo warfare eventually caught the eye of Tirpitz, and Scheer was drafted to the Admiralty's torpedo office. This led to promotion and his first command, the cruiser *Gazelle*. Finally, Scheer's star was beginning to rise.

He became a captain in 1905, and two years later he was given command of the battleship *Elsass*. In 1909, he was named as Chief of Staff to Admiral von Holtzendorff, the High Seas Fleet commander, and the following year he reached flag rank. As a Rear-Admiral, Scheer soon found himself back in the Admiralty, where he spent a year serving as Chief of the Navy Department before returning to the fleet in early 1913 as commander of a battle squadron. His promotion to Vice-Admiral came later that year. After the war began, he served under von Ingenohl, a commander he criticised for being too cautious. Then came von Pohl, who made his predecessor look like a rash adventurer. It was clear that now Scheer was in charge, these days of remaining in port were over. He planned to use his fleet much as von Ingenohl had done, only Scheer intended to do so far more aggressively. So began the sequence of events which would lead to the greatest naval clash since Trafalgar.

The aggressive stance was not decided upon a whim. After the Dogger Bank battle, Tirpitz wrote a memo saying he thought the battle was a final missed opportunity. He argued that the naval balance had shifted markedly in Britain's favour, thanks to the newly commissioned dreadnoughts which had recently joined the Grand Fleet. The fleeting moment had passed and the High Seas Fleet was now too badly outnumbered to have a chance of winning the naval war. This was a message which von Pohl welcomed, and it spurred him to concentrate his efforts on waging a U-Boat campaign. During von Pohl's year-long tenure the naval balance had shifted even further in Jellicoe's favour. However, Scheer realised that to cede control of the North Sea to Britain meekly was a betrayal of the huge resources Germany had poured into the creation of a battle fleet. By pursuing a more active strategy, he hoped to justify the fleet's very existence.

Since taking charge, von Pohl had strengthened and expanded the defences of the Helgoland Bight. The minefields were pushed further forward along the neutral Dutch coast until they stretched 170 nautical miles in a great arc from the Dutch island of Terschelling to the coast of the Danish peninsula of Jutland. Minesweeping patrols sortied from behind this defensive perimeter to keep its exits clear of British mines, while the same channels were guarded by torpedo boats. Scheer continued this policy, but rather than seeing it as defensive barrier, he regarded it as a safe haven where he could gather his fleet before sending them out into the North Sea. Scheer had other assets too: U-Boats were stationed off Harwich, Rosyth and Scapa Flow to provide him with an early-warning system of British naval movements; and the zeppelins of the Naval Airship Division now conducted regular long-range sweeps over the North Sea, ranging as far west as the British coast.

In fact, zeppelins lay behind Scheer's first aggressive sortie. In late January, nine zeppelins crossed the North Sea and bombed towns in the Midlands. Although these caused little damage and there were few casualties, the Admiralty was pressured into taking action. The small warships that regularly patrolled as far east as the edge of the German minefields were reinforced and told to provide early warning of any future raids. Scheer reacted to this by organising a sweep of the area to the west of Helgoland. On the night of 10–11 February, three torpedo boat flotillas drove the British patrols away, sinking a minesweeper in the process. Although this little skirmish was given the imposing title of the Second Battle of Dogger Bank, it was not really a battle at all. However, Jellicoe took no chances and the Grand Fleet put to sea, as did Beatty' battlecruisers and Tyrwhitt's Harwich Force. By then, though, the German torpedo boats were already heading back to port.

Baiting the Lion

By March, Scheer was ready to conduct a sortie using the whole High Seas Fleet. His plan was to send Hipper's battlecruisers south to fall upon the pre-dreadnoughts guarding the eastern end of the English Channel. Unlike von Ingenohl, though, Scheer supported Hipper properly, with his dreadnoughts following 30 miles behind the Scouting Groups. The sortie began on the night of 4–5 March, and by mid-morning Hipper had passed the Dutch barrier islands and turned south towards Dover. A pair of Zeppelins had flown ahead to bomb Hull and as they passed over Hipper's Scouting Group they reported that no enemy warships had been seen. So it proved. The southern portion of the North Sea seemed unusually devoid of British ships. Tyrwhitt stayed in port and, although Jellicoe and Beatty put to sea, they remained well to the north of the Dogger Bank.

On 6 March, the German fleet returned home, the seamen in high spirits after what they saw as a successful sweep.

This sortie was important for Scheer. The long year of idleness had taken its toll on morale. Both press and public had criticised this naval inactivity while German soldiers were fighting and dying in Flanders and Poland. Now the High Seas Fleet was fighting back. Scheer was disappointed that he had not managed to lure Beatty south. This, after all, had been a stated secondary aim. It was clear that Beatty was reluctant to move too far away from the cover of Jellicoe's dreadnoughts. So, for his next sortie, Scheer planned to strike further north. He was still wary of operating too close to Jellicoe's base in Scapa Flow, but a glance at the chart and a few calculations showed that if he provoked a response from Beatty by appearing in the right place, then he might be able to overpower him before Jellicoe could come to Beatty's rescue.

On 24 April, Scheer put to sea again. Back in November 1914, Hipper's battlecruisers had conducted a singularly ineffective bombardment of Great Yarmouth, when hundreds of tons of beach sand were thrown around, but otherwise the town was unscathed. Now Scheer planned to bombard the town again. Its advantage over British coastal towns further north was that it lay closer to Wilhelmshaven than either Scapa Flow or Rosyth. If an attack there could lure Beatty south, there was a chance the British battlecruisers could be overwhelmed before Jellicoe could intervene. The plan was not a new one, it was just that Scheer was keener on carrying it out than his predecessors. This time, though, Scheer would coordinate the raid with a zeppelin raid on East Anglia. Even if Beatty didn't intervene, it might force Jellicoe to divide his fleet in order to cover the whole of the British North Sea coast.

The German battlecruisers slipped out of Wilhelmshaven on the morning of 24 April. For once Hipper wasn't in command; he was sick, and so Rear-Admiral Friedrich Bödicker led the Scouting Groups. He now had five battlecruisers in the 1st Scouting Group, as *Lützow* had just entered service. These capital ships were preceded by the six light cruisers of the 2nd Scouting Group and ringed by two flotillas of destroyers. Scheer had also put to sea with the rest of the High Seas Fleet and planned to wait for Hipper off Terschelling, just outside the western edge of his minefields. However, at 4 p.m., Bödicker's flagship *Seydlitz* struck a mine in a field recently sown by the British and a hole was ripped in her bow. The flooding was contained, but *Seydlitz* had no option but to turn back, escorted by two destroyers and a zeppelin. Bödicker shifted his flag to the *Lützow* and the sortie continued.

Shortly before dawn the remaining six zeppelins forged ahead, and began their bombing raid on a number of East Anglian towns. While nobody was killed in the attack, it stirred up a hornet's nest of indignation. At 4 a.m., the German battlecruisers had come within sight of the coast and formed a line parallel to the Lowestoft seafront. The Polish-born Captain Hans Zenker of the *Von der Tann* described the bombardment; 'Mist over the sea and smoke from the ships ahead made it difficult to make out our targets as we steered for Lowestoft. But, after we turned the Empire Hotel offered us an ample landmark for an effective bombardment.' The hotel, which first opened in 1900, dominated the seafront from its perch at the top of Kirkley Cliff to the south of the harbour. A primary school now stands on the site of the five-storey hotel.

Zenker continued; 'At 5.11 a.m. [4.11 a.m. in Britain] we opened fire with our heavy and medium calibres on the harbour works and swing bridges. After a few "shorts" the shooting was good. From the after-bridge a fire in the town, and from another vantage point a great explosion at the [harbour] entry were reported.' The bombardment only lasted nine minutes. The battlecruisers then headed eight miles up the coast until they reached Great Yarmouth. Here, the bombardment was even shorter; it began at 4.42 a.m. and finished three minutes later. It was cut short due to the unexpected arrival of Commodore Tyrwhitt's Harwich Force. This appeared from the south, firing as it came, but as soon as Tyrwhitt spotted the battlecruisers, he ordered his ships to turn away. Before they escaped, though, the brand-new light cruiser *Conquest* was hit by a 12-inch shell from either *Derfflinger* or *Lützow*, but she was able to limp away to safety. The bombardment over, Bödicker headed back out to sea.

The passage across the North Sea was uneventful, and the battle-cruisers re-joined the rest of the High Seas Fleet to the west of Terschelling. Scheer lingered there as long as he could, but after British submarines were sighted he decided to bring the sortie to an end and return home. Meanwhile, both Jellicoe and Beatty were at sea. The Grand Fleet had made its own sortie the week before, a fruitless sweep as far as far as Horn Reef that made no contact with the enemy. The west coast of Jutland was blanketed by thick fog, and in the murk the battlecruisers

Australia and *New Zealand* collided. *Australia* was damaged badly enough to need dry docking in Rosyth when she returned. Jellicoe returned to Scapa Flow on 24 June, and before his flagship *Iron Duke* had hooked on to her usual buoy he learned that the Germans were at sea.

After a hurried taking on of coal and oil, his ships passed through Hoxa Sound for the second time in twenty-four hours, and after clearing the Pentland Firth they set a course to intercept Hipper off Terschelling. By noon on the 25 April, the main body of the Grand Fleet were 100 nautical miles to the east of Berwick, steering towards the south-east at 20 knots. Ahead of Jellicoe were three other groups of warships. Seventy miles ahead of him was the 5th Battle Squadron – consisting of four of the new Queen Elizabeth class 'fast battleships'. In between was a squadron of pre-dreadnoughts, ships which were already on passage south when the orders came to follow the 'fast battleships'. Even further in front were the two squadrons of the Battlecruiser Fleet, accompanied by a small screen of cruisers and destroyers. Beatty was going at full speed, and was therefore drawing away from the rest of the British fleet. This meant that the Grand Fleet was badly strung out and vulnerable to just the kind of attack Scheer had been dreaming of.

Unfortunately for Scheer his ships lacked the fuel to linger off Terschelling long enough to stay and fight. If they had and if Beatty had made contact, then there is little doubt that he would have suffered badly before he could withdraw. Even with the support of the other two advance squadrons of 'fast battleships' and pre-dreadnoughts, the odds would have been stacked heavily against him. Still, it wasn't to be. By the time Scheer led his ships back into port on 25 April, Beatty was still 200 nautical miles away, a full eight hours of fast steaming. When the news was passed on to him by his submarines, Jellicoe ordered his own ships to return to their bases. In the end, the Lowestoft and Yarmouth operation achieved little. It certainly hadn't produced the favourable encounter Scheer had been hoping for.

Although only four civilians had been killed, twenty-one fewer than on board the *Conquest*, public outrage in Britain was immense, and political pressure forced Jellicoe to react. His solution was to send the pre-dreadnoughts of the 2nd Battle Squadron to Sheerness, where it could intercept any further German attacks. The eight King Edward VII class battleships that made up the squadron were collectively known in the fleet as 'the wobbly eight', due to their propensity to roll heavily in anything but the calmest of seas. To bolster these vulnerable ships, Jellicoe also despatched the *Dreadnought* with them to serve as the squadron flagship. First though, she was sent for a much-needed refit. So the ship that started it all would miss out on the great clash of dreadnoughts off Jutland less than a month later.

On 26 May, Jellicoe wrote to Beatty, explaining his recent criticism of Beatty's performance in his report to the Admiralty; 'I hope you do not think that because I criticise and wish to discuss these points that I am in any way disloyal . . . It cannot be patriotic to sit down and say nothing when we . . . cannot retaliate when somebody else endeavours to strike us.' On Beatty's rashness in outstripping the dreadnoughts behind him, Jellicoe commented; 'The leopard cannot change its spots.' Turning to reacting to Scheer's sorties, he said; 'Changing of bases won't do it. Commodore (T) from Harwich wasn't in time. We from here weren't, and both of us could have been.' He ruled out leaving Scapa Flow, as no other base on the North Sea was suitable, then encouraged Beatty to communicate freely with him. Beatty, annoyed at being criticised, did nothing. A few days later, his reluctance to communicate with Jellicoe would have profound repercussions.

By then four of the new Queen Elizabeth class 'fast battleships' had joined the Grand Fleet, with a fifth due in May. In fact, like *Dreadnought*, this fifth ship – *Queen Elizabeth* – would be undergoing a refit when her sister ships sailed off to Jutland. The term 'fast battleship' was used to refer to a third generation of dreadnoughts because, with a top speed of 23 knots, they were marginally faster than their predecessors and were therefore grouped into their own distinct squadron. More importantly, they carried eight 15-inch guns apiece, the largest calibre gun in either Jellicoe or Scheer's fleets.

The Royal Sovereign class had a similar speed and armament to the Queen Elizabeths, although they were slightly less well armoured. The first of these, the *Revenge* joined the Grand Fleet in March, and Jellicoe expected two of her sister ships to join him during May. So Jellicoe could afford to lose *Dreadnought* from the Grand Fleet by stationing her in Sheerness in order to appease his political masters.

There was almost as much public outcry over the zeppelin raid on East Anglia as about the bombardment of two of the area's seaside towns.

This led to yet more political pressure, and so, a week later, Jellicoe took his fleet to sea again on a mission of revenge. His target was the zeppelin base at Tondern (now the Danish town of Tønder) in Schleswig. The base became operational in the spring of 1915, and consisted of three large hangars, plus a fourth smaller one for a flight of fighters used for base defence. There was also a sizeable gasworks on the edge of the field, a small barracks and a radio tower. In early May 1916, there were just four zeppelins based there, but unlike the much larger Nordholz base near Cuxhaven, the Tondern facility lay at the very edge of Germany's protective minefields. So Jellicoe decided to attack it using bomb-carrying seaplanes, launched from his two seaplane carriers *Engadine* and *Vindex*.

The whole of the Grand Fleet sailed from Scapa Flow during the afternoon of 2 May, with the battlecruisers sailing early the following morning. The two groups rendezvoused later that day, and screened by destroyers and cruisers they made their way to the coast of Jutland. By dawn on 4 May the fleet lay off Horns Reef, but the seas were rough, and conditions were getting steadily worse. This made launching the seaplanes almost impossible. *Engadine* and *Vindex* carried eleven Sopwith Baby floatplanes between them, but only three of them were launched successfully. Of these, one was damaged when it clipped the mast of an escorting destroyer, while another developed mechanical problems. Both had to land and were winched back on board, but the third aircraft carried on with its mission.

The zeppelin base lay 48 miles to the south-east of the launch position, which the plane covered in half an hour. When it reached the base, it dropped its single 65-pound bomb outside a hanger, but this caused no real damage. The zeppelins were away on a raid, so the field was empty of better targets. The frail little plane returned, and with some difficulty it was winched back on board *Engadine*. However, this was not the only aircraft to feature in the operation. That morning, as the Grand Fleet approached Horns Reef, it was spotted by one of the Tondern zeppelins, the *L-7*. She approached closer to the fleet than she should have and was badly hit by fire from the light cruisers *Galatea* and *Phaeton*. She caught fire, lost altitude, and crashed in the sea just off the Danish coast. A British submarine surfaced and rescued seven survivors from the crashed airship. The Tondern raid itself was a failure, but at least Jellicoe could now say he had lessened the zeppelin threat. Jellicoe and Beatty returned to Scapa Flow and Rosyth, where they waited for Scheer to make his next move.

What these spring operations showed was that Scheer was certainly more aggressive than his predecessors, and that he was willing to use the dreadnoughts of the High Seas Fleet to provide proper support for probes by his Scouting Groups. He also seemed eager to bring on a battle – in fact that was the primary aim of the Lowestoft and Yarmouth raid. That a naval clash didn't happen was down to time and distance. It was almost 400 nautical miles from Scapa Flow to the coast of East Anglia or the Dutch barrier island of Terschelling. That meant it would take the Grand Fleet twenty hours to reach these places, while Hipper's battlecruisers could make the crossing to East Anglia in six hours. Beatty in Rosyth would take almost twelve hours to get there. However, Scheer's 'window of opportunity' was a small one. He couldn't wait for long due to fuel consumption, particularly by his destroyers, and the longer he lingered, the greater the threat of a British submarine attack became.

To Scheer, it also seemed that Jellicoe was reluctant to operate further south than Dogger Bank. So, if the two fleets were going to meet, then it was more likely to happen further north, above the latitude of 55° North, which ran through Newcastle, Dogger Bank and the German island of Sylt, off the coast of Schleswig. Jellicoe seemed quite happy crossing the North Sea above this line, and going as far east as Horns Reef, within sight of the shores of Jutland. Scheer realised this, and so he decided to conduct his next sortie towards the north, where the chances of bringing Jellicoe to battle would be much greater. First though, he had to deal with the problem of intelligence. Like the British, the Germans used a string of directional wireless stations to gain some information about British movements. To help him though, he really needed to know when Jellicoe and Beatty put to sea. That way he could work out where the fleets might meet. Fortunately, he had already had the means at hand to do just that.

Taking the Bait

Admiral Scheer's predecessor Hugo von Pohl had been a great advocate of the U-Boat, and had countered Britain's blockade of Germany by imposing one of his own. This, though, would be an undersea blockade, the first of its kind in the history of warfare. His fleet of U-Boats would be his blockading force, prowling the waters around the British Isles in search of prey. More controversially, von Pohl also planned to lift the humanitarian restrictions placed upon his U-Boat commanders. Until then, U-Boats had followed the international legal rules on 'commerce raiding', which meant unarmed merchant ships had to be warned before an attack was made, and their crews given the chance to abandon ship. Instead, von Pohl declared that it would not always be possible to warn the passengers and crew of a ship that they were in danger. This was the start of 'unrestricted U-Boat warfare', in which boats could sink enemy ships without any kind of warning.

Grand Admiral Tirpitz was opposed to this dramatic change in the rules of war. So too was Kaiser Wilhelm, especially after US President Woodrow Wilson protested that this was an act unprecedented in naval warfare. So the Kaiser ordered von Pohl not to target neutrals, particularly American ones. For the moment a diplomatic disaster was averted, and the U-Boat commanders who enforced the undersea blockade limited their attacks to Allied ships. This was successful enough though; between May and September 1915 these U-Boats sunk over 780,000 tons of shipping. They suffered losses themselves; fifteen U-boats were lost, including *U-29*, which had sunk three British cruisers earlier in the war. In March 1915, she was rammed and sunk by the *Dreadnought*, the only time Fisher's great ship ever took on a German opponent. Another casualty of the campaign was Tirpitz, who resigned when the Kaiser refused to stop unrestricted U-Boat attacks.

Still, by the autumn of 1915 it was clear that the campaign was not working. The sinking of the great Cunard liner RMS *Lusitania* in May – labelled by Churchill the greatest single atrocity of the war – led to a major rift between Germany and the United States. Of the 1,198 people who died, 128 were American citizens. In the United States, public opinion instantly turned against Germany, and American politicians became increasingly supportive of Britain. This proved too much for Kaiser Wilhelm, and in September he ordered von Pohl to end his campaign. When Scheer took over command of the High Seas Fleet, he used his U-Boats to attack British warships, to conduct reconnaissance patrols, or to screen the movements of his surface ships. Now he planned to merge the first two of these roles into one. His boats would report when Jellicoe and Beatty put to sea, and then they would attack them. That way they might even the odds before the two great dreadnought fleets met in battle.

For much of May, a large portion of the High Sea Fleet busied itself conducting an exercise in the Baltic. Scheer, though, was planning

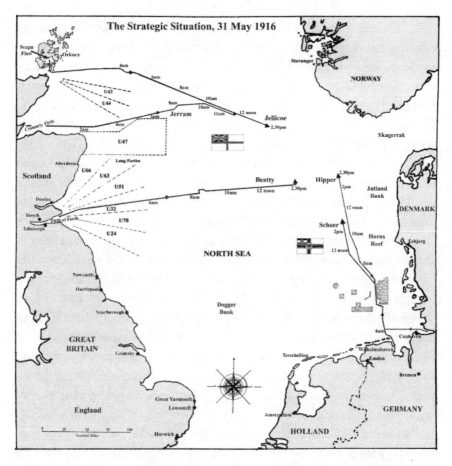

The Strategic Situation, 31 May 1916

another raid, this time on Sunderland, just south of Newcastle. He'd already sent out ten U-Boats to lie off the eastern approaches to the Pentland Firth and the Firth of Forth. Three other boats would lay mines off Orkney, the Firth of Forth and the Moray Firth, while five more boats would keep an eye on the Harwich Force and screen the southern flank of Scheer's operation. The Sunderland attack was cancelled at the last minute as the *Seydlitz* was not ready. However, the U-Boats were already at sea and by 1 June they would have to return to their bases. It was now 23 May, and so if Scheer was to make a sortie and still use his U-Boats to help him, then he had less than a week to make his move. So when he was told *Seydlitz* would be able to join the fleet on 29 May, he decided to go ahead with the operation.

This time, though, the problem was the weather. A strong wind blowing from the north-east made it impossible to send his zeppelins ahead of him when he reached the British coast, to give him advance warning of Jellicoe's approach. While he waited for a change of wind, Scheer drafted a second plan, just in case the wind refused to change. This involved taking his fleet north towards the Skagerrak, the 60-mile wide gap between Norway and Denmark. British merchant ships regularly used the channel, and so the move would force Jellicoe and Beatty to put to sea, where the U-Boats were waiting for them. Scheer would leave it until 30 May to decide which plan to follow, but in the meantime his fleet prepared for sea. Orders for both operations were issued on 28 May, and the following day *Seydlitz* rejoined Hipper's squadron. Finally, with no change in the weather, Scheer abandoned the Sunderland plan. Instead, the High Seas Fleet would be heading for the Skaggerak.

Late in the afternoon of 30 May, as the High Seas Fleet assembled in the Jade Estuary, Scheer's flagship *Friedrich der* Grosse sent out a wireless signal which said '31 May GG 2490'. This was the green light; the Skagerrak operation was about to start early the following morning. So at 1 a.m. on the morning of 31 May, Hipper's Scouting Groups got underway. The Vice-Admiral flew his flag in the *Lützow*, which led the 1st Scouting Group to sea, followed by the battlecruisers *Derfflinger*, *Seydlitz*, *Moltke* and *Von der Tann*. The four light cruisers of the 2nd Scouting Group came next, accompanied by three destroyer flotillas, led by the light cruiser *Regensburg*. Hipper's job was to scout ahead of the rest of the fleet, and once he got closer to the Skagerrak, Scheer would cut him loose to sweep through the channel, sinking any British ships he could find.

At 2.30 a.m. – well before dawn – Scheer ordered the rest of the High Seas Fleet to sea, led by the sixteen dreadnoughts of the I and III Battle Squadrons. The five light cruisers of the 4th Scouting Group followed, then three and a half destroyer flotillas clustered around their flagship, the light cruiser *Rostock*. Thirty miles to the north-east, the six pre-dreadnought battleships of II Battle Squadron had already put to sea from the mouth of the River Elbe, and were now steaming past Cuxhaven. These two groups would rendezvous at 4 a.m. within sight of Helgoland. Finally, Scheer sent a signal warning his U-Boats that the

High Sea Fleet was at sea. That meant they were as ready as they could be for the inevitable British response. What he didn't know was that the British were already at sea, and the U-Boat trap had failed utterly. Now, both great fleets were heading towards the same patch of sea to the west of Jutland.

7

Enemy in Sight!

In Room 40 of the British Admiralty, the signal '31 May GG 2490' caused something of a stir. The cryptographers knew 'GG' stood for *Grösst Geheim* ('Most Secret'), and '31' was the date that operation '2490' would begin. Beyond that, they were in the dark. They'd also intercepted a high level of radio traffic from U-Boats, which also suggested that another large-scale operation was about to start. In the War Room of the Admiralty where a great table-top map of the North Sea was laid out, it was also noted that in the past 24 hours patrolling British submarines had reported a lot of minesweeping activity around the northern exits of the German defensive minefields. They'd also learned that the High Seas Fleet had left Wilhelmshaven and was assembling in the Jade Estuary. This suggested that if Scheer was about to sortie, then the likelihood was that he would be heading up the Danish coast. So in the late afternoon of 30 May, Admiral Sir Henry Jackson, the First Sea Lord, ordered Jellicoe to put to sea.

Jellicoe's Sortie

Strangely, Jellicoe had been planning a sortie of his own, which was due to begin early on 1 June. He was heading to Horns Reef for another attempt at drawing Scheer out. Now, the German admiral seemed to be doing the job for him. So at 9.30 p.m., the British fleet began to weigh anchor. An hour later, the boom defences of Hoxa Sound were lowered, and one by one the ships of the Grand Fleet headed out of Scapa Flow. An hour after that they were in the Pentland Firth, having passed the

Pentland Skerries, and were now heading east, into the North Sea. It was still twilight, as the long Orkney summers had begun. One seaman in the fleet remembered a sense of awe when he looked at the sky; 'The eve of Jutland I always remember – blazing red and orange-colouring caused by storm clouds – indeed, very wonderful and beautiful.' He added that it was; 'a sky which seemed a foreboding that something dreadful was about to happen'. For many men in the fleet he was absolutely right.

Not all of Jellicoe's forces were in Scapa Flow. Vice-Admiral Beatty's Battlecruiser Fleet was in Rosyth, with his capital ships divided into three squadrons: two of battlecruisers, and one – Rear-Admiral Hugh Evan-Thomas' 5th Battle Squadron – consisting of four fast battleships. These large ships were accompanied by three light cruiser squadrons and three destroyer flotillas. After the bombardment of East Anglia, Jellicoe had moved Vice-Admiral Jerram's 2nd Battle Squadron to the Cromarty Firth, four hours closer to the English east coast. Jerram's eight dreadnoughts put to sea at the same time as Jellicoe, accompanied by a light cruiser squadron and a destroyer flotilla. One of Jerram's dreadnoughts was the *Conqueror*, where Boy Seaman Arthur Sneesby feared that this would be another fruitless sortie; 'But, after all these false alarms, at the end of May we didn't turn back, but went straight on towards the Jutland coast, and everybody keyed up.'

That left Jellicoe with his two remaining dreadnought squadrons, a small battlecruiser squadron, two cruiser squadrons (one light, the other armoured), and two destroyer flotillas. They formed the core of the fleet. They would head east from Scapa Flow, and Jerram's squadron would join them a little after noon the following day. There, the twenty-four dreadnoughts of the battle fleet would reform into one block of ships, before continuing on towards the Danish coast. In Rosyth, Beatty's Battlecruiser Fleet would rendezvous with the rest of the fleet that following afternoon, where it could scout ahead of Jellicoe's battle fleet. Thanks to the team in Room 40, the whole great British armada of 151 warships was at sea over two hours before the High Seas Fleet even weighed anchor.

In theory, the Grand Fleet should have run straight into a line of waiting U-Boats. Two ought to have been waiting to the east of the Pentland Firth, one in the Moray Firth and no less than seven off the Firth of Forth. However, the recent spate of bad weather had driven many of them off their allotted stations. To make matters worse, only two picked up Scheer's signal of 30 May, warning them that he was putting to sea and therefore to expect the British to do likewise. One of these was *U-32*, which was lying off the Firth of Forth. Each of the U-Boats in the area had an assigned patrol area, the lines of which radiated out from the mouth of the Forth. At 3.30 a.m. *U-32* spotted two British cruisers, and the boat fired two torpedoes at them. Then the periscope jammed, the cruisers turned to ram the boat, and so it dived out of harm's way. When *U-32* surfaced, it saw two battlecruisers, but they were too far away to intercept.

The same thing happened to *U-66*; she spotted a whole line of dreadnoughts approaching, but the escorting destroyers forced the boat to dive. By the time she surfaced, the dreadnoughts had gone. These had been Jerram's 2nd Battle Squadron on its way to join Jellicoe – a perfect target and a missed opportunity. Worse was to come. Attacking the British was only part of the job. The U-Boats' main task was to warn Scheer if either Jellicoe or Beatty put to sea. As soon as it could, *U-32* surfaced and sent a radio report that two battleships, two cruisers and several destroyers were at sea, 60 miles east of the Firth of Forth and heading towards the south-east. *U-66* did the same, reporting eight battleships, plus cruisers and destroyers 60 miles east of Peterhead, steering towards the north-east. In fact, these reported courses meant little, as both group of British ships were zig-zagging, since U-Boats had been reported in the area. Scheer had to work out what the information actually meant.

As no reports had come from the U-Boats off Orkney, Scheer assumed that Jellicoe was still in Scapa Flow. This was not just a wrong assumption; it was a dangerous one. He guessed that the dreadnoughts off Peterhead were Jarvis' squadron, and the battlecruisers off the Firth of Forth belonged to Beatty. That meant that while he was pretty sure Beatty was at sea, and probably Jerram too, because they were heading in different directions this was probably just a routine sweep by two independent groups of ships. Scheer was fairly confident he could overpower each or even both of these forces if the two sides met at sea. Even that was unlikely, though, as the British ships had put to sea well before him, which suggested these sorties had nothing to do with his own fleet's movements. Scheer knew nothing about Room 40 and the ability of the British to intercept his signals.

Jellicoe had his own intelligence problems. When he left Scapa Flow, the High Seas Fleet was assembled in the Jade Estuary, but had not yet put to sea. Then, at noon on 31 May, a signal from the Admiralty told him that Scheer and his flagship *Friedrich der Grosse* was still in port. The problem lay with Captain Thomas Jackson, the 'insufferable' director of the Admiralty's Operations Division. That morning he visited Room 40, and demanded the cryptologists tell him where German radio call sign 'DK' was located. This was Scheer's flagship, at least when it was in port. When the fleet put to sea, the call sign was changed to 'RA', and the old one adopted by the port's harbour office. The cryptologists knew this, but Jackson didn't give them the chance to tell him. Instead, he walked off and sent his misleading signal to Jellicoe. As a result, Jellicoe had no idea that the German commander was just 250 nautical miles to the south-east and that the two fleets were closing fast.

By noon, Jerram's 2nd Battle Squadron had come in sight of the rest of the Grand Fleet, and within the hour the two formations would combine. Jellicoe's ships were following a south-easterly course, which was taking them in the direction of the Skagerrak. On board the dreadnoughts any excitement slowly gave way to the usual routine of life at sea. Approximately 90 nautical miles to the south, Beatty's Battlecruiser Fleet was heading west, bound for the same place. Beatty's orders were to continue until 2 p.m., and then, if no German ships were sighted, he would head north to join Jellicoe.

After the Admiralty signal, Jellicoe thought that while Hipper's Scouting Groups might be at sea, Scheer's dreadnoughts were not. He hoped to intercept Hipper before the German battlecruisers could flee south to safety. For his part, Scheer thought Beatty was at sea, but that Jellicoe was still in Scapa Flow. Strangely then, both sides then sought an encounter battle where the enemy battlecruisers, far from the support of their fleet, could be overwhelmed and destroyed.

On the German battlecruiser *Derfflinger* her Senior Gunnery Officer, Commander Georg von Hase, was enjoying the peaceful day. At sea he had no particular duties unless the ship went to action stations; 'For me, therefore, every cruise of this kind was a complete rest. If there was news of the enemy, or if there was anything unusual to be seen, or in particularly fine weather, of course I kept to the bridge. For the rest, however, I slept, read, or played chess in the wardroom, and made a round of all the guns only about once every two hours.' On the British fast battleship *Warspite*, Torpedoman Harry Hayler remembered the day; 'The morning breaks fine and clear and the two fleets commenced exercising. How little did any of them think that this mimicry would soon become grim reality . . . so they went on in blissful ignorance to the fact that the German fleet was even then on its way to give battle. All this time the sun had been shining, and the sea is as calm as a millpond – everything seems so peaceful.' That was about to change.

First Contact

At noon on 31 May, Beatty's Battlecruiser Fleet and Hipper's Scouting Groups were a little over 100 nautical miles apart. Unknowingly, both forces were heading towards the same little patch of sea – about 65 miles to the west of the northernmost tip of Jutland – the British approaching it from the west and the Germans from the south. If both stuck to their present courses, the two groups of ships would sight each other at around 3 p.m. Meanwhile, Jellicoe was about 80 miles north of Beatty, and Scheer 50 miles south of Hipper. So the pieces were on the board, and they were moving closer to each other.

Hipper had passed through the channel through the German defensive minefields at 7 a.m., and by 11 a.m. the Scouting Groups were 35 miles to the west of Horns Reef. As the main body of the High Seas Fleet was 50 miles behind Hipper, they passed the same points roughly three hours after the battlecruisers. This also meant that if Hipper got into trouble, it could take two to three hours for Scheer to come to his rescue unless the battlecruisers fled southwards. This, of course, was what Hipper hoped to do if he met Beatty – to draw him south towards the waiting guns of the German dreadnoughts. For Scheer, the biggest problem he faced was his lack of information about the enemy. Were they at sea, and if so where? In an attempt to answer this, he ordered four land-based zeppelins to fan out across the North Sea, searching for the enemy. High winds kept them grounded until 11 a.m., so by the time airships began their reconnaissance, the two fleets were already on a collision course.

As Georg von Hase put it; 'That the entire English fleet was already at sea and bearing on the same point as ourselves, not a man in the German fleet suspected, not even the Commander-in-Chief. And, in the same way, according to all published reports, no-one in the English fleet knew that the German fleet had put to sea. There is no reason to believe that this was not the case, and yet in the inland parts of the country the question is always being asked: How did the English get to know that we were off the Skagerrak?' It was a fair question, and even after the battle, von Hase and his colleagues remained blithely unaware that the boffins in the British Admiralty's Room 40 had not only cracked their signal codes, but knew that at least some elements of the High Seas Fleet were at sea.

What happened that afternoon was largely due to the formations adopted by Beatty and Hipper. Hipper's five light cruisers were deployed in a convex arc eight miles across with a small group of destroyers clustered around each of the cruisers. Behind them, like the arrow to this curved bow came Hipper's five battlecruisers, deployed in line astern behind his flagship, the *Lützow*. Yet more destroyers were ranged around the battlecruisers, forming an anti-submarine screen. Beatty's larger force was in a more complex formation. Three light cruiser squadrons – twelve ships in all – were steaming in six columns, each with two cruisers in it, all heading west, but echeloned in a line running from south-west to north-east, spread over twenty-five miles of sea. The 2nd Light Cruiser Squadron was on the right, the 3rd in the middle, and the 1st on the left. The column on the north-east end of the line consisted of the squadron flagship *Galatea*, followed by *Phaeton*. This meant these two cruisers were the closest ships to the unseen enemy.

Some eight miles behind the centre of this cruiser line came the four 'Splendid Cats' of Beatty's 1st Battlecruiser Squadron. Like Hipper's battlecruisers, they were deployed in line behind the flagship *Lion*, and were surrounded by a cluster of destroyers. Between three and five miles ahead, and slightly to port of Beatty were two more clusters of ships: off Beatty's port quarter were the four fast battleships of the 5th Battle Squadron, screened by a light cruiser and destroyers; while off *Lion*'s port beam were the two ships of the 2nd Battlecruiser Squadron, screened in the same way. This meant that Beatty's capital ships were deployed in a triangle, behind the long sloping line of light cruisers. So far the sweep had been uneventful, and Beatty's ships had steamed across an empty sea. So, at 2 p.m., Beatty gave the order to alter course to the north in fifteen minutes. Nobody realised that the peace of the afternoon was about to be shattered.

At 2.15 p.m., Beatty altered course. He was now heading north, with the three squadrons of capital ships in the lead. The triangle was still there, all that had changed was the direction it was heading. The light cruiser screen was still angled in the same way, but the 1st Light Cruiser Squadron was now on the right of the line, with *Galatea* and *Phaeton* on the eastern end of the long cruiser screen. Although nobody knew it, had Beatty kept on his original course, then he would have cut between Hipper and the rest of the High Seas Fleet. More importantly, the eastern edge of the British cruiser screen and the western edge of the German one were now just 16 miles apart. Only the haze kept these cruisers from seeing each other. Both Beatty and Hipper were now heading north on roughly parallel courses. The two groups of warships might not have made contact if fate had not intervened in the shape of a neutral tramp steamer.

At 2 p.m., lookouts on the light cruiser *Elbing* spotted a merchant ship off their port beam. The cruiser was on the western end of Hipper's screen, and it signalled its flagship *Frankfurt* for instructions. Standing on the *Elbing's* bridge was Lieutenant Heinrich Bassenge, whose turn it was to stand the afternoon watch. He moved over when the captain, Commander Rudolph Madlung, came on to the bridge, and peered at the strange ship through his binoculars. The lieutenant recorded; 'Madlung had just sent *B-110* to investigate. Through our binoculars we watched, with excitement, our torpedo boats circling the steamer, going alongside it and examining their papers.' On *Frankfurt*, Rear-Admiral Bödicker had already ordered *Elbing* and her two attendant destroyers to break formation and investigate. At the same moment, the steamer was spotted off the starboard beam of *Galatea*, and the 1st Light Cruiser Squadron was ordered to take a look.

So *Galatea* and her consort *Phaeton* headed east towards the steamer, with *Inconstant* and *Cordelia* following off their starboard quarter. The destroyers *B-109* and *B-110* outpaced the *Elbing*, and so at 2.20 p.m. the two German destroyers and the two leading British cruisers spotted each other when they were just over five miles apart. So it was that the crew of the neutral Danish steamer SS *N.J. Fjord* witnessed the opening shots of the greatest naval battle of its age. On the *Elbing*, Heinrich

Bassenge described the moment; 'After a short time a signal came from *B-110* – we thought they must have found something important. I read the message myself, but all it said was "Smoke clouds from the west. It looks like an enemy battleship."' He added, with a fine display of understatement; 'This message was unexpected.' It certainly was. Until that moment, nobody knew that the peace of the afternoon was about to be shattered, and that they were about to be pitched into the battle of their lives.

The *NJ Fjord* was closer to the German force than the British one, and the destroyers had pulled alongside the steamer and had lowered boats to inspect her when they spotted smoke to the west. They recovered their boarding parties and set off to investigate, signalling the news to *Elbing* as they went. A few minutes later, they spotted the *Galatea* and *Phaeton* and turned away. On board the *Galatea*, Commodore Edwyn Alexander-Sinclair ordered the signal 'Enemy in Sight' to be hoisted. The message was relayed from squadron to squadron until it reached Beatty's flagship. The *Galatea* then opened fire. Seconds later, British 6-inch shells began falling around the two destroyers as they sped back towards the *Elbing*, which was three miles away, next to the steamer. Then, lookouts on the *Elbing* spotted the *Galatea* and *Phaeton*, and the sighting was passed on to Bödicker and Hipper. By now, the British cruisers had turned their guns on the *Elbing*, and at 2.32 p.m. she returned fire. Both sides were now unleashing their first salvos of the battle.

The first hit was scored by the *Elbing*. Three minutes after opening fire one of her 5.9in (15cm) shells struck the *Galatea* below her bridge. This first hit of the battle was a dud; the shell failed to explode. On the *Elbing*, Bassenge watched the salvo strike; 'We managed to direct the first hit of the battle at the *Galatea*. The shell hit the bridge through two or three decks.' He added; 'Both English cruisers returned fire, but didn't hit us.' On the *Galatea*, Stoker Thomas Farquhar was off duty when his ship was hit; 'They put a shell through our ship's side – through our dispensary, through another bulkhead and finally made a dimple in the other side of the ship, but lucky for us it didn't explode, as it was right over the 4-inch magazine chamber.' Had the shell worked, the *Galatea* might have been the first casualty of the twelve-hour battle.

At that moment, Alexander-Sinclair spotted further Germans cruisers to the east, with more smoke behind them. He ordered his squadron to turn away to the north-west, hoping to lure the Germans closer to Beatty's battlecruisers. To the west of *Galatea*, Beatty didn't react to the news at first; it was only when Alexander-Sinclair reported several German cruisers were in sight that he ordered his battlecruisers to intervene. At 2. 32 p.m., the same moment that *Elbing* and *Galatea* were exchanging fire, Beatty ordered his capital ships to swing round to the south-west. His plan was to come round behind the enemy cruisers and cut off their escape route.

Meanwhile, the *Elbing* turned to shadow *Galatea* and her three consorts, while Bödicker brought *Frankfurt* and *Pillau* up to join her, followed later by the rest of the 2nd Scouting Group. When he heard the sighting report from *Elbing,* Hipper ordered his battlecruisers to alter course towards the south-west, where his ships were better placed to support his cruiser screen. This meant that the battlecruisers were on course to meet each other well to the south of the patch of sea where the *NJ. Fjord* was rolling in the swell with her engines stopped. Confused messages meant that Hipper was not precisely sure what kind of British ships were firing at his cruisers. Some signals said armoured cruisers, another indicated a whole fleet of dreadnoughts. The dreadnought sighting was unlikely, but British cruisers of any kind could meant battlecruisers were also in the area. He decided to move up to support his cruisers, his ships ready to intervene if they got into trouble.

As the battle began moving away to the north, Hipper moved his ships round to the west, then the north-west. Beatty altered course as well, in response to a report from *Galatea* that thick clouds of black funnel smoke could be seen to the east. At 3 p.m., his battlecruisers turned towards the north-west. This meant that the two rival groups of battlecruisers were approaching each other at right angles and on converging courses. Both Hipper and Beatty, though, had no real idea what they were facing. So far a handful of light cruisers and some destroyers had made contact, exchanged fire and then disengaged. Now these same light forces were running on parallel courses towards the north-west. In fact, Beatty and Hipper were just 25 miles apart, and closing fast. Beatty was to the west of *Galatea*, while Hipper was to the south-east. With both surging forward at around 24 knots, contact was just a few minutes away.

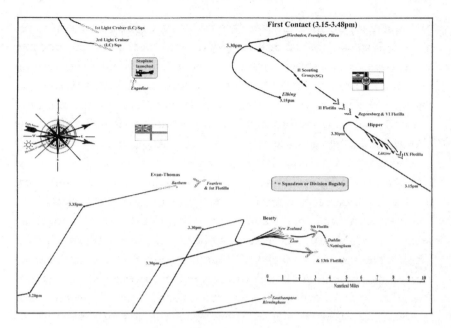

First Contact (3.15–3.48 p.m.)

A Collision of Battlecruisers

In theory, Hipper should have been heavily outnumbered. He had just five battlecruisers while Beatty had six, supported by four powerful, fast battleships. The odds had temporarily changed, though, as Beatty had lost contact with Rear-Admiral Hugh Evan-Thomas and his four fast battleships. The problem was, when Beatty altered course at 2.32 p.m., the thick smoke pouring from the flagship's funnel meant that his flag signal couldn't be seen from the bridge of Evan-Thomas' flagship *Barham*, which was then five miles away off Beatty's port bow. So when the battlecruisers turned away to the south-east, the fast battleships remained on their original course. It took several minutes to realise the mistake, but by then *Lion* and *Barham* were ten miles apart, and as Beatty had increased speed, the gap was increasing.

Evan-Thomas was furious at Beatty's failure to keep him informed. After the battle he wrote; 'Lion had been signalling to *Barham* with a searchlight previously to the turn, and had made all alterations of course by that method. There was no reason why a signal should not have been made for *Barham* to turn with *Lion*.' With even greater forthrightness, Evan-Thomas posed a rhetorical question; 'After all, isn't it one of the fundamental principles of naval tactics that an admiral makes sure that his orders are understood by distant parts of his fleet before rushing into space, covered by a smoke screen?' Cursing, Evan-Thomas signalled his own ships to follow him as he set off after Beatty, but at this critical moment the battlecruisers were on their own. This communications error was only the first of what would be a long catalogue of signalling blunders made by Beatty during the long battle.

On board the *Princess Royal,* action stations had been sounded at 2.45 p.m., as the 'Splendid Cats' raced towards the south-east. Until then, the crew had been expecting the sortie to prove uneventful, and the men had been enjoying a 'make and mend', where those not on duty could relax. Some men slept on the deck, while others played cards or chatted. The *Galatea's* signal changed all that. The British ships battlecruiser cleared for action, even though the only enemy anyone had seen by then were the light cruisers and destroyers of the 2nd Scouting Group. These German ships were already in action, but Hipper felt there was no need for the crews of his battlecruisers to prepare for battle until the enemy were actually in sight. After all, his ships were fully ready, and sending the men to their battle stations would just take a few moments. So the men of the 1st Scouting Group enjoyed a last few minutes of leisure as their ships steamed towards their light cruiser screen.

Beatty's force included the seaplane carrier *Engadine*, one of the two nascent carriers that had taken part in the bombing of Tondern. Beatty ordered her to launch an aircraft, and at 3.08 p.m. a frail two-seater Short Type 184 floatplane struggled uncertainly into the air and set off in the general direction of the *Elbing*. Ten minutes later, the observer sighted the German cruisers, and closed in to take a better look. The Germans opened fire and so, with shrapnel bursting around him, the pilot veered away out of range. He kept shadowing the cruisers for another 25 minutes, until a broken fuel pipe forced him to return to the *Engadine*. Strangely, neither the pilot or the observer spotted the approaching German battlecruisers, just a few miles away to starboard. That sighting, though, was made by masthead lookouts while the floatplane was still in the air.

The pilot, Lieutenant Frederick Rutland, described what happened after he sighted the enemy; 'Clouds were at 1,000 to 1,200 feet, with patches at 900 feet. That necessitated flying very low. On sighting the enemy it was hard to tell what they were, and so I had to close within a mile and a half at a height of 1,000 feet. They then opened fire on me with anti-aircraft and other guns, my height enabling them to use their anti-torpedo armament . . . I flew through several of the columns of smoke caused through bursting shrapnel.' On the *Elbing,* Bassenge noted; 'A little enemy seaplane came up from the south-west . . . The aircraft inspected us from front to back . . . and then disappeared into the mist.' After this exploit, the seaplane pilot was known in the service as 'Rutland of Jutland'.

At 3.18 p.m., lookouts on the German battlecruisers spotted thick funnel smoke to the south-west. Two minutes later, four modern cruisers were spotted by *Elbing,* and then two more were sighted behind them. The news was passed to the *Lützow,* but Hipper remained unconcerned. After all, they were just cruisers. *Frankfurt* was astern of *Elbing,* and she opened fire on these new targets. It was not until 3.28 p.m. that these British light cruisers came close enough to *Lützow* for her lookouts to realise they were not light cruisers at all. What was advancing towards them was a force of six British battlecruisers. On the *Derfflinger,* the ship's gunnery officer Lieutenant Commander Georg von Hase was lounging on a leather sofa in the battlecruiser's wardroom, sipping 'an excellent cup of coffee'. Suddenly; 'At 4.28 p.m. [3.28 p.m. in British ships] alarm bells rang through the ship, both drums beat for action, and the boatswains of the watch piped and shouted "Clear for Action!"' Battle was about to be joined.

Von Hase raced to the bridge, and learned that 'isolated enemy forces had been sighted to the westward.' He ordered the guns to be trained round on to the bearing the enemy were approaching from, a bearing marked by their funnel smoke. He still could not see the British yet, so he set his gunnery direction periscope to its maximum visibility. 'Suddenly my periscope revealed some big ships. Black monsters – six tall, broad-beamed giants steaming in two columns. They were still a long way off, but they showed up clearly on the horizon, and even at this great distance they looked powerful, massive.' A minute later, the British lookouts on *New Zealand* spotted the German battlecruisers steaming at right angles to them and about 18 miles away to the north-east. On both sides the great guns trained round, and gunnery direction teams began the methodical process of working out range, bearing and angle of fire.

On the British side, *New Zealand* and *Indefatigable* of the 2nd Battlecruiser Squadron were still three miles ahead and to starboard of the four 'Splendid Cats' of the 1st Battlecruiser Squadron. The four fast battleships of the 5th Battle Squadron should have been to their left, but instead they were ten miles away to the west, desperately trying to catch up. So Beatty signalled *New Zealand* and ordered Rear-Admiral William Pakenham to tuck his two lighter ships in behind the more powerful 'Splendid Cats' – *Lion, Princess Royal, Queen Mary* and *Tiger*. In the *New Zealand*, Midshipman George Eady was in the Transmitting Station, deep in the heart of the ship. As he sailed into action for the first time in his life, he wondered if he was really in the safest place; 'As there was a 12-inch magazine on each side of us, a 4-inch one below and the foremost boiler equally close, we should probably have all been blown to glory together.'

Several miles away to the north-east, the German battlecruisers were already in battle formation, with the flagship *Lützow* followed by *Derfflinger, Seydlitz, Moltke* and *Von der Tann*. As the two flagships radioed the news to Scheer and Jellicoe, the two groups of battlecruisers drew closer to each other, with the British heading almost directly towards Hipper's line. On the *Seydlitz*, Captain Moritz von Egidy remembered seeing the British battlecruisers make their appearance; 'The British cruisers came in view, and behind them dense clouds of smoke. Then, tripod masts and huge hulls loomed over the horizon. There they were again – our friends from the Dogger Bank.' Von Egidy had a score to settle; at Dogger Bank his ship had been pounded hard, and many of his men had been killed. Now he had the chance to avenge them.

8

Our Bloody Ships

The largest guns carried in any battlecruiser were the 13.5-inch calibre weapons on Beatty's "Splendid Cats". On paper these big guns had an effective range of 13,650 yards (almost seven nautical miles), and a maximum range of 23,820 yards. However, the chances of hitting a target depended on a host of other factors, all of which were dependent on good gunnery direction. That involved parties of spotters relaying information to a team below decks, who processed the ever-changing details of range, bearing, course, speed and target direction to produce a firing solution. On *Warspite*, Able Seaman Harry Hayler described the scene in the Transmitting Station 'Imagine then . . . a room eighteen feet square, in the centre of which was a table. On one side of it is a roll of paper that is stretched across the table to another roller, which is being revolved by a motor, and so keeps the paper constantly on the move. On this is plotted out all the information which the men at the guns want to know.'

This Transmitting Station was the nerve centre of the ship – the key component in the chain that led to the guns being fired accurately at their target. It was from here that the firing solutions were sent to the gun turrets, which were all trained round to the required angle and the guns elevated to the right position. First though, the turret crews were ordered to load their guns, and the turret trained on to the approximate bearing of the enemy. As Gunner John Hazelwood inside one of *Warspite*'s turrets remembered; 'When the guns are brought to the ready you simply wait for the [order to] open fire . . . We were keen – this was the day we were waiting for.' Then, on the command of the Gunnery

Officer, all the turrets in the ship that were trained on the enemy would fire a single co-ordinated salvo. In an ideal world, the shells would then land on their target, or at least on and around it. That though, rarely happened on the first salvo.

In both fleets the accuracy of the guns depended on the information fed into the analog computers below decks. The key piece of information was the range, and in both fleets special optical stereoscopic magnified range-finders were used to judge the distance as accurately as possible. The difficulty was that this wasn't a simple operation, particularly if the target ship was difficult to see. In the British fleet, the ships were silhouetted against the afternoon sun, making them appear crisp and clear in the German rangefinders. The German ships, on the other hand, were obscured by a slight haze, making it difficult to get an accurate reading. For the British, this problem was exacerbated by the destroyers which were now racing ahead of the battlecruisers to form a protective screen, billowing clouds of funnel smoke as they went. Even more importantly, the optics on the German rangefinders were of a much higher quality than those on the British ones. This gave the Germans a distinct edge.

Opening Salvos

At 3.20 p.m., the rival battlecruisers were still seventeen nautical miles apart, well out of range of the big guns. However, the two sides were closing rapidly and the range fell steadily with each passing minute. In ten minutes, the range had dropped to thirteen miles, and on both sides the gun crews in the great battlecruisers were poised, waiting for the order to unleash their first deadly salvo. Meanwhile, the other smaller ships were either forming a screen or getting out of the way. Hipper ordered the cruisers and destroyers of the 2nd Scouting Group to reverse course towards the south-east, and form up a mile to starboard of the battlecruisers. Beatty's ships were even more scattered, but as the two battlecruiser squadrons formed into a single line, two destroyer flotillas formed a line ahead of them, while a squadron of light cruisers struggled to keep pace. Some twelve miles to the north, the 1st and 3rd Light Cruiser Squadrons were ordered to shadow their German counterparts.

News of the coming fight had been radioed to Jellicoe and Scheer, whose battle fleets were 70 miles to the north-east and 50 miles to the south respectively. Both commanders had been following developments ever since the first sighting by *Galatea* and *Elbing*, and both increased speed so they could bring the weight of their dreadnoughts to bear in support of their battlecruisers. Jellicoe was quite pleased that the Germans were heading in his general direction; that would make the job of intercepting them much easier. Then at 3.33 p.m., Hipper swung *Lützow* round to starboard, and the rest of his battlecruisers followed her turn, until the whole squadron had settled on its reciprocal course. He also reduced speed to 18 knots, to give the cruisers a chance to catch him up. The Germans were now heading towards the south-east, with the British approaching them at right angles off their starboard beam.

This made it much more unlikely that Jellicoe would be able to catch Hipper before he broke off the fight. So, with his dreadnoughts cracking on at maximum speed, he sent Rear-Admiral Sir Horace Hood's 3rd Battlecruiser Squadron ahead, in an attempt to support Beatty. These three small battlecruisers would have been vulnerable enough fighting their German counterparts. If they ran into dreadnoughts, they wouldn't stand a chance. Strangely, neither Jellicoe nor Scheer suspected the enemy dreadnoughts were at sea. Both commanders believed they faced a force of enemy battlecruisers and lighter ships, and planned to ambush them with their dreadnoughts. Now that Hipper was running towards the south-east, this would bring him further from Jellicoe, and closer to Scheer. The question was, would Beatty take the bait and chase Hipper, or would he keep clear and link up with Jellicoe?

For Beatty, the decision was clear. A little over a year before, his battlecruisers had got the best of their German counterparts at the Battle of Dogger Bank. Although both sides had suffered, the *Seydlitz* had only escaped thanks to a British signalling mistake. Now Beatty had ten capital ships to five if he included his missing fast battleships, and he had unfinished business with Hipper. So the British battlecruisers continued their headlong charge towards the Germans, and the range kept dropping. At 3.29 p.m., Beatty had turned his ships to starboard, so that the two sides were still converging, but the guns of all six of his battlecruisers could now bear on the enemy. *New Zealand* and *Indomitable* were closer to the Germans than the four larger battlecruisers, but after a deft change of course to starboard, Rear-Admiral Pakenham tucked them in behind the 1st Battlecruiser Squadron. Now it was all a matter of waiting for the order to open fire.

On the bridge of Vice Admiral Beatty's flagship *Lion* there was a certain amount of confusion, as the thick coal smoke obscured their view of the German battlecruisers some eight nautical miles away to port. Beatty preferred the open compass platform to the armoured confines of his flagship's conning tower, and it was from here that he peered at the enemy warships, which had settled on a parallel course almost directly on Beatty's port beam. A thin white mist hung in the air, too humid for the afternoon sun to disperse. This same mist had hidden the enemy until they were almost within range. The Germans saw their opponents first; Beatty's ships were picked out by the sun and their paintwork was darker than that of their opponents. However, both sides were now ready for action.

A few minutes before, Beatty had just swung his 'Big Cats' into line, with *Lion* leading, followed at precise 500-yard intervals by five other battlecruisers: *Princess Royal, Queen Mary, Tiger, New Zealand* and *Indefatigable*. On the bridge of each ship, as the gun crews waited for the order to fire, a midshipman was holding up a little hand-held device which showed just how high the ship in front should be when it was almost exactly 500 yards away. Any change resulted in orders being passed to the engine room, so the speed of the ship could be adjusted accordingly. Even when going into battle, pride in the ship demanded perfect station-keeping. On the German flagship *Lützow*, Vice-Admiral Franz von Hipper was also keeping a close eye on the relative position of his ships and those of the enemy. He then turned to his flag captain, and gave the order to open fire.

At 3.48 p.m., a ripple of fire erupted from the five German battle-cruisers. At that range, it took less than half a minute for the shells to reach their destination – 20 large shells, each weighing 660 to 880 pounds, the equivalent of a very large fully-stocked fridge freezer. The difference was, these armour-piercing shells were packed with high explosives, and when they hit a ship they were travelling at a speed of almost 1,500 feet per second. Armour-piercing shells didn't explode on impact. Instead, they were designed to burrow through the ship's armour, and explode deep inside her hull. On Hipper's flagship, Commander Günther Paschen, the ship's Gunnery Officer recorded the moment in his gunnery log; 'Estimated Speed: 26 knots, Course 110°. This made the rate of closing 4hm [hundred metres] a minute. At a range of 167hm by our

calculations the first turret salvo from "A" and "B" turrets was fired at
4.48 [3.48 p.m.]. Time of flight – 22 seconds.'

Beatty still hadn't given the order to open fire, but acting on their
captains' own initiative the British ships opened fire just a few seconds
later. In fact, it was Beatty's own Flag Captain Alfred Chatfield who fired
first; 'The range was 16,000 yards. I could wait no longer, and told
[Commander] Longhurst to open fire. At the same moment the enemy
did so. [Lieutenant Commander] Seymour hoisted the "5" flag (engage
the enemy), and off went the double salvos.' In the *Lion*'s foretop,
Midshipman Anthony Combe heard the order being given; 'Almost
immediately after the enemy had opened fire the Captain said "Open
Fire" to the foretop . . . You could hear the firing bell in the Transmitting
Station ring and the direction layer [gunner] pressed the trigger, at which
the guns went off with a tremendous crash.' The duel between the two
lines of battlecruisers had begun.

There were six battlecruisers in the British line, and five in the
German one, eight miles (or 16,000 yards) away to port. Ideally, each ship
would fire on a single opponent in the enemy line. The accuracy of
shooting was determined by the fall of shot, so more than one ship firing
at the same target risked confusing the spotting teams of both of the
firing ships. The opening German salvo fell about 200 yards short of
the British ships, but already the German gunners were almost ready to
fire again. On board the *Tiger*, Able Seaman Victor Hayward was at his
station in the battlecruiser's foremost gun turret when the first German
shells fell; 'A blinding flash through our gun port and a rattle of a hail of
shell splinters on our ship's side told us that Jerry was already straddling
us with a near miss. Our guns thundered out, the great 13.5-inch heavies
speaking for the first time.'

On both sides range takers, plotters and gun layers worked as a
team, so that the next salvo would land closer to the target. At least
that was the theory. On board the *Derfflinger* – the second battlecruiser
in the German line – the target was the *Princess Royal*, which was
directly behind Beatty's flagship *Lion*. Georg von Hase, in the direction
platform in *Derfflinger*'s foretop, noticed that the *Princess Royal* had not
fired at him, but both she and *Lion* had fired on the German flagship
Lützow instead, just ahead of him. 'By some mistake we were left
being out. I laughed grimly, and now I began to engage our enemy

with complete calm, as at gun practice, and with continually increasing accuracy.'

This was down to Beatty. He wanted to concentrate fire on the German flagship, so both *Lion* and *Princess Royal* fired at her. He had a signal hoisted on *Lion*'s foremast, ordering his last four battlecruisers to fire at the last four German ships, but the flags were hidden by funnel smoke, and the signal went unnoticed. Instead, the third and fourth British ships, *Queen Mary* and *Tiger*, fired at the third and fourth German ones, *Seydlitz* and *Moltke*. Behind them, obeying standing instructions, *New Zealand* took aim at *Moltke*, while the final British ship, *Indefatigable*, trained her guns on the final German ship, the *Von der Tann*. For their part, the first four German ships fired at the first four British ones, while *Von der Tann* concentrated on *Indefatigable*. This meant that for the moment nobody was firing at either the *New Zealand* or the *Derfflinger*. The job of aiming and firing was much easier if nobody was firing back at you.

Both sides fired their guns in groups of four or five, correcting the range before unleashing another partial salvo. Once they found the range, all the guns would open up on the target. Some crews were better at it than others. The other shells sent up columns of water 200 feet high, which hung as if suspended for several seconds before crashing back into the sea. *Moltke* straddled *Tiger* with her second salvo, hitting her with two of her four shells. On *Derfflinger*, a frustrated von Hase watched his first five partial salvos miss their target, thanks to a young officer who messed up the rangefinding corrections. Once this was dealt with, *Derfflinger*'s gunnery improved dramatically.

'The sixth salvo, fired at 5.52pm [3.52pm] straddled – three splashes over the target, one short!' That, though, was four minutes into the fight, and precious minutes had been lost. Fortunately for von Hase and his shipmates his target, the *Princess Royal*, was still firing at the German flagship, 400 yards in front of the *Derfflinger*. If this process of observing, plotting, calculating, adjusting and firing might have seemed like some abstract exercise on board *Derfflinger*, on other battlecruisers the brutal realities of naval gunnery were being driven home with awe-inspiring force.

First Blood

By the time von Hase's guns found the range four minutes into the fight, *Tiger* and Beatty's flagship *Lion* had both been hit four times apiece by

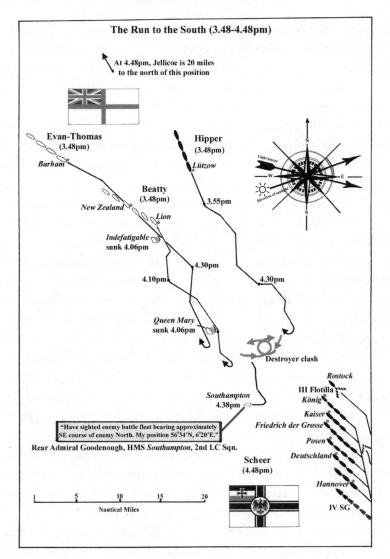

The Run to the South (3.48–4.48 p.m.)

shells fired by *Moltke* and *Lützow*. Most of these hits were not particularly serious – or at least they didn't reduce the fighting ability of the two ships. For anyone caught in their blast, the destructive power unleashed by these huge Krupp shells was horrific. Thomas Bradley, the young and normally ebullient Roman Catholic chaplain on board *Tiger*, saw their effect at first hand in the ship's forward casualty station; 'The cries of the wounded and burnt men were very terrible to listen to . . . They were brought in, sometimes with feet or hands dangling off.' The medical orderlies did what they could, sending the worst cases down to the surgeons in the sick bay, while the dead were laid out in a nearby mess deck as yet more casualties were brought in.

Lion had been the first ship hit, when at 3.50 p.m. a shell from *Lützow* passed clean through her forecastle without doing any serious damage. However, the German flagship now had her range, and *Lion* was hit again a minute later, and then twice more in quick succession. Fortunately for her, most of *Lützow's* semi armour-piercing shells were faulty, and failed to explode. So Beatty's flagship was spared any serious damage for now. Three ships behind her was *Tiger*, which was being fired on by *Moltke*. The German battlecruiser had found *Tiger's* range after three minutes, when a shell plunged through her forecastle and burst in her forward sick bay. Fortunately, it was empty, but the compartment was completely wrecked. She was hit twice more in the next few minutes, but then at 3.54 p.m. *Moltke* fired another full salvo. This time, the German shells struck a near-mortal blow.

The salvo fell neatly around *Tiger*, and hits were scored, both on gun turrets. One struck the roof of 'Q' turret – the midships turret on the battlecruiser – but, while the plating was holed, the steel protected most of the men inside and only three of them were killed. Still, the turret was effectively put out of action as all her sighting and communication equipment was wrecked. The second shell struck 'X' turret on its barbette, the armoured collar that ran between the gun turret and the magazines, several decks below. It hit just where the barbette rose out of the upper deck, piercing its armour and entering the gun-house behind it. The gunners were incredibly lucky; it failed to explode, but just lay there malevolently on the gun-house floor. After seven minutes, the turret was back in action, but damage to the gun-laying equipment meant that its guns shot wildly for the rest of the battle.

Father Bradley joined a doctor rushing aft to help the wounded in 'Q' turret, and in the shell-handling spaces beneath it. One of the casualties was a young boy, a midshipman. 'The poor fellow was wounded in several places. I took off his sea boots and found a piece of shell had gone through his foot. He was also wounded in the arm and side. His left eye was lying on top of a mass of bruised flesh that filled the cavity of the eye.' The priest took the boy to his cabin, where he died during the night.

Meanwhile, the German shells kept falling. Of all the German battle-cruisers, *Moltke* was the most accurate that morning. Her initial salvo had fallen slightly short, but this had been corrected, and her guns straddled *Tiger* with their third salvo. She continued to pound her target, hitting *Tiger* repeatedly as the two lines of battlecruisers continued their ferocious duel.

By contrast, with the exception of *Queen Mary* whose gunnery was well-regarded, all the British battlecruisers fired a mile or more over their targets with their opening salvo. In fact, shells fell dangerously close to the light cruiser *Regensburg* and the German destroyers, steaming two miles beyond their own battlecruisers. Although the accuracy of British salvos improved as the battle continued, German fire was both more accurate and effective. The *Queen Mary* was generally regarded as the best gunnery ship in the battlecruiser fleet, and so it was no real surprise that she was the first British ship to hit her target. She straddled the *Seydlitz* at 3.55 p.m., and one shell ripped a 10-foot diameter hole in her battery deck, killing several gunners manning her 6-inch guns. Miraculously, it left the ship's chaplain unscathed, even though the shell exploded right next to him.

Two minutes later, at 3.57 p.m., another shell from *Queen Mary* struck the *Seydlitz* on the barbette of 'Caesar' turret, just above the upper deck. In effect, it was an identical hit to the one scored by *Moltke* against *Tiger* just three minutes earlier. The blast ignited a powder cartridge, and the resulting flash swept through the turret, killing almost all of its crew. On the bridge, Captain von Egidy remembered the aftermath; 'The Gunnery Central Station [the "Transmitting Station" in British ships] deep down reported "No answer from 'C' turret".' Smoke and gas poured out of the voice pipes from 'C' turret. It was clear that the turret had been knocked out of action. Then, quick thinking by the ship's Gunnery Officer, Lieutenant Commander Richard Foerster, may have saved lives. When smoke from 'Caesar' turret began seeping through the voice pipes, he knew exactly what had happened, and immediately ordered the turret's magazines to be flooded.

Moments earlier, *Seydlitz*'s commander Captain von Egidy had been hoping for vengeance. Now, he simply considered himself lucky. At the Battle of Dogger Bank earlier the previous year, 'Caesar' turret had been hit in the same place and the explosion ignited most of the cordite charges in the turret's handling room. That day 190 men had been burned to death and two turrets put out of action. Both von Egidy and Foerster had been there and knew how disastrous a turret hit could be. This time, thanks to Foerster, the blast never reached the magazine and just twenty men were burned alive or left with severe injuries. The turret was put out of action, but the human cost of that devastating shell hit could have been very much worse. Just how bad it could get was demonstrated three minutes later when a salvo of 12-inch shells from *Lützow* straddled Beatty's flagship *Lion*. One of the shells ripped the top of her midships turret and began the dramatic sequence of events that could have spelled disaster for Beatty and his flagship.

Essentially, the entire turret crew were killed or badly wounded and only the quick thinking of a dying officer of marines saved the flagship from disaster. His final order, to seal and flood the magazines, was all that stopped *Lion* from being torn apart by a flash fire reaching the turret's magazines. Almost half an hour later, as damage control parties were trying to clean up the mess, a ripped cordite charge ignited, and the resulting fireball killed yet more men, but also raced down the turret shaft and broke harmlessly against the doors of the now inert magazines. Had it not been for that marine, Vice-Admiral Beatty would have become one of the first casualties of the battle. So, both Beatty and a now badly damaged *Lion* would survive and would continue to fight.

Watching the fighting unfold was Commander Alan Mackenzie-Grieve, the First Lieutenant of the light cruiser *Birmingham*. He was about a mile from the *Lion*, watching her from the after conning tower of his ship; 'The enemy's shooting at *Lion* became extremely accurate, and she sheered a little to starboard . . . Just as she came back again she was heavily hit, and I saw a large plate, which I judged to be the top of a turret, blown into the air. It appeared to rise very slowly, turning round and round, and looked very much like an aeroplane. I should say it rose some 400 or 500 feet, and looking at it through glasses I could distinctly see the holes in it for the bolts. My attention was drawn from this by a sheet of flame by her second funnel, which shot up about 60 feet, and soon died down, but didn't immediately disappear.' Mackenzie-Grieves had just watched the aftermath of the hit which immolated virtually the entire crew of the flagship's middle turret.

A Double Calamity

Since the fighting started, the two lines of warships had been drawing closer to each other, but at 3.57 p.m. Beatty ordered his flagship to turn two points (22½°) to starboard, to widen the range slightly. One after the other, the rest of Beatty's battlecruisers followed *Lion's* lead, turning in succession when they reached the spot where *Lion* had been when she altered course. Two minutes later, at 3.59 p.m., Hipper also turned away slightly, ordering a course change of one point (11°) to port. Although the two lines of battlecruisers were now edging away from each other, this didn't presage any drop in the intensity of the battle. Quite the reverse. The two sides now had the range of their opponents, and the fight was reaching a dramatic crescendo.

In the British line, *Princess Royal* was struck by three shells in three minutes, the last of which struck at 4 p.m., piercing the barbette of 'B' turret and killing eight men and injuring 38 more. A fire began, but there was no repeat of the carnage in *Lion*, *Tiger* and *Seydlitz*. Hipper's flagship *Lützow* was hit twice at 4 p.m., just as her own shells smashed into Lion's 'Q' turret. Two 13.5-inch shells from *Lion* tore through her forecastle, one landing between 'Anton' and 'Bruno' turrets before plunging through the deck, killing most of the medical team in the forward dressing station. Two minutes later, a shell from either *Tiger* or *New Zealand* exploded in the water beneath *Moltke*, buckling steel hull plates and springing rivets along her double bottom. Water began gushing in, but *Moltke's* well-trained damage control teams soon stemmed the flooding and the battlecruiser fought on.

At roughly the same moment as the salvo from *Lützow* fell around *Lion*, and a shell ripped 'Q' turret apart, another salvo from *Von der Tann* straddled the *Indefatigable*, the last ship in the British line. The German battlecruiser had just found the range and was firing full salvos at the aftermost British ship. Most of these shells splashed harmlessly into the sea around the British ship, but one of them struck her – exactly where is not clear. It was probably struck somewhere towards the stern of the ship, near her aftermost turret. *Indefatigable* was firing back, but her salvos still had not got the range of *Von der Tann*. Then, at 4.02 p.m., the German battlecruiser struck again. This time two shells struck *Indefatigable*, somewhere behind her funnels between the mainmast and 'X' turret. Smoke started billowing from the superstructure below her mainmast, and observers in the *New Zealand* – the closest ship to her – thought *Indefatigable* was on fire.

They also noticed that she was not keeping her station any more. A few minutes earlier, Beatty had ordered the battlecruisers to turn slightly to starboard, and one after the other the great ships followed the turn made by the flagship. *Indefatigable*, at the back of the line, never made the turn, but instead she kept on her original course, which was bringing her closer to the Germans, rather than away from them. They also saw that when the smoke cleared slightly, the *Indefatigable* was down by the stern, as if she was taking on water, or even sinking. The hits might have ripped a hole in her underside, or perhaps her after magazines were being deliberately flooded. We will probably never know for sure. In any case, it was clear that the battlecruiser was in serious difficulties.

Then a fresh German salvo arrived and at least two shells struck *Indefatigable* again, this time around 'A' turret. At 4.03 p.m. she began listing markedly to port and then, a few heartbeats later, there was an almighty explosion. Crimson and orange flames shot well above her foremast, then quickly turned into thick black smoke. The fatal blow might have come earlier, with the hit to the stern, but these new hits or an earlier fireball must have ignited a magazine. As hundreds of shocked onlookers on both sides watched, the heart of the battlecruiser was ripped out and she quickly rolled over to port and sank. On *Von der Tann* the initial cheering tailed off, as the full implications of the blow they had meted out became clear. In an instant, just over a thousand sailors like themselves had been killed or were about to die as the sea closed over them. Only two men survived – both masthead lookouts who had been thrown clear when the ship rolled over and sank beneath them.

Those who saw the disaster would never forget it. Others never noticed, as they were too caught up in their part of the great duel. On board the *Lion*, the assistant navigating officer Lieutenant William Chalmers glanced aft along the line of British ships, and saw a huge pall of smoke behind them; 'I gazed at this in amazement, and at the same time tumbled to the fact that there were only five battlecruisers in our line.' Still, there was no chance to pause as the battlecruisers raced on, their guns still firing their deadly salvos at each other. However, the odds had shifted; there were now five battlecruisers a side, and the British advantage in numbers had gone. That, though, was about to change as a new squadron entered the fray. Having struggled to catch up with Beatty, the four fast battleships of Evan-Thomas' 5th Battle Squadron were now in range, and at 4.06 p.m. the first of their 15-inch shells began falling around the aftermost German ships, the *Von der Tann* and the *Moltke*.

This took Hipper by surprise. Until then, he had watched the battle unfold with a degree of stoicism, standing on the bridge of *Lützow* with a cigar clamped between his teeth. This display of sangfroid was challenged when Evan-Thomas' shells began falling. First of all, he had not expected them to be there at all. Then, as he had tucked his cruisers on the disengaged side of his battlecruisers, he deprived himself of the cruiser screen that could have warned him the fast battleships were approaching. Evan-Thomas opened fire just moments after he was spotted by lookouts on the German cruiser *Frankfurt*. At the time, the fast battleships had altered course to the south-south-east, and so by training their guns on to their port bows they could all fire at the Germans battlecruisers. The range was 9½ miles (19,000 yards) and just within their maximum range. *Barham* and *Valiant* targeted *Moltke*, while *Warspite* and *Malaya* fired at *Von der Tann*.

Two miles away, Lieutenant Bassenge watched the arrival of the fast battleships from the bridge of the *Elbing*; 'Out of the blue came a heavy barrage of fire . . . we were suddenly surrounded by high fountains of water. Out of the distance four big ships appeared . . . the very modern battleships of the 5th Battle Squadron – of the Queen Elizabeth class. The distance was about seventeen kilometres (9.4 miles) – we could just see the enemy on the horizon. With our 15-cm [5.9-inch] guns . . . we were not equipped for anything like this. We turned quickly, glad to get out of it.' Moments later, the fast battleships trained their guns on the German battlecruisers, and after calculating the firing solution for their great 15-inch guns, they opened fire.

Their shells straddled their targets with the first salvos, and at 4.09 p.m., *Von der Tann* was hit below the waterline close to her stern. The explosion made the whole ship vibrate like a tuning fork, and hundreds of tons of seawater poured into her. The steering compartment was flooded, but quick thinking by her damage control teams averted any further disaster. The battlecruiser was still able to steer, just avoiding the fate of being left helpless, and served up as a victim to Evan-Thomas' squadron. Seven minutes later it was the turn of the *Moltke*. This time, a shell struck a coal bunker, ignited a small secondary magazine and destroyed a 15 cm gun casemate, killing all its crew. By then, both *Moltke* and *Von der Tann* were zig-zagging wildly, trying to throw off the aim of the British gunners. For the moment they succeeded.

The intervention of the fast battleships might have altered the odds in the battle, but it certainly didn't change its tempo. Both lines of battlecruisers – five on each side now – were still hammering away at each other. While *Von der Tann* turned her guns on the *New Zealand*, and *Lützow* and *Moltke* continued to pound *Lion* and *Tiger* respectively, both *Derfflinger* and *Seydlitz* concentrated on the *Queen Mary*, leaving *Princess Royal* untouched. For their part, each of the British ships was firing at its counterpart in the German line: *Lion* at *Lützow*; *Princess Royal* at *Derfflinger*; *Queen Mary* at *Seydlitz*; *Tiger* at *Moltke*; and *New Zealand* at *Von der Tann*. The pace of fire had slackened though, largely because the increasing range and all the smoke and spray made accurate gunnery harder, and so the shooting became more deliberate. So, at 4.12 p.m., Beatty ordered his ships to steer two points closer to the enemy. Once again, the battlecruisers were edging closer to each other. When the gap between them dropped to 16,000 yards, Beatty turned away again to keep the range steady.

Of all the British battlecruisers that afternoon, the *Queen Mary* was proving the best at gunnery. She had long been regarded as the best gunnery ship in Beatty's command, and she was proving her worth that afternoon. She had been the first to find the range of the enemy, and her guns had already scored four hits on *Seydlitz*, including the one at 3.57 p.m. which put one of her after turrets out of action and forced the ship to flood its magazine. Another shell from *Queen Mary* struck the German battlecruiser at 4.17 p.m., destroying a secondary gun and forcing a turbine room to be cleared of men while the smoke and fumes dissipated. However, despite the loss of one of her guns, *Seydlitz* had the range of the *Queen Mary* and was starting to pound her without mercy. So too did *Derfflinger*. At 4.17 p.m. the British battlecruiser was hit by at least three shells, one landing outside 'X' turret, and another damaging the after 4-inch battery. The gunners in *Seydlitz* noticed a fire had started near the battlecruiser's stern.

At 4.21 p.m., the *Queen Mary* was hit again, this time by a 12-inch shell from *Derfflinger* which hit 'Q' turret. The shell didn't seem to penetrate the turret itself, but the right-hand gun and its elevating and training mechanisms smashed, and so it was put out action. The left-hand gun continued to fire though, at least for a few minutes more. Since the battle began, the *Queen Mary* had been hit at least five times, but apart from the last hit to 'Q' turret no serious damage had been inflicted. That though, was about to change. At 4.26 p.m. Midshipman Jocelyn Storey in 'Q' turret heard a terrific explosion somewhere forward in the ship. He thought it might be a magazine. The blast swept over the turret, and the barrel of the remaining left-hand gun was sheared off. The right-hand gun slipped off its mounting, and a cordite charge ignited, killing many of the men in the turret. Storey escaped though, and clambered out onto the turret roof. From there he was able to watch the death of his own ship.

The sight was incredible. The ship had broken in two beneath the foremast, and the stern section – which he was still standing on – was rising out of the water. Then, from behind him, there was another huge explosion and he was thrown into the water. The first explosion was the result of two 11-inch shells from *Seydlitz* hitting the battlecruiser, one of which may have struck amidships and sheared the barrel off Storey's remaining gun. The other struck the battlecruiser further forward, near 'A' or 'B' turrets or their barbettes. That was the shell that destroyed the ship. The shell must have penetrated the turret armour and exploded inside it, or in the shell hoist beneath. The resulting fireball reached one of the magazines and both of them exploded within fractions of a second of each other. This blast split the ship in two just forward of the foremast, and much of the forward section was ripped apart by the explosion, including the bridge and the forward turrets.

The stern section rose quickly into the air after the blast from the explosion swept across its decks. This force of this wrecked 'X' turret, and started a fire there. A minute later, this caused another explosion to erupt in 'X' turret. It was this that catapulted Midshipman Storey into the water and saved his life. He and eighteen others were the only survivors from the battlecruiser's 1,275-man crew. Gunner's Mate Ernest Francis, who was in 'X' turret, remembered experiencing the shock of the explosion outside the turret at 4.17 p.m., and feeling the thump four minutes later when 'Q' turret was hit. Then came the big explosion. 'Immediately after that came what I termed the big smash, and I was dangling in the air on a bowline, which saved me from being thrown to the floor of the turret.' The power failed and he noticed how quiet everything had become. He stuck his head through the hatch in the roof of the turret and took in the scene of devastation outside. It was clear the ship was sinking.

Francis clambered back and told the turret officer what was happening. The order came to clear the turret, but by now the stern was rising out of the water and it was becoming harder to clamber up the ladder. Eventually, Francis made it on to the open deck, and from there he half clambered, half fell over the side into the water. Midshipman John Lloyd-Owen was part of the same turret crew, and he reached the quarterdeck behind the turret. From there, he looked forward, and saw the ship – what was left of her – was lying on her side; 'She was broken amidships – her bows were sticking up in the air and the stern was also sticking out at an angle of about 45° from the water.' The deck was red hot from internal fires and explosions beneath him. 'A few moments afterwards a tremendous explosion occurred in the fore part of the vessel, which must have blown the bows to atoms. The stern gave a tremendous lurch, throwing me off into the water.'

Other explosions of varying sizes rippled through what was left of the ship, 'X' turret's magazine proving the final blow to many of the men still clustered on the after part of the ship, or in the water beneath it. When the forward magazines exploded, a great eruption of red flame was seen shooting upwards, followed by a mass of black smoke. The two forward turrets were thrown at least a hundred feet in the air, the masts collapsed inwards, and then the bows seemed to disappear. A huge mushroom-shaped cloud hovered over the shattered remnants of the stern, which rose out of the water, its propellers still turning slowly, despite the loss of power to them. When the *Queen Mary* exploded, *Tiger* was just 500 yards astern of her, making 24 knots. Captain Henry Pelly ordered the wheel turned hard over to port, and *Tiger* swept past the wreckage as pieces of burning debris cascaded onto her deck.

On the *New Zealand*, following behind her, the bridge crew were able to make out the name of the sinking battlecruiser, picked out in red letters on the port side of her stern. Men in the water must have been run over by the two battlecruisers, and many others were pulled under by the sinking remnants of their ship. The shattered stern section slipped beneath the oil-slicked water soon after *New Zealand* surged past her, and all that remained of the 26,000 ton, 700-foot long battlecruiser was a circle of wreckage, bodies and a small handful of survivors. Above them lingered that black cloud of smoke, which Georg von Hase described as looking like a monstrous black pine tree. Most of the nineteen survivors were rescued by the British destroyers *Laurel* and *Petard*, but two were found later by the German destroyer *G-89*. One of the men rescued by *Laurel* was Ernest Francis, amazingly the only uninjured survivor to be hauled out of the water.

In the popular imagination, while most people do not know the details of this great clash of battlecruisers, they remember that British ships blew up, taking most of their crew with them. The reason this sticks in the mind is the pithy quote attributed to Vice-Admiral Sir David Beatty, as he watched the battle unfold. Losing one battlecruiser in this way was unfortunate. To lose two – a third of his force – was something akin to a disaster. Still, Beatty was not a man to show his feelings, even though the sinking of *Indefatigable* and *Queen Mary* must have been a real shock. So, instead of reacting in horror, he uttered a phrase that has gone down in the history books, one that perfectly summed up this stage of the battle. The man it was uttered to, Beatty's Flag Captain Alfred Chatfield recalled the moment; 'Beatty turned to me and said; *There seems to be something wrong with our bloody ships today!*'

Of course there are other versions. The two signallers present remember a different version – 'What's the matter with our bloody ships today?' was heard, and some claim he added Chatfield's name at the end. Later, British history books felt this was not dignified enough, and added 'Steer two points closer to the enemy' afterwards, an unnecessary but understandable embellishment, mirroring the Nelsonic 'Engage the enemy more closely' signal. This though, was never uttered, as a study of the ships' logs will reveal. Still, the almost ludicrous degree of under-statement appealed to the British psyche, and the phrase – or Captain Chatfield's version of it – became Beatty's official response to these twin disasters. One thing was clear, though. As Chatfield wrote next, after the phrase was uttered it was; 'A remark which needed neither comment nor answer. There was something wrong.'

9

The Run to the North

Although Hipper now had five battlecruisers to Beatty's four, the appearance of Evan-Thomas' fast battleships had changed the whole situation. In theory, the German battlecruisers could all make 25 knots or more, but successive hits had taken their toll, and the fast battleships eight miles behind them were gradually closing the range. *Moltke* was hit by three 15-inch shells in ten minutes, so that by 4.26 p.m., the moment the *Queen Mary* exploded, she was listing 3° to port, and a thousand tons of seawater had to be pumped into her port side to restore her to an even keel. *Von der Tann* was lucky just to suffer the one hit from *Barham*, but shells were falling all around her as she zig-zagged through the towering spouts of water. It was clear that Hipper's squadron could not take this battering for long without suffering serious damage. So, at 4.30 p.m., he ordered his ships to turn simultaneously to port. This was his only chance to break off the uneven fight.

A Wild Scene

The only way this could work would be if Beatty could be distracted while Hipper's battlecruisers made their escape. Fortunately, Hipper had the ideal tool to hand. Two of his three destroyer flotillas were too far to the east to intervene, but Commodore Heinrich's IX Torpedo Boat Flotilla was close to hand, clustered round the flotilla's flagship, the light cruiser *Regensburg*. Hipper ordered Heinrich to cover the retreat of the battlecruisers. The two lines of battlecruisers were now about six miles apart (12,000 yards). This space would become Heinrich's arena. His cruiser and nine small destroyers entered it by racing past the stern of the line of friendly battlecruisers, and they fanned out, ready to launch a torpedo attack on Beatty's ships. However, Beatty could play that game too. He ordered the 13th Destroyer Flotilla into action, led by Captain John Farie in the light cruiser *Champion*. These small, sleek warships would now have a chance to fight their own duel between the battlecruisers.

Like their German counterparts, the twelve British destroyers had been following the battlecruisers on their disengaged side. Now they sped in front of Beatty's flagship, and raced at top speed – 34 knots – towards the Germans. The two groups clashed, and soon the sea was filled with them, swirling around like fighter planes in a dogfight over the trenches. The naval historian Julian Corbett vividly captured the spectacle; 'It was a wild scene of groups of long low forms vomiting heavy trails of smoke, and dashing hither and thither at thirty knots or more through the smother and splashes, and all in a rain of shells from the secondary armament of the German battlecruisers, as well as from the *Regensburg* and the destroyers, with the heavy shell of the contending squadrons screaming overhead. Gradually a pall of gun and funnel smoke almost hid the shell-tormented sea, and beyond the fact that the German torpedo attack was crushed, little could be told of what was happening.'

The intervention of the British destroyers came in the nick of time. Heinrich's boats were forced to fire their torpedoes at a longer range than they wanted, before the British boats reached them. All of these German torpedoes missed Beatty's battlecruisers. Then came the great swirling clash, and by its end two German boats – *V27* and *V29* – had been sunk and the remainder were pulling back, covered by fire from the German battlecruisers. The battle had lasted just a few minutes, but the greater size and more powerful armament of the British had proved its worth. Now it was their turn to harass the enemy's larger ships. From *Champion*, Farie ordered his undamaged destroyers to launch a torpedo attack on the German battlecruisers, which were now heading towards the south-east in line abreast. The Germans responded by opening up a withering fire on the racing destroyers with their secondary gun batteries. The destroyers pressed home their attack amid a fury of shells.

These twelve M-Class destroyers carried four 21-inch torpedoes apiece, but only twenty of them managed to launch successfully, at a fairly long range of 6,000 yards. Of these, only one – a torpedo fired by the destroyer *Petard* – actually hit its target. At 4.57 p.m., it struck *Seydlitz* on her starboard side, beneath her forward turret. It ripped a hole in her, but behind her outer hull there was an inner defence, a torpedo bulkhead. This bulged, but held, and so the damage was contained. Still, several of her outer hull compartments were flooded, and the ship was now leaking badly below the waterline. For the moment though, *Seydlitz* was still in the fight. The destroyers paid a price for this though; several of them were damaged and two – *Nestor* and *Nomad* – were left dead in the water after crippling hits from the battlecruisers' 5.9-inch guns.

Lieutenant Commander Paul Whitfield, commander of the *Nomad*, described the moment his boat was hit; 'Our misfortune lay in getting a shell from one of their light cruisers clean through a main steam pipe, killing instantly the Engineer Officer and, I think, a Leading Stoker . . . The ship finally stopped, though steam continued to pour from the engine room.' Despite being dead in the water, Whitfield still wanted to fight; 'With the ship stopped, bad luck had it that the only gun that would bear was the after one, and that couldn't be fought owing to the steam from the engine room obliterating everything . . . I then noticed we had started to list to port considerably, and so thought that rather than let the torpedoes go down with the ship . . . I would give them a run for their money.' He fired all four of them at the German battle-cruisers, but didn't score any hits. So he was left wallowing impotently as the tide of battle swept on past his crippled destroyer.

Goodenough's Surprise

During the destroyer battle, Hipper's five battlecruisers had altered course to the south-east, then the east, but at 4.38 p.m they began turning back onto a more southerly course. On their port side the remaining destroyers and cruisers of the 2nd Scouting Group were closing with them in case they were needed. For his part, Beatty's ships were also now heading due south; they had made no attempt to mirror Hipper's change of course. This meant that soon the two lines of battlecruisers were almost 10 miles apart, both running south, with the Hipper to the north-east of Beatty. Ten miles astern of Beatty were Evan-Thomas' four fast battleships, which were now pretty much following Beatty's course – so much so in fact that at around 4.40 p.m. they steamed past the patch of wreckage that marked where the *Queen Mary* had sunk.

The destroyers of both sides had pulled back and were now regrouping on the disengaged side of their respective lines of battlecruisers. Ahead of Beatty, about two miles away, the four light cruisers of Commodore William 'Barge' Goodenough's 2nd Light Cruiser Squadron were acting as the scouts of the fleet, and ignoring the battle raging astern of them. Goodenough's flagship *Southampton* was in the lead, followed in line astern by *Birmingham, Nottingham* and *Dublin*. At 4.30 p.m., as the *Queen Mary* was sinking and the destroyer fight was just getting under way, lookouts on *Southampton* spotted smoke to the south-east. It turned out to be a German light cruiser, the *Rostock*. Then the lookouts spotted more smoke behind her – lots of it. Goodenough trained his binoculars on the *Rostock*, then looked beyond her. Appearing over the horizon were the topmasts and then the upper works of what seemed a compact mass of dreadnoughts. It was the High Seas Fleet.

The long line of ships seemed endless, but in fact the dreadnoughts were steaming in several separate divisions of four ships apiece; they only looked like a massed column from Goodenough's perspective. Destroyers screened their flanks, and the whole powerful battle fleet was now heading directly towards the *Southampton*. Goodenough's instincts told him to turn and run, but for the moment he held his course, counting the dreadnoughts as they appeared. He reached a total of sixteen of them, although there were clearly more ships further astern. So far the Germans had not opened fire, but that could not last. Already the British could see the guns of the leading divisions pointing towards them. It was a terrifying spectacle, and an impressive one. Beatty had to be told, but Goodenough wanted to make sure the report was as accurate as he could make it. Finally, an officer on the bridge could not take the tension any longer, and said; 'If you're going to make that signal, you'd better do it now, sir. You may never make another.' Finally, Goodenough gave the order.

So, at 4.38 p.m., *Southampton* sent the signal to Jellicoe and Beatty that transformed the whole nature of the battle. It read 'Have sighted enemy battle fleet [bearing] SE. Enemy's course North.' It then added the cruiser's estimated position: 56° 34' North, 6° 20' East. With that,

Goodenough ordered his ships to turn simultaneously to starboard and make their escape. In the High Seas Fleet, Rear-Admiral Behncke's König and Kaiser class dreadnoughts were in the lead, following close behind the *Rostock*. Their gunlayers had been following the British cruisers for some minutes, but as they were head on the gunners could not be sure of they were friend or foe. It was only when Goodenough turned away that they saw they all had four funnels, the tell-tale mark of a British Town class light cruiser. The range was now just six miles. Behncke gave the order to open fire.

In less than a minute huge pillars of water rose around the four cruisers as the first salvos landed near them. The German gunnery was good, but a fast-moving light cruiser was a difficult target. This was made more so because all four ships were now zig-zagging furiously to throw off the enemy's aim. They used every trick to survive – for instance steering towards the patch of water where the last salvo had landed, in the hope that the German gunners would reduce the range before shooting again. On the *Southampton*, Lieutenant Stephen King-Hall was in the secondary gunnery control position below the mainmast, where he was painfully aware that the steel plate protecting him was just a tenth of an inch thick. In a display of sangfroid he tried to nibble at a piece of bully beef. 'However, my throat was so dry that I could not get much down, and we could not get any water.'

He added; 'About once a minute – or perhaps thrice in two minutes, a series of ear-splitting reports would indicate that another salvo had burst around the ship.' He felt the need to see the shells land; 'Against my will I could never resist hanging over the edge, and then I saw a half dozen . . . muddy foamy-looking circles in the water, over which black smoke hung. Sometimes the pools were on one side, sometimes the other.' He and his companions were drenched by the water thrown over them. King-Hall summed up the situation perfectly; 'I should say (and this is a carefully reasoned and considered estimated) that 40 large shells fell within 75 yards of us within the hour, and many others varying distances out. We seemed to bear a charmed life, but it was obvious that such a position could not last forever.' Incredibly, the only damage Goodenough's four cruisers suffered was a glancing blow to the stern of *Southampton*, which did no serious damage.

Gradually, the British cruisers began pulling out of range; in theory the range of these German 12-inch guns was up to 17,700 yards, but their effectiveness was reduced when firing at small fast-moving targets. Once out of range, Goodenough began shadowing the German battle fleet from a safe distance, and sending regular reports to Jellicoe and Beatty. As for Beatty himself, at first he refused to believe Goodenough. After all, the Operations Department in the Admiralty had assured him that Scheer's battle fleet was still at anchor off Wilhelmshaven. It took Beatty five more minutes before he realised Goodenough was absolutely right. Ahead of him the might of the High Seas Fleet appeared, heading directly towards him, while in between, about 5,000 yards away, the four ships of the 3rd Light Cruiser Squadron were racing back towards him, with a forest of shell splashes falling all around them.

The Hunter becomes the Hunted

So, at approximately 4.40 p.m., Beatty hauled *Lion* around to starboard, followed by his remaining three battlecruisers. Soon his ships were racing towards the north-west, ending what has become known as 'The Run to the South'. Effectively, the first stage of the battle was over. A few minutes before, despite his losses, Beatty was fairly confident that he would eventually overpower Hipper's battlecruisers. Now the hunter had become the hunted. Just as Evan-Thomas had rescued Beatty, now Scheer's arrival saved Hipper. Later – much later – when the fleets returned to port, a detailed analysis of what had just happened would make grim reading in the British Admiralty. There was little doubt that the Germans had won the first round. During the hour-long action, the British had scored seventeen hits, and the Germans fifty-four. Six of these British hits had been made by the fast battleships. This meant that Hipper's battlecruisers had outshot Beatty's by a factor of roughly four to one.

Now, though, the game had changed. Beatty's next task was to extricate his ships and flee northwards towards Jellicoe. This was his hidden card. While he knew roughly where Jellicoe was, neither Scheer or Hipper was aware that the Grand Fleet was at sea. Now it was Beatty's turn to lead the Germans into a trap. Jellicoe was approximately 45 miles to the north-west, which meant that if Jellicoe and Beatty closed with each other at something close to full speed, they would make contact in about an hour. All Beatty had to do was to keep out of trouble, and to draw both Hipper and Scheer northward towards the

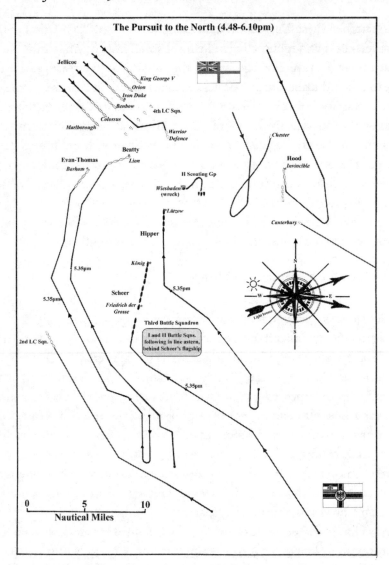

The Pursuit to the North (4.48–6.10 p.m.)

waiting guns of Jellicoe's dreadnoughts. The situation was complicated slightly by Beatty's inability to contact Jellicoe. *Lion*'s wireless transmitter had been knocked out, and his reserve set had a very limited range. So radio messages had to be forwarded through the *Princess Royal*, which increased the chances of messages being lost, delayed or misunderstood. Beatty's staff were not particularly good at signalling, and this didn't help.

Another signalling failure that afternoon was about to place four modern dreadnoughts in harm's way. In the *Barham*, Evan-Thomas had been too far to the north to pick up Goodenough's warning. Although Beatty heard it, he didn't believe it, and even altered course slightly to the east, so he could more easily check Goodenough's report for himself. When the lookouts in *Lion* sighted the High Seas Fleet steaming towards them, and Beatty decided to reverse course, he or his signalling team forgot to pass the message on to the fast battleship squadron, which was then seven miles astern of *Lion*. So, when the battlecruisers suddenly reversed course, Evan-Thomas was perplexed. At the time he was still running to the south, firing at Hipper's battlecruisers as he went. The Germans were on a parallel course, about 18,000 yards to the east, off *Barham*'s port beam. Why then had Beatty suddenly turned about?

The two small columns of four capital ships, one led by *Lion*, the other by *Barham*, were now approaching each other, and at 4.48 p.m. the columns passed to port. As the fast battleships raced by, Beatty realised that nobody had warned Evan-Thomas what lay ahead. So he hoisted a signal, telling him to follow him to the north, taking station behind the rearmost battlecruiser, the *New Zealand*. The trouble was that this was a 'preparatory' signal, and officially Evan-Thomas had to wait until he was told to 'execute' it. So he kept on his old course to the south, and each passing minute brought Evan-Thomas and Scheer 1,400 yards closer to each other. Two minutes later, Evan-Thomas realised why Beatty was now racing in the opposite direction. Shortly before 4.50 p.m. the masts of the German dreadnoughts appeared through the haze to the east, steaming towards them at full speed.

When Beatty made his turn away to the north, the closest German dreadnought was about 20,000 yards away (10 miles). Had he told Evan-Thomas, then the fast battleships would have stayed out of range too. Instead, they were left to close the range with the enemy, and then run the gauntlet of German fire. While this would take the pressure off Beatty and his battlecruisers, it did little for the crews of the four fast battleships. Already, the opening German salvos had started to fall around the *Barham*. The shooting was accurate, and it was heavy too, as twelve dreadnoughts were now firing at Evan-Thomas' flagship. When Beatty's order finally came, it increased the danger even more. They were told to reverse course, turning in succession to starboard. As the

German dreadnoughts were already targeting the leading British ship, the risk was that they would all fire at the same turning point, pounding each of the fast battleships as it passed through *Barham's* position.

At 4.58 p.m., or just after *Barham* turned, she was hit by three 12-inch shells fired by the dreadnoughts *Kronprinz* and *Kaiserin*. The first knocked out her wireless office, the second ignited ready-use charges for the dreadnought's 6-inch secondary guns. Another punctured *Barham's* starboard side on her upper deck and passed through the ship, blowing a jagged hole on the waterline on the far side of the ship. Strangely though, Evan Thomas' worst fears were not realised, and the other ships made their turn without being hit, despite the ferocity of the German fire. On board *Warspite*, the third ship in the line, the ship's First Lieutenant (or second-in-command), Commander Humphrey Walwyn watched as the whole of the enemy fleet was arrayed before them; 'Very soon after the turn, I saw on the starboard quarter the whole of the High Seas Fleet – at least I saw masts, funnels and an endless ripple of orange flashes all down the line.'

The four fast battleships made that agonisingly slow turn and hauled round to the north, and, with *Malaya* bringing up the rear, they set off in pursuit of Beatty's battlecruisers. They now formed the rearguard of Beatty's Battlecruiser Fleet as it raced northwards towards Jellicoe, pursued by the entire High Seas Fleet. Before Evan-Thomas arrived, Scheer's advancing dreadnoughts had opened fire on Beatty's battle-cruisers, but they lacked the range to hit them. Now the fast battleships had obligingly come even closer. They were also fired at by Hipper's battlecruisers, which had altered course again, and were now heading north, to maintain contact with both Beatty and Evan-Thomas. He was now leading the German fleet towards the north. It must have seemed as if the whole eastern horizon was filled with large enemy ships, all firing at the fleeing British.

The Fighting Rearguard

Hipper was about 17,500 yards to the east of Evan-Thomas, while Scheer's leading dreadnoughts were 19,000 yards to the south-east, with the rest following in an echeloned line of columns to the south. It was Hipper who scored the first hit at 4.58 p.m., when a 12-inch shell from *Derfflinger* struck the *Barham*, the first of four from von Hase's guns in the space of just over twenty minutes. It was also the most destructive, ripping through the starboard side of her upper deck to explode beneath the main deck, and putting a 6-inch gun out of action. The resulting flash also killed all the men in the Dynamo Room. Lieutenant Commander Stephen Tillard was in *Barham*'s conning tower at the time; 'I saw all four rounds which hit *Barham* in mid-air as they came. One hit penetrated the deck six feet from where I stood. It went on to explode below without doing much harm.' The next few minutes would see *Barham* hit three more times, with each blow seemingly more serious than the last.

Tillard saw these other salvos from *Derrflinger* hit the ship too. The last of these almost proved a fatal blow; 'Another hit below the waterline, and blew a hole in the opposite side of the ship, causing jagged edges which might have slowed us up. It wiped out a torpedo detachment.' What he could not see was that damage these hits were inflicting below decks. The first hit at 4.58 p.m. ignited the charges of 6-inch guns, and the blast ripped down a trunk to the Dynamo Room, killing everyone inside it. Another punched a hole in the armoured deck, just above a 6-inch shell magazine. Evan-Thomas was lucky though; shell fragments penetrated the magazine but didn't cause an explosion. The other three fast battleships remained unscathed – for the moment. The British captains zig-zagged furiously to avoid the shells, and through a combination of luck and good seamanship they managed to avoid any more hits.

By 4.57 p.m., Beatty's four battlecruisers had passed the spot where *Queen Mary* had sunk, and were about 18,000 yards to the west of Hipper. They opened fire on their old foes again and Hipper promptly switched targets. The battlecruiser duel had started all over again, but this time the ships were running towards the north. The conditions still favoured the Germans, but gradually that changed, as the sun sank lower, making it harder for the German rangefinding teams to get an accurate reading. Still, in just four minutes a shell from *Lützow* had hit *Lion*, and Beatty turned away to port to increase the range. He also increased speed to 26 knots. The duel continued as the battlecruisers pulled apart, with *Seydlitz* hitting *Tiger* and Hipper's flagship scoring two more hits on *Lion*. None of these hits were serious though, but it showed that, despite the light, Hipper's gunnery was still better than Beatty's. During this brief exchange, the British failed to hit anything.

By 5.10 p.m., Beatty had drawn out of range. He was starting to think tactically, probably for the first time since the battle started. He, Evan-Thomas and Goodenough were fleeing towards the north-east, with Scheer's battle fleet in pursuit. Now though, only the 5th Battle Squadron was still in range of the Germans, leaving Beatty free to pause and think. Jellicoe was approaching from the north-east, and by Beatty's reckoning he was about 30 miles away. This meant that contact would be made some time after 6 p.m. The less warning Scheer had of Jellicoe's approach, the better. Ideally, the Germans would only discover the Grand Fleet was approaching them when it was too late to evade it. So Beatty planned to use the funnel smoke from his ships to screen Jellicoe's approach from Hipper, thereby buying time for Jellicoe to deploy. That meant driving Hipper away from Jellicoe's path.

For his part, Hipper was unwilling to draw too far ahead of the rest of the High Seas Fleet. His five battlecruisers had all suffered varying degrees of damage, and their fighting ability was not what it had been ninety minutes earlier. He was also fairly wary of the fast battleships of the British 5th Battle Squadron, whose fire had proved disturbingly effective – far more so than the battlecruisers. Still, however powerful it was, this British squadron was within range of both Hipper's battlecruisers to the north-east and Behncke's III Battle Squadron to the south-east. The British ships were effectively outnumbered by three to one. So Hipper's battlecruisers turned their guns back on this isolated British rearguard, which was already under fire from Behncke's pursuing squadron of dreadnoughts – the vanguard of Scheer's battle fleet. Having effectively been abandoned by Beatty, Evan-Thomas and his men would simply have to hold off the cream of the High Seas Fleet until Jellicoe arrived.

Evan-Thomas' four ships were following Beatty towards the north-west, and for the second time in an hour they passed the flotsam marking where the *Queen Mary* had sunk. Goodenough's light cruisers were following him, while small clouds of British destroyers tried their best to keep out of the way. By now, though, the light was gradually beginning to favour the British, and the gunnery direction systems on the Queen Elizabeth class fast battleships. This time it was Hipper who got the worst of the exchange, as *Barham* and *Valiant* engaged his battlecruisers, leaving *Warspite* and *Malaya* to hold off the German dreadnoughts. Over the next thirty minutes, both sides scored telling hits, but it was Hipper's battlecruisers which suffered the most, as their armour was no match for

Evan-Thomas' 15-inch guns. This was particularly so as at 18,000 yards the fast battleships were beyond the range of some of the older battle-cruisers' guns. In other words, they could be shot at, but could not shoot back.

Seydlitz, Lützow and *Derfflinger* were hit six, four and three times respectively during this duel, and they scored eleven hits in return, two on *Warspite*, and four each on *Barham* and *Malaya*. The German dreadnoughts also exchanged hits, scoring there more hits on *Malaya*. In return, shells from *Warspite* and *Malaya* caused minor damage to three German dreadnoughts: *König, Grosser Kurfurst*, and *Markgraf*. In all this it was *Seydlitz* and *Malaya* that suffered the most. The German battlecruiser was struck at 5.06 p.m., and the shell punched a hole in her bow near the waterline. Two more 15-inch shells landed in the forecastle, adding to the damage. In all, the *Seydlitz* was hit six times during this phase of the battle.

Richard Foerster described the devastation on board; 'One of the 38cm [15-inch] shells struck the armour of the port IV [5.9-inch gun] casemate and detonated in the room; the ship quivered and twitched below decks and the sides trembled just as thin sheet metal. At the rear of the aft funnel a group from turret "C" fought to extinguish a fire that was threatening *Fahnrich zur See* [Midshipman] Schmidt, *Bootmannsmaat der Reserve* [Petty Officer] Corinth and some sailors ran over the deck to the casemate, and attempted to enter from above, through a coal man hole, to advance into the casemate as they could hear whimpers, moans and cries for help from inside. The detonation pressure had hurled the cover off, however sheet metal scrap had jammed the opening and they couldn't get through. The complaints from their injured comrades urged the men on and won't rest.'

It was an ugly situation, but then somebody noticed a way in; 'They could see over the side that the shell had penetrated the hull and perhaps they could enter through the shell entrance hole. *Fahnrich* Schmidt and *Matrose* [Seaman] Neumann fitted gas masks and provided with hand lanterns went down the hull side, where they groped their way in. In the weak light of the hand lanterns a gruesome picture offered itself to them; around the totally destroyed gun lay horribly mutilated corpses, the entire serving crew seemed to have been killed by the detonating shell. However, from the space behind the gun a lamentable moaning sounded again, and there lay four motionless, badly wounded men, injured by shell splinters. Carefully but quickly they were carried through the darkness to the man hole, where the sheet metal was bent aside from below. With the assistance of the others standing on deck the injured were taken above and then to the battle dressing station.'

The *Seydlitz* had been pounded hard and, despite all her damage control crews could do, the flooding increased. As the evening wore on *Seydlitz* gradually dipped her bows until the forecastle was almost awash. Things were almost as bad on board the *Von Der Tann*. She had been suffering hydraulic problems, and her turrets kept malfunctioning. Her last working turret jammed, and so her main guns were silenced until they could be repaired. Now, she stayed at the end of Hipper's line, drawing fire from other ships still capable of fighting back. On the *Derfflinger*, von Hase described this phase of the action as 'depressing, nerve-wracking and exasperating'. After all, he was fighting an out-numbered enemy, but one whose more powerful guns had a longer range.

Still, they were hitting back, and one hit on *Malaya* at 5.30 p.m. silenced most of the starboard secondary battery, and came within a hair's-breadth of igniting a magazine. It would probably have been the end of the ship had the shell breached one more bulkhead. *Barham* and *Warspite* suffered too, but no major damage was inflicted. Assistant Clerk Gilbert Bickmore described one of the hits to his ship; 'The *Warspite* received one hit from an 11-inch shell which hit tight aft. Even in "A" turret at the other end of the ship we felt the hit, which made the ship give a sort of wriggle, very like a trout on the end of a line.' Both hits on *Warspite* during that phase of the battle were caused by 11-inch shells. Still, good armoured protection and a fair amount of luck meant that Evan-Thomas' squadron were giving as good as they got, and were gradually making their way closer to Jellicoe.

One little incident briefly drew the focus away from the four fast battleships. Forty minutes earlier, destroyers of the German XI half-flotilla made a half-hearted attack on Beatty's withdrawing battlecruisers, just as Evan-Thomas' fast battleships were passing Beatty during their run towards the south. Despite this rich selection of targets, none of their torpedoes hit anything, although on board *Valiant*, torpedoes were seen passing close to both her bow and stern. Meanwhile, the British destroyers *Moorsom* and *Nicator*, decided to have a go at the approaching German dreadnoughts. On the *Moorsom*, Sub Lieutenant Hilary Owen remembers his big moment; 'I remember seeing *Nicator* making an attack, but no sign of *Nestor* or *Nomad*. Then the High Seas Fleet opened fire and our gunner (Mr. Condon) related how he saw a salvo of 11-inch "like a flight of wild duck", which fell only about a hundred yards short, and the large shell splinters found lying about the deck bore him out.'

It was a near-suicidal gesture, but the two sides were approaching each other at a rate of a mile a minute, so there was no time to have second thoughts. Owen continued; 'Then, at a range of about 6,000 yards we turned to port, and fired two torpedoes – one from each tube – and then we legged it for the safety of our own line.' *Moorsom* was hit, but got away, but less fortunate were two crippled destroyers – *Nestor* and *Nomad*. The two boats had been immobilised earlier that afternoon, and the tide of battle had swept past them. Now it had returned with a vengeance. On the *Nestor*, Commander Barry Bingham saw the German battle fleet bearing down on him; 'Their course necessarily led them past first the *Nomad*, and in another ten minutes the slaughter began. They literally smothered the destroyer with salvos. On the destroyer, Lieutenant Commander Paul Whitefield recalled; 'The ship was sinking fast. I gave the order to abandon her and pull clear. About three minutes later she went down vertically by the stern.'

Then it was *Nestor*'s turn. Commander Bingham made the Carley floats ready, got rid of his signal books, and waited for the inevitable. 'Very soon we were enveloped in a deluge of shellfire. Any reply from our own guns was absolutely out of the question . . . to have answered . . . would have been as effective as the use of a peashooter against a wall of steel.' However, Bingham had one last trick. During the past hour his men had reloaded one of his torpedo tubes; 'Just about this time we fired our last torpedo at the High Seas Fleet, and it was seen to run well.' With this last gesture of defiance, the destroyer began to settle by the stern, and heel over to starboard. Bingham gave orders to abandon ship. At 5.30 p.m. the destroyer sank, leaving what remained of her crew to be picked up by a German destroyer during the night. Commander Bingham survived, and was later awarded a Victoria Cross for his defiant last stand.

This was not the only rash destroyer attack that afternoon. Two more British destroyers had been left behind to escort the seaplane carrier *Engadine*, but now they re-appeared to the north of the battle arena and decided to launch an attack on Hipper's battlecruisers. So, the little destroyers *Onslow* and *Moresby* surged forward, drawing a great deal of fire from any German ship in range. Eventually, the volume of fire proved too much, and both destroyers turned away, but not before *Moresby* managed to let off a torpedo. It missed, but the rash, foolhardy, gallant attack forced Hipper to turn away slightly towards the east. By 5.15 p.m., it was all over, and as the destroyers made good their escape, the High Seas Fleet pressed on, although by now Evan-Thomas' ships had largely pulled out of range. What followed was a brief lull in the fighting, the first since the firing began almost two hours before.

This was about to change. First, now that Beatty had pulled ahead of the German battlecruisers, he altered course slightly to starboard, bringing his four ships on to a north-easterly course and within range of Hipper. Beatty opened fire at 5.41 p.m., when the ships were eight miles (16,000 yards) apart. So did Evan-Thomas. At the time, Hipper was advancing with his five ships in echelon, but he quickly reformed them into a line, running parallel to Beatty. Four minutes later, the *Princess Royal* scored a hit on the *Lützow*, the shell striking just below her conning tower, but causing no serious damage. However, Hipper's battlecruisers were in bad shape and he had no real desire to renew the fight at such bad odds. Visibility was also poor towards the west. So Hipper broke off the fight, leading his battered ships away to the east. This was exactly what Beatty had wanted. Jellicoe's approach was now completely screened from the Germans.

At 5.47 p.m., when Hipper altered course away from Beatty, his battlecruisers had pulled almost seven miles ahead of the German battle fleet, which was now steaming northwards in a single line. The battle fleet's recent manoeuvrings had disordered its perfect spacing, and now the leading dreadnoughts were now well ahead of the slower ships towards the rear of the line – the older dreadnoughts and pre-dreadnoughts. Hipper's own cruisers and destroyers were ahead of him, steering towards the north-east, while Beatty's light cruisers and destroyers were either ahead of him, astern, or keeping well out of the way somewhere off his port side. For the past two hours, Hipper and Scheer had been fighting various elements of Beatty's Battlecruiser Fleet, which had always been to the west of them. Now, without warning, a new adversary would make a surprise appearance from the east. For Hipper and his men, the battle was about to take a very unexpected turn.

10

Jellicoe enters the fray

As Hipper broke off contact with Beatty, a new threat appeared out of the murk towards the north-east. A little after 5.30 p.m., the light cruisers of Rear-Admiral Bödicker's 2nd Scouting Group saw a ship approaching them from that unexpected direction. It was the British cruiser *Chester* – one of the two light cruisers which formed the screen of an entirely new force – Rear-Admiral Sir Horace Hood's 3rd Battlecruiser Squadron. Earlier that afternoon, Jellicoe had detached Hood from the rest of the Grand Fleet with orders to find Beatty and to give him whatever support he needed. Hood had expected to make contact with Beatty about forty minutes before, based on the dead-reckoning position supplied by Beatty two hours earlier. Unfortunately, Beatty didn't give any more reports on his position, course or speed, and so neither Jellicoe or Hood knew exactly where to find him. Hood had radioed Beatty asking for an update, but Beatty never replied.

Hood and Bödicker

So Hood had gone further east than intended, but after finding no sign of Beatty he altered course towards the south-west. The core of his force consisted of three Invincible class battlecruisers – his flagship *Invincible*, followed by *Inflexible* and *Illustrious*. Four destroyers screened them, while about five miles in front were two light cruisers off the flagship's port and starboard bows. *Chester* was on the starboard bow, making her the closest to Hipper. When her captain heard gunfire to the south-west, he set off to investigate. It was too hazy to see properly, but *Chester's* lookouts suddenly spotted a cruiser and a destroyer flitting through the murk to starboard. The ghostly outlines of three more cruisers could be seen behind them. At first, Captain Lawson thought it might be part of Beatty's cruiser screen, but a minute later, at 5.38 p.m., these mystery cruisers opened fire.

At that range (just 7,000 yards), the Germans could hardly miss, especially as the *Chester* was now clearly visible. Captain Lawson immediately increased speed and turned away to starboard, but this only made things worse, as by turning he made his ship a better target. In the space of just a few minutes the cruisers *Frankfurt*, *Elbing*, *Pillau* and *Wiesbaden* hit his ship seventeen times. Four of *Chester*'s ten 5.5-inch guns were knocked out, and seventy-eight of her crew killed or wounded. On *Chester*'s bridge Signalman Charles Rudall survived an explosion that killed or wounded twelve signal staff, leaving two lookouts unscathed. 'Exposed cordite was exploded, and flames shot up about 200 feet. Gun crews were walking over the side, blinded or hurt.' He added; 'During this action I saw a man's hair stand on end – a thing I never thought possible.'

Surgeon Lieutenant Bloomfield went on deck with a first aid team to do what he could. One of his assistants was Wardroom Steward Reg Gulliver, who recalled the scene, which, he said; 'will remain in my memory forever'. He continued; 'An officer was lying dead, with both legs severed in sea boots. I stepped over a body that had been disembowelled. I had to hold a seaman's foot while the doctor cut it off, as it was just hanging.' Other dead bodies were scattered around the upper deck. The wounded were taken below for treatment, and the first aid team did what they could for them. Fortunately for *Chester*, her engines were undamaged, and she used them to power away to the north at full speed, towards Hood's battlecruisers. In *Frankfurt*, Bödicker ordered his cruisers and destroyers to give chase.

Five miles to the north-east, Hood heard the sound of gunfire, and saw the faint flashes of gunfire piercing the gloom. He realised that *Chester* had run into trouble and so, when the cruiser raced out of the murk to the south-west, he swung his line of three battlecruisers round to the north-west, so they lay broadside on to whatever was chasing Captain Lawson's beleaguered ship. On Hood's other attached light cruiser, the *Castor*, an officer recalled seeing her battered consort reappear; 'The *Chester* came close across our bows from east to west, with big holes in her along the main deck, and her ship's company cheering through the holes as she passed us.'

Then, at 5.55 p.m., the pursuing German cruisers appeared through the murk some 10,000 yards away. On the *Inflexible*, the Gunnery Officer spotted the *Chester*, then her pursuers; 'We sighted gun flashes, and the next minute the *Chester*, surrounded by shell splashes, came out of the mist on our port bow, heading across the bows of the squadron from port to starboard, and was followed a minute later by three German light cruisers.' Hood immediately gave the order to open fire. A few minutes earlier Bödicker had ambushed *Chester*. Now it was his turn to suffer. When he saw the three battlecruisers he immediately turned away, but by then it was too late; the shells were already falling around him. The 12-inch shells from *Indomitable* and *Invincible* straddled *Wiesbaden*, and their second salvos hit her. One of these shells exploded in her engine room, disabling her and leaving the cruiser dead in the water.

A shell from *Illustrious* also hit *Pillau*'s boiler room, destroying six of her ten boilers, but for the moment the cruiser could still function and she limped away, furiously making smoke to hide herself from the enemy. To cover his withdrawal Bödicker ordered his supporting destroyers to launch an immediate torpedo attack. The six destroyers fired twelve torpedoes and, although these all missed, their tracks were spotted by the battlecruisers, who all turned away to avoid them. So, with his three remaining cruisers pumping out smoke as fast as they could, Bödicker fled to the south. The first Hipper knew of all this was at 6 p.m., when he received a signal from Bödicker which read 'Am under fire from enemy battleships'. Two minutes later the signal from *Frankfurt* was repeated. Hipper had no real idea what was going on. He doubted the accuracy of the report, but he thought it meant some of Beatty's ships had got ahead of him and were lying across his path.

So, just before 6 p.m., Hipper ordered his battlecruisers to turn away and move closer to the battle fleet, which was coming up astern of him. He'd no wish to be cut off from it, particularly when it was now so difficult to make out much to the west, due to a combination of the murk and the low angle of the sun. Once the *König* came in view, the flag of Rear-Admiral Behncke flying from her foremast, Hipper turned his battlecruisers about again, effectively becoming the new vanguard of the battle fleet. Meanwhile, Bödicker's three remaining light cruisers were forced to abandon the stricken *Wiesbaden*, and raced for cover behind Hipper's larger ships. While some of the 2nd Scouting Group's destroyers fled south too, the commander of the IX Flotilla had come up to see if they could help the *Wiesbaden*. Instead they spotted the battle-cruisers, and Lieutenant Commander Herbert Goehle led his eleven boats into the attack.

Simultaneously the four destroyers escorting the battlecruisers appeared, and Commander Loftus Jones of the *Shark* led them forward in a counter-attack. The two groups of destroyers were both making almost 30 knots, and the two sides closed within seconds. Before they did, Goehle was able to fire off six torpedoes, but none of them hit. Then the two groups were in amongst each other, firing as they went. Goehle was supported by the light cruiser *Regensburg*, the flotilla flagship, which joined in the fight by firing at the British light cruiser *Canterbury*, which briefly appeared through the mist. The British destroyers were larger, but they were heavily outnumbered, particularly as Commander Bruno Heuberer in *Regensburg* sent in two more half flotillas as reinforcements. A flurry of 4-inch and 8.8-cm shells later, and the *Shark* was left dead in the water, having been riddled by hits from the German guns.

Coxswain Bill Griffin was at the wheel at the time; 'I reported "Steering gear gone, sir!", on which the captain gave orders to man the after wheel. It was then that I got wounded in the head, over the right eye. We then went to starboard, making use of the guns on the port side.' Amazingly, the *Shark* was still fighting back. This though, only lasted a moment, as Griffin added; 'This was when the forecastle guns' crew were completely blown away, gun and all.' The British destroyers were certainly getting the worst of the battle. On the *Ophelia*, a few hundred yards from the *Shark*, Able Seaman Bill Clement-Ford saw their own bow gun being hit, and; 'The gun crew lying dead around it except for one of the loading numbers, who was standing up with his arm jammed in the breech of the semi-automatic gun . . . It was a sickening sight to look down on this from our small bridge.'

On the destroyer *Acasta*, her commanding officer, Lieutenant Commander John Barron found the situation rather desperate. He wrote; 'The [German] destroyers were supported by cruisers, and things very quickly became unpleasantly warm. The German shooting was undoubtedly good, their salvos falling close together – perhaps too close together, really – but at first we were little hit, although a piece of shell scalped a signalman on our bridge, and a lot of shell splinters were flying about. We afterwards picked up 30 to 40 pieces from the mattresses slung around the bridge. Also on the bridge, we were all soaked through by the spray thrown up by shells, causing the sub lieutenant to remark that "an umbrella would be handy".' Moments later, the *Acasta* was hit in her bows, near the waterline, and Barron remembered that it; 'It gave us the feeling that the ship had been pushed bodily sideways.'

Seeing the *Shark* was in trouble, the *Acasta* fired off a torpedo, then came alongside the shattered destroyer. Barron offered to tow her to safety, but Commander Loftus Jones of the *Shark* waved them away, shouting out 'Don't get sunk over us.' He was right; *Acasta* was damaged herself, and the attempt would have been suicidal. Two destroyers would be lost instead of one. In the destroyer *Ophelia*, Commander Lewis Crabbe saw *Shark* being hit, but was unable to help her or *Acasta*, as both his destroyer and the accompanying *Christopher* were already damaged and shrapnel was bursting overhead. So, he veered away, covering *Acasta* as she withdrew to safety. As Jones thought, *Acasta* had been hit twice as she lay alongside the *Shark*, the shells wrecking her steering gear and filling her engine room with steam, scalding most of the men inside it. Barron nursed what remained of his steam power to coax his boat away towards the safety of the British battlecruisers.

At that point the *Shark* was hit by a German torpedo and she began sinking. Jones had a leg ripped off by the explosion, and both he and over half his crew went down with their ship. Two weeks later, the body of Loftus Jones was washed up on a beach near Gothenburg in Sweden. He was buried there with full military honours and was later awarded a posthumous Victoria Cross for his gallantry.

Another posthumous winner of that famous medal was sixteen-year-old Boy Seaman (1st Class) John Cornwell of the *Chester*. The young East Ender was operating the gun sight of the cruiser's forward 5.5-inch gun when the gun was hit by a 15 cm shell fired by one of Bödicker's cruisers. All of the crew were killed or badly wounded, many of them cut down by shrapnel which scythed off their lower limbs, exposed below the weapon's small gun shield. Young Cornwell was grievously wounded in the chest, but he stayed at his post, and once the cruiser limped to safety, a first aid team found him there, the only survivor of his gun crew. He died two days after the battle, but his example of devotion to duty led to his posthumous medal, which his mother received from the king on his behalf. *Chester* is long gone – she was broken up for scrap in 1921 – but the gun crewed by 'Boy Cornwell' was preserved and is now on display in London's Imperial War Museum.

Taking Stock

This little action might have temporarily unnerved Hipper, but it also changed the general course of the battle. Hipper placed little faith in the 2nd Scouting Group's reports of 'battleships', but he did think they might have made contact with Hood's 3rd Battlecruiser squadron, which he knew normally formed part of Beatty's command, or possibly even a part of Jerram's 2nd Battle Squadron, sent forward to support Beatty. He never suspected that this mysterious force could be part of Jellicoe's Grand Fleet. The other, often unconsidered result of Hood's sudden appearance was that without it, Hipper might have been able to prevent Beatty pushing him further to the east. After all, the 2nd Scouting Group's destroyers were still a formidable force, and a determined attack against Beatty might have forced him back to the west.

That would have meant that Hipper might have spotted Jellicoe before the British battle fleet had a chance to deploy from its cruising formation into a line of battle. That in turn would have meant that Hipper and possibly the leading dreadnoughts of the German battle fleet might well have been in a perfect position to cross Jellicoe's 'T' as the British dreadnoughts struggled to sort themselves out into a fighting formation rather than a manoeuvring one. In crossing the 'T' of an adversary, a fleet would be able to fire all of its broadside guns at the enemy advancing towards them, while only the leading enemy ship could fire back. This was exactly the battle-winning situation the Japanese had engineered during the Battle of Tsushima nine years earlier, a clash that led to the complete annihilation of the Russian fleet. It was the dream of every admiral, and unknowingly Hipper and Scheer might have found themselves in exactly that position. Now, thanks to Hood, that wasn't going to happen.

Still, over the past hour, during this 'Run to the North', the tide of battle had swung a little in favour of the Royal Navy. After extricating his battlecruisers from Scheer's ambush, Beatty's ships had sped northwards towards Jellicoe, or rather where Beatty's staff navigators thought Jellicoe might be. Arguably, Beatty could simply have broken contact and fled to the west and, barring any unforeseen disaster, he could have evaded his pursuers. Instead, by steaming north he tried to lure both Hipper and Scheer into a trap of his own. Hipper's battlecruisers and Evan-Thomas' fast battleships had been firing at each other throughout the 'Run to the North', but Beatty had temporarily broken contact. Then he edged to the east, and at 5.41 p.m. had moved close enough to open up on Hipper's ships again. This should have made Hipper suspect that Beatty was trying to drive him eastward, and he should have asked the question: 'Why?'

Hipper's ships were now slower than Beatty's remaining battlecruisers, and it was perfectly possible that he might be trying to work around to the north of Hipper, to cross his 'T'. That, though, seemed unlikely, as Scheer was following behind Hipper. If he tried that, then Beatty risked letting the Germans cut him off from Rosyth or Scapa Flow. The appearance of these reported 'battleships' provided something of an answer. Surely Beatty was trying to make contact with a missing element of his fleet, and not hiding anything more sinister. Still, both Hipper and Scheer were uneasy. It was Scheer who summed up the uncertainty perfectly when he turned to his Flag Captain Theodor Fuchs after looking into the haze to the north and said simply; 'Something lurks in that soup.' He never suspected though, that it might be the entire British battle fleet.

That the tactical situation now slightly favoured the British was down to the 15-inch guns of Evan-Thomas' 5th Battle Squadron. During the 'Run to the South', the British battlecruisers had been pounded heavily by Hipper, and two of them had been blown to pieces. The intervention of the fast battleships had altered the situation, as the accuracy of their gunnery proved far superior to that of Beatty's battlecruisers. Now, during the 'Run to the North', they had continued to fire fast and accurately, and their 15-inch shells not only outranged the German big guns, but were more destructive too. Salvos from *Barham* and *Valiant* had scored thirteen hits on Hipper's battlecruisers, while *Warspite* and *Malaya* had had struck Scheer's dreadnoughts five times. In return – largely thanks to the long range and the worsening light – Hipper's ships had only achieved five hits on his British opponents. For once, Hipper was losing the gunnery duel, and his ships were now suffering badly.

Still, the 12-inch guns of Behncke's dreadnoughts had evened the score slightly by managing to inflict seven more hits on the *Malaya*, the most badly-battered of the four fast battleships. Overall though, Evan-Thomas' powerful squadron was more than holding its own against two powerful enemy squadrons. Less impressive was the performance of Beatty's battlecruisers. During the 'Run to the North', Hipper had hit Beatty's ships six times, while only the *Princess Royal* managed to strike back, scoring a solitary hit on the *Lützow*. This though, was less important than the fact that, despite losing two battlecruisers, Beatty still had four more to command. True, *Lion* had lost 'Q' turret during the earlier duel with Hipper, and both *Tiger* and *Princess Royal* had lost a turret apiece too – each from malfunctions rather than enemy fire. Otherwise, all three were still in good shape, and *New Zealand* was largely undamaged, having suffered only one minor hit during the whole afternoon.

By contrast, Hipper's five remaining battlecruisers had all been badly knocked about. During the 'Run to the North', the flagship *Lützow* had been hit by four 15-inch shells plus another at 5.45 p.m. by one from *Princess Royal*. She was down by the bows due to heavy flooding and was leaking badly. Both *Derfflinger* and *Moltke* had suffered flooding during the 'Run to the South', and now they both had several hundred tons of water inside them and were listing slightly. *Seydlitz* was in an even worse state. By 5.55 p.m. she had taken six hits from 15-inch shells and her forward compartments were completely flooded. Her foredeck was alarmingly close to the water, and although the flooding had been contained – for the moment – her damage control teams were working flat out to keep her afloat. Although *Von der Tann* was relatively unscathed, her guns were silent due to malfunctions. In other words, the 1st Scouting Group was suffering badly and barely able to remain in the fight.

Still, despite the damage to his scouting forces, Scheer was fairly confident he had Beatty on the run. After all, earlier that afternoon Hipper had sunk two British battlecruisers, and some of Beatty's other ships – either the fast battleships or the battlecruisers – must have been taking a fair degree of damage. With his own eyes he had seen Beatty's own flagship *Lion* with thick black smoke hanging over her midships section, a sure sign that she had been dealt a major blow. At 5.15 p.m., he had ordered his dreadnoughts to pursue Beatty's retreating forces. Although the 'Splendid Cats' and the Queen Elizabeths were much faster than his own 20-knot dreadnoughts, there was a good chance that one or two of them had suffered enough damage to slow them down. Then, although the rest of Beatty's Battlecruiser Fleet might get away, Scheer and Hipper could add one or two more capital ships to the day's tally. That would be enough to turn this running fight into a major German victory.

Fleet Action Imminent

While neither Scheer or Hipper knew they were steaming directly towards the dreadnoughts of the British battle fleet, Jellicoe himself was struggling to work out exactly what was going on just a few dozen miles to the south-east of him. When the sortie began, he thought Scheer was putting to sea with his entire fleet. Then came the signal from the Admiralty, telling him the German fleet commander was still in port. He suspected Hipper might be at sea, but Jellicoe was confident that Beatty had the ships he needed to deal with the German Scouting Groups. With the addition of the 5th Battle Squadron, the Battlecruiser Fleet outnumbered Hipper by two to one. That was enough of a margin virtually to guarantee victory if the two forces met. It seemed that for the dreadnought battle fleet this would be just another fruitless sortie. Then, at 2.28 p.m., wireless signals were picked up from German ships. That meant something was out there.

Jellicoe ordered the fleet to prepare to increase speed, something that was achieved through the sweat of stokers, shovelling tons of coal into the boiler furnaces. Moments later came the report from *Galatea* that enemy ships had been sighted. This was followed by the news that these enemy ships included battlecruisers. So Hipper was at sea after all. At 3 p.m., he ordered the Grand Fleet to 'Assume complete readiness for action'. In the unique seven-turreted *Agincourt*, a dreadnought built first for the Brazilians and then the Turks before being appropriated, gunnery officer Lieutenant Angus Cunninghame Graham recalled the preparations; 'This consisted of clearing away guard rails, frapping and rigging, placing shot mantlets where not already done, rigging hoses which were left running on the upper deck to keep it wet as a fire precaution.' Finally, 'three or four extra white ensigns were hoisted at the mast and yards'.

At 3.55 p.m., Beatty sent a wireless message to Jellicoe, telling him 'Am engaging enemy'. Jellicoe knew by then that both Beatty and Hipper were heading towards the south-east, away from the Grand Fleet. That meant that the battle fleet probably would not see action after all. Still, he increased speed to 20 knots, and ordered Hood to 'Proceed immediately to support battlecruiser force'. By rights, Rear-Admiral Hood should have been with Beatty. His three-ship Squadron – the first and smallest battlecruisers in service – had been sent up from Rosyth to Scapa Flow a week before to conduct gunnery practice. When the Grand Fleet put to sea late on 30 May, Hood's 3rd Battlecruiser squadron was attached to the battle fleet. That afternoon, sending them speeding forward to help Beatty was probably all Jellicoe thought he could do to influence the coming battle.

Then, Jellicoe waited for news. For several months, in fact ever since the Dogger Bank battle, Jellicoe had tried to impress on Beatty the need to send him regular and timely sighting reports and information on enemy numbers, position, course and speed. When the crunch finally came, Beatty ignored his crucial role of being the 'eyes and ears' of the fleet. Instead, he became engrossed in fighting his own duel with Hipper, a duel he was losing until Evan-Thomas arrived to save him. Then, at 4.48 p.m., came the signal from Commodore Goodenough that changed everything; 'Have sighted enemy battle fleet [bearing] SE. Enemy's course North.' This was Jellicoe's first inkling that Vice-Admiral Scheer's dreadnoughts were at sea. Goodenough kept sending reports – three in the next hour – but they were frustratingly vague. They confirmed, though, that Scheer's dreadnoughts were still steaming northwards. Beatty never sent a single message during this whole crucial hour.

When Jellicoe heard the sighting report from *Southampton*, he sent a signal to the Admiralty telling them 'Fleet Action Imminent'. Of course there was nothing the Admiralty could do apart from warn the dockyards and the hospitals, and lay on stocks of extra coal and oil. The whole grave responsibility for what would happen next rested on Jellicoe's shoulders, the man Winston Churchill had described as 'the only man on either side who could lose the war in an afternoon'. Now that afternoon had come, but Jellicoe had no thought of defeat; all his efforts were concentrated on bringing the guns of his mighty fleet of dread-noughts to bear on the enemy. He had a vital decision to make, and just a few minutes to make it in. His dreadnoughts were steaming in their cruising formation, six columns steaming abreast of each other, with each column made up of four dreadnoughts in line astern. The trouble was, this wasn't a battle formation.

The cruising formation was used so that this tight box of ships could be tightly controlled by the fleet flagship; Jellicoe's *Iron Duke* was in the front and centre of the formation. It was also protected from U-Boats by a screen of destroyers, while an outer screen of cruisers gave Jellicoe warning of any threat. The trouble, of course, was that before deploying into battle formation – a long line of dreadnoughts arrayed in line astern – Jellicoe needed to know where the enemy was. That way he could put himself directly across their path, and ideally cross their 'T'. If he got it wrong, the enemy could either evade him, or worse, be in a position to cross Jellicoe's own 'T'. Jellicoe's decision on how and when to form up into this formation relied on information of the enemy. That was something he simply was not being given, except in the vaguest terms. Jellicoe needed news – or Beatty.

Then, at 5.55 p.m., Jellicoe and his staff heard the sound of gunfire. Strangely, it was coming from two directions – from the south-east and the south. This was Hood firing at Bödicker, ten miles to the south-east, and Beatty firing at Hipper, seven miles to the south. The running battle to the north was about to reach the Grand Fleet. Jellicoe signalled Vice-Admiral Sir Cecil Burney, whose flagship *Marlborough* was leading the battle fleet's right-hand column. He asked, 'What can you see?' A few minutes later came the reply Jellicoe had been waiting for; 'Our battlecruisers, bearing SSW, steering E, *Lion* leading ship'. It was Beatty. The two British commanders had finally made contact. Jellicoe reckoned that if Beatty was close by and was firing, then Hipper couldn't be far away either. Behind him – somewhere – would be the rest of the High Seas Fleet.

Men on both groups of ships realised the importance of the moment. On the dreadnought *Benbow*, Lieutenant Thomas Norman wrote; 'I must confess it was a magnificent sight, seeing the *Lion*, slightly on fire forward, leading the other ships and firing salvo after salvo, with the enemy's flashes visible in the haze, but not the ships themselves.' On the dreadnought's bridge, Norman's friend Lieutenant Patrick Lawder was trying to keep station with the other lead ships of *Benbow's* neighbouring columns. Still, he noticed the *Lion*, and remembered; 'The enemy could not be seen without glasses against the misty background, but a few columns of smoke could be seen.' He added; 'The flashes of both sides showed very clearly, as a sort of deep orange, and also the splashes of the enemy's shots, and a few of our own.'

At 6.06 p.m., Jellicoe could see *Lion* herself, and was taken aback to see the thick black smoke still hovering over her waist. He also noticed she was firing, and running up a signal. If the junction of the two British forces was a relief for Jellicoe, it was even more so for the sailors in the British battlecruisers. Despite the losses of so many shipmates and the disasters of the 'Run to the South', it all seemed worth it, as they had led the Germans into Jellicoe's path. As Captain Walter Cowan of the *Princess Royal* said; 'With the Grand Fleet in sight and within striking distance, we felt like throwing our caps into the air. It looked a certainty we had them.'

Of course, the two battle fleets were still hidden from each other. Jellicoe could now hear gunfire beyond Beatty, towards the south-east, and minutes later he could make out the orange flashes of a still hidden enemy firing at unseen British ships. In fact, it was Scheer taking aim at the fast battleships. At that point Jellicoe turned to his staff with exasperation and exclaimed; 'I wish somebody would tell me who is firing, and what they are firing at.' That of, course, should have been Beatty's job. Instead, when Jellicoe signalled Beatty asking him, 'Where is enemy's battle fleet?', Beatty could not tell him. He had had lost touch with Scheer an hour before, soon after he began his 'Run to the North'. Instead, Beatty sent the ambiguous reply 'Enemy's battlecruisers bearing south-east'. That was not what Jellicoe wanted to know. So the British commander-in-chief had to make the judgement call of his life, based on guesswork and intuition rather than reliable information. By 6.10 p.m. the time to reach that crucial decision had finally arrived.

Dreadnoughts in Action

Deploying a fleet of two dozen fast-moving dreadnoughts into battle formation is not a job for a beginner. The manoeuvre had been practised with monotonous regularity during fleet exercises and by now every dreadnought captain and admiral knew exactly what was expected. Above all, Jellicoe was utterly familiar with the complex operation, so much so that he had no doubt it would be carried out. His only concerns were with the timing of the manoeuvre, and the final course his long battle line would steer. His great fear was that he would be forced to lead his ships into battle when they were still deployed in their cruising formation of six columns. If that happened, only the front guns of the six leading ships – and possibly the ships in the far right-hand column – could fire at the enemy. Jellicoe calculated that it would take twenty minutes to complete the manoeuvre, from the moment the 'Deploy' signal was flown. His mind was full of calculations and probabilities.

The Deployment

Jellicoe had two options. His six columns were currently steering towards the south-east at a speed of 18 knots. The columns were spaced out sufficiently to let each column make a 90° turn without colliding with their neighbours. The idea was, when the 'Deploy' order was executed, the lead ship in each column would begin making its turn at the same time, and the dreadnoughts behind it would turn in succession when they reached the same spot. That would bring the whole fleet into a huge line twenty-four dreadnoughts long, steaming at right angles to its present course. Once the turn was made, the long battle line could then be turned again on to the course Jellicoe had chosen for it. So Jellicoe actually had to make two tough decisions. The first was whether to turn to port (the north-east) or starboard (the south-west). The second was what course to steer afterwards. If he sent the battle fleet steaming in the wrong direction, he could be putting his whole fleet in danger.

Turning to starboard was appealing, as it would bring his dreadnoughts into action quickly. That would help Beatty. The drawback though, was that they might be so close to the enemy that Scheer could launch a flurry of torpedoes at his ships. That would risk the loss of several dreadnoughts. If he deployed to port, then his ships would be two miles further away from the enemy – the distance between his first and sixth column – but this would greatly reduce the risk of a surprise torpedo attack. Just as importantly, his Flag Captain Frederic Dreyer, the fleet's leading gunnery expert, had recommended it. Dreyer's reasoning was that it would make the British ships hard to see in these hazy conditions, while the Germans would be to the south-west of Jellicoe, and clearly silhouetted by the low early evening sun. All these calculations took Jellicoe about a minute. He reached his decision and at 6.15 p.m., he gave the necessary order. The Grand Fleet would deploy to port.

A minute earlier, Jellicoe's decision was made a little easier when Beatty belatedly signalled 'Enemy battle fleet to the south'. Given the patchy visibility, that meant that Scheer was roughly six to eight miles south of *Lion*, and Jellicoe could see Beatty's flagship crossing his path two miles to the south-east. On *Iron Duke*, Captain Dreyer recalled the moment Jellicoe gave the order; 'I heard at once the sharp, distinctive step of the Commander-in-Chief approaching – he had steel strips on his heels. He stepped quickly onto the platform around the compasses and looked in silence at the magnetic compass card for about twenty seconds. I watched his keen, brown weather-beaten face with tremendous interest, wondering what he would do. With iron nerve he had pressed on through the mist with his 24 huge ships, each weighing some 25,000 tons or so, until the last possible moment, so as to get into effective range, and make the best tactical manoeuvre . . .'

It certainly required strong nerves. However, Dryer continued; 'I realised when I watched him that he was as cool and unmoved as ever. Then he looked up and broke the silence with the order, in his crisp, clear cut voice.' That order was given to the Fleet Signals Officer, Commander Alexander Woods. According to Dreyer, it read; 'Hoist equal speed pendant south-east.' Woods thought about it, and made a suggestion; 'Would you make it a point to port, sir, so that they will know it is on the port wing column?' Jellicoe replied at once; 'Very well. Hoist equal speed pendant south-east by east.' This change was not really necessary, as the *Iron Duke* would begin the turn to port anyway, and the other captains would be watching her. Still, it removed any chance of confusion. Within seconds, three signal flags were climbing up the flagship's mainmast halyards.

Next, Jellicoe ordered Dreyer to begin the fleet flagship's turn to port. To port and starboard, the captains of *Orion* and *Benbow* were waiting for this, and they ordered their ships to turn to port as well. The three other leading ships did the same, and the whole great manoeuvre was underway. This put the leading ship of the left-hand column, Vice-Admiral Jerram's flagship *King George* V, at the head of the line. The *Iron Duke* was ninth in what was fast becoming a giant steel conga line of twenty-four dreadnoughts. Once the turn was completed, the line of ships would cover six miles of sea. It was the decisive moment of the battle and of the entire naval campaign, if not the war. Dreyer noted the strange fact that at the time the manoeuvre began; 'We had not sighted any German ship.' This was about to change. If Jellicoe's calculations were correct, then the German fleet would blunder out of the mist to find the whole British battle fleet arrayed across their path.

Arbuthnot's Folly

While the dreadnoughts of the Grand Fleet were making this impressive and stately manoeuvre, a small fracas was taking place a few thousand yards to the south-east, hidden from Jellicoe's view by the swirling patches of mist and smoke. Before Jellicoe ordered the battle fleet to change formation, the destroyers screening it peeled away and reformed behind the dreadnoughts. Once reorganised into their three component flotillas, they shadowed the battle fleet, keeping a mile off its port beam. The cruiser screen also moved out of the way. The five light cruisers of the 4th Light Cruiser Squadron raced ahead to take up position ahead of the battle line, once it had settled on to its new course, which Jellicoe had established as the east-south-east. The four armoured cruisers of the

2nd Cruiser Squadron pulled away to the north, where they reformed and waited for orders. That left the four armoured cruisers of Rear-Admiral Sir Robert Arbuthnot's 1st Cruiser Squadron.

The 52-year-old Sir Robert was a keen sportsman and pioneering rally driver, but as a naval commander he had a reputation both as a stickler for orders and for impetuosity. At Jutland he rashly decided to dispense with caution to lead a headlong charge towards the enemy. It was a gesture that would cost him his life, his ship and his crew. His squadron had been protecting the starboard wing of the battle fleet until its redeployment, and he was now expected to reform astern of it. However, at 6.20 p.m., he spotted enemy light cruisers through the mist, seven miles to the east. These belonged to Bödicker's 2nd Scouting Group, which had just turned about after encountering Hood's battle-cruisers. Arbuthnot ordered his ships to turn broadside on to the enemy, and gave orders to open fire.

After just two salvos he saw the German cruisers turn away into the mist. Refusing to be robbed of his moment, he ordered his squadron to pursue. His flagship *Defence* was followed by the *Warrior*, and together they sped off towards the east. Of his two other cruisers, the *Duke of Edinburgh* eventually set off after them, but the *Black Prince* never saw the signal, and stuck to its original orders to form up astern of the battle fleet. Arbuthnot's course took him across the path of Beatty's battlecruisers, and *Lion* actually had to swerve to avoid a collision as the two ageing armoured cruisers raced past her. After a few minutes, they spotted the crippled *Wiesbaden*, 5,000 yards to the south-east. Both *Defence* and *Warrior* opened fire and pumped several salvos into her, leaving her blazing fiercely. The two armoured cruisers were still firing at her when several even larger shapes loomed out of the mist behind the burning cruiser. It was Scheer.

At that range – just four miles – Arbuthnot's two cruisers stood no chance. The four König class dreadnoughts of Rear-Admiral Behncke's III Battle Squadron opened fire. Each of the dreadnoughts opened up with ten 12-inch guns apiece, and at that range almost every shot struck home. On board the *Malaya*, Lieutenant Patrick Brind watched the spectacle unfold. 'When I first saw them I felt they were doomed. They were steaming at their utmost speed between the lines, endeavouring to get clear round us, i.e. round the end of the Grand Fleet, smoking very heavily, being continually straddled and frequently hit. They were soon on fire in several places, especially the *Defence*, but still they continued to fire to the very last.' Within minutes, the two cruisers were reduced to blazing hulks, their engines wrecked and their now-blazing hulls ripped open by numerous shell holes.

At 6.20 p.m., the *Lützow* and *Derfflinger* caught sight of the armoured cruisers, and Hipper's flagship opened fire. On *Lützow*, the Gunnery Officer Commander Günther Paschen ordered the killing salvo; 'At first glance I recognise an old English armoured cruiser, and give the necessary orders. My arm is clutched – "Don't fire, that's the *Rostock!*" But, I can see the [large calibre] turrets fore and aft. "Action! Armoured Cruiser. Four Funnels. Bow left. Left 30. Range 76hm [hundred metres]. Salvo!" . . . Fire salvos rapidly follow, of which three straddled, then there was repeated the now familiar sight of a ship blowing up.' According to Brind; 'The *Defence* suddenly disappeared in an immense column of smoke and flame hundreds of feet high. It appeared to be an absolutely instantaneous destruction – the ship seeming to be dismembered at once.' It was all over in an instant, and when the smoke cleared there was nothing left of Arbuthnot's flagship.

On the *Derfflinger*, von Hase's gunnery team also mistook her for the *Rostock*, until they realised the ship was an enemy armoured cruiser. Von Hase remembered the moment the target exploded; 'The secondary armament was trained on the target . . . Then, just as we were about to give the order "Fire!", something terrific happened. The English ship, which I had meanwhile identified as an old English armoured cruiser, broke in half with a tremendous explosion. Black smoke and debris shot into the air, a flame enveloped the whole ship, and then she sank before our eyes.' Watching from the *Malaya*, Brind added; 'Wreckage continued to fall into the water for quite a considerable time after the explosion, but when the smoke cleared there was absolutely nothing to be seen, where only a minute before had been the *Defence*.' There were no survivors.

Warrior was probably spared a similar fate because she was now shrouded in thick black smoke. Several of the fifteen 12-inch shells that struck her pierced her on the waterline, and both her engine rooms and magazines were now completely flooded, while her decks were ablaze and a huge column of smoke rose from her quarterdeck. The cruiser had become a charnel house; the ship's surgeon recalled that a shell striking the aft dressing station had killed forty people in a single explosion.

Men tried to fight the fires and contain the flooding, but the escaping steam, raging fires and choking smoke in the engine rooms made it impossible to get down there. Some of the stokers survived by clambering through holes torn in the decks. Others were not so fortunate.

The cruiser would never have survived another salvo, as the German gunnery had been highly effective. Fortunately for *Warrior*'s crew, at that moment a worthier target appeared. *Warspite* suddenly loomed through the mist just a few thousand yards from the stricken *Warrior*. Behncke's dreadnoughts immediately switched their fire to her, and *Warrior* was given a reprieve. After the tide of battle had moved on, the *Engadine* took *Warrior* in tow. She never made it home; her damage was so great that the following morning the cruiser foundered some 160 miles east of Aberdeen, after *Engadine* had taken off her surviving crew. The other armoured cruiser in the group was the *Duke of Edinburgh*. She was some way behind her two consorts, and when she saw the German dreadnoughts, her captain put his helm hard over. Shells flew her way, but she was able to escape back into the mist. She would be the only ship in her squadron to make it back to Scapa Flow.

Warspite

The reason *Warspite* drew the German dreadnoughts' fire from *Warrior* was not altruism or self-sacrifice; it was a matter of mechanical reliability. After Jellicoe began deploying his battle fleet, Evan-Thomas realised he was in the wrong position. The battlecruisers had forged ahead to take up their allotted station near the head of the line of British dreadnoughts, and the fast battleships were expected to be there too. However, they had been too far to the south of Beatty to make it into position before Jellicoe's dreadnoughts deployed into line. Having no wish to mask Jellicoe's line of fire, Evan-Thomas decided to form up at the rear of the battle fleet rather than at its head. By 6.15 p.m., his four fast battleships were a little to the east of the point where Jellicoe had made his turn, and so, with *Barham* in the lead, he altered course to port, to tuck himself in behind the *Agincourt*, the last ship in the long line. That was the moment when *Warspite*'s steering failed.

While her three sister ships steamed away to the north, *Warspite* began turning to starboard in a large, lazy circle. The ships of the 5th Battle Squadron had been close enough to watch *Defence* and *Warrior* race off to their doom, and as they turned away they could even make out the looming shapes of enemy ships through the haze to the south-east. Now *Warspite* was turning towards the enemy, and her crew could see them clearly. They could also see her. The German ships opened up at a range of five miles. At the time, Scheer was altering course a little to starboard, and *Warspite* was on their port beam. One after another, the German dreadnoughts opened fire at her as they passed, before continuing on into the haze towards the north-east. *Warspite* performed two complete circles in front of the massed guns the High Seas Fleet, as her crew worked feverishly to free her jammed rudder. It is little wonder that this was later described as *Warspite*'s 'Death Ride'.

Commander Humphrey Walwyn was *Warspite*'s First Lieutenant. He wrote; 'The steering gear episode was rather extraordinary. The hit by the port wing engine room had buckled the after bulkhead of the centre engine room, on which the steering engine is secured. This gave it a hot bearing and it was labouring heavily.' This problem was highlighted when *Warspite* turned to port to avoid *Valiant*, which was just ahead of her. As Walwyn described it; 'The Quartermaster got a bit rattled and forced the wheel too quick, which overrode the telemotor gear due to the engine lagging with a hot bearing.' The ship turned, but when her captain tried to straighten out, the steering system refused. As Walwyn put it; 'The ship had therefore ten degrees port helm on, and completed the circle twice, turning through 32 points towards the enemy's fleet.'

Over the next fifteen minutes, *Warspite* was hit by thirteen 12-inch shells, and several smaller ones. Captain Edward Phillpotts tried to use his engines to counteract the jammed rudder, but it did little good. His best form of defence was to keep moving, but still his ship was surrounded by fountains of water from near misses, and the 12-inch shells kept on slamming into her. One of the shells hit the casemate of No. 6 gun, on *Warspite*'s starboard side. Midshipman John Bostock was nearby, leading a damage control team. The biggest danger was an ammunition explosion, so Bostock ordered fire hoses to be aimed at the shattered casemate. Later, he wrote; 'We knew that the gun crew must be burnt pretty badly, and this didn't altogether make a pleasant job spraying cold salt water into the casemate. But still, it had to be done, because if the rest of the cordite had caught fire there was no knowing what might have happened.' Only then did they tend to the wounded.

By now, the *Warspite* was being pounded hard. Commander Walwyn recalled; 'The upper deck and superstructure looked perfectly awful, holed everywhere. I think at this time the firing had slackened, but the noise was deafening – shells bursting through tons of water over the ship.' The *Warspite* was certainly in a bad way. Her superstructure was peppered and ripped, and below decks her sick bay was destroyed, several secondary guns were knocked out and she was struck near the waterline. One of the barrels in 'Y' turret was knocked out, and she suffered minor flooding. Amazingly though, she survived without suffering any more serious damage. The ship had been saved by her thick armour and by a certain degree of luck. Eventually Phillpotts managed to nurse her away to the north-west, shrouded by smoke and pursued by shells from the *Ostfriesland* and Scheer's flagship *Friedrich der Grosse*.

Invincible

After dealing with Arbuthnot, Hipper had formed his battlecruisers in front of Scheer's battle fleet, and by 6.20 p.m. he was steaming towards the north-east. Smoke was lingering in the area, and the combination of the low sun to the west and the misty conditions meant that visibility was patchy, and changing by the minute. They passed the stricken *Wiesbaden*, on fire and almost hidden in smoke, but her after gun was still firing at a hidden enemy, probably the *Warrior*. In the *Derfflinger*, von Hase was still reeling from the sight of the *Defence* blowing up, but suddenly he saw other ships – even larger ones – appear to port, as the mist briefly cleared. As his guns swung into action again, he had time to ponder the colour of paint. These ships were dark grey, and, as von Hase explained; 'It is my opinion that our light grey colour was more favourable than the dark grey of the English ships. Our ships were much more quickly concealed by the thin films of mist which were now driving across the sea from east to west.' Then his guns opened fire.

The ships he spotted were the three battlecruisers of Hood's squadron. Having crippled the *Wiesbaden* and driven off the rest of the 2nd Scouting Group, Hood altered course to the west in an attempt to find Beatty. At 6.15 p.m., he sighted the *King George V*, leading Jellicoe's great line of dreadnoughts, approaching him off his starboard bow. Harold Webber, a seventeen-year-old signaller stationed in the *Indomitable*'s mast, remembered when he first saw Jellicoe's ships; 'Two columns of smoke appeared – the Grand Fleet. To me at my action stations, armed with one set of semaphore flags and Morse flags, and not even a canvas screen between me and the enemy, it was a welcome sight.' Moments later, Beatty appeared off the port bow, steaming almost at right angles to Jellicoe's battle line. It was soon clear that Beatty was planning to take station ahead of the dreadnoughts.

Hood thought for a moment. His correct station was astern of Beatty, but that would put him in the line of fire of the dreadnoughts. So, at 6.21 p.m., he ordered his squadron to reverse course, and placed himself ahead of Beatty. Minutes later, the swirling mist cleared, revealing a line of enemy five battlecruisers 9,000 yards off their starboard beam, almost due south of them. By then, Hipper's battlecruisers had already been spotted by Beatty, whose flagship was two miles behind Hood's *Invincible*. The British had been waiting for just this moment, and within seconds the four British battlecruisers opened fire, concentrating on the aftermost three German ships – *Seydlitz, Moltke* and *Von der Tann*. Hood saw this, and ordered his own three battlecruisers to fire on the *Lützow* and *Derfflinger* at the head of the German line.

Moments later, the Germans opened up too, splitting their fire between the two groups of British battlecruisers. On the *Derfflinger*, Georg von Hase noted; 'At 8.24 p.m. [6.24 p.m.] I began to engage large enemy battleship [battlecruiser] to the north-east. Even though the ranges were short, from 6,000 to 7,000m, the ships often became invisible in the slowly advancing mists, mixed with the smoke from the guns and funnels. It was almost impossible to observe the splashes.' He noticed that the British had now found the range of Hipper's line, and were scoring hits. 'At 8.25 p.m. [6.25 p.m.], Lieutenant von der Decken, in the after control, reported *Lützow* heavily hit forward. Ship on fire – much smoke' Then, even more ominously; 'Three heavy hits on the *Derfflinger*.' As von Hase put it; 'We were being subjected to a heavy, accurate and rapid fire from several ships at the same time. It was clear that the enemy could see us much better than we could see them.'

The *Lützow* was being hit hard. Her Senior Gunnery Officer, Commander Paschen, said of it; 'There began a phase compared with which all that had hitherto happened was play. While our own smoke completely hid the target from me so that I had to hand over to the after control, a hail of hits descended on us from port aft and port ahead.' In other words, both Beatty and Hood were firing at Hipper's flagship, and causing serious damage. Still, Pashen, von Hase and others were firing back, with some ships concentrating on Beatty's ships, and others on Hood's squadron. The whole situation was summed up with British understatement by young Harold Webber, watching from the *Indomitable*. 'On the starboard bow we had the German fleet throwing everything they had, including their toothbrushes at us' he recalled, 'and the Battlecruiser Force returning the complement.' He could not resist adding; 'As one can imagine there was a lot of smoke and flame around.'

Still, for Hipper this was an untenable position. He found himself out-numbered again, and his ships were in no condition to endure another prolonged duel. The two protagonists were on parallel courses, so he began turning away towards the south-east. It would take time to complete the turn though, and meanwhile Hipper's flagship was being struck repeatedly; *Invincible* alone hit her eight times in as many minutes. On *Invincible*'s bridge, Hood used the voicepipe to congratulate the ship's Gunnery Officer, Commander Hubert Dannreuther, whose station was in the fire control director high up in the foremast. 'Your firing is very good!' the admiral shouted, 'Keep it up as quickly as you can! Every shot is telling!' Dannreuther, the thirty-five-year-old son of a German-born concert pianist, did just that. Dannreuther noted though; 'This was the last order heard from the Admiral or Captain, who were both on the bridge at the end.'

On *Derfflinger*, von Hase remembered just how ferocious the shooting was. 'Several heavy shells pierced our ship with terrific force and exploded with a tremendous roar which shook every seam and rivet.' To throw off the aim of the British gunners, Captain Hartog briefly had to pull his ship out of line. *Invincible* was being hit too, though. *Lützow* and *Derfflinger* were concentrating their fire on *Invincible* – her consorts *Illustrious* and *Indomitable* were left alone – and she was hit several times, but to no discernible effect. Just before 6.30 p.m. a salvo straddled her stern. From his perch in the foremast, Dannreuther could not see any sign of damage, but on *Derfflinger* the spotters noted two hits. Then, von Hase fired again. This time, Dannreuther had a grandstand view of the salvo coming in, and watched as one of the shells struck the roof of 'Q' turret just behind him. Seconds later, *Invincible* blew up.

The 12-inch shell hit the battlecruiser at 6.30 p.m. It ripped the roof off the turret and exploded inside, killing all but one of the turret crew. This ignited powder charges, and the flash raced down the hoist towards the shell-handling rooms and magazines below. The magazine exploded, followed a split-second later by the one serving neighbouring 'P' turret. The whole central section of the ship erupted in a gigantic burst of crimson flame. In *Derfflinger*, von Hase and his team watched spellbound as the ship was ripped apart by a rapid chain of explosions. Debris including gun turrets and boilers was hurled in the air, the huge flame was followed by an even bigger column of black smoke, and, surprisingly, coal dust spurted in all directions. The ship was broken in half and the two tripod masts collapsed towards each other. Severed from each other, the bow and stern sections of the battlecruiser raised up out of the water. As the smoke cleared slightly, hundreds of horrified onlookers saw them form a giant 'V' shape in the water.

At the rear of Hood's line was the *Indomitable*. On board her was Midshipman John Croome, who had clambered on top of a turret roof to take a photograph. As he watched; 'There was a terrific flash from the *Invincible* . . . and she went up in a column of smoke several hundred feet high, decorated at the edges by bits and pieces of what a second before had been a battlecruiser and the flagship of our squadron.' The teenager raised his camera and took a picture – one that showed the huge geyser of smoke and debris at its height. Seconds later, he was forced to take shelter as fragments of debris began falling all around him. Von Hase picked up the telephone, and told his turret crews 'Our enemy has blown up!' A great cheer thundered through the ship. Von Hase let the men have their moment, then calmly ordered them to switch targets to the ship on the left, the *Inflexible*.

In the *Invincible*, Marine Bryan Gasson was perched in the roof of 'Q' turret manning a rangefinder when the 12-inch shell from *Derfflinger* struck just the turret just in front of him, between its twin gun barrels. The roof of the turret appeared to be lifted off and then another shell struck the same place. He described what happened almost immediately; 'The flashes passed down to both amidships magazines, containing 50 tons of cordite. The explosion broke the ship in half.' Gasson was almost at the epicentre of the explosion that blew up his ship, but against all the odds he survived. He added; 'I owe my survival, I think to the fact that

I was in a separate compartment at the back of the turret, with my head through a hole cut in the top . . . the rangefinder and myself only had a light armoured covering. I think this came off, and as the ship sunk I floated to the surface.' Although badly burnt, the marine was incredibly fortunate – one of very few lucky men on board.

Of the battlecruiser's complement of 1,032 men there were just six survivors. One of them was Commander Dannreuther. 'She went down with a crash and I was pushed out of her' he recalled, 'I was a bit out of breath and I saw a target floating by, so I went and got on it, finding two other fellows there.' He estimated *Invincible* took just fifteen seconds to sink, apart from the bow and stern sections. The sea was only 180 feet deep there, and so the two severed edges of the bow and stern sections were now resting on the seabed. They were still there the following morning, a temporary gravestone marking the spot of the disaster. Amazingly, as *Inflexible* and *Indomitable* raced past, the handful of survivors in the water or clinging to the bow and stern waved and cheered at them. They did the same for *Lion*, even as some were swept off by the battlecruiser's wash. This display of spirit prompted Beatty to despatch the destroyer *Badger* to pick up what survivors she could find.

A few minutes later, the leading ships of the Grand Fleet drew level with the wreck. At first, many sailors thought the wreckage was part of a German ship. Then they saw the name *Invincible* on her stern. On the dreadnought *Monarch*, the sixth ship in the British battle line, sailors watched men die in front of them; 'Right aft she was crowded with men' remembered Able Seaman John Myers, 'but many of these poor fellows fell into the water, and soon the sea around was alive with bobbing heads of swimming men . . . although a destroyer was picking up survivors, many were drowned before our eyes.' When he clambered aboard *Badger*, Dannreuther downplayed his escape. He told his rescuers that he merely stepped off into the water when the foretop came down. They were just hauling him out of the water when *Iron Duke* sped past. Jellicoe signalled *Badger*, asking: 'Is wreck one of our own ships?' Commander Albert Freemantle of the *Badger* replied, 'Yes. *Invincible*.'

The Battle Line

The salvo that destroyed *Invincible* was one of the last fired by Hipper's battlecruisers in the exchange. His ships were already turning away,

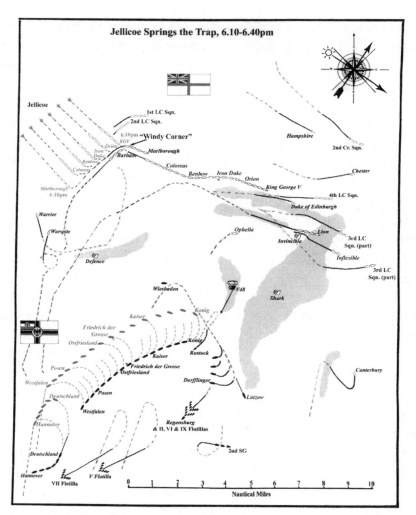

Jellicoe Springs the Trap (6.10Ω–6.40 p.m.)

and a minute later they slipped into the bank of mist which hid them from view. Hipper took stock. His own flagship *Lützow* was badly damaged and barely afloat. *Seydlitz* was in a similarly bad way, and both battlecruisers could only steam at reduced speed; any faster and water would pour in through the many holes in their bows. The *Derfflinger* was also badly damaged, but at least she could still manoeuvre. *Moltke* and *Von der Tann* were relatively unscathed, although the latter still had trouble with her turrets; only one of them was able to fire. There was now a very real danger that *Lützow* would founder if her crew could not stem her flooding, and that could not really be done when she was still steaming at full speed. If Hipper had not broken off the action with Beatty, there was every chance that his flagship would have sunk beneath him.

This turning away by the battlecruisers robbed Scheer of the last chance he had of tripping the ambush waiting for him in the mist. In fact, the poor visibility was playing into Jellicoe's hands now, as he was able to complete his deployment without being seen. While all the other columns turned to port, the left-hand one led by Vice-Admiral Jerram in King George V maintained its original course to the south-east. As each successive column flagship – Orion, Iron Duke, Benbow, Colossus and Marlborough – reached the spot where she had been, they turned hard to starboard to follow her. So the long snake-like line of dreadnoughts appeared to make a right-angled turn one after the other, until they were all following in line behind flagship. By 6.20 p.m., Iron Duke had made the turn at the spot later dubbed 'Windy Corner', as Jellicoe peered intently into the murk to the south, waiting for his first glimpse of the enemy.

Then, at about 6.25 p.m., he spotted the first grey shapes appearing through the mist to the south. Scheer's dreadnoughts were still advancing in a single line, led by Rear-Admiral Behncke in the König. His III Battle Squadron was made up of two divisions: the four Königs and then the four dreadnoughts of the Kaiser class. These were the most modern dreadnoughts in the High Seas Fleet, and included the Friedrich der Grosse, the eighth ship in the German line and Scheer's fleet flagship. Behind her came the eight older dreadnoughts of the I Battle Squadron, commanded by Vice-Admiral Erhard Schmidt in the Ostfriesland, while bringing up the rear were the six obsolete pre-dreadnoughts of the II Battle Squadron commanded by Rear-Admiral Franz Mauve, who flew his flag in the Deutschland. Until that moment, Scheer and his commanders thought they were fighting Beatty's Battlecruiser Fleet. Collectively, they were about to receive the shock of their lives.

In the König, at 6.28 p.m., Behncke began to make out a vague line of grey shapes about 13,000 yards off his port bow. Visibility was poor, but it was still clear enough for him to make out a line of orange flashes ripple down the same line. There was no doubt about it. Ahead of him, deployed in battle formation, were the dreadnoughts of the Grand Fleet. Two minutes before and seven ships behind him, the transcript of a wireless message was handed to Scheer as he stood on the bridge of the *Friedrich der Grosse*. It was from Lieutenant Commander Oskar Heinecke, the commander of the 5th Destroyer Flotilla, whose flagship *G-11* had picked up survivors from the British destroyers sunk during the 'Run to the North'. It proved singularly unwelcome news. The message read; 'According to statements of prisoners from destroyer *Nomad*, there are 60 large ships in the vicinity, including 20 modern battleships and 6 battlecruisers.' This was the first inkling Scheer had that Jellicoe was at sea.

Moments later, he spotted the enemy. The first salvos of heavy calibre shells began to fall around Behncke's flagship. For Jellicoe, this was a moment of quiet triumph. He had guessed correctly, and his deployment of the battle fleet had put his ships in a long line of battle, directly across the path of Scheer's dreadnoughts, and at an ideal range. He had achieved the great naval prize of crossing the enemy's 'T'. Now every gun in his battle fleet was able to concentrate its fire on the head of the German line. All Behncke could fire back with were his forward-facing guns. One after the other the great dreadnoughts began opening fire. The reason they didn't all fire at once was down to visibility; not all the ships could see a target, and masked arcs of fire; a by-product of Jellicoe's one error during this stage of the battle.

Just as *Iron Duke* made her turn at 'Windy Corner', Jellicoe decided to alter the course of his battle line from south-east to south-south-east. He made the signal, then cancelled it half a minute later, when he realised this would bring the head of the line into the path of Beatty. The temporary confusion this caused, as well as the problems of turning exactly at the right place with dreadnoughts of varying levels of responsiveness, meant that the line became slightly ragged. So when the enemy were sighted, *Thunderer's* line of fire was temporarily blocked by *Conqueror*, the next dreadnought ahead of her. Then, the last division of dreadnoughts were still steaming away from Scheer, as they were still lining up to make their turn to starboard at 'Windy Corner'. So, while *Conqueror* opened fire at 6.25 p.m., others in the line began firing a few minutes later. By 6.30 p.m. though, at least ten dreadnoughts were firing salvos at the head of the German column.

Most of these were the dreadnoughts which had originally been in the second, third and sixth columns. The *King George V* and the four other ships of her division were waiting for Beatty's battlecruisers to get out of the way, while most of those of the four and fifth columns were still completing their turn at 'Windy Corner'. Still, *Benbow* and *Colossus*, the two lead ships of their columns, both opened fire at 6.30 p.m. The German Official History lucidly summed up the situation Behncke found himself in; 'Suddenly the German van was faced by the belching guns of an interminable line of heavy ships extending from north-west to north-east, while salvo followed salvo almost without intermission, an impression which gained in power from the almost complete inability of the Germans to reply to this fire, as not one of the British dreadnoughts could be made out through the smoke and fumes.'

This point about the inability to see the British ships was well made. At 6.30 p.m., Scheer on the bridge of the *Friedrich der Grosse* might not have been able to see clearly the British ships for himself, but he certainly spotted the flashes of their great guns. If the signal from his destroyer commander had unnerved him, the sight of this great line of British dreadnoughts must have felt like his heart had been ripped out. Standing next to him was Captain Adolf von Trotha. He remembered this key moment in the battle. 'Admiral Scheer had stood freely on the open upper bridge. Now, however, the enemy's shells began to fall around *Friedrich der Grosse*, and a salt water torrent rained over the ship, reminding us to seek the shelter of the [armoured] conning tower . . . it was a narrow intimate space, measuring only a few metres in area, with the front protected by armour almost half a metre thick.' It was from here that Scheer surveyed the ruins of any hopes of victory.

After the battle Scheer wrote; 'It was now quite obvious that we were confronted by a large portion of the English fleet, and a few minutes later their presence was indicated on the horizon directly ahead of us by rounds of firing from guns of a heavy calibre. The entire arc stretching from north to east was a sea of fire. The flash from the muzzles of the guns was distinctly seen through the mist and smoke on the horizon, though the ships themselves were not distinguishable.' He added, with the benefit of hindsight; 'This was the beginning of the main phase of the battle.' It was a terrible situation for him, but afterwards he tried to put a brave face on it; 'There was never any question of our line veering round to avoid an encounter. The resolve to do battle with the enemy stood firm from the first. The leaders of our battleship squadrons, the

Fifth Division, turned at once for a running fight, carried out at about 13,000 metres.'

This was exactly what Jellicoe had wanted. Flag Captain Dreyer, his gunnery expert and the inventor of the Dreyer Fire Control System, had recommended the deployment to the left and the subsequent turn to the south-east as it would make the British ships hard to see, while the Germans would be sharply defined by the low-lying sun to the west. For all its critics, the Dreyer Fire Control System fitted to Jellicoe's dreadnoughts was proving its worth now. *Iron Duke* alone fired nine salvos in less than five minutes, despite the swirling mist, and her fire control teams were delighted that their target – Behncke's flagship the *König* – was illuminated clearly. One of her 13.5-inch shells glanced off the roof of the flagship's conning tower and exploded further aft. The flying shrapnel wounded Rear-Admiral Behncke as he was standing on the bridge, together with several of his officers. For the moment, Rear-Admiral Hermann Nordmann in the *Kaiser* would command the German vanguard.

The *König* was hit seven more times in five minutes, with most of the hits being scored by *Iron Duke*, which thanks to Dreyer was a crack gunnery ship. By the end of this fusillade, the German dreadnought was holed on the waterline, compartments were flooded, and she was listing almost 4° to port. Some of her secondary magazines had been flooded after ready-use charges were ignited in her secondary gun casemates, a fire was raging in her forward compartments and dozens of her crew were killed or wounded. Given that as many as 228 heavy-calibre guns were aimed at her, she was very fortunate to have suffered so little damage from those opening salvos. Further down the line, Scheer was recovering from the shock of this unexpected encounter, and was busy working out how to respond. Clearly, to continue on his present course was suicidal. He needed to extricate his battle fleet, and do it while he still had a fleet to command.

12

Gefechtskehrtwendung

Winston Churchill was wrong. Jellicoe wasn't the only man who could lose the war in an afternoon. Vice-Admiral Scheer carried a similar weight of national expectation on his shoulders; it was just that for him the stakes weren't quite so high. Germany was still primarily a land power. A crushing defeat at sea would mean the country would still die a slow lingering death thanks to the naval blockade, but at least it wouldn't lose an overseas empire and lay itself open to invasion. Still, Scheer realised that the decision he made over the next few minutes could make or break the Imperial German Navy. Get it right, and the High Seas Fleet might survive to fight another day. Get it wrong, and it faced an annihilation as complete as that suffered by the Russians at Tsushima, or the French and Spanish at Trafalgar. As he peered intently at the line of gun flashes piercing the murk to the north, his mind was racing, working out the course of action that could save his fleet, his reputation and even his life.

Scheer's Trump Card

The head of the German line was almost hidden by the towering shell splashes, but Scheer could see it was starting to curve slightly to the right as if bowing under the pressure of the British fire. From the air, this would have given the German column the appearance of a giant fishhook. This was understandable; it meant that if the turn continued, the dreadnoughts would soon be able to bring their broadside guns to bear. The Königs had five twin turrets on their centreline, while the less-advanced Kaisers behind them had four twin turrets, or five if they fired their starboard 'in echelon' turrets across their boat decks. Still, it would mean the ships would at last be able to fire back, even if they were still unable to see their assailants properly. However, if the whole battle line made the same turn to starboard at the same point where *König* had been, then the British could just keep aiming at the same point and pound each German dreadnought in succession as it made its turn.

At that moment, Commodore Andres Michelsen, commander of the fleet's destroyers, decided to help Scheer by launching an attack. He flew his pennant in the light cruiser *Rostock*, which served as the mother ship for several flotillas. At 6.32 p.m. the cruiser lay directly behind the *König*. Michelsen ordered Lieutenant Commander Wilhelm Holmann's III Flotilla into the attack, even though he still couldn't see the British ships. When Holmann asked for directions, he was told to head towards the port bow, towards the mist and the gun flashes. Minutes later, the seven boats roared forward, passing between the *König* and the battlecruisers, which were half a mile to the east, having pulled away from Beatty a few minutes earlier. The destroyers spotted Beatty's battlecruisers ahead of them, but as they got within torpedo range, Michelsen ordered their recall. He'd decided to save his torpedoes for use against Jellicoe's dreadnoughts instead.

Three of the destroyers either didn't see the recall in time or, more likely they didn't want to waste the opportunity. These three – *V-48*, *V-73* and *G-88* – all closed to within three miles and fired off one torpedo each. The torpedoes all passed astern of the *New Zealand*, the last of Beatty's four battlecruisers. Although the destroyers couldn't see her, the spread also narrowly missed the armoured cruiser *Duke of Edinburgh*. An officer in the foretop of the armoured cruiser described the near miss; 'At 6.47 p.m., the track of a torpedo was sighted coming directly towards us from starboard. We altered course to port, and it passed close astern of us.' At the time, the cruiser was 600 yards in front of the *King George V*, the leading dreadnought in Jellicoe's battle line. Had Michelsen known it and held his nerve, or sent in the rest of his destroyers, then he might have struck a really telling blow.

In fact, this half-hearted attack achieved something tangible after all. As the destroyers sped off, they poured out great clouds of smoke to cover their withdrawal. On the upper bridge of his flagship, Jellicoe had been bothered by the murk for several minutes. 'At this time,' he wrote, 'owing to smoke and mist, it was most difficult to distinguish friend from foe, and quite impossible to form an opinion on board the *Iron Duke*, in her position towards the centre of the line, as to the formation of the enemy's fleet.' This was before the mist cleared enough to allow his ships to open fire. Now, just a few minutes later, the enemy ships were once again being hidden from view. The oily black smoke screen laid by the German destroyers was augmented by the mist, the funnel smoke of hundreds of warships, and the smoke and flames still billowing from the *Wiesbaden*, stranded midway between the two battle fleets. This helped to hide what would happen next.

Back on the bridge of the *Friedrich der Grosse*, Scheer noted all this, and continued rapidly to weigh up his limited options. His battle fleet was sailing into a trap, and he had to do something and do it quickly. He considered a turn on to a course parallel to Jellicoe, but ruled it out for the reason given above; one after the other his ships would be pounded by a huge number of enemy guns as they reached the turning point. Turning to port was ruled out for the same reason, plus that would mean that his battle fleet would lose contact with Hipper's badly mauled Scouting Groups, which were somewhere off his starboard beam. Also, a running battle with Scheer to the west of the British would mean his ships would be clearly defined by the setting sun. So, he couldn't turn to the left, or turn to the right. To keep going was to invite piecemeal destruction. Somehow though, he had to find a way to escape, and find it within the next few minutes.

Clearly he wasn't going to win a stand-up fight against the whole British battle fleet. That had never been his intention; his aim had been to lure just a part of it onto the guns of the High Seas Fleet. Now it was his fleet which had its head in the lion's mouth, and the jaws were about to close. So he had to break off the action. That, though, was no easy thing. He was about 150 miles from Wilhelmshaven, which meant that even his fastest dreadnoughts would take almost eight hours to reach home. He couldn't just run away, as he had Rear-Admiral Mauve's II Battle Squadron with him. Its six under-gunned pre-dreadnoughts added very little to his fighting potential, and they were woefully slow. To turn and run would mean sacrificing them – and the lives of the 4,500 German sailors who crewed them – to the faster British fleet. Somehow, he had to protect these vulnerable ships, while still keeping his fleet intact.

It was early evening, though, and dusk was only a few hours away. If he could somehow keep the British at bay until nightfall, then he would have a fighting chance of escaping under cover of darkness. Scheer calculated all this in a matter of moments. After the battle, he was accused of being so shocked by Jellicoe's appearance that he didn't know what to do. That certainly wasn't the case now. As Scheer wrote later; 'While the battle is progressing a leader cannot obtain a really clear picture, especially at long ranges. He acts and feels according to his impressions.' So Scheer acted, making the decision – the only decision – that could save his fleet. At 6.33 p.m., he called over his Signals Officer and ordered an immediate general signal to be given. It read 'Turn together 16 points to starboard.' The German battle fleet was about to carry out a *Gefechtskehrtwendung* ('Battle About Turn').

This wasn't a manoeuvre for the faint of heart. It involved a simultaneous turn, in this case to starboard, by every ship in the battle line. There was a very great risk that several of the ships could collide, particularly as the battle fleet was made up of ships with different manoeuvring abilities, speeds and idiosyncrasies. It had been practiced before; in fact it was devised specifically to escape exactly the situation in which Scheer found himself. However, these practice manoeuvres had been carried out during fleet exercises, in near-perfect conditions. Now Scheer was planning to perform it in the middle of a raging sea battle, in poor visibility and with enemy shells falling around his leading ships. The whole operation depended on quick thinking on the part of the ship captains, and perfect timing. One mistake, and the whole manoeuvre could end in disaster as ships collided, or swerved out of the way, losing all semblance of order and formation.

In the official German history, though, it all sounded simple; 'The exceptional training of the German fleet . . . made Scheer feel confident that, in spite of the bend in the line and the enemy's tremendous counter-activity, it would be possible to carry out the intended movement without serious difficulty, even under the heaviest of hostile fire.' The armchair admiral who penned this was writing with the benefit of hindsight. For Scheer, standing on the bridge of his flagship, the whole manoeuvre must have seemed more like a reckless gamble. He just had to hope that in the heat of battle his ship captains could pull it off.

To reduce the risk of collision, the last ship in the line would begin the manoeuvre, and commence the turn to starboard. Once the ship ahead of her saw that she had started to turn, her helm would be put over too, and this was repeated all the way up the line to the leading ship in the formation. In theory, the pre-dreadnoughts of Rear-Admiral Mauve's II Battle Squadron were at the back of the line, and so they should have turned first, beginning with the *Hanover*, the last ship in the nine-mile-long line. However, the slower pre-dreadnought had fallen behind the ships ahead of them, and so a 3,000-yard gap had appeared between Mauve's flagship *Deutschland* and the *Westfalen*, the last dreadnought in Scheer's battle line. So, acting on his initiative, Captain Johannes Redlich began turning the *Westfalen* to starboard. Moments later, Captain Richard Lange in the *Posen* did the same, and the whole manoeuvre was repeated all the way up the line of German dreadnoughts.

In the end, the whole German line turned about like a well-drilled squad of soldiers on a parade ground. What worried Scheer the most were his leading ships – soon to be his rearguard. They had been the ones under fire, and at the northernmost end of the line the curve in it would make it harder for the captains to make the turn and then find their assigned station. When the moment came, they performed the manoeuvre with considerable skill. The only real problem was the *Markgraf*, three ships behind Rear-Admiral Behncke's flagship *Kaiser*. Her port engine was overheating and she had to complete the manoeuvre using just two of her three propellers. Still, Captain Carl Sieferling managed it. The same armchair admiral said that in response to Scheer's order; 'his subordinate leaders and the captains of individual ships fully justified the reliance he placed in them'. This was something of an understatement.

Rather pompously, the official history stated that the *Gefechtskehrt-wendung* was 'one of the many tactical movements practised for the various eventualities of an action', and added that it was an emergency measure, as the tactical doctrine of the High Seas Fleet demanded that; 'On encountering the enemy, deploy from a wide preparatory formation [in other words a column] into a line of battle, from which all the guns could be brought to bear simultaneously.' This plays down the effectiveness of the 'Battle About Turn', just as much as it regarded it as simply another manoeuvre. It wasn't. It was one the British had never practised, and didn't even know about. It was one that Scheer used only as a last resort, and even then it was a manoeuvre that was fraught with danger. Still, his gamble paid off. By 6.40 p.m. at the latest, the entire German battle fleet was now steaming in line towards the south-east, with the *Westfalen* in the lead and the *Kaiser* bringing up the rear.

Losing Contact

It took some time for the British to work out what had happened. The same mist that had shrouded the British dreadnoughts from view now obscured what was taking place to the south. Meanwhile, the smoke screen laid by Holmann's III Flotilla hid the *Kaiser* like a swirling black shroud. As they lost sight of their targets, the firing of the British dreadnoughts petered out. *Iron Duke* ceased fire at 6.36 p.m., but a few dreadnoughts kept firing, even though they couldn't see a target. *Barham*, for instance, now tucked in behind the battle line, kept firing salvos until 6.50 p.m. at the spot where the *König* had been. These ships, though, were just wasting their ammunition. Later, Jellicoe said; 'I could not see his turn away from the top of the charthouse, nor could anyone else with me. I had imagined the disappearing of the enemy to be due to the thickening of the mist, but after a few minutes I realised that there must be some other reason.' It was all very perplexing; one moment the German ships were there, then the next they had vanished.

Five miles to the east, Beatty's battlecruisers had also lost sight of Hipper's battlecruisers. Another mile further on, Rear-Admiral Trevylyan Napier in the light cruiser *Falmouth* could still see Hipper's ships about five miles to the south-west, having watched them break off the fight after sinking the *Invincible*. He never informed Beatty, though, presuming the enemy could also be seen from the *Lion*. It was only at 6.40 p.m., when Beatty signalled Napier, that he discovered Hipper was now heading away from him. Four minutes later Beatty ordered his three battlecruiser squadrons to alter course to the south-east. He also cut his speed to 28 knots, to avoid getting too far away from Jellicoe's dreadnoughts. Beatty might well have regained contact with Hipper, but a few minutes later, *Lion*'s gyro compass failed, and the flagship steamed in a circle. The other battlecruisers dutifully followed, and, by the time *Lion* straightened out, the Germans had gone.

On the far side of the band of smoke and mist, Hipper was in serious trouble. His flagship *Lützow* was barely afloat, and her forecastle had dipped so low it was almost underwater. In the foretop, Commander Paschen watched his ship struggle to keep afloat; '*Lützow* sheers out of the line to slacken speed – the water is pouring in too fast at our bows. Four of our destroyers put up an enormous black veil of smoke between us and the enemy, and for once we were out of the heavy fire.' Having broken off his duel with the British battlecruisers, Hipper had turned away to the south-east, and then to the south-west. He was therefore about three miles to the east of the *König* when the battle fleet made its 180° turn, and Hipper decided to stay on a westerly course so he could maintain contact with Scheer. That meant, of course, that he completely lost sight of Beatty. This done, though, he was able to take stock.

The flagship was not the only ship in serious difficulties. *Seydlitz* was well down by the bow and *Derfflinger* also had a large hole in her bows. More immediately, her port propeller was in danger of becoming entangled and jammed by the trailing wreckage of a damaged wire torpedo net, which was now hanging over the ship's side. Clearly, something had to be done and done quickly. Von Hase described what happened; 'The Captain gave the order "All engines stop". I surveyed the horizon through the periscope. There was nothing of the enemy to be seen at this moment . . . It was a very serious matter that we should have to stop like this in the immediate neighbourhood of the enemy, but if the torpedo net was to foul the propeller all would be up with us.'

These steel nets were hung over the side from booms when the ship was at anchor, to protect her against torpedoes. They didn't work properly, though, and the British had abandoned theirs before the battle. Now they were putting the *Derfflinger* in grave danger. The crew worked fast though, to secure the net, while von Hase surveyed the damage aloft; 'The masts and rigging had been badly damaged by countless shells, and the wireless aerials hung down in an inextricable tangle so that we could only use our wireless for receiving – we could not transmit messages.' Looking down, things were even worse; 'A heavy shell had torn away two armour plates in the bows, leaving a huge gap quite six by five metres, just above the waterline.' Then, the vital work at the stern was done, and the propeller was free. *Derfflinger* got underway as quickly as she could, and re-joined the rest of the Scouting Group.

It was now clear that the *Lützow* had to head for home, and there was no guarantee she would make it. She was certainly no use as a flagship; her wireless room had been destroyed and she could only steam at reduced speed, for fear of causing more flooding. So Hipper's Chief-of-Staff, Lieutenant Commander Erich Raeder, persuaded the Scouting Group commander to haul down his flag from the *Lützow* and transfer to another ship. Hipper reluctantly agreed, but before he left he sought out Captain Viktor Harder, shook his hand and wished him luck. Harder would certainly need it. Meanwhile, Raeder had called the destroyer *G-39* alongside, and Hipper stepped aboard. He looked back to see his old flagship edge away, smoke still billowing from her wrecked and almost submerged forecastle. Michelsen's destroyers had already formed a protective ring around her, and began laying smoke to screen her exit from the battle. Hipper would never see his flagship again.

Jellicoe's Pursuit

Jellicoe's response to the disappearance of the German battle fleet was slow. The last he'd seen of the German battle fleet, it was under fire, and its head was beginning to bend to starboard. At first Jellicoe thought that Scheer had put his battle fleet onto a parallel course to his, and so when the destroyer smoke cleared, he expected to see the German dreadnoughts moving onto a new easterly course. It took several minutes for Jellicoe to realise that Scheer simply was not there. The tail of his own battle fleet was still negotiating 'Windy Corner', and ordering another course change had to wait until this first manoeuvre was complete. Finally, at 6.55 p.m., Jellicoe gave the order to turn by divisions onto a new course with a heading of south-south-east. This meant that the flagship of each division of four dreadnoughts would turn simultaneously, and the three remaining ships in the division would follow her. Jellicoe had finally set off in pursuit.

Jellicoe still didn't know where the enemy was, though. As he ordered the turn, he signalled *Marlborough*, Vice-Admiral Burney's flag-ship near the rear of the battle line. In response to Jellicoe's signal reading 'Can you see any enemy battleships', Burney gave a one-word reply – 'No'. Had he known that the *König*, now at the rear of the German battle line, was now almost ten miles away from the *Iron Duke*, heading towards the south-west as fast as she could manage, then Jellicoe would have realised that his pursuit was futile. Thanks to his successful

Gefechtskehrtwendung, Scheer had got away. In fact, the only German warship anyone could see was the stricken, burning *Wiesbaden*. For several minutes the British gunners took out their frustration on her, the dreadnoughts pummelling the burning cruiser with their secondary batteries as they steamed past.

Wiesbaden took several direct hits, while even the destroyer *Onslow* had a go, firing a torpedo into her from 2,000 yards. Even then, *Wiesbaden* fought back. Her after gun, the only one still firing, scored a hit on the destroyer, damaging her engine room and forcing her to pull away. Lieutenant Commander John Tovey – the man who a quarter of a century later would mastermind the sinking of the *Bismarck* – described his destroyer's torpedo attack. Only one of his torpedoes launched successfully, and he 'saw the torpedo hit the light cruiser below the conning tower and explode'. It was almost inconceivable that *Wiesbaden* could survive all this, but she did, at least for a while. The gallant little cruiser finally rolled over and sank during the night, taking most of her surviving crew with her. By the time a Norwegian freighter came upon the life raft carrying her survivors late the following day, there was only one man left alive.

The *Wiesbaden* may well have been responsible for the attack that left a hole in the side of Vice-Admiral Burney's flagship. At 6.54 p.m, a minute before Jellicoe's change of course, *Marlborough* was steaming towards the south-east, the 17th dreadnought in the British battle line. She was about 10,000 yards to the north of the *Wiesbaden*, which at the time was hidden by a pall of smoke. Directly astern of her there was a loud clang on the starboard side of the *Revenge*. The likelihood is that this brand-new dreadnought had been struck by a torpedo which failed to detonate. There was no question about the second torpedo in the spread being a dud; moments later it struck the starboard side of the *Marlborough*. It ripped a 30-foot hole in her hull below the waterline, punctured the torpedo bulkhead behind it, and water poured into the boiler room.

In *Marlborough's* 'B' turret, Midshipman Angus Nichol remembered; 'A sudden tremendous shock. I was almost thrown off my feet, and the shells, which were halfway into the loading cages, were up-ended and jammed against the tops of the cages.' This jolt could have easily caused a shell to drop and explode, causing untold damage in the turret. Fortunately for Nicholl and his men, nothing exploded. As the midshipman remembered it; 'For a second there was a tense silence, then the voice of [Gunner] Jimmy Green, "There go my flippin' eggs!". With a shout of laughter, we set about righting the shells to keep the guns in action.'

One of the dreadnought's crew was Medical Orderly George Fox, who recalled the moment when the explosion; 'Simply lifted the ship like a ball and bounced her up and down . . . we felt the ship going further over and over.' In fact, *Marlborough* took on an 18° list to starboard. Fox and his shipmates feared the worst and dreaded being trapped below decks as the ship capsized. Quick thinking by Captain Percy Grant saved the day; he ordered tanks on the port side to be counter-flooded, and eventually the dreadnought rolled back 10° or so. The flooding was contained in one boiler room and an adjacent compartment, and the dreadnought limped on at reduced speed, but for the moment she was still able to keep her place in the line. *Marlborough* even managed to make her turn to starboard when Jellicoe ordered it. The ship had the distinction of being the only British dreadnought hit by a torpedo during the battle.

After his course change at 6.55 p.m., the battle fleet was running south in six divisions of four ships, while Jellicoe prayed for the mist and smoke to lift so he could see the enemy. At the time he had cruisers and destroyers on either side and astern of him, while Beatty's battlecruisers were also 10,000 yards off *Iron Duke*'s port beam, steaming in the tight circle caused by *Lion*'s faulty gyro compass. On all of these sixty dreadnoughts, battlecruisers and cruisers, lookouts were scanning the southern horizon for any sign of the Germans. All they saw was grey seas, white mist and drifting black smoke. Evan-Thomas' fast battleships were astern of Burney's damaged flagship, apart from the badly damaged *Warspite*, which was still trying to re-join her squadron. When she did reach the 5th Battle Squadron, Evan-Thomas ordered her to head back to Rosyth, as she was too badly damaged to fight. Strangely though, at that moment she was the closest British warship to the German fleet.

As the great dreadnoughts sped south they passed a life raft, containing the surviving crew of the destroyer *Shark*. One of the most poignant letters of the battle was written to Lieutenant-Commander Arthur Onslow of the *Onslaught* by Able Seaman Joseph Howell, one of the men on the raft. It read; 'I have often wondered if my simple signal was ever read. . . . When you passed us, sir, I made with my arms, the best I could, the simple message "We are British" . . . Would you kindly ask your Yeoman of Signals if he read it? We had quite a lot alive on the raft at that time, but they were fast dying off from exposure. I was badly wounded in the knee . . . So, dear sir, if I am not asking too much would you kindly answer this note, if you were informed of my little signal "We are British"?' Unfortunately, Onslow, like the other ship commanders in the Grand Fleet, had orders to pursue Scheer. When the survivors were eventually rescued, only Howell and five others were left alive on the raft.

So Jellicoe continued on towards the south. Inexplicably, he had lost contact with Scheer, who was now somewhere to the west. This meant that the Grand Fleet was now between Scheer and Wilhelmshaven. Jellicoe's big fear now was not a meeting with Scheer's dreadnoughts; that was something he relished. It was a surprise attack by destroyers striking suddenly out of the mist. So the Grand Fleet remained at battle stations, and its commander remained wary. He was also acutely aware that sunset that evening was due at 8.17 p.m. At that time of year, dusk would come slowly this far north, and so Jellicoe expected he could still have enough light in which to fight a battle until about 9.30 p.m. That was still two-and-a-half hours away. He still had that long to fight and win a battle. A renewal of the action, though, now looking unlikely, at least until dawn the following morning. Jellicoe could never guess that Scheer was just about to give him another chance of victory.

13

A Second Chance

Having lost contact with each other, Jellicoe and Scheer only had a rough idea where the other was. The two great fleets were reduced to playing a giant game of hide and seek in the mist. Jellicoe knew that the Germans had somehow managed to reverse course and were heading towards the west. His own response, when he finally realised what had happened, was to turn the Grand Fleet's dreadnoughts towards the south, steaming in columns or divisions of four battleships. In effect, the fleet had returned to the cruising formation they were in before Jellicoe deployed them into line. This way, the fleet could cover a wider area as it moved south, and it was also better placed to react to a threat from an unexpected quarter. Jellicoe also reduced the fleet's speed to 17 knots so that the damaged *Marlborough* could keep pace with the others.

Beatty and his battlecruisers were a mile-and-a-half ahead of the *King George V*, which was leading the first column of dreadnoughts. The other five columns were parallel to the first one, only each of them after the first was a little astern of the column off their port bow. In effect, the whole battle fleet was in echelon. The fleet flagship *Iron Duke* was now leading the third column. The fleet was now spread over five miles (10,000 yards) of sea. Behind them, the three remaining fast battleships of the 5th Battle Squadron formed a seventh column, following astern of the dreadnoughts. In front of Burney and Beatty, two squadrons of light cruisers probed ahead of the battle line searching vainly for the enemy fleet, which appeared to have been swallowed up by the mist.

Scheer's Gamble

That afternoon, both Jellicoe and Scheer were badly let down by their cruiser commanders. All of them failed to carry out their primary duty to act as the 'eyes of the fleet' and discover where the enemy battle fleet had gone. Certainly, the light cruisers had to keep out of the way of the battle line if the dreadnoughts began firing at each other, but in both fleets the light cruisers were now safely out of the way. The German cruisers were to the east of their battle fleet, while their British counterparts were to the south of theirs. Unfortunately, the commanders of these squadrons showed almost no initiative, and certainly never tried to provide their respective admirals with an answer to their big question – where was the enemy? There was one exception. Astern of the British fleet, Goodenough's light cruiser squadron deployed into line abreast at 7 p.m., and began moving south, heading towards the spot where the German battle fleet had last been seen.

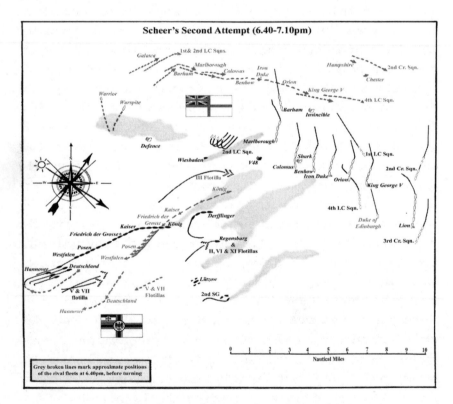

Scheer's Second Attempt (6.40–7.10 p.m.)

Then, at 6.45 p.m., Captain Johannes von Karpf of the *Moltke* sent a signal to Scheer. It read; 'Enemy's van bears East by South.' At the time, the German battlecruisers were within sight of Scheer's flagship, about three miles due east of her. Large banks of smoke lay to the north and east, most of it laid to cover the withdrawal of the German battlecruisers and dreadnoughts. Still, through it all, von Karpf's lookouts caught a brief glimpse of the leading ships of Jellicoe's battle fleet, which were then seven miles to the north-east. When von Karpf saw them, the British ships were steering towards the south-east. Seconds later, the mist and smoke hid the British dreadnoughts from view. This crucial signal explains the seemingly strange thing Scheer did next.

Scheer now had something to go on. He knew that before the *Gefechtskehrtwendung*, Jellicoe's dreadnoughts had been steaming at twenty knots. The High Seas Fleet was now heading towards the south-west at eighteen knots. As Jellicoe was heading towards the south-east, then the two fleets were moving further apart. A glance at the tactical plot would have shown that if Jellicoe kept on that course, then in about twenty minutes the front of the British line would be due east of Scheer's current position. That knowledge, that assumption of Jellicoe's course and speed, was all based on von Karpf's fleeting sighting. Thanks to his *Gefechtskehrtwendung*, the German commander-in-chief had avoided disaster, but he was now heading in the wrong direction. The British were now between the High Seas Fleet and their base. So if the two fleets kept heading southwards, then the Germans would have to fight their way past Jellicoe, either during the night or at dawn the next day. That was an encounter Scheer didn't relish.

So the other option was to double back somehow, and work behind the British fleet. That way, the Germans would be to the east of the British, and closer to Horns Reef. From there, they could run south towards the entrances to the German minefields off the Danish coast. It would be dark soon – in less than two hours – and the Germans would be steaming into familiar waters, while the British would be heading towards enemy minefields. First though, Scheer had to slip past Jellicoe's battle fleet. Having weighed up the situation, Scheer reached his decision. At 6.55 p.m., ten minutes after von Karpf's sighting, he issued the general signal; 'turn together 16 points to starboard'. It was a second *Gefechtskehrtwendung*. A few minutes earlier, Scheer had ordered his battle fleet to alter two points to starboard. This meant that this new 'battle about turn' would put the German battle fleet on east-north-easterly heading. That, by Scheer's reckoning, would place his dreadnoughts astern of the British fleet. Instead, thanks to factors of which Scheer was unaware, Jellicoe's battle fleet would lie dead ahead of him.

In the ten minutes between Captain von Karpf's sighting and Scheer's change of course the whole tactical situation had changed. Jellicoe had just altered course to the south. Now his battle fleet was spread out in six columns, and thanks to the torpedo damage inflicted on the *Marlborough*, the whole fleet had reduced speed to 17 knots. So, at 7 p.m., Scheer thought Jellicoe's flagship was about 12 miles away to the northeast. He was, only he was no longer steaming away from Scheer. Now the two flagships were approaching each other again, as were the dreadnoughts formed up around them. Even though neither commander knew it yet, within twenty minutes the *Friedrich der Grosse* and the *Iron Duke* would be within sight of each other. Scheer's change of course meant that his battle fleet was now heading directly towards Jellicoe's dreadnoughts. Just as importantly, Jellicoe would get a second chance to cross Scheer's 'T'.

This second 'battle about turn' left Behncke's flagship *König* once again at the front of the German battle line. The lumbering pre-dreadnoughts of the II Battle Squadron were far to the rear. In fact, they were not in the line at all; having been left behind earlier, they were just about to take station ahead of the battle fleet when Scheer ordered his change of course. So, once again the six pre-dreadnoughts were lagging behind the faster-moving battle line. Ahead of Behncke was the 1st Scouting Group. Its four remaining battlecruisers were still commanded by Captain von Hartog of the *Derfflinger*; Hipper was in his destroyer, impatiently waiting for the chance to board his new flagship. His old one, the *Lützow*, was three miles to the south, limping her way to safety at half speed. *Derfflinger* was two miles to the east of Behncke's flagship when Scheer made his about turn. This meant that, when the two fleets met, the battlecruisers would once again be in the lead.

After the battle, much of the criticism levelled at Scheer concerned his repeated ability to put his fleet in harm's way. Having your 'T' crossed once was unfortunate, to do it twice within an hour was nigh-on suicidal. In his official report to the Kaiser, he explained his decision by arguing that; 'The enemy could have compelled us to fight before dark – he could have prevented us exercising our initiative, and finally he could have barred our retreat to the German Bight.' This was all true, but then Scheer spoiled it by adding; 'There was only one way to avoid this; to strike a second blow at the enemy with a second onslaught, carried through regardless of cost, and to bring all the torpedo boats against him with full force.' There had been no first blow. Instead, Scheer's battle fleet had blundered into the British dreadnoughts arrayed across its path. Now Scheer was about to do it again.

The addition of the massed torpedo boat attack was written with the benefit of hindsight. The flagship's signal logs reveal that order was given later – much later. Before his second encounter with Jellicoe, Scheer's only orders to his destroyers were to despatch a flotilla to offer whatever assistance it could to the *Wiesbaden*. Instead, in his report to the Kaiser, Scheer claimed his destroyers would do that and more; 'This would surprise the enemy, throwing his plans into confusion for the rest of the day, and, if the blow fell heavily enough, would make it easier to disengage for the night. It also offered the possibility of a final attempt to bring help to the hard-pressed *Wiesbaden*, or at least of rescuing her ship's company.' This same fiction was repeated in the German Official History of the battle, which added that; 'Scheer now advanced with the . . . intention of inflicting another forcible blow.' Instead, Scheer was steaming towards disaster.

In fact, this same Official History also claimed that Scheer; 'knew that this movement would very soon expose him to a second crossing of the "T".' It then quoted Vice-Admiral Nelson, who writing before the Battle of Trafalgar stated; 'I think it will surprise and confound the enemy. They don't know what I'm about.' Citing Nelson was all very well, but this was no battle in the Age of Fighting Sail. At Trafalgar, Nelson deliberately sailed towards the enemy, having his 'T' crossed, in a move calculated months in advance in order to break the enemy's line and bring about a decisive action fought out yardarm to yardarm. In 1805, these tactics were as revolutionary and dangerous as they were decisive. In 1916, they were nothing short of suicidal. For the official historians to explain Scheer's actions in this way – claiming it was premeditated – was an insult to the intelligence of both Scheer and his men. Instead, the German admiral took a daring gamble, and it didn't pay off.

A Regular Death-Trap

Jellicoe's first inkling that Scheer was about to cross his 'T' came a few minutes later. At 7.05 p.m., Goodenough's squadron was approaching the stricken *Wiesbaden* from the north. She was 3,000 yards away, and still on fire, with thick black smoke covering the water to the east of her. Then, to the south-west – behind the burning cruiser – he spotted a formation of German destroyers, heading towards him at high speed. This was the III Flotilla, sent north by Scheer to 'Rescue *Wiesbaden's* crew'. Lieutenant Commander Hollmann who commanded the flotilla saw Goodenough's four cruisers, too, and thought they were preparing to attack the *Wiesbaden*. His six remaining boats were outmatched, though, and he altered course to the east, to hide behind the smoke billowing from the burning cruiser. It was then that Goodenough spotted what lay behind the destroyers.

A long line of German dreadnoughts could be seen, about four and a half miles to the south, their line curving slightly as it steamed towards the east. He also spotted the German battlecruisers, a little closer to him, but also heading east. It must have seemed as if the whole southern horizon was filled with large enemy ships. As Goodenough watched, these same ships opened fire and soon large-calibre shells were falling all around *Southampton* for the second time that afternoon. Goodenough spun his squadron around and headed back towards the north, praying for the mist to cover his retreat. Meanwhile at 7.08 p.m., he radioed the news of the sighting to Jellicoe. The British commander-in-chief now knew Scheer's dreadnoughts were heading towards him, and in a few minutes would appear out of the mist to the west. Seconds later, a second sighting report reached him from Beatty in *Lion*, who had just sighted the approaching German battlecruisers, nine miles to the north-west.

That meant that as the minutes ticked by, Jellicoe was anticipating what would happen next, while Scheer, seven ships behind the leading German dreadnought, was blissfully unaware of the impending clash. A few minutes earlier, Jellicoe had ordered a two-point course change to starboard, but at 7.09 p.m., he countermanded the order, and the British dreadnoughts resumed their southerly course. On board *Marlborough*, the crew could see the *Wiesbaden* and the German destroyers to the south of her. Their presence was reported to Jellicoe, but strangely

Hollmann never passed on his sighting of the British fleet to Scheer. Instead, Hollmann turned away, but not before two of his destroyers fired four torpedoes at the closest British dreadnoughts. These all missed, but three passed close to the *Neptune*, forcing her to jink out of the way.

This is how Scheer described the action; 'The *Wiesbaden* and the boats making for her were in the midst of such heavy fire that the leader of the destroyers thought it useless to sacrifice his boats. In turning to go back, *V-73* and *G-88* together fired four torpedoes at the Queen Elizabeths.' In fact, the target was Rear-Admiral Burney's 1st Battle Squadron, the closest capital ships to the two German destroyers. A midshipman stationed in the *Neptune*'s foretop described the attack; 'Our secondary armament opened fire and scored a hit or two, but their attack was successfully made, and a number of torpedoes were fired, which gave us a few anxious minutes. One torpedo crossed the line immediately under *Neptune*'s stern, and directly afterwards two parallel tracks were seen which seemed to be coming straight for us. The ship was turned under full helm and our stern put towards the track of the torpedoes, which we only avoided by inches.'

It was at that moment that the front of the German line loomed out of the mist. The first to appear were the battlecruisers, led by *Derfflinger*. On her bridge was Georg von Hase, his telephone headset keeping him in contact with his spotters, fire control teams and gun crews. His lighter 5.9-inch guns were already firing at Goodenough's cruisers, 7,000 yards to the north-west, but then more cruisers were sighted to the north. Although it hardly seemed a worthy target, von Hase ordered his main guns to engage these new ships. He recalled the moment later; 'the enemy ships were again at the extreme limit of visibility. Now they opened a lively fire, and I saw that the ship I had selected as a target was firing full salvos from four double turrets. The light round the enemy cleared for a moment, and I saw distinctly that they were dreadnoughts of the heaviest class, with 38cm [15in] guns! Fire was now flashing from them.' The 'light cruiser' he spotted was actually the brand-new dreadnought *Revenge*.

Behind their battlecruisers came the German dreadnoughts, emerging out of the mist to be confronted with a flaming arc of gun flashes. The time was 7.10 p.m., just forty minutes since Scheer had found himself in the same predicament. Jellicoe's dreadnoughts were still in their six columns, but where a few minutes before they had been neatly arrayed in echelon, the recent course change and torpedo attack had forced some ships to veer off course. So not all of the ships could fire at the enemy. For instance, *Erin*'s line of fire was blocked by *Orion*. However, the rest of the fleet were presented with a perfect target. Engine Room Artificer Harold Wright was on deck when the Germans appeared, and recalled that; 'We were steaming on a southerly course with the whole battle fleet stringing out behind us. The Germans fleet was to the westward, apparently in single file, silhouetted against the setting sun – a perfect target, each ship standing out black and clear.'

Some of the British ships never saw the Germans; on the *Conqueror*, for instance, an officer in 'A' turret recalled seeing nothing between 7 p.m., when they passed the *Wiesbaden*, and 7.14 p.m., when 'We observed German destroyers attacking the battle fleet . . .' In between, he declared that; 'There was a lull in the fighting for a quarter of an hour, with nothing to be seen, and the turrets' crews were given permission to fall out on top of the turrets to see a sunken ship, reputed to be German, which we were passing, its two ends sticking out of the water.' In fact, the sinking ship was the *Invincible*. On the *Posen*, Leading Seaman Albert Blessman was alarmed by what he saw; 'Suddenly we were practically surrounded. We were being fired at from every side. The entire British fleet had suddenly appeared. We were in a tight corner, and I said to myself "You will be a lucky fellow if you get out of this".'

When the British saw the Germans, they opened fire. There was no firing plan, no orders were given – the British dreadnoughts simply opened up on the leading German ships as they appeared. This meant that several ships were firing at the same targets, which made it almost impossible for the British spotters to work out which of the many salvos were their own. The first ships opened fire shortly after 7.10 p.m., and within two minutes the firing had become general, with at least a dozen dreadnoughts targeting the enemy. The leading German ships were surrounded by shell splashes. With those many shells descending on them, it was inevitable that the British would score numerous hits. During the next few minutes, Behncke's flagship *König* was hit once, while the ship astern of her, the *Grosser Kurfurst*, was struck seven times. This suggested that that the British salvos were overshooting the leading ship, and hitting the one behind.

The *Grosser Kurfürst* was left with a 4° list to port thanks to the flood-ing of her forward compartments. She had just overtaken the *Markgraf,* which had a damaged engine. Lieutenant Beissel von Gymnich said; 'The English fleet knew this and concentrated heavily on us. After a few minutes we were hit eight times by their 38cm shells. We had nineteen dead, among which were two officers. Water was flooding the ship due to a hit near the waterline.' He added; 'Due to so many misses a wall of water had built up restricting their view, which was an advantage for us which nobody had reckoned upon.' Being deluged by shell splashes from British heavy guns was no real advantage. At that point, the British were only firing at the head of the line, and the *Kurfürst* was merely just behind the *König*, the main aiming point for many of the British guns.

Further astern, the *Markgraf* took one hit from a 12-inch shell fired by *Agincourt*, while the same seven-turreted dreadnought also scored two hits on the *Kaiser*, following astern of her. Strangely, the *Helgoland*, the eleventh dreadnought in the German line, was also hit, in her case by a 15-inch shell, possibly fired by either *Barham* or *Valiant*. Back on the *King George V*, Artificer Wright watched the shells strike home, claiming; 'One was able to distinguish the difference between the flash of the German guns and the resulting explosion when one of the German ships was hit.' If the German dreadnoughts were suffering, the battlecruisers should have got a hard pounding. They were 4,000 yards to the north-east of Behncke's flagship and therefore closer to the British; *Marlborough*, for instance, was just 4,000 yards away from them. Several British dread-noughts targeted them, but amazingly none of the battlecruisers were hit. That though, was only a temporary respite.

The German ships had been firing back with the few guns that could bear, but a combination of poor visibility towards the east and the volume of fire directed at them reduced the potency of their own salvos. During those hectic few minutes, both the battlecruisers and the leading dreadnoughts managed to fire a few salvos, but no hits were scored. Meanwhile, each passing minute brought the High Seas Fleet another 750 yards closer to the British guns. On the bridge of the *Friedrich der Grosse*, Scheer could now see the British ships, and realised he would have to take immediate and drastic action. Von Hase summed up the situation perfectly; 'The Commander-in-Chief realised the danger to which our fleet was exposed. The van of our fleet was shut in by the semicircle of the enemy. We were in a regular death trap.' Scheer's solution – the only one available to him – was to sacrifice von Hase and his shipmates in order to save the rest of his fleet.

14

Hartog's Death Ride

Vice-Admiral Scheer was in an unenviable position. For the second time that afternoon his battle fleet was in mortal danger, and he needed to do something quickly if he had any hope of extricating it. The most obvious solution was to order another *Gefechtskehrtwendung*. That, though, wasn't going to be as easy as it had been earlier. The vanguard of his battle line of dreadnoughts was much closer to the British than it had been forty minutes before. *Iron Duke* was about seven-and-a-half miles ahead of his leading ship the *König*, and a little under nine miles from his own flagship. Other British columns were much closer though, and these were already firing full salvos of heavy calibre shells. Essentially, it was the same situation that had faced him before, only the shorter range made his ships far more vulnerable to British fire. If he ordered the 'battle about turn', he would have to find some way of distracting the British, to hide the movement and to protect his leading ships.

The most obvious way to do this was to order his destroyers to launch a massed attack on the British battle line. Three flotillas were on hand, escorted by the light cruisers *Rostock* and *Regensburg*. They were 3,000 yards to the south-east of the *König*, off her starboard bow. It would take a few minutes to form the boats up for the attack, though, and every passing minute increased the risk to his battle fleet. The other tools at his disposal was the battlecruisers, deployed in a line heading east two miles to the north-east of *König*, off her port bow. They were already badly damaged and British shells were beginning to fall around them. Scheer had seconds to decide what to do, but frankly he had run out of options.

So, at 7.13 p.m., Scheer sent a signal which read; 'Battlecruisers – turn towards the enemy. Attack!' The German commander planned to sacrifice his battlecruisers, in order to save the rest of his fleet.

The Ships Will Fight to the Death!

Captain Paul Hartog was still in temporary command of the battered 1st Scouting Group. When he received the order he didn't hesitate. With *Derfflinger* in the lead he swung his ships to starboard to cross the path of the German battle fleet. It was a mission that was almost guaranteed to end in the sacrifice of all four battlecruisers. Standing close to Hartog on the *Derfflinger's* bridge was von Hase, and he was able to describe the moment; 'At about 9.12 p.m. (7.12 p.m.) the Commander-in-Chief gave the fleet the signal to turn about on the opposite course and almost at the same time sent by wireless to the battlecruisers and destroyers the historic order; "Close the enemy!" The signalman on our bridge read the message aloud, adding the words which stood against it in the signal book: "And ram! The ships will fight to the death!" Without moving an eyelid, the captain gave the order: "Full Speed Ahead – Course South-East".' Hartog's 'Death Ride' had begun.

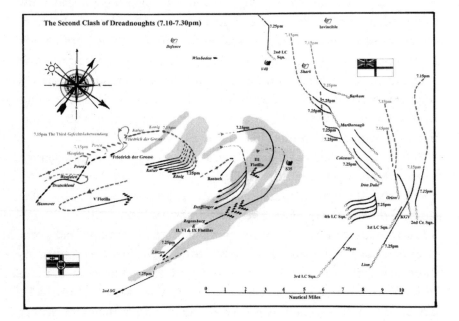

The Second Clash of Dreadnoughts (7.10–7.30 p.m.

Unlike its British counterpart, the Imperial German Navy had considered the role of battlecruisers in a modern war and so they viewed them in a different light. It was envisioned that they would be used in the North Sea, acting as the core of the fleet's scouting forces. This made it likely that they would come up against British battlecruisers, and so they carried enough armour to perform well in that kind of duel. However, they had another role. The dreadnoughts were considered the very heart of the High Seas Fleet, and so their protection was all-important. So in the fleet's tactical doctrine, it was laid down that the battlecruisers should be prepared to cover the withdrawal of the battle fleet if the need arose. In other words, in a general engagement the battlecruisers could be expected to hold off the enemy battle fleet while the rest of the German dreadnoughts slipped away. It says much for German thoroughness that this sacrificial role was enshrined in German doctrine.

When this dramatic order reached him, Captain Hartog was leading his four battlecruisers towards the west. He immediately ordered a course change of four points (45°) to starboard, onto a south-easterly heading. His alteration of course put him across the path of the German dreadnoughts. There was no risk of collision; the battlecruisers were well ahead of the head of the German battle line, Hartog had increased speed, and anyway Scheer intended to follow this order with a second – to perform another *Gefechtskehrtwendung*. Hartog was not exactly steering towards the enemy as he had been ordered. Instead, he was doing something more useful – screening Scheer's withdrawal. As Commander Hans Scheibe, an officer in the squadron, later wrote; 'The battlecruisers, temporarily under command of the captain of the *Derfflinger*, while Admiral Hipper was changing ship, now hurled themselves recklessly against the enemy line, followed by the destroyers. A dense hail of fire swept them all the way.'

It was true. Before, while most of the British heavy guns had been targeting the head of the German battle line, most now switched their targets to the four charging battlecruisers. As she was leading the charge, the *Derfflinger* attracted most of the British fire. The battlecruiser seemed to be lost amid a foaming profusion of shell splashes as heavy shells of at least three different calibres began falling around her. Von Hase put it dryly; 'Followed by the *Seydlitz*, *Moltke* and *Von der Tann*, we altered course south at 9.15 p.m. [7.15 p.m.] and headed straight for the enemy's van. The *Derfflinger*, as leading ship, now came under a particularly deadly fire. Several ships were engaging us at the same time.' He tried to shoot back, even though the British ships were hard to see in the fading light. 'I selected a target and fired as rapidly as possible. At first the ranges recorded were 12,000 [metres], from which they sunk to 8,000. And all the time we were steaming at full speed into this inferno, offering a splendid target to the enemy while they were still hard to make out.'

Astern of *Derfflinger* was the *Seydlitz*, followed by the *Moltke*, with the *Von der Tann* bringing up the rear. All of their guns that still worked fired steadily at the British, who were only really visible as a line of twinkling orange gun flashes. On the *Seydlitz*, von Egidy noted that; 'Visibility decreased, and there seemed to be an endless line of ships ahead. But we saw only incessant flashes, mostly four discharges in the peculiar British rippling salvos. Our ship received hit after hit, but our guns remained silent as we could not make out any targets. This put us under a heavy strain, which was relieved to some extent by ship handling, changes of formation and zigzagging towards and away from previous salvos.' Like Commodore Goodenough's light cruisers had done earlier that afternoon, the German battlecruisers were using every trick they could to avoid the curtain of shells falling around them. Inevitably though, some of the British shells struck home.

On the *Derfflinger*, von Hase was in the armoured fire control position behind the bridge, controlling the fire of his own guns, more in hope than expectation of scoring a hit. He recounted the sheer weight of fire coming towards them; 'Salvo after salvo fell around us, hit after hit struck our ship. They were stirring minutes.' Communications were lost with the spotting team in the foretop, so von Hase had to direct the fire himself. Then, at 7.15 p.m., just two minutes after the 'death ride' began, a 15-inch shell from *Revenge* struck the roof of *Derfflinger's* after turret. 'A 38cm [15in] shell pierced the armour of "Caesar" turret and exploded inside. The brave turret commander, Kapitanleutnant von Boltenstern, had both his legs torn off, and with him nearly the whole gun crew were killed.'

That though, was merely the initial shell strike. Von Hase continued; 'The shell set on fire two shell cases in the turret. The flames from the burning cases spread to the transfer chamber, where it set fire to four more cases, and from there to the case chamber, where four more were

Right: As Commander-in-Chief of Britain's Grand Fleet, Admiral Sir John Jellicoe (1859–1935) had to lead this untried modern fleet into battle, while juggling difficult subordinates and an over-expectant public.

Left: Jellicoe's rival Vice-Admiral Reinhard Scheer (1863–1928) was a skilled tactician, but he had the unenviable task of fighting a battle he never expected, against a numerically superior enemy.

Left: On occasion the commander of Britain's Battlecruiser Fleet, Vice-Admiral Sir David Beatty (1871–1935) could be strong-willed and impulsive – traits that displayed themselves at Jutland with fatal consequences.

Right: The commander of Germany's Scouting Forces, Vice-Admiral Franz Hipper (1863–1932) had clashed with Beatty before. He now felt he had his measure, and planned to entrap his rival.

The "battlecruiser" was as vulnerable as it was powerful. At Jutland the crew of the *Princess Royal* (pictured) watched their sister-ship *Queen Mary* blow up next to them.

What saved Beatty at Jutland was Evan-Thomas's four "fast battleships". This post-Jutland picture of the 5th Battle Squadron was taken from *Warspite*; *Valiant* can be seen in the foreground.

Jellicoe's flagship HMS *Iron Duke* – the namesake of her class – was one of a new generation of "super dreadnoughts", armed with 13.5-inch rather than 12-inch guns.

Like many of the dreadnoughts at Jutland, the SMS *Kaiser* had her 12-inch gun turrets amidships echeloned slightly, so theoretically their guns could be fired to either side.

This evocative picture by maritime artist Claus Bergen shows the battlecruiser SMS *Seydlitz*, viewed from her quarterdeck, late in the afternoon, after two of her turrets were silenced.

At Jutland *Invincible* was one of three British battlecruisers to be ripped apart in a sudden explosion. This photograph was taken just a few minutes later.

Left: The new generation of "super dreadnoughts", including these Queen Elizabeth class "fast battleships", had their main gun turrets mounted on their centreline – a much better layout than before.

Left inset: This dramatic photograph captured the moment at 4.26 p.m. when the battlecruiser HMS *Queen Mary* blew up after being hit by a salvo of shells fired by the *Derfflinger*.

Right: Many of the injuries suffered by seamen during the battle came from white-hot shell fragments, or from flying pieces of debris such as this 6-inch casemate gun housing.

Below: The battlecruiser SMS *Seydlitz* was lucky to make it back to Wilhelmshaven. In this photograph taken after the battle, the heavy damage she suffered is still clearly visible.

In this photograph of the German battlecruiser *Seydlitz* taken from one of her consorts late in the battle, fires can be seen raging on her battle-scarred upper decks.

The scuttling of the High Seas Fleet in Scapa Flow in June 1919 was the final act of the naval war. Here the battlecruiser *Derfflinger* is seen sinking by the bow.

ignited.' Each of these shell cases was packed with up to 126 kilograms (or 277 pounds) of explosives, divided between a large silk bag and a smaller brass cartridge. If one of these ignited, it could cause devastation inside the confines of the gun turret, or in the cramped working or transfer chamber below it. Von Hase continued; 'The burning cartridge cases emitted great tongues of flame which shot up out of the turrets as high as a house.'

The *Derfflinger* was lucky. A hit like this could easily have destroyed a British battlecruiser, but good handling practice and rigorous safety procedures meant that the blast vented upwards, rather than down through the hoist to the magazines. As von Hase put it; 'They only blazed – they didn't explode, as had been the case with the enemy. This saved the ship, but the result of the fire was catastrophic. The angrily searching flames killed everyone within their reach. Of the 78 men inside the turret only five managed to save themselves by climbing through the hole in the turret provided for throwing out empty shell cases, and of these several were severely injured. The other 73 men died together, like heroes in the fierce fever of battle.' In truth, most of them would have been killed instantly, either by the explosion or the resulting fireball. Von Hase was wrong; only two men escaped rather than the five he reported, and both of them suffered from severe burns. One of them died just hours later, leaving just a single maimed survivor to tell the tale.

The next hit was also from a 15-inch shell fired by the aptly named *Revenge*. It struck just over a minute later. Again Von Hase recounted what happened; 'A 38cm shell pierced the roof of 'Dora' turret, and here too exploded inside the turret. The same horrors ensued. With the exception of a single man, who was thrown by the concussion through the turret entrance, the whole turret crew of eighty men including all the magazine men, were killed instantly. The crew of the "Dora" turret, under the leadership of their brave turret officer Stückmeister [Warrant Officer] Arndt, had fought heroically up to the last second.' This meant that in the space of just two minutes, *Derfflinger* had lost both her after gun turrets – half of her main armament. Von Hase continued; 'Here too, the flames spread to the cartridge chamber, and set fire to all the cases which had been removed from their protective packing.' As a result; 'From both after turrets great flames were now spurting, mingled with clouds of yellow smoke – two ghastly pyres.'

The yellow smoke was from picric acid, used in the Lyddite-capped shells employed by both sides. The smoke and fumes seeped through the ship's ventilation trunking. As von Hase described it; 'At 9.15 p.m. [7.15 p.m.] I received a message from the Transmitting Station "Gas danger in the heavy gun Transmitting Station – Station must be abandoned." This gave me a shock. Things must be in a pretty bad way in the ship if the poisonous gases had already penetrated the Transmitting Station, which was carefully protected.' It was sited deep inside the ship's armoured citadel, where it was reasonably safe from enemy fire. Clearly the naval architects never considered the impact of picric acid fumes. The Transmitting Station was a key link in the fire control chain. Without it and without the spotters in the foretop, von Hase had to direct his guns deprived of the aid of mechanical computers or high-powered rangefinders that had made these weapons so accurate during their duel with Beatty.

The British fire was now ferocious. Von Hase described the experience; 'Now hit after hit shook the ship. The enemy had got our range excellently. I felt a clutch at my heart when I thought what the conditions must be in the interior of the ship . . . Suddenly we seemed to hear the crack of doom. A terrific roar, a tremendous explosion, and then darkness, in which we felt a colossal blow. The whole conning tower seemed to be hurled into the air as though by the hands of some portentous giant, and then to flutter, trembling, into its former position. A heavy shell had struck the fore control about 50 cm in front of me. The shell exploded but failed to pierce the thick armour, which it had struck at an unfavourable angle, though huge pieces had been torn out.' The door of the tower – kept ajar for ventilation – was also wrenched open, and refused to close again. Derfflinger's armoured conning tower was protected by 30 cm (12 inches) of Krupp steel. That kept out the 12-inch shell fired by Bellerophon. If the shell had been larger, though, then von Hase might not have survived.

Because of the yellow poisonous fumes lingering after this near miss, von Hase and his team donned gas masks, but he found it almost impossible to yell orders through his telephone headset while wearing this rubber mask. He cautiously peeled it off and discovered he could breathe clearly. He noted that one effect of the near miss had been that the heavy armoured door to the fire control position had been blown shut.

It refused to move, but a few minutes later another 12-inch shell fired by *Colossus* struck the deck below the bridge and exploded in the sick bay beneath it. The blast ripped up a large section of deck on the battlecruiser's starboard side, and the concussion blew von Hase's heavy steel door shut again. Von Hase noted; 'A polite race, the English! They had opened the door for us, and it was they who shut it again.' This black joke kept them amused as they sheltered from the storm of shellfire and splinters raging outside their armoured box.

Von Hase was still trying to fire back though, and needed a target for what remained of his ship's guns; 'I looked towards the enemy through my periscope. The salvos were still bursting around us, but we could scarcely see anything of the enemy, who were disposed in a great semi-circle around us. All we could see was the great reddish-gold flames spurting from the guns. The ships' hulls we saw but rarely.' Ever the professional, von Hase kept his guns in action, despite the lack of a suit-able target. 'I had the range of the flames measured. That was the only possible means of establishing the enemy's range. Without much hope of hurting the enemy I ordered the two forward turrets to fire salvo after salvo. I could feel that our fire soothed the nerves of our ship's company . . . the secondary armament were firing too, but of the six guns on that [port] side, only two could be used.'

The *Derfflinger* was not the only ship to suffer. *Seydlitz* was hit four times during the 'death ride', and once more while making her escape. The first four were from 12-inch shells fired by *Hercules* and *St Vincent*, and they struck the battlecruiser in her superstructure, on her hull, and on 'Caesar' turret, which had already been disabled. The concussion knocked out the ship's electric lighting, plunging its compartments into darkness. Still, as von Edigy explained, the crew were trained to work in the dark; 'Our men called these exercises "blind man's buff" because they were blindfolded to learn handling valves etc. by touch. The stokers and coal trimmers deserved the highest praise, for they had to wield their shovels mostly in the dark, often up to their knees in water without knowing where it came from and how much it would rise.' This sea water was seeping aft from the extensive flooding further forward caused by the torpedo hit earlier that afternoon.

Still, *Seydlitz* had been relatively lucky; none of these hits matched the one which had knocked out 'Caesar' turret during the 'Run to the South' three hours before. The next hit, though, a 15-inch shell from *Royal Oak,* came close to destroying another turret, and possibly even the whole ship with it. At 7.27 p.m., it struck the right-hand gun of 'Bertha' turret, the ship's starboard 'wing turret', and destroyed the barrel. Another few feet further aft, and the shell would have penetrated the turret itself. As von Egidy explained, for a moment it was thought the turret itself was about to blow; 'In "Bertha" turret there was a tremendous crash – smoke, dust and general confusion. At the order "Clear the turret" the turret crew rushed out, even using the traps for the empty cartridges, then they fell in behind the turret.' When the smoke cleared, the crew returned to their turret, and found the gunlayer dead at his post.

The ship's Senior Gunner Officer Richard Foerster, also described the hit; 'There was a huge blow to turret "Bertha", and the crew were shaken up, and at the same time a thick poisonous yellow gas penetrated into the turret . . . "Smoke danger in turret B, turret evacuated," ordered the turret commander, *Oblt z S* [Sub-Lieutenant] Kienitz. Just as at battle training all left the turret through all the available exits including cartridge traps, and in a few seconds the serving crew stood on deck. From below compressed air hissed and was blown through the turret . . . all the poisonous substances were quickly removed from the turret and the air was again pure. The gun leader of the right turret was dead, a piece of armour had struck him in the chest. However, the other damage was only marginal, the shell had hit the turret brow and had been so weakened that it remained outside the turret.' The gunlayer's body was removed, and the remaining gun was soon back in action.

Then, at 7.14 p.m., the signal 'Battlecruisers to operate against the enemy's van' appeared on the signal shrouds of the *Friedrich der Grosse*. This was a reprieve; the faint hope of survival for Captain Hertog's command. The signal was passed from *Derfflinger* and the other battle-cruisers, and at 7.17 p.m., the *Derfflinger* hauled round a little onto a more southerly course. When the order came, the ship was only 7,500 yards from the closest British dreadnought, the *Colossus*. This was point-blank range, at which even 12-inch shells could penetrate the belt and turret armour of the German battlecruisers with ease. That, at least, was the theory. In practice, the British were let down by their shells. Many of their armour-piercing shells exploded too early – on contact – rather than waiting for a few seconds while the armour-piercing shell buried itself deep in the heart of the enemy ship. These faulty shells were what saved Hertog and his battlecruisers – the shells and sound German shipbuilding.

As they made the turn *Von der Tann* was hit by a shell from the *Revenge*. It struck the ship just behind the After Conning Tower, and splinters flew through its sighting slits, killing or wounding everyone inside. Splinters also blasted through the ventilation trunks into the engine room, which was filled with choking black smoke. Seaman Carl Melms, forming part of a damage control party recalled; 'Our ship was in great danger during the evening. It was so bad that I thought our time had come and we would sink. We received a direct hit in the foundations immediately behind the Commander [the First Lieutenant, in the After Conning Tower]. I heard afterwards that nearly everybody there had been killed.' The whole battlecruiser rocked from the blow, and from the concussive blasts of the many near misses which sent towers of water cascading over her decks. The hardest thing for her crew was that because all her guns had been silenced, she could not even fight back.

The only hits scored by the battlecruisers during the 'Death Ride' came from a salvo fired by *Seydlitz*. At 7.16 p.m., two 11-inch shells struck *Colossus*; one on the port side of her signal deck, the other just behind her forward funnel. A fire began, a 4-inch gun was damaged, and five men were wounded. The Assistant Paymaster Harold Foot helped one of them; 'The range-taker, who was standing next to me in the bridge had his right arm completely shattered, and another man in the foretop was severely wounded.' Foot assisted the wounded man, then raced off to help put out the fire. Meanwhile, the *Colossus* kept on firing at the enemy battlecruisers as they hauled away to the south. Interestingly, these five wounded men were the only casualties suffered on any of the British dreadnoughts during this key phase of the battle.

The situation was very different in the German battlecruisers. *Motlke* had not been hit, but her consorts were all suffering badly. Even the poor *Lützow* was fired at, after being spotted by *Monarch* and *Orion* 18,500 yards to the south-west. She was hit five times in three minutes, the explosions cutting power to her after turrets, while damaging 'Anton' and temporarily knocking out 'Bertha' turrets. The escorting destroyers laid more smoke, and the now mortally wounded battlecruiser limped off. By 7.20 p.m., the German battlecruisers were also pulling away from the British dreadnoughts, covered by smoke from their destroyers. Captain Hertog's ships were now duelling with Beatty's four battle-cruisers, but thanks to the smoke screen neither side managed to hit the other. The British dreadnoughts also gradually ceased fire as their target became obscured. By then, though, their captains had something else to worry about, as the same destroyers formed up for an attack.

All in all, though, the 'Death Ride' had been a success. While the four battlecruisers were acting as a decoy, the rest of Scheer's battle fleet managed to extricate themselves, and were soon heading back the way they had come. Certainly, three of the four ships had been cruelly pounded, particularly the *Derfflinger*, but all four ships survived the curtain of fire falling around them and managed to break off the action before they suffered a crippling hit, or worse. The human cost though, had been high; *Derfflinger* lost 157 of her crew at Jutland, most of whom were killed during those few tense minutes. This had been a climactic moment in the battle, a crisis for Scheer which could only be met by offering his battlecruisers as a sacrifice. If they had failed to distract Jellicoe's battle fleet while Scheer carried out his *Gefechtskehrtwendung*, then the Grand Fleet might well have destroyed their German opponents. Thanks to Hertog's actions, Scheer was given a reprieve.

The Third *Gefechtskehrtwendung*

Scheer made the decision to order another *Gefechtskehrtwendung* just two minutes after his battle fleet first came under fire from Jellicoe's dreadnoughts. A minute later, at 7.13 p.m., he ordered the signal; 'Turn together 16 points to starboard' to be hoisted. This was a preparatory signal; the evolution would only begin when the signal came down. Meanwhile, the signal halyards running up the *Friedrich der Grosse*'s foremast were also used to display the signal to Captain Hertog, to 'Attack!'. The *Gefechtskehrtwendung* signal was still flying when the 'Death Ride' began, as Scheer needed to judge the moment perfectly. The British needed to be distracted, and he hoped that the smoke from the battlecruisers would hide his manoeuvre. At 7.18 p.m., the signal was suddenly hauled down, and the *Gefechtskehrtwendung* got under way.

This would never be as neat a manoeuvre as it had been before. Several of the leading ships had now been damaged, and so their engine performance varied. Also, when they came under fire at 7.10 p.m., the leading ships tended to slow down slightly, or weave out of the line a little, to avoid the conflagration ahead of them. So this was going to be no textbook manoeuvre. It was, though, a vitally important one, as the survival of the battle fleet depended upon its success. As before, the manual called for the ships at the end of the battle line to begin their turn first, to reduce the risk of a collision. This time, there was no time for such niceties. As soon as the signal came down, Vice-Admiral Schmidt in the *Ostfriesland* began turning immediately. His ship was ninth in the column – directly astern of Scheer's flagship – and behind her stretched the rest of the 1st Battle Squadron. This set the tone, and within seconds other ships ahead and astern of him began turning too.

In the *Friedrich der Grosse*, Scheer was concerned that the ships ahead of him had bunched up under pressure of the enemy fire and so, to give them more room, he ordered his flagship to turn to port. It says a lot about the proficiency of the German commanders that none of the other ships followed their flagship's lead. Just as Behncke's flagship *König* began her turn at 7.18 p.m., she was hit by a 13.5-inch shell from *Iron Duke*, which struck the ship near her mainmast. This caused extensive damage to her upper deck around the mast, but this proved relatively superficial. As the lumbering dreadnought turned, the next salvo landed in the empty patch of sea where she would have been if she had gone straight ahead. The *Grosser Kurfürst* was also hit four times while she made her turn, all the hits caused by 15-inch shells fired by the 5th Battle Squadron, six miles to the north-east. The German dreadnought seemed to stagger under these blows, but kept moving away from her tormentors.

Captain Karl Sieferling of the *Markgraf* began his turn a little early, but weaved as he did so to avoid the salvos landing ahead of him. His ship was also labouring slightly as one engine had already been knocked out. For a moment it looked like the *Kronprinz* – the ship directly ahead – might collide with her, but quick-thinking by both helmsmen avoided disaster. An accident at this critical moment could well have been fatal. Somehow, all the four leading dreadnoughts made their turn successfully, despite the shells falling all around them. However, before the order came they had been formed in line astern. They were now in a huddle abreast of each other, heading towards the south-east. The trouble was, they could not complete their turn until the ships that had been astern of them got out of their way.

Behind them in the line were the four Kaiser class dreadnoughts that formed the other division of Behncke's squadron. The last of these four ships was Scheer's flagship *Friedrich der Grosse*, which at Scheer's orders had deftly turned to port, to give the others more room. The *Kaiser* was in the lead, followed by the *Kaiserin* and the *Prinzregent Luitpold*. The *Prinzregent Luitpold* began turning as soon as the *Friedrich der Grosse* did, but ahead of her the *Kaiserin* was out of line, having jinked to starboard because the *Kaiser* ahead of her had just slowed down to avoid ramming the *Markgraf*. She was also slow to begin her turn, and her consorts were already altering course. Here the dreadnoughts were so crowded together that a collision seemed inevitable. However, quick thinking and good ship handling saved the day. The *Kaiser* slowed down a little, the *Prinzregent Luitpold* sped up, everyone altered course slightly and disaster was averted.

By the end of the manoeuvre the three dreadnoughts were steaming in line abreast, and one after the other they would alter to starboard, with the *Prinzregent Luitpold* leaving enough space between her and the *Ostfriesland* ahead of her to let Scheer's flagship slot back into the gap. Like thundering steel dodgems, these great dreadnoughts jostled their way back into their assigned places, constantly adjusting course and speed to keep clear of their consorts. In the confusion, though, the *Grosser Kurfürst* and the *Kronprinz* had managed to swap positions in the line. Unlike the III Battle Squadron, who had to perform this tricky manoeuvre under heavy fire, the eight older dreadnoughts of the I Battle Squadron made their turn with precision, and their neat line was soon joined by the *Friedrich der Grosse*. She became the ninth ship in the German battle line, while the *Westfalen* was now in the lead for the second time in an hour.

Once more the six pre-dreadnoughts of the II Battle Squadron were too far astern of the faster dreadnoughts to get in the way, and they turned independently, even though at the time they were advancing with each of three-ship division steaming in line abreast. Rear-Admiral Franz Mauve would deftly reform his ships into line, and then take up position off the starboard bow of the *Westfalen*. He would also follow the same south-westerly course as the dreadnoughts. By 7.25 p.m., Behncke's seven dreadnoughts were now in echelon rather than line abreast, as they raced to catch up with the rest of the battle fleet. The lead ship, the *Prinzregent Luitpold*, was now a mile and a half astern of Scheer's flagship, and they were struggling to catch up with her. The front of the battle line was heading south-west, but its tail – the fleet flagship and the ships just ahead of her – were still heading west. So Behncke altered course slowly, until his ships were heading towards the south-west, effectively cutting the corner of the battle line.

It would take the best part of half an hour before the German battle fleet was able to sort their battle line completely. One reason for this was that all the dreadnoughts were steaming at full speed, in an effort to put as much distance between themselves and the British guns as they could. Before they finally slipped from view, Captain Friedrich Brüninghaus in the *König* veered a little to port and laid a smoke screen to cover the fleet's retreat. The British fire slackened almost immediately. This was only partly due to the fraught but ultimately successful *Gefechtskehrt-wendung*. To cover the whole manoeuvre, Scheer had launched his battlecruisers on their 'death ride'. That, though, was only part of his hastily improvised plan. As the dreadnoughts were busy turning, Scheer ordered another signal to be hoisted. It read: 'Torpedo Boats to Attack!'

Attack with Torpedoes!

The signal had been flying from *Friedrich der Grosse's* halyards for at least five minutes, but it came down at 7.21 p.m., the signal to 'execute' the attack. At that moment, the battle fleet was halfway through its turn. The recipient was Commodore Andres Michelsen, commander of the fleet's destroyers, whose broad pennant flew from the masthead of the light cruiser *Rostock*. She was two miles to the south of the fleet flagship, and clustered around her were thirteen destroyers – elements of the VI and IX Flotillas. They immediately hared off to the west at full speed, their funnels belching thick black smoke. Two minutes later, five more destroyers from III Flotilla raced after them. The British saw their approach and answered with a wall of fire, mainly from secondary 4-inch and 6-inch guns, but a few larger calibre guns joined in as well. The leading destroyer, flotilla leader *G-41*, took a direct hit and slewed away, her wheel spinning as her helmsman fell wounded.

On the *Benbow*, Midshipman Geoff Congreve watched the attack; 'After we had fired about four salvos, ten or so destroyers then came right across between the line, going very fast, pouring out clouds of black smoke and hiding the whole horizon. They were being fired at by the secondary armament of nearly the whole fleet, and several must have been hit, but they did their job . . . They must have fired their torpedoes too – I think we were hit by one that failed to explode.' In fact, only *G-41* and *G-86* were hit as they roared towards the British, but when the time came both destroyers were still able to launch their torpedoes. On the battered *G-41*, Lieutenant Commander Max Schultz ordered the boats of his VI Flotilla to fire their torpedoes, and then to make their escape back through their own smoke screen.

On the *Iron Duke*, Petty Officer Arthur Brister watched the attack; 'As they approached to within torpedo range they appeared bent on suicide, but I only had time to see one of them pull up suddenly and drift away helplessly.' Brister was called away to send a signal, but he'd seen enough to be impressed by the Germans' bravery. Later, he wrote; 'I remember that German torpedo attack as the most exciting and bravest incident I saw at Jutland . . . It was the kind of dashing naval action prominent in boyish dreams.' Three miles to the north-west, the fast battleships were a little closer to the German destroyers, and were involved in shooting at them as they roared towards the British ships. On the *Malaya*, Sub Lieutenant Caslon watched the attack; 'Only one destroyer got within close range, although I think they all fired torpedoes.' He said of that destroyer that; 'Splashes were falling all around her like rain falling in a puddle of water.'

Caslon had been watching the attack by Lieutenant Commander Herbert Goehle's IX Flotilla, which took place a little to the north of Shultz's VI Flotilla's torpedo run. The flotilla leader *V-28* took a direct hit from a 6-inch shell and turned away. She was more fortunate than her companion *S-35*, which was hit by a heavy calibre shell and was ripped in two, sinking almost immediately. Caslon, watching from the *Malaya*, said; 'She was hit by several shells at once, and sank.' However many shells hit her, it was a swift end. She was already carrying the survivors of the *V-39* on board, a destroyer sunk three hours earlier during the 'Run to the South'. This time, there was nobody left to rescue. Another of Goehle's boats, the *S-51*, was hit in the engine room, but managed to limp away into the cover of the smoke screen before the British shells found her range.

Still, between them these frail little destroyers of VI and IX Flotillas managed to launch a total of thirty torpedoes at the British dreadnoughts; eleven from Shultz's boats and the rest by Goehle's flotilla. Each of these destroyers carried six 50 cm torpedoes, in two twin and two single launchers. Most boats had managed to fire three off, at a range of between three-and-a-half to five miles. There could have been even more. However, when III Flotilla came up to the smoke screen, it met the other destroyers racing back through it, having launched their torpedoes. So, the III flotilla turned around as well, but not before one of its boats, the *S-54*, caught a glimpse of the enemy and launched a single torpedo at them. That brought the total up to thirty-one torpedoes.

They were launched one after the other at around 7.27 p.m. – the German boats were not designed to launch all their tubes at one time. However, a combination of the smoke, the shell splashes all around them and the poor light made accurate aiming all but impossible. The torpedoes in this huge spread were merely launched in the general direction of the British ships, rather than carefully aimed at specific targets. Actually, there was little point; at that range the torpedoes would take a while to reach their targets. The G-7 torpedoes had a range of 9,842 yards and a speed of 28.5 knots. That meant they covered a half mile in just over a minute, and so it would take eight minutes for them to reach the closest British ships. In fact, as Midshipman Congreve of the *Benbow* suggested, the British didn't see the torpedoes launch; they only saw the boats turn away amid a dense cloud of smoke.

Not seeing the torpedoes being launched reduced the British reaction time a little. When the destroyers broke off the action, though, it was clear that the torpedoes were already in the water. Fortunately, by then Jellicoe had already given his orders. In 1916, the standard procedure for dealing with a torpedo attack was to turn the ships away from the oncoming torpedoes. The advantages were obvious. Instead of a closing rate of 28.5 knots, this reduced the speed of the dreadnought – usually 20 knots – to just 8.5, or a little over 280 yards per minute. That gave the dreadnoughts a fighting chance to jink out of the way of the torpedoes' path. These German torpedoes also threw up a clear white wake which was visible to lookouts on the British ships, so the dreadnought captains could decide which way to turn.

Another option, and one that became common practice during World War Two, was to head towards the torpedoes, and try to 'comb' the torpedo tracks. That seemingly suicidal tactic could work, but speed and manoeuvrability were crucial, neither of which were particularly impressive in coal-fired dreadnoughts. Above all, this increased the closing speed to a startling 1,600 yards a minute. This was not really a viable option for Jellicoe, despite the suggestions by 'armchair admirals' after the battle. Besides, a turn away was the course laid down in the Grand Fleet's Battle Orders, so that was the order Jellicoe's captains were expecting.

So, as soon as he saw the destroyers, Jellicoe made the only logical decision open to him. At 7.22 p.m. – even before the torpedoes hit the water – Jellicoe ordered the battle fleet to turn simultaneously two points (22.5°) to port. Three minutes later, he ordered a second two-point turn, a total of 45° in all. Before the order, the fleet had been steaming in six columns, each of four ships, with the leading ships angled to form a sort of echeloned line, from the *Marlborough* in the north-west to the *King George V* to the south-east. This was a reasonably good formation for gunnery, but a vulnerable one when the enemy were firing torpedoes at you. By turning his ships simultaneously towards the south-east, the oncoming torpedoes were heading towards a large column of dreadnoughts, five miles long and one and a half miles wide. Even at this slower closing speed the prospects for the British didn't look good.

It was 7.33 p.m. before the first torpedo wake was sighted approaching the *Marlborough*. She was the closest ship in the battle fleet to the spot where the destroyers had launched their torpedoes. The lookouts in the foretop and maintop had telephones, and gave Captain George Ross a steady stream of reports as the torpedoes crept closer. *Marlborough* had already been hit by one torpedo that afternoon; a second blow could be fatal. When they were almost upon her, the helmsman turned the wheel to starboard and the dreadnought lumbered out of the way, or tried to. One passed ahead of her, another close under her stern. In fact, as Ross put it; 'we should certainly have been hit if the stern had not been swinging'. There was no avoiding the third, but by some miracle it passed underneath the ship without detonating. Ross thought its depth settings had malfunctioned. In any case it was a close shave – and *Marlborough* was only the first of several vulnerable ships.

Revenge was a few hundred yards off *Marlborough*'s port quarter. At the critical moment the helmsman turned the wheel to port, and two torpedoes missed her, passing close to both her bow and stern. Off her port quarter were the other two ships of the column, *Hercules* and *Agincourt*. Captain Montagu Doughty of *Agincourt* felt particularly vulnerable, as his dreadnought was the longest in the battle fleet, and therefore the biggest target. Still, she 'combed' the two approaching tracks by turning to port, and so one torpedo passed on either side of her. A Royal Marine gunner on board saw one of them pass the ship by, but added; 'A little later another torpedo came straight at us, but luckily for us it surfaced 200 yards away, having spent its run. It was another lucky escape.'

This same spread of torpedoes continued on, and four of them were spotted heading towards Evan-Thomas in the *Barham*, whose ships were following the battle fleet a few thousand yards astern of the fifth column led by *Colossus*. However, Captain Arthur Craig of the *Barham* had sufficient warning to keep out of their way. *Neptune* was the third ship in the fifth column, and Captain Vivian Bernard thought a torpedo hit was inevitable when he saw one approaching his stern. There was no time to turn out of its way. The torpedo was; 'following exactly in our course . . . coming closer and closer . . . we could do nothing but wait, mouths open.' Then, he added; 'Nothing happened.' The torpedo was no longer there, probably having reached its maximum range just before impact. It was not an experience Bernard wanted to ever repeat.

Further down the line of columns, another torpedo passed close to Jellicoe's flagship the *Iron Duke*, then continued on towards the *Thunderer*, the last ship in the next column, a few hundred yards off *Iron Duke's* starboard bow. Captain James Fergusson ordered a hard turn to port, and the torpedo passed harmlessly by *Thunderer's* side. Almost certainly there were other torpedoes that had not been spotted, but none of them hit their targets. Of the thirty-one torpedoes fired, all – by some miracle it seemed – had missed. Actually it was not a miracle at all. By turning away, Jellicoe had given his captains the best possible chance to evade the incoming torpedoes, and by moving his ships away from the launching point he'd made it far more likely the torpedoes would run out of range before they struck one of his ships. Thanks to his quick reactions, none of his dreadnoughts were hit. The problem, though, was that he had now lost contact with the enemy.

By the time the torpedo attack ended the two fleets were sailing at right angles to each other, the Germans to the south-west, the British to the south-east. Between them was a dense bank of smoke and a pile of floating debris, the last remnants of German destroyer *S-35*. Behind the smoke was the mist – with no German ship in sight. To the south, the sea was covered by another even bigger smoke screen, laid by the remnants of Rear-Admiral Bödlicker's 2nd Scouting Group. His light cruisers were playing their part in hiding Scheer's battle fleet and the shattered battlecruisers from view. The British guns had been silent for some minutes now, as the last of their targets had disappeared from sight. Jellicoe would soon resume his old southerly course, and ahead of the battle fleet Beatty's battlecruisers and light cruisers were already chasing after the fleeing enemy. However, the light was now fading, and unless contact was regained soon, then it would be too dark to fight.

Part III

Scheer's Escape

15

Fading Light, Fading Hope

It was now 7.30 p.m. Scheer's battle fleet had survived his second near-disastrous encounter with Jellicoe's dreadnoughts, and he was now steaming away from them. Thanks to the German torpedo attack, the British battle fleet was now heading in virtually the opposite direction. Amazingly, despite all that frenetic activity – the 'death ride', the *Gefecht-skehrtwendung* and the destroyer attack – only twenty minutes had passed since the two fleets blundered into contact. Now though, with the dreadnoughts heading away from each other, each passing minute made a further clash less likely. Sunset was at 8.17 p.m., so all Scheer had to do was to keep his distance for another hour until the night brought an end to the battle. He would then have a chance of escaping from the British under cover of darkness. For his part, Jellicoe knew that as the light began to fade, so too would his hopes of crushing the German battle fleet.

Beatty's Signal

At first Scheer had steamed almost due west, heading directly away from the British. Then, at 7.27 p.m. he turned towards the south-west and reduced speed at 17 knots. This allowed his pre-dreadnoughts and any damaged ships to keep up. In fact, the damage wasn't as bad as it might have been. Seven German dreadnoughts had been hit that afternoon, but their speed was largely unimpaired. Just as importantly, their main guns were still fully operational. Scheer had got off extremely lightly. Now, though, the vulnerable pre-dreadnoughts of Rear-Admiral Mauve's II Battle Squadron were in the lead, Vice-Admiral Schmidt's I Battle

Squadron was in the middle, and once again Rear-Admiral Behncke's III Battle Squadron brought up the rear. Scheer knew that Jellicoe was somewhere to the east, so he ordered Mauve to take station off the starboard bow of the line of dreadnoughts. That way, they would be screened if Jellicoe suddenly appeared again.

Less satisfactory was the placement of his battlecruisers. Hartog's four ships were 6,000 yards off the port beam of the battle line, which placed them between it and Jellicoe. So Scheer's most heavily damaged ships were still at the point of greatest danger. To protect his vulnerable battlecruisers Scheer ordered Commodore Michelsen to screen them with three of his destroyer flotillas, the same boats that had launched the attack on Jellicoe's battle fleet. Now they were a thousand yards off the port beam of *Derfflinger*, where they could protect the battlecruisers and also launch an attack if Jellicoe's ships suddenly broke through the mist. Hipper was still in the destroyer *G-39*; for forty minutes he had been impatiently waiting for a lull in the fighting so he could resume command of his ships. These destroyers and the four shattered battlecruisers were all that lay between Scheer and the massed guns of Jellicoe's dreadnoughts. These ships, and a swirling soup of mist.

Seven miles or 14,000 yards west of the German battlecruisers, Jellicoe's flagship the *Iron Duke* was now heading away from Scheer, his battle fleet steering towards the south-east. That though, was about to change. Jellicoe had just ordered his dreadnoughts to turn south by divisions. This meant he was reforming his battle line, with Vice-Admiral Jerram in *King George V* in the lead. Eight thousand yards in front of Jerram was Beatty's flagship *Lion*, leading his six battlecruisers – his own four plus the two survivors of Hood's squadron. Beatty had already turned towards the south-south-west, as had the three squadrons of light cruisers accompanying him. Of these, Rear-Admiral Napier's cruisers were 6,000 yards off his starboard bow, Commodore Le Mesurier's squadron was off his starboard beam, and Commodore Alexander-Sinclair was following astern. For the next half hour, these little ships would be thrust into the very heart of the battle.

Although the two flagships were about thirteen miles apart, and their courses were still diverging slightly, the area between them contained a squadron of German dreadnoughts, the German battlecruisers, the badly damaged *Lützow* and her escorts, plus several squadrons of light cruisers and flotillas of destroyers. Only the smoke and mist kept them from seeing each other. However, Commodore Charles Le Mesurier in the *Calliope* was now leading his four light cruisers towards the west-south-west, which meant he was heading almost directly towards the screen of German destroyers. Here, the two groups of ships were just 9,000 yards apart. Before they met though, a brief gap in the mist began an even more dramatic chain of events. At 7.32 p.m., the destroyer *V-30* signalled Commodore Heinrich on the *Regensburg*, reporting the sighting of 'large enemy vessels to the south-east'. These were Beatty's six battle-cruisers, about 15,000 yards off the German destroyers' port quarter.

At the time, Heinrich's destroyers were on the starboard beam of the German battlecruisers, which were hidden from Beatty by the mist. The two groups of battlecruisers were on parallel courses, though and a few minutes later another brief rent in the mist gave lookouts on the *Lion* a glimpse of the German destroyers. More importantly, beyond them they saw a line of capital ships. These were the German battlecruisers. The nearest dreadnought was three miles or 6,000 yards further away to the north-west, but for some reason Beatty believed this brief glimpse had revealed Scheer's main battle fleet. So, at 7.40 p.m., he ordered a signal to be sent by searchlight to the armoured cruiser *Minotaur*. It read; 'Enemy bears from me NW by W, distant ten to eleven miles. My position Lat 56° 56' N, Long 6° 16' E. Course SW, speed 18 knots.' *Minotaur* was used to relay the signal, as *Lion*'s wireless had been knocked out. This signal was directed at Jellicoe, five miles behind Beatty's flagship.

Minotaur duly passed the message on to the *King George V*, which was two miles astern. From there, a wireless message was sent to Jellicoe on board the *Iron Duke*. This all took time though; the signal only reached the flagship's wireless room at 7.54 p.m. Another five minutes passed before it was deciphered and delivered to Jellicoe. During these nineteen minutes, Beatty had become convinced that he was just a few miles to the south-east of Scheer, and he alone was in a position to intercept the Germans before nightfall. For his part, Jellicoe was perplexed. This was the first sighting of the German battle fleet since its last *Gefecht-skehrtwendung*, but it also made little sense. For a start, Beatty's position was wrong – it was actually north of Jellicoe, instead of south. Was Beatty's sighting as inaccurate as his navigation? Jellicoe decided to alter course slightly to starboard, just in case.

To confuse things further, a minute earlier Jellicoe had been handed another signal, this time from the normally reliable Commodore Goodenough on board the light cruiser *Southampton*. He was to the north-west of the British battle fleet, and he'd just reported sighting enemy ships steering towards the north-west. Did this mean Scheer had turned his fleet to the north and was trying to work his way around the back of the Grand Fleet? Was it merely a force of light cruisers or destroyers, screening the rear of the High Seas Fleet. Jellicoe had no way of knowing, at least not until a more reliable sighting report reached him. So, to play it safe, at 8 p.m., Jellicoe ordered his dreadnoughts to alter course to starboard by divisions, and to steer a west-south-westerly course at 17 knots. Given the poor visibility, this was something of a gamble. Jellicoe had no idea exactly what was waiting for him in the mist, but at least this gave him a chance of finding out before dark.

A few minutes later, Jellicoe received another signal from Beatty – perhaps the most controversial communiqué of the battle. It read; 'Urgent. Submit van of battleships follow battlecruisers. We can then cut off whole of enemy's battle fleet.' The message suggested that Beatty knew exactly where the enemy battle fleet was, and was in a position to engage them. It also implied he was ahead of Scheer, and might therefore be able to cross his 'T' again. At the very least, that he could block Scheer's progress until Jellicoe joined in the fight. If it sounded almost too good to be true, then it was. When the signal was sent at 7.48 p.m., Beatty was 18,000 yards from the nearest German dreadnought, well beyond the range of visibility. Even the official German account commented on this; 'It was by no means clear on what Beatty based his expectations of being able to cut off the whole German fleet. When he sent the wireless message containing this assurance, he had lost touch with the enemy.'

In other words, when Beatty sent the signal, he'd only the vaguest idea where Scheer's battle fleet was, and had no contact with it. He might have glimpsed the German battlecruisers, but that was all. Later, Beatty's supporters claimed that if Jellicoe had heeded it, then the battle could have ended in a final dramatic clash. Jellicoe's supporters rightly pointed out this was nonsense, as Beatty was merely making wild and unjustified demands for support, without any reason for them. To many, his signal smacked of rank insubordination. Jellicoe ignored it for two very good reasons. First, the 'van', Jerram's 1st Battle Squadron, had lost contact with Beatty as the battlecruisers raced ahead of the rest of the fleet. Second, the whole battle fleet had just altered course to the west, and the six columns of British dreadnoughts – seven if you included the fast battleships to the north – were now spread out over five miles of sea, making contact with the enemy a near certainty.

Jellicoe though, had no desire to leave Beatty unsupported. So, he ordered Jerram to 'follow the battlecruisers'. Jerram expected this order, but he'd no intention of carrying it out. After all, he'd no clear idea where the battlecruisers were; now he was heading west, they were somewhere off his port beam. So to link up with Beatty, Jerram would have had to alter course to port, and then try to find the battlecruisers further to the south. This wouldn't really be possible, as the dreadnoughts were slower than Beatty's ships; there was no guarantee they'd catch them up. So Jerram decided to stay where he was, on the southern wing of the battle fleet, at least until Beatty could be found. As a senior officer put it after the war, the battle fleet was already doing what Beatty asked, and more.

What neither Jerram, Beatty or Jellicoe knew though, was that the British dreadnoughts were now heading almost directly towards the enemy, who was now 14,000 yards away and steaming across the British path. The reason for this was a change of course. At 7.48 p.m., Scheer ordered his battle fleet to head due south. This meant that when Jellicoe altered course twelve minutes later, the British were almost at right angles to the Germans, and closing with them at just under 600 yards a minute. Technically, this meant that if the two sides met, Jellicoe was about to have his 'T' crossed. In practice though, as the fleet was sailing in divisions, then as soon as contact was made it could swing neatly into line, forming on a parallel course to the Germans. Then, the superior weight of metal of the British broadsides would really tell. Fortunately for Scheer, the renewed clash that Jellicoe hoped for would not happen. Instead it would be the lighter forces of both sides who would make contact and begin the last clash before nightfall.

A Clash of Cruisers

When he turned to the south, Scheer took care to keep his fleet closed up in a compact formation. Essentially, the dreadnoughts, pre-dreadnoughts and battlecruisers formed three neat and parallel columns, with the battle fleet in the centre, the vulnerable pre-dreadnoughts to starboard, and the battlecruisers to port. The other important element on the naval chessboard that evening was the *Lützow*, surrounded by her escort of destroyers. She was now passing astern of the battle fleet, where she would be fully protected if Jellicoe suddenly made an appearance. In front of both the pre-dreadnoughts and the dreadnoughts, a squadron of light cruisers probed for the enemy, while the destroyers were divided into two groups, one on each flank of the three columns of the German battle fleet. British ships, probably battlecruisers, had already been sighted off the fleet's port beam, and so Scheer expected an encounter before darkness hid him from the enemy.

A few minutes after 8 p.m., funnel smoke was spotted from the bridge of the light cruiser *Castor*. She flew the broad pennant of Commodore Jack Hawksley, commander of the 11th Destroyer Flotilla. He immediately turned to investigate, accompanied by eight destroyers. The smoke had been spotted five miles to the west-north-west, and as he headed that way, Hawksley reported the sighting to both Beatty and Jellicoe. About 2,000 yards to the south was the *Calliope*, flagship of Commodore Charles Le Mesurier's 4th Light Cruiser Squadron. Le Mesurier turned his flagship round to support Hawksley, and was followed by the *Constance* and the *Comus*. At that moment, Beatty was on Le Mesurier's port beam, his battlecruisers still racing towards the south-west. To increase his chances of making contact, Beatty ordered Rear-Admiral Napier's four-strong 3rd Light Cruiser Squadron to fan out to the west in a last-ditch attempt to locate the enemy fleet before dark.

Ten minutes later, at 8.15 p.m., Hawksley sighted a line of German destroyers – the twelve boats of the V Flotilla, commanded by Lieutenant-Commander Oskar Heinecke. The Germans turned away and the British chased them, firing as they went. Heinecke led his boats towards the light cruiser *Rostock*, which then shepherded its charges towards the cover of the nearest friendly capital ships, the dreadnoughts of Behncke's III Battle Squadron. The British didn't score any hits on the German destroyers, but they kept up their pursuit. The sun had now set and the light was beginning to fade. Hawksley was surprised that the Germans didn't put up a fight. Then he found out why. At 8.26 p.m., he sighted a line of German dreadnoughts about four miles in front of him.

Heinecke had led him on to the guns of the German battle fleet. Seconds later, orange flames rippled along the German line as three dreadnoughts opened fire.

On the *Comus*, Lieutenant Reginald Servaes watched the scene from the bridge. 'We, half the squadron, and half a flotilla were sent off again to bear off another destroyer attack, Personally I was too busy keeping station, and never saw any destroyers. Our leading ship [*Calliope*] opened fire about three minutes later. Almost as soon as she had opened fire I saw three Hun battleships, who promptly opened fire on our leading ship. Our destroyers had already turned back, as the Hun destroyer attack had failed to develop.' As he watched, the Germans got the range of the Commodore's flagship; 'His ship started getting straddled, and as she turned she was hit once or twice, and we were straddled. One salvo burst close astern of us, and I heard the splinters going pit-a-pat against the funnels and casings.' It was only a matter of time before a cruiser was torn apart by a salvo of large calibre German shells.

On the *Calliope*, an officer on the bridge recalled; 'We were in sight of the German battleships for about ten minutes, and under fire during this time from two Kaiser class battleships and one Helgoland, whose shooting was very accurate. Only our high speed and zigzagging saved us from annihilation. As it was, we seemed to be in the middle of splashes, and the noise of the bursting shell and flying fragments was absolutely deafening. . . . For the last five minutes that we were under fire we were in sight of our own ships, although the two battle fleets were invisible to each other, and we were told afterwards that at times we were hidden in spray from the flashes.' What saved the British cruisers and destroyers was the growing twilight. The spotters on the *Prinzregent Luitpold*, *Kaiser* and *Markgraf* could barely see the dim outlines of the destroyers heading towards them; they were shooting more at their white bow waves than at the vessels themselves.

Still, they fired both their main guns and their secondary batteries. Water spouts broke all around the British flotilla, and Hawksley ordered it to turn away. The flotilla survived, but it missed a splendid opportunity to launch a potentially devastating torpedo attack against Behncke's dreadnoughts. Then Le Mesurier's light cruisers spotted the German line, and vice versa. The German spotters switched targets, and opened fire at a range of 6,500 yards. Le Mesurier ordered his cruisers to turn away, but before he did *Calliope* fired a single torpedo at the enemy battle line from one of her submerged tubes. Then, as the anonymous lieutenant from *Calliope* put it; 'Having fired our torpedo, we turned and proceeded full speed, zigzagging two points each way on an eastern course to join our own ships, which by this time were out of sight.' The *Calliope* eventually reached the safety of the British battle line, black smoke billowing over her shell-riddled deck.

Le Mesurier described the encounter in a letter to his wife; 'Our second little excursion came soon after 8 o'clock – another German destroyer attack. This time I only took out three ships [*Calliope, Constance* and *Comus*]. We pushed the German destroyers back, when suddenly, out of the haze, loomed large the High Seas Fleet about four miles off. We held on a bit and fired torpedoes at 'em – the *Calliope* has good ground to think that hers got home – and then ran like billy-oh for shelter, with at least three big battleships plunking at us.' In fact, the torpedo missed, or at least failed to explode, but as she turned away *Calliope* was struck by a salvo of 5.9-inch shells fired by the *Markgraf.* Two of her 4-inch guns were silenced, and a dozen men were killed or seriously wounded. One of the badly wounded – a boy bugler from South London – was later awarded a bugle inscribed by the king, in recognition of his gallantry that evening. The other British ships escaped unscathed.

This was merely the first of several clashes that rippled up and down the German line as the sun set in the west. As Hawksley and Le Mesurier were beginning their sortie, Rear-Admiral Napier's flagship *Falmouth* was a few thousand yards to the south-west. He'd just finished deploying his squadron into line abreast, each cruiser a mile apart. They were heading due west in an attempt to locate the head of the German battle fleet. *Falmouth* was at the right or northern end of the line. The mist swirled and eddied in front of them, but at 8.09 p.m., lookouts on his flagship spotted a line of ships dead ahead of them, about six miles to the west. Then the mist closed again. A few minutes, later it cleared; this time long enough for Napier to make out they were German light cruisers – five of them, steaming in line astern. He turned his squadron onto a roughly parallel course, heading towards the south, and waited for the mist to thin enough to be able to open fire.

These five ships were the light cruisers of the IV Scouting Group. They were led by Commodore von Reuter, who flew his pennant in the

Stettin. The *München*, *Frauenlob*, *Stuttgart* and *Hamburg* followed astern of von Reuter's flagship. These ships constituted the vanguard of the High Seas Fleet, charged with probing ahead of Scheer's battle fleet as it steamed southwards. It was not until 8.17 p.m., two minutes after sunset, that lookouts on the *Stettin* sighted the approaching line of British ships. They spotted five of them, as Napier's squadron had been temporarily joined by the *Canterbury*. So the two light cruiser squadrons were evenly matched, or rather they would have been if Rear-Admiral Bödicker's II Scouting Group hadn't been in the area, its leading ship 2,000 yards off the port quarter of the *Hamburg*, and therefore closer to Napier's flagship than von Reuter. However, thanks to the mist, Bödicker hadn't yet spotted the British cruisers when von Reuter sent Scheer his sighting report.

Von Reuter immediately turned his ships towards Napier, and the Germans charged at the British, firing as they went. Napier remained on his existing course, but both groups of five light cruisers were now rapidly drawing closer to each other; each passing minute brought the two groups a thousand yards closer to each other. When the charge began they were about 9,000 yards apart. Within minutes this had dropped to less than 6,000 yards. The gunnery duel, though, was one-sided. Thanks to the setting sun, the German ships were clearly visible to the British against the western sky, while the British light cruisers were largely invisible – only a few dim shapes could be made out. Visibility varied; for instance, *Stettin* and *München* were able to fire off several salvos with their forward-facing guns, while off their port beam *Frauenlob*, *Stuttgart* and *Hamburg* couldn't make out any clear targets at all. The British enjoyed a clear advantage, and it soon began to tell.

München was hit twice by British 6-inch shells, one wrecking a ship's boat, the other tearing a hole in her aftermost funnel. Steam pressure dropped and *München* began to fall behind. By now, Napier's five ships were almost crossing the 'T' of von Reuter's squadron, and so, a little after 8.30 p.m., von Reuter ordered his ships to turn away. They turned to starboard, hauling round simultaneously until they were all steaming westwards. Within minutes they had disappeared into the mist again and Napier's ships were left without anyone to fire at. An officer on board the *Falmouth* described the clash in almost dismissively perfunctory terms; 'At 8 p.m., we were ordered to sweep to the westward and locate the head of [the] enemy line before dark. At 8.08 p.m. we sighted, and until 8.38 p.m. engaged four light cruisers, but then some enemy battle-cruisers arrived in support of the light cruisers, and we retired.' He added that 'the enemy were firing shrapnel during this evening action'.

This little clash, although hardly an important event in the long-running battle, marked a significant turn of events. Von Reuter's cruisers had been scouting ahead of the German battle fleet, hoping to guide Scheer safely towards the south. The arrival of Napier's squadron forced the Germans to turn away, and at 8.21 p.m. von Reuter sent a signal, reporting 'Four enemy light cruisers in [square] 007E'. This would add to Scheer's unease about what was lurking through the mist a few miles ahead of him. By now though, even bigger guns were firing a few thousand yards to the north. This next phase of what was fast becoming a running skirmish began at 8.18 p.m., the moment von Reuter began his charge. For the past forty minutes Beatty's six battlecruisers had been steaming towards the south-west at high speed, hoping to work their way ahead of the German battle fleet. Now Beatty's last chance for glory had arrived.

Beatty's Last Chance

At 8.18 p.m., Beatty's lookouts sighted two groups of ships to the west. About seven miles off the starboard bow were the three remaining light cruisers of Bödicker's II Scouting Group. Then, the mist parted again, and six miles or 12,000 yards off *Lion's* starboard beam were the German battlecruisers. Better still, they weren't moving – the British were presented with a sitting target. Once again the poor visibility worked in favour of the British; their ships remained hidden, while the Germans were clearly visible. Beatty altered course to starboard slightly and closed the range to 8,500 yards. At 8.20 p.m., three British battlecruisers opened fire, followed a minute later by *New Zealand* and *Indomitable*. Because of funnel smoke swirling around her *Inflexible* had problems ranging in, but the other five British battlecruisers all had clear targets. Now, surely, Beatty would be able to avenge the destruction of two of his ships.

The Germans had been taken completely by surprise. When the British shells started falling around them, the three German battle-cruisers had briefly heaved to, to let Hipper transfer from the destroyer *G-39* to the *Moltke*. One minute Hipper was taking advantage of a lull in the fighting, the next he was facing the final annihilation of his battered squadron. The first he knew of the threat was the line of orange gun flashes which lit the darkening sky to the south-east. The British battlecruisers were virtually invisible, but at least the German spotters could aim at the gun flashes. So, within a minute, a frustrated Hipper was veering away again in his destroyer, the four German ships in line astern, with *Derfflinger* leading, were getting under way again, and both sides were locked in their final duel of that long and bloody day.

On the *Derfflinger*, von Hase was in the conning tower when the British battlecruisers opened fire. "'Clear for Action!" sounded once more throughout the ship, and a few seconds later I had trained the "Anna" turret on the target and fired. In the thick mist the "Bertha" turret could not find their target ...' Effectively, the ship was down to one working turret. Then, 'a heavy shell struck the "Anna" turret and bent one of the rails on which the turret revolves, so that it was stuck. Our last weapon was snatched from our hands!' A working party used crowbars to free it, and the uneven duel continued. Rangefinding was a real problem. Von Hase recalled; 'I had to shoot almost entirely by estimated range, for only rarely was the Bg. (*Basis Gerät*, or Rangefinder) man able to get the range of a gun flash . . . It was impossible to observe the splashes.' With some understatement he added; 'The situation had once more become very uncomfortable.'

With the German ships outnumbered three to two, the British were able to group their fire. So, *Princess Royal* targeted *Derfflinger*, *Tiger* took on *Moltke*, while *New Zealand* and *Indomitable* fired on the *Seydlitz*. *Inflexible* engaged whatever target her spotters were fleetingly able to see. Thanks to a communications error, *Lion* began by firing on the light cruiser *Pillau*, but she soon turned her guns on the *Derfflinger*. After just four minutes, *Moltke* was struck amidships by a 13.5-inch shell, and moments later *Derfflinger* was hit on her sole remaining turret, jamming her training gear. The German ships were moving now, and Captain Hartog – still in temporary command – ordered the squadron to disengage by making a hard turn to starboard. Bödicker's cruisers had already jinked out of the way to give their battlecruisers a clear angle of fire. As Bödicker took cover behind the pre-dreadnought squadrons, Hartog's battlecruisers began their turn away.

The German battlecruisers were still dangerously exposed though, and they were now taking the full brunt of Beatty's fire. At 8.30 p.m.

Seydlitz was hit twice, one shell striking her after turret without causing serious damage, the other exploding over her bridge, killing or wounding most of her bridge crew, but sparing Captain von Egidy. What probably saved the Germans from more serious damage was Hartog's quick decision to disengage. That, and the fact that of the British ships, three had one or more turrets disabled or knocked out. *Seydlitz* and her consorts were hitting back, though; *Derfflinger* fired eight salvos, and *Von der Tann* three partial ones. *Moltke* and *Seydlitz* managed two salvos apiece. Thanks to the poor light, German fire was largely ineffective, with most salvos landing well behind the British ships. In fact, the armoured cruisers 2,000 yards beyond Beatty's battlecruisers altered course to port to avoid the German shells landing close to them.

Relatively ineffective though they might be, on the *Tiger* Midshipman John Ouvry found the German fire disconcerting; 'When we were engaged on the starboard side some German battleships engaged us in failing light, and opened fire on us. I remember seeing the flashes of the German guns firing, and wondering whether the shell was on its way to blow me up – whether I'd actually seen the gun fire that was going to cause me to pack up.' The gunnery officer on the *Inflexible* didn't have a clear target, but noted; 'Few shots came near us, although there seemed to be firing at some ship or other going on all around. I looked aft once, and saw a lot of splashes falling way astern of us in the smoke, but didn't appear to be any ships there. Also, a number of shots fell a long way over us. . . . at about 8.45 p.m. we seemed to lose the enemy altogether, and we didn't sight them again before it finally became dark.'

The only verified hit came at 8.24 p.m. when a 5.9-inch (15-cm) shell from one of the German ships' secondary batteries struck *Lion*, without causing any significant damage. By then though, the German battle-cruisers were heading westwards at full speed, and the British spotters found themselves without any clearly visible targets. This was only a temporary lull. One unforeseen result of Hartog's alteration of course was that it placed his battlecruisers directly in the path of the German battle fleet, which before the firing began was 4,000 yards off Hartog's starboard beam. The line of dreadnoughts was led by the *Westfalen*, which was forced to alter hard to starboard to avoid a collision. The rest of the German dreadnoughts followed her example, turning in succession when they reached the same spot. As a result, by 8.30 p.m., all the

German dreadnoughts or battlecruisers were either steaming westward, or were about to turn that way.

Scheer's plan of running towards the south was now in disarray. Thanks to the battlecruisers turning away to the west, the bulk of the High Seas Fleet was now heading in a direction its commander really didn't want to go. The aim of his southerly course was to try to avoid getting too far away from Wilhelmshaven. Now each mile the fleet headed west, the harder it would be for Scheer to reach his home port. Still, the withdrawal of the four battlecruisers was vitally necessary. The bows of the *Seydlitz* were almost under water, while *Derfflinger* was also barely afloat. A few more hits and both ships might sink, while the other two – with several guns knocked out – were ill equipped to defend themselves. As Hartog tried to escape, Beatty would have pursued him, if a new force hadn't suddenly appeared. This new squadron – one that was no match for Beatty's ships – bravely offered itself as a target for several vital minutes, while Hartog and his battlecruisers limped away to safety.

16

Duelling in the Dusk

Although Scheer didn't know it, at exactly 8.26 p.m. his fleet was facing disaster. If Beatty changed course right away, he could harry the German battlecruisers to destruction. To avoid colliding with Hartog's ships, the dreadnoughts of Scheer's battle fleet had just been forced to make an emergency 90° turn to starboard. One after another, the dreadnoughts were making the turn at the exact point where *Westfalen* had altered course. Scheer had no clear idea what was happening; he saw his battlecruisers firing at an enemy, but he couldn't make out what they were shooting at. However, one after the other, the ships of his battle line were turning away from the British, while the unseen enemy kept pounding the German battlecruisers. Scheer's flagship was ninth in the line of dreadnoughts, which meant her captain had no choice but to follow the ships ahead of him. Had Scheer known where Jellicoe was, his concern would have turned to dread.

The Five-Minute Ships

While all these skirmishes had been taking place Jellicoe's dreadnoughts had been steaming towards the west-south-west, and steadily closing the range with Scheer's battle fleet. The two lines were now just 4½ miles or 9,000 yards apart. A rent in the mist would reveal the German ships, which were also still silhouetted in the fading twilight. Fortunately for Scheer, the mist still stopped the two sides from seeing each other . . . or most of them. The exception was the one portion of the German battle fleet which was still steaming towards the south. While the rest of

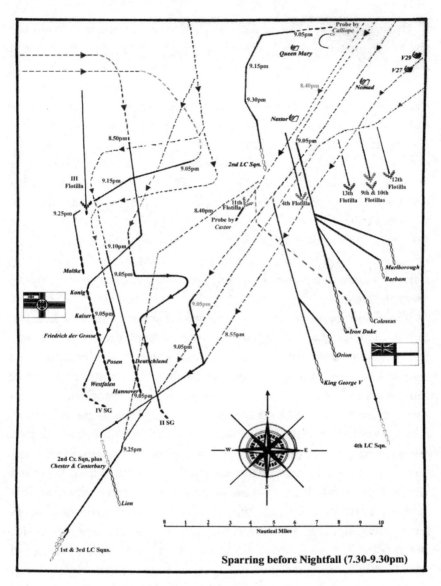

Sparring Before Nightfall (7.30–9.30 p.m.)

the fleet altered course to the west, the six old pre-dreadnoughts of Rear-Admiral Mauve's II Battle Squadron stayed on their old course. At 8.26 p.m. their lead ship, the *Hannover*, was 5,000 yards in front of Hartog's battlecruisers, and a little further to the west than the German dreadnoughts behind her. That meant they were on their own when Beatty sighted them.

During the last half hour the six German pre-dreadnoughts and the six British battlecruisers had been gradually drawing closer to each other, so that by 8.26 p.m. they were just over five miles or 10,000 yards apart. During the past few minutes, Mauve on board his flagship *Deutschland* had seen Hartog's battlecruisers firing at the enemy, but he had no idea what they were firing at. This gunnery duel told him that British dreadnoughts or battlecruisers were somewhere out there to the east; he just didn't know where. Just before 8.30 p.m., he found out; *Tiger* and *Princess Royal* spotted the German squadron and opened fire. This was a particularly uneven contest; despite the damage they had suffered, Beatty's battlecruisers still packed a powerful punch – one much larger than the poorly-armed and lightly armoured pre-dreadnoughts. These old battleships had been dubbed 'five-minute ships' by the German Navy – an estimation of just how long they would last in a fight with modern dreadnoughts.

The accuracy of that nickname was about to tested. When the British sighted Mauve's squadron, Beatty's battlecruisers were still firing at their German counterparts, and Hartog had already turned away to the west, forcing the German battle line immediately north of him to do the same. British shells were falling around the German battlecruisers and occasionally hitting them, while a few were also falling dangerously close to the leading German dreadnoughts. In fact, *Westfalen* had already been straddled, and splinters had struck her upper deck. Of all the German dreadnoughts, only the *Posen* fired back, but with absolutely no effect, as her assailants were invisible. Now, though, as the German battlecruisers limped away, the fresh target of Mauve's six pre-dreadnoughts proved too tempting a target for Beatty to resist. While a few battlecruisers still fired at Hartog's ships, most switched targets to Mauve's squadron.

The range was now a little under five miles, or 10,000 yards, well within range of the British guns. There was no clear order of firing. Beatty issued no orders, so the selection of targets was down to individual captains. *Princess Royal* fired on the *Hannover* at the front of the six-ship German line, while *Tiger* just astern of her fired on the *Hessen*, the fifth ship in the enemy line. *New Zealand* aimed at the *Schleswig-Holstein*, then after scoring a hit she switched targets to the *Schlesien*, the second German ship. *Indomitable* targeted *Pommern*, just ahead of *Hessen*, while *Lion* and *Inflexible* kept firing at the German battlecruisers. Despite being ambushed, Mauve was an experienced commander, and he immediately took in the situation. His ships were on their own and they had no real chance of firing back at the British ships with any real chance of success. Still, the six pre-dreadnoughts offered Hartog a lifeline by drawing fire away from the German battlecruisers.

So until Hartog managed to disengage, Mauve was determined to hold both his course and his nerve. He worked out it would take about five minutes for Hartog's ships to escape from Beatty – and that, coincidentally, was the life expectancy the sceptics had given his ships. Still, as the heavy shells began to fall around his near-defenceless battleships, Mauve had little choice but to see the gamble through. Later, the German official history put a brave face on it; 'Owing to interference from smoke and the indifferent visibility, the *Pommern* and *Schleswig-Holstein*, and the *Deutschland* fired only one, and the *Hessen* five, the *Hannover* eight and the *Schlesien* nine rounds from their 11-inch guns.' In fact, this return fire was an invention; the German squadron's battle reports – a conscientious series of returns – show that no shots were fired. This is hardly surprising; Beatty's battlecruisers were completely invisible against the darkening eastern horizon, apart from the flash of their guns.

In one of the *Indomitable*'s 12-inch gun turrets, the turret officer jotted down a brief account of the action as it developed; 'Many of our squadron's salvos hit, and large fires were observed on board several of their ships, and their speed seemed to decrease. By 8.42 p.m., a distinct shock and muffled explosion could be felt and heard, but no damage could be discovered, nor could any definitive cause be assigned to the occurrence.' Oddly, fifteen minutes before a similar thing happened to *Inflexible*. Her gunnery officer wrote; 'About 8.30 p.m. we all felt a violent bump, which we at first thought might have been a mine or torpedo.' One possible explanation was that both ships struck a piece of floating wreckage, left behind during the 'Run to the South'.

On board the *Derfflinger*, von Hase watched the one-sided fight. He later wrote a particularly glowing account of it. According to him, as *Derfflinger* and her consorts turned away; 'Help came from the quarter from which it was least expected. After the fleet had turned about on a southerly course our II Squadron, the old ships of the Deutschland class, found themselves in the van of the fleet. Admiral Scheer now thought the moment favourable to dispose the fleet in the best tactical formation for the withdrawal south. The II Squadron was therefore ordered to take station astern of the two modern squadrons. The officer commanding the II Squadron was carrying out this manoeuvre at this very moment, bringing his squadron west of the remainder of the fleet and of us. In doing so he came between us and the enemy, who were now pressing us hard. Suddenly the enemy saw seven big ships heading for them at top speed.'

This was not strictly true. First, the two squadrons were approaching each other fairly gradually, and as soon as he sighted the British battlecruisers, Mauve ordered his ships to turn three points (34°) to starboard, to keep the two columns from closing any further. Also, Scheer gave no such orders; until the involuntary turn to the west his whole fleet had been heading south, with the II Battle Squadron ahead of the dreadnoughts on account of the *Gefechtskehrwendung* half an hour earlier. Finally, Beatty had six battlecruisers under his command, not seven. Von Hase's account became even more tangled as he went on to describe what happened next; 'At the same time the tireless destroyers again pressed home the attack. This was too much for them – the enemy turned about and disappeared into the twilight. We didn't want to see any more of them, but felt a great relief at this sudden improvement in our situation.' This was wildly inaccurate, and very misleading.

During their gunnery duel with the pre-dreadnoughts, Beatty's ships kept on their original heading; in fact, they didn't change course for another half hour. They certainly didn't turn away and break off the action. The problem for Beatty, though, was one of speed. His battlecruisers were making about 25 knots, close to their top speed. By contrast, on a good day Mauve's squadron could make 18 knots, and it appears when the two sides clashed, his ships were steaming at about two knots less than that. At 8.30 p.m., the pre-dreadnoughts were a little behind the beam of the British, and throughout the five-minute exchange the British ships kept drawing ahead. Then, after enduring their fire for five minutes, it was Mauve rather than Beatty who turned away, an alteration from 212° to 263°. That meant that since first sighting Beatty, the pre-dreadnoughts had altered course by a total of 60°, or just over five points. If anyone turned away it was Mauve – and with good reason.

Von Hase's account was no doubt coloured by his willingness to show his old squadron in a good light. This comes across in what he wrote next; 'I saw all the good friends of my old squadron coming up, the good old *Hessen*, in which I served for five years, the *Pommern*, the *Schleswig-Holstein* and others. They were shooting vigorously and themselves came under a heavy fire. But it was not long before the enemy had had enough. I wonder if they would have turned about if they had known what kind of ships these were! They were the famous German five minute ships, to settle which the Englishmen could not spare five minutes, but bravely withdrew!' In fact, what brought the firing to an end was a combination of widening range, the mist, the growing darkness and a general inability to spot the fall of shot. One by one, the British battlecruisers ceased fire; the last shot was fired by the *New Zealand* at 8.39 p.m.

Two of the German pre-dreadnoughts were hit during those long, fraught minutes. *Schleswig-Holstein* and *Pommern* both suffered one hit apiece. *Pommern* was barely damaged, but the hit on the *Schleswig-Holstein* was more serious; at 8.32 p.m., a 12-inch shell from *New Zealand* struck her amidships, ripping a hole in her upper deck and putting a secondary gun out of action. Three German sailors were killed and nine wounded. By then, the German ships – both the pre-dreadnoughts and the battlecruisers – had ceased fire. Von Hase recorded that; 'At 10.31 p.m. [8.31 p.m.] my faithful log keeper recorded the last shot fired by the *Derfflinger's* heavy guns.' The hit by *New Zealand* was a historic one. At the time nobody would have credited it, but this was the last clash between British and German capital ships during the battle. In fact, apart from a skirmish with Russian pre-dreadnoughts off Riga in 1917, it was the last clash of its kind of the entire war.

By now, it was too dark to see the enemy ships, and as von Hase put it; 'The long northern day came to an end.' This last gunnery duel was a strange way to end the day, but Mauve's intervention had probably saved Scheer's battle fleet. It had almost certainly rescued the German battlecruisers from piecemeal destruction. Before the sortie began, Scheer had been reluctant to bring along his pre-dreadnoughts; only Mauve's persuasiveness led to them being included. Now though, their presence had been justified, as it had drawn Beatty's fire from the German battlecruisers at a critical moment. More importantly, Mauve's appearance prevented Beatty from altering course in pursuit of the enemy battlecruisers, and so bringing Scheer to battle during the last minutes of twilight. If he had, then Jellicoe could have caught the still disorganised High Seas Fleet between two fires. Mauve, though, was never properly credited by Scheer for his fleet-saving intervention.

Jerram's Great Chance

Since his skirmish half an hour before, Commodore Le Mesurier's 4th Light Cruiser Squadron had been formed up on either side of Vice-Admiral Jerram's dreadnoughts. This meant they were at the head of the British battle line. A little before 9 p.m. they were still there – two light cruisers to port of Jerram's flagship, and three to starboard. Suddenly, lookouts on the *Caroline* spotted three enemy ships appear out of the gloom off their starboard quarter. They were about 10,000 yards away, and the lookouts thought they might be enemy pre-dreadnoughts. Just in front of them were low shapes that looked suspiciously like enemy destroyers. Captain Henry Crooke of the *Caroline* radioed the sighting report to Le Mesurier, whose flagship *Calliope* was over on the far side of the dreadnoughts. He also sent a warning to Jerram's flagship, *King George V*, that an enemy torpedo attack was likely. Another clash now seemed inevitable.

For some reason the message never reached Jerram. However, Commodore Hawksley of the 11th Destroyer Flotilla in the light cruiser *Castor* intercepted it easily enough. He watched the *Caroline* turn to investigate, accompanied by her two consorts *Comus* and *Royalist*, both part of Le Mesurier's squadron. Hawksley ordered his destroyers to follow. This was the second probe by Le Mesurier's squadron into the gloom to the west. It soon turned out these weren't pre-dreadnoughts at all. They were dreadnoughts – the leading three ships of the German battle fleet. At 8.45 p.m., having avoided colliding with the German battlecruisers, the front of the German dreadnought column had turned round to the south again. What Crooke's lookouts had seen were the *Westfalen*, *Nassau* and *Rheinland*, leading the long column of German dreadnoughts.

Crooke was still not sure what these ships were. So he ordered the searchlight on his bridge wing to flash a recognition challenge. The only response was a star shell fired from one of the secondary guns of the *Nassau*. That clinched it; at that stage of the war British ships weren't equipped with star shells, but the Germans were. Crooke immediately gave the order to attack. As light from the star shell bathed the sea with its glow, *Caroline* and *Royalist* spurred forward, with German shells falling all around them. Amazingly none of the shells hit them, and the range dropped rapidly. A little after 9.05 p.m., they swung round to unleash their torpedoes. Each carried four 21-inch Mark IV torpedoes, and these were launched at a range of about 5,000 yards. Then the cruisers turned away, weaving through the shell splashes. For the moment, though, Hawksley's destroyers didn't join the attack.

On the *Caroline*, the ship's carpenter Fred Fielder remembered those tense moments; 'The shells screamed over our heads, some dropping between us and our own ships . . . by this time we had set up a smoke screen, and escaped from an extremely perilous position'. He added; 'The small ship would have been literally blown off the water had any of the broadsides fired at us got home.' This gallant little attack could well have resulted in the crippling of a German dreadnought. Two of the torpedoes almost hit the *Nassau*; one streaked in front of her bows, the other – thanks to a faulty depth setting – passed underneath her hull. Nassau and *Westfalen* turned hard to starboard to avoid the torpedoes, and by the time they turned back onto their old course the British cruisers had gone. Fred Fielder put the poor German shooting down to 'a state of panic or blue funk', but it was more likely that this brief turn away had thrown off the gunners' aim.

The reason Hawksley hadn't taken part in the torpedo run was because he expected the British dreadnoughts behind him to open fire, and didn't want to get in the way. Later he explained; 'I turned the flotilla away from the battlecruisers and expected the fleet to open fire at them.' However, Jerram's big guns remained silent. Hawksley then decided; 'It was not dark enough to make an attack unsupported by fire from the fleet.' He added; 'The battlecruisers turned off to starboard and were lost sight of.' These were not battlecruisers of course; they were powerful dreadnoughts. So the German I Battle Squadron was spared a determined attack just as darkness began to cloak their ships from the enemy. Just as importantly, thanks to Jerram, a last gasp chance to deal a crippling blow to the High Seas Fleet was about to be missed.

A few minutes later, lookouts on the *King George V* spotted the line of enemy ships again, now 11,000 yards off their starboard bow. Crooke sighted them too, and ordered his cruisers to make another attack. Within seconds a signal from the *King George V* countermanded this order. Instead, Jerram signalled Jellicoe that the ships his men had sighted were actually Beatty's battlecruisers. This made no sense. Minutes before, Jerram had watched as Crooke had carried out his torpedo attack, and he must have seen the German star shell. He'd lost touch with Beatty over an hour before, but Beatty had been well ahead of Jerram when he disappeared. There was no reason to expect him to reappear off the beam of the slower-moving dreadnoughts. Jerram's flag captain Frederick Field begged him to open fire, as did several other officers, but Jerram was adamant. These were British ships, and he wouldn't fire on them.

Four ships astern of Jerram was the *Orion*, flagship of Rear-Admiral Arthur Leveson, commander of the 2nd Division – half of Jerram's squadron. On her bridge, the same scene was repeated; Captain Oliver Blackhouse and his First Lieutenant, Commander Home, both implored Leveson to turn a Nelsonian blind eye to Jerram's orders and to open fire. They could clearly see they were enemy dreadnoughts, and Leveson probably could too. The admiral was even begged to ignore orders, just like Nelson at the battles of St Vincent and Copenhagen, and so make his name 'as famous as Nelson's'. These stirring words were uttered in vain; Leveson was a product of the Victorian navy, and to him obedience and discipline were everything. He thought for a moment, then declared; 'We must follow our next ahead.' There would be no last-minute gunnery duel, and a last golden opportunity to wreak destruction on Scheer's fleet slipped away.

This was particularly unfortunate as, while the German dreadnoughts could still be dimly seen, the British battle line was invisible to their opponents. Even a very brief engagement might well have forced the German battle line to alter course to the west again and sow confusion in the German line. So the two fleets kept steaming on virtually parallel courses until darkness finally cloaked the enemy. The long hours of daylight were over and the last chance of an effective gunnery duel had passed. As darkness fell, both Jellicoe on the *Iron Duke* and Scheer on the *Friedrich der Grosse* considered their options. Of the two, Jellicoe was in the more enviable position. He knew that darkness would last for just five hours. When dawn came, he felt confident that he'd be able to finish the battle and destroy the High Seas Fleet once and for all. For his part, Scheer was trapped, and only a miracle – or some deft manoeuvring – could save his ships from destruction.

17

The Cover of Night

Jellicoe should have felt pleased with his fleet's performance that afternoon. He had outmanoeuvred Scheer throughout the long day and had
outfought him too. The German admiral had been forced to make three
emergency battle turns away, two of them under withering British fire.
Despite these, the British still lay between the German fleet and its base.
That evening, Chief of Staff Rear-Admiral Charles Madden remembered
that at sunset, Jellicoe declared; 'Everything that had happened had been
according to expectation.' Certainly there had been setbacks; Jellicoe's
own flagship had passed close by the wreckage of the *Invincible*, and he
had watched helplessly as the *Defence* blew up. Both *Warspite* and *Warrior*
had been badly damaged, and were now detached from the fleet and
heading home. *Marlborough* had been torpedoed, but she was still keeping
up with the rest of her squadron. All this though, did very little to reduce
the deadly fighting potential of the Grand Fleet.

Jellicoe still didn't know about the loss of *Queen Mary* or *Indefatigable*,
or of the damage suffered by the rest of the Battlecruiser Fleet. Beatty
simply hadn't told him. In fact, the Vice-Admiral had been singularly
uncommunicative all day. Even now, Jellicoe didn't really know where
Beatty was, other than somewhere ahead of him. Still, he knew about
the pounding taken by Hipper's ships, three of which were barely able to
stay afloat. Jellicoe had seen them during their 'death ride' and knew
they couldn't take much more punishment. The German dreadnoughts
had also suffered, and Jellicoe was confident that come morning he
would be able to finish what he'd started. All he had to do was to make

it through the next five hours of darkness. That meant avoiding a night action and enemy torpedo attacks. If he stayed between Scheer and Wilhelmshaven, then when dawn came, the High Seas Fleet would be at his mercy.

Jellicoe's Deployment

The Grand Fleet could have pressed home an attack that evening, angling its line through the darkness to the west until it made contact with Scheer's dreadnoughts. Both fleets had large numbers of destroyers and most of the boats still had torpedoes. However, Jellicoe simply didn't want to risk everything in a night action, a form of sea battle he saw as little more than a lottery. The High Seas Fleet had practised night fighting, and were well-versed in manoeuvring their ships in the dark. They had superb searchlights and had practised using them to direct the fire of their guns in the dark. By contrast, the British had almost no training in this key area. This lack of expertise seemed to be particularly apparent among the destroyer flotillas, a weakness which was soon to become all too apparent.

Bill Bennet, a boy seaman on the cruiser *Comus* reinforced this point about the searchlights when he wrote; 'When we switched off our searchlights we had to find tarpaulins to throw over them to hide the glowing carbons that stood out like full moons, and gave the enemy the chance to have a bang at us. When the German searchlights were switched off, there was damn all to see – we learned later his lights had iris shutters fitted.' As for the lack of training, this was illustrated by Lieutenant Stephen King-Hall from the cruiser *Southampton*. He recalled; 'At approximately 9.45 p.m. we suddenly saw a flotilla of destroyers rushing at us. Just as we were about to open fire, we saw that they were our own. As they dashed past our line (how we cursed their haphazard behaviour) one of them fired a 4-inch at us, but didn't hit anyone.' He added; 'I imagine a gunlayer lost his head.'

Another problem in the Grand Fleet was its primitive approach to night-recognition signals. Signal challenges and responses were flashed between ships by Aldis Lamp, and this was far more visible than the standard German method – the hoisting of green lights from the masthead. This became even more critical when the Germans worked out what evening's recognition signal was being used by the British.

Lieutenant Heinrich Bassenge of the *Elbing* remembered his cruiser's nocturnal encounter with the *Castor*; 'We showed them the English recognition signals which they acknowledged. As we were sure it was the enemy we opened up a heavy fire . . .' So Jellicoe rightly feared that a night action would inevitably be costly, and would lead to chaos; ships colliding with each other, unseen destroyers launching torpedo attacks at point-blank range, and a general atmosphere of confusion and chaos. That really was not Jellicoe's style at all.

In the Grand Fleet's *Battle Orders* issued before Jutland, Jellicoe described the exact situation facing his fleet that evening. In a section entitled *If the action has been indecisive*, he wrote; 'It may be necessary to force or accept action so late in the day that a decisive stage will not be reached before darkness necessitates breaking off the main engagement.' In these circumstances; 'It may be desirable to retire the fleet at dark, if the enemy still possesses a great preponderance of torpedo craft with which to attack.' This was Jellicoe's real fear; he was confident that in a daylight gunnery duel his numbers and heavier guns would ensure victory. He could just as easily lose this edge though if some of his dread-noughts were sunk by enemy torpedoes, fired under cover of darkness. So he resolutely avoided a night action he saw as unnecessary. Instead, he would block Scheer's route to Wilhelmshaven, and the battle would be renewed at dawn, on Jellicoe's terms.

At 9 p.m., Jellicoe firmly rejected the launching of a night action. That was when he ordered his battle fleet to turn away from the enemy by divisions and steer towards the south-south-east. This meant that instead of drawing closer to Scheer, the British dreadnoughts were now gradually pulling away from him. This was not just about avoiding a night action; Jellicoe was also thinking strategically. In a letter to the Admiralty written after the battle, Jellicoe explained his thinking. 'At 9 p.m., light being very bad, mist increasing, fleet was turned to a course South, to pass between Mine Area 1 and Horns Reef, in order to intercept enemy should he return by either Sylt or Ems Channels. Flotillas were disposed five miles astern of the fleet.' In other words, while he didn't want to risk a night battle, he wanted to make sure he kept remained firmly between Scheer and his base. Jellicoe was playing a waiting game. After all, he could afford to, as it was Scheer who was trapped and unable to escape.

Fifteen minutes later, as the six divisions or columns of the British battle fleet maintained their course, Commodore Goodenough reported that his cruisers had lost sight of the enemy. During the last minutes of twilight, his four cruisers had fought a running skirmish with German destroyers, but the enemy pulled back, and since then everything had been quiet. For Jellicoe this confirmed that the two fleets had broken contact for the night. So, two minutes later, he ordered his battle fleet to assume its night cruising formation. The six columns of divisions would form into three columns of squadrons, each of eight dreadnoughts, with a mile separating each one. The cruiser squadrons would take station in front, behind and on the sides of the battle fleet, while the destroyers – usually positioned with the cruisers – would now obey Jellicoe's new orders and follow astern of the dreadnoughts, just in case Scheer tried to work his way round the back of the Grand Fleet.

Jellicoe's other fear – apart from a torpedo attack – was that Scheer might evade him during the night. A close examination of the chart showed that Scheer had four routes back to his base – four options. The first was easily discounted; the transit of the Skagerrak, and a voyage around the Danish peninsula. At 9 p.m. the High Seas Fleet was just over 340 miles from the Lillebaelt (Little Belt) between the island of Funen and the eastern coast of the Danish mainland. Not only would this passage be lengthy, but it meant that the slower-moving or badly damaged German ships would never make it home. Jellicoe's fleet could easily overhaul and destroy them the following morning. In the end only one group of German destroyers, the II Flotilla, returned home that way, after being isolated from the rest of the High Seas Fleet during the night. That left three other routes, all of which led through or round the British and German minefields to reach the German Bight.

The two main channels were known as the Ems and Sylt routes. The first of these skirted the western side of the known British minefields, the outer limit of which ran westwards from the Amrum Bank for 25 miles, and then down to the south-west in the direction of the Dutch Frisian Islands. The Amrum Bank was 25 miles from the island of Sylt, which lay just off the coast near the Danish-German border. The gap between the island and the bank was known as the Amrum Channel, and German minesweepers regularly swept the area to keep it clear. The Amrum lightship, on the southern end of the bank, marked the beginning of the German defensive minefields. To reach the Amrum Channel, the German fleet would have to pass close to the Horns Reef Lightship, which marked the western end of Horns Reef, 35 miles from the Danish coast. This option, the Sylt route, was Scheer's shortest way home.

Scheer's other option was the Ems route. He would reach it by steaming southwards, down the western edge of the British minefields, to within sight of the Dutch Frisian Islands. From there, the route followed the swept channel close to the coast that passed through the German minefields. This route led east past the mouth of the River Ems to reach the Jade Estuary and Wilhelmshaven. Jellicoe knew that the Germans also used a fourth route which went through a cleared channel in the British minefields from its north-western corner that led to the island of Helgoland. However, he was not sure exactly where it started. Blocking it was fairly easy, though, as was preventing Scheer from reaching Horns Reef. All Jellicoe had to do was to keep his British fleet to the east of the Germans.

Jellicoe considered Scheer might try to take the Sylt route by way of Horns Reef, but he felt this was a high-risk option, as it meant fighting his way past the Grand Fleet. Twice that afternoon Scheer had clashed with Jellicoe's dreadnoughts. Both times he had cried off. Therefore, Jellicoe felt it unlikely Scheer would make a third attempt, even under the cover of darkness. So Jellicoe's night-time deployment was based on Scheer's taking one of the two southern routes home; the Ems route or the less well-defined channel through the British minefields leading to Helgoland. However, just in case Scheer tried sneaking past him in the night, Jellicoe's destroyers were now strung out astern of him, acting as a tripwire to warn him of any German move towards the Horns Reef. So Jellicoe felt he had done all he could to bottle up Scheer, until dawn allowed him to finish the destruction of the German fleet.

His dispositions done, Jellicoe sent a general signal to the fleet; 'No night intentions'. This effectively told his captains that if all went well there would be no battle until morning. That meant they could do what they could to repair any damage to their ships, tend to their wounded, or give their men a few hours of much-needed rest. On most ships, the men remained at action stations throughout the night, but at least they could be fed – with soup, sandwiches, rum and cocoa – a welcome respite after so many hours of tension and drama. This arranged, Jellicoe lay down fully dressed on his sleeping cot in his little night cabin located immediately behind the *Iron Duke*'s bridge. Before he retired, he left orders to be woken up if there was any significant development. He would certainly need his sleep. He wanted to be fresh and ready for battle when dawn broke in less than four hours' time.

Scheer's Great Gamble

Vice-Admiral Scheer had also been considering his options that evening, and knew perfectly well how precarious his position was. Dawn would come a little after 2 a.m., and soon after the British would have enough light to renew the battle. With his fleet outnumbered and encumbered by his damaged battlecruisers and vulnerable pre-dreadnoughts, it was a battle Scheer stood little chance of winning. Scheer was faced with the four options Jellicoe had worked out. Of these, he immediately dismissed the Skagerrak route, for the same reason as Jellicoe; it would mean the sacrifice of his slower ships. However, unlike Jellicoe he also saw the two southern options as unpalatable. First, the channel leading through the British minefields towards Helgoland was a one-way route. Scheer had used it the previous night, but the seaward entrance to this swept channel was unmarked, and so finding it after a day of navigational dead reckoning was nigh-on impossible.

At 9 p.m., the start of the Ems route was 180 miles away, the equivalent of twelve hours of steaming, or more if his slower and damaged ships tried to keep up. With sunrise a little after 2 a.m., by 3 a.m. there would be enough light for the gunnery direction teams on both sides to ply their trade. This meant that if he went south, Scheer would have to fight a running battle lasting more than six hours. That would destroy his fleet. Also, Beatty's battlecruisers were somewhere ahead of him, between his fleet and the mouth of the Ems channel. He would have to fight these battlecruisers, and Beatty had the strength to delay Scheer until Jellicoe could intervene. Given the numerical superiority of the Grand Fleet and the vulnerable state of many of his warships, the prospect of a fight with Beatty, then a running battle with Jellicoe was unacceptable. That left Scheer with the Sylt route option, the riskiest one of them all.

Still, Scheer knew something that gave the option a very faint chance of success. During the last of the twilight skirmishes, two German destroyer flotillas deployed behind the battle line carried out a reconnaissance to the east. They tangled with Commodore Goodenough's light cruisers, and achieved nothing concrete, but at least this probe gave Scheer an impression of just how far the British battle line stretched. The destroyer crews had managed to peer beyond the British cruisers, and had seen the end of Jellicoe's dreadnought columns heading towards the south. Scheer wrote later that this information told him where Jellicoe's battle line ended. 'If we could succeed in warding off the enemy's encircling movement, and could be the first to reach Horns Reef, then the liberty of decision for the next morning was assured to us.' Scheer made up his mind. He would try to slip past Jellicoe's battle fleet in the night. Failing that, he would fight his way through it.

Fighting though, was not really a viable option for at least one of the German capital ships. On board the *Derfflinger*, von Hase remembered just how bad the situation was; 'The gun firing had ceased, but now a stubborn struggle was waged against fire and water. Although as far as possible everything inflammable had been taken out of the ship, the fire continued to spread, fed principally by linoleum, the wooden decks, clothing and oil paints. About ten o'clock we had practically mastered the flames, the fire now only smouldering in a few isolated places. The "Caesar" and "Dora" turrets were still smoking, and giving out clouds of thick yellow gas from time to time, but this gradually ceased after the ammunition chambers had been flooded. No-one could have believed the ship could endure so much heavy fire.' He rightly added that this was a splendid testimony to the shipbuilders. Still, if *Derfflinger* was to survive, she needed to break through the British fleet.

This daring manoeuvre began with a deceptively simple order. At 9.14 p.m., Scheer ordered his battle fleet to steer 'SSE¼E – this course is to be maintained. Speed 16 knots. II Squadron take station at the rear of the line. Battlecruisers are to prolong the line astern.' This was just the opening move. Now, though, instead of angling away to the south, his fleet was running parallel to the British battle fleet. Next, Scheer needed to reorganise his fleet before it reached the British line. At 9.20 p.m., *Westfalen*, the leading ship of the column of German dreadnoughts, was ordered to alter course to the south-west, to pass clear of the pre-dreadnoughts ahead of her. Scheer wanted to form his battle fleet into one unbroken line, and knew he needed his best ships at its head.

Normally that would be the more modern dreadnoughts of Behncke's III Battle Squadron, but they had suffered damage, and so he decided to lead with Schmidt's I Battle Squadron instead.

On board the *Deutschland*, Mauve acknowledged the order and kept steadily on his course, but he reduced speed slightly, to make it easier for the dreadnoughts to overtake him. They were now approaching him off his starboard quarter, having jinked back onto a parallel course. In front of his six pre-dreadnoughts were the cruisers of the II and IV Scouting Groups, while the destroyers raced past, ordered forward by Scheer to form a protective screen ahead of the fleet. He saw something else, too. Ahead of him in the dark he glimpsed a light, revealing the presence of British warships. He didn't know it, but this was the masthead light of the armoured cruiser *Shannon*, part of the 2nd Cruiser Squadron which was then steaming southwards to join up with Beatty. While the rest of the Grand Fleet was to the east, Beatty's battlecruisers and now *Shannon* and her three consorts were to the south of the High Seas Fleet. Thanks to that light, Mauve and Scheer also now knew they were there.

At 9.29 p.m., Scheer sent another signal, ordering the pre-dreadnoughts to join the line behind Behncke's dreadnoughts. So, at 9.40 p.m., Mauve gave the order for his own *Gefechtskehrtwendung*, as the column of German dreadnoughts lay off his starboard quarter. With an easy precision borne of practice, the six pre-dreadnoughts turned to port, and formed a new line, heading in the opposite direction. Now *Deutschland* was back in the lead again, and the *Hannover* brought up the rear. His aim was to turn to circle to port and tuck his squadron in at the back of the German battle line. As he did so, he was surprised to see two battlecruisers approach out of the darkness ahead of him. It was *Moltke* and *Seydlitz*, which had approached from the north, then manoeuvred around to the east slightly to avoid the pre-dreadnoughts as they raced past. As Mauve peered at *Moltke*, he noticed she was flying the pennant of Vice-Admiral Hipper.

While the German battle fleet was being reordered, Hipper had seized the chance to reclaim control of his command. At 9.30 p.m., he ordered the *Moltke* to haul out of line and heave to, and as the destroyer *G-39* came alongside, Hipper and his staff scrambled up the nets strung along the battlecruiser's side. His first order was for his battlecruisers to

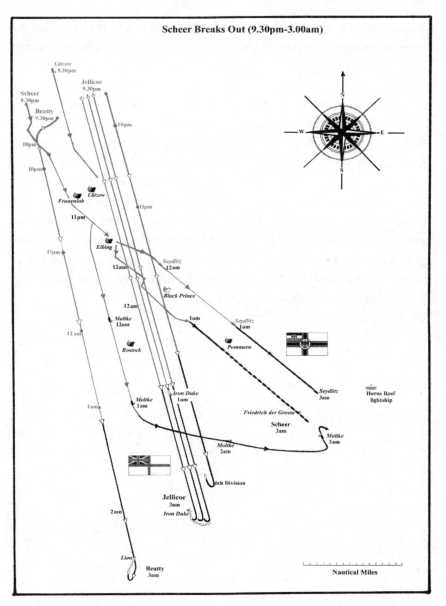

Scheer Breaks Out (9.30 pm– 3.00 a.m.)

increase speed, to work their way forward to their proper place at the head of the German battle line. *Derfflinger* and *Von der Tann* were in no condition to comply with these orders though, and as the *Moltke* steamed off, followed by the *Seydlitz*, Captain Hartog quietly formed up astern of the line of German dreadnoughts. The cruiser *Regensburg* did likewise, as Commodore Heinrich's destroyers were now either far ahead or astern of the battle line. Until they returned, the battle line itself was the safest place to be.

Next, Scheer angled his battle line a little further towards the east, onto a new heading of south-south-east by ¾ east (a course of 150°). This was only a small change, of course, but it meant that even though the fleets were still 14 miles apart, their courses were converging. If seen from the air, the two courses would have formed a 'V', which would bring the two fleets together about 20 miles to the south. That meeting, though, depended on the two fleets sailing at the same speed. In fact, the British were steaming at 17 knots, one knot faster than the Germans, and so they were very slowly drawing ahead. Jellicoe would reach the apex of the 'V' before Scheer, while the German fleet would turn the 'V' into an 'X' by crossing Jellicoe's wake some time before midnight. Then the breakout attempt would begin in earnest.

18

Probing the Line

The two fleets were moving closer to each other, one side anticipating a clash, the other unaware that the opposing fleet was heading nearer. Meanwhile, the protective screens of light cruisers and destroyers were also drawing together between the two fleets. While the dreadnoughts might still have been several miles apart, these screening forces were much closer, and were moving closer still. On the eastern side of the German fleet, von Reuter's IV Scouting Group steamed through the darkness. He should have been further to the south-west, ahead of the dreadnoughts, but a navigational error meant that his five light cruisers now lay between the two fleets. They were joined by others. The light cruiser *Rostock*, flagship of the battle fleet's destroyer flotillas was in the same area, as Commodore Michelsen struggled to stay within range of his destroyers, now spread out in a screen ahead of the fleet. For some mutual support he decided to join von Reuter's force, bringing Reuter's strength up to six ships.

Rear Admiral Bödicker's II Scouting Group was also between the two battle fleets, but after losing the *Wiesbaden*, his strength was down to just three ships. Shortly before 10 p.m., he was reduced to two, as the *Elbing* developed a condenser problem and had to drop astern of her faster-moving consorts. Like Commodore Michelsen of the *Rostock*, Commander Madlung of the *Elbing* didn't want to blunder around on his own in the darkness, with the British somewhere out there to port. So, when he saw von Reuter's line of cruisers, he joined them, taking up station between the *Frankfurt* and the *Rostock*. With just two ships left,

Bödicker didn't fancy running into a British cruiser squadron either, but still he headed east until he saw the dim shapes of British dreadnoughts ahead of him. He turned away to port, and then looped round to steam on a reciprocal course to the British. He did that for ten more minutes, just to make sure of the enemy's heading. He then turned away without being seen and headed back towards his own fleet.

Tension was mounting in the German fleet, as everyone sensed that the two battle fleets were approaching each other. However, according to Vice-Admiral Adolf von Trotha, Scheer's Chief of Staff, the atmosphere on the bridge of the *Friedrich der Grosse* was one of readiness; 'The next [dreadnought] ahead was visible only as a black silhouette, accompanied by the weak shimmering light of her stern lantern playing on the foam of the propeller wash, and a point of light on the forecastle which gave the helmsman the correct line for our own ship – but otherwise there was complete darkness.' He added; 'the engineers . . . were careful not to produce any sparks from the funnels, which would betray our position . . . Silent darkness! Tense attentiveness! . . . Hundreds of eyes spied into the night, hundreds of senses tensed themselves in the highest expectation and readiness.' Still the great column of warships steamed on through the night, drawing ever closer to the enemy.

Far ahead of the Germans, the bridge crew of the battlecruiser *Princess Royal* realised they didn't know that evening's night-recognition signals, as their signal book had been destroyed by an enemy shell. So Captain Walter Cowan ordered his yeoman to ask the flagship. At 9.30 p.m., the request was sent to the *Lion* using an Aldis signal lamp. Two minutes later, the information was flashed back. Other eyes saw the message too. Both messages were sent in plain English, rather than in code. The German light cruiser *Elbing* was a few miles astern, and her lookouts spotted the exchange, or at least most of it. They certainly saw enough to learn that the British recognition challenge that night began with the letter 'Ü'. This was passed on to the *Frankfurt*, and at 10.22 p.m. she transmitted the news to the rest of the fleet. After some bright officer pointed out the letter didn't exist in English, the challenge was changed to 'UA'. Minutes later this little nugget was used to startlingly good effect.

A Flurry of Destroyers

Seven miles north of Bödicker in the *Frankfurt*, another far more dramatic encounter was taking place. An hour before, German destroyers from the II and V Flotillas had carried out a reconnaissance towards the east, only to run into Commodore Goodenough's light cruisers. After a brief but furious exchange of fire they withdrew into the mist, and Goodenough continued on towards the south-west, screening the eastern flank of Jellicoe's dreadnoughts. Goodenough maintained this course until 10 p.m., when he turned onto the same heading as the rest of the British fleet. This, though, meant that he was now almost due north of Bödicker and von Reuter. More significantly, *Frankfurt* and *Pillau* were now heading towards the north-west, having confirmed the position of the British battle line. This meant that Bödicker and Goodenough were now on a collision course. This, though, wouldn't be the first clash of the night.

Three miles to the north-east of Goodenough in the *Southampton*, a line of British destroyers were racing northwards to take up their assigned position five miles astern of their own dreadnoughts. These were the boats of the 4th Destroyer Flotilla, commanded by Captain Charles Wintour, whose flagship was the destroyer *Tipperary*. His twelve boats were deployed in a long column, and had been steaming at 20 knots as they surged northwards. At 9.45 p.m. the column reached its allotted station and Wintour gave the order that would turn it about onto its new heading. The boats were halfway through their turn when the Germans struck, having approached unseen from the north-west. The attackers were the nine destroyers of Lieutenant-Commander Gottlieb von Koch's VII Flotilla, who were making a fresh probe to the west in an attempt to locate the British dreadnoughts. Instead they came upon Wintour's flotilla, whose crews were too taken up by their own manoeuvring to notice the approach of the German destroyers.

At first, von Koch thought the destroyers ahead of him were those of the II Flotilla, which had become detached from the rest of the German fleet. Von Koch flashed a recognition signal from the bridge of his flagship *S-24* but it went unanswered. Seconds later, he realised that the boats ahead of him were British destroyers. He ordered his flotilla to attack, and his nine boats swooped in just as the British column was completing its turn. The four leading boats, including the *S-24*, fired a single torpedo each at the enemy. As these torpedoes began racing towards the British column von Koch ordered his boats to disengage, and they turned away. He had no wish to be drawn into a close-range fight with better-armed British destroyers. Besides, he and his men had a long night ahead of them. The torpedoes missed, but Lieutenant Commander Reginald Goff, commanding the British destroyer *Garland*, watched two of them pass close under his stern. If he had turned a few seconds later, he could have been blown to pieces.

Goff was at the back of the column, and while several boats must have seen von Koch's flashing signal lamp, he was the only commander to react. He fired his after 4-inch gun at the departing Germans, and radioed his sighting report to Wintour in the *Tipperary*. By then though, the Germans had gone, and so Wintour followed his orders and stayed on his allotted course. After all, there was a bigger picture here. His flotilla was only the first of four that were deployed five miles astern of the Grand Fleet. To the east the 9th, 10th, 12th and 13th flotillas were moving north to take up station to the east of Wintour. The idea was that if Scheer tried to work his way past the British dreadnoughts, then he would fall foul of this solid mass of destroyers. Given that the visibility on that moonless night was less than a thousand yards, then Scheer's dreadnoughts could well face a massed torpedo attack, launched at point-blank range if they came within range.

On the destroyer, *Broke*, the navigating officer never even noticed the German boats. Instead, he saw the flames thrown up by the burning *Southampton*; 'At about 9.50 p.m. a very violent explosion was seen almost right ahead, flames reaching a height of several hundred feet.' This was an exaggeration; observers on other British cruisers recall a fierce blaze, but no notable explosion or huge tower of flame. Less explicably, the *Broke* then hit something in the water; 'For one moment the ship suddenly seemed to stop dead. Then, giving a series of short heaves, she went on again. On the bridge we immediately thought that we had fouled some submerged obstruction, but the engine room reported that it felt like an underwater explosion. At all events, no damage was done.' Although there is no clear explanation for this, one of the German torpedoes might have exploded prematurely, and these were the shock waves from the underwater blast.

What this little clash did reveal was that the Germans were better trained at night fighting, and were less likely to make blunders in the darkness. Just as importantly, they now knew roughly where the British ships were, while their opponents expected the short night to pass without any major incident, and were largely unprepared for a night battle. After all, Jellicoe himself had signalled he had no intention to initiate a night-time action, and while the British crews remained at action stations, the general feeling was that there would be no more fighting before the morning. Certainly, there might be the odd clash between cruiser or destroyer screens, encounters like the one between Wintour and von Koch's flotillas, but the chances of anything more substantial were seen as remote. Soon, when Scheer finally made his move, this dangerous combination of poor training and general complacency would cost the British dear.

Castor in the Spotlight

At the same moment these destroyers were clashing, the light cruiser *Castor*, flagship of the 11th Destroyer Flotilla, was a few miles to the south, leading her own charges into position astern of the Grand Fleet. The *Castor*, flagship of Commodore Hawksley, was at the head of the line, with fifteen destroyers divided into two half-flotillas following astern of her. Like Wintour's boats, they were moving north to take up station, in their case on the starboard beam of the battle fleet. They weren't alone, though. The *Frankfurt* and the *Pillau* were silently watching them. When the range was just 1,200 yards, the two German cruisers launched their torpedoes at the *Castor*, and then turned away into the darkness. They weren't seen; Bödicker had given orders not to use searchlights or to open fire. To do so would reveal their presence and attract a swarm of British destroyers. At that moment, though, the cruiser altered course to port, and the torpedoes ran past her unseen.

Having reached their station at 10 p.m., Hawksley's destroyers neatly reversed course and formed a new line heading towards the south-south-east. They were now running parallel to their battle fleet, the nearest column of which – Jerram's 2nd Battle Squadron – was five miles to the south-east. *Castor*'s lookouts hadn't spotted Bödicker's two cruisers because they were looking the wrong way. The Germans had got between Hawksley's destroyers and Jerram's dreadnoughts. As Bödicker crept away, a new group of German cruisers entered the arena. Von Reuter's IV Scouting Group, now reinforced by *Elbing* and *Rostock*, was a few thousand yards to the west of Hawksley, and following a similar heading. By then, von Reuter's column of seven light cruisers had split into two groups. At 10.15 p.m., the *Castor* and her charges materialised out of the darkness on the port side of the second group, the light cruisers cruisers *Hamburg*, *Elbing* and *Rostock*.

The two sides were less than 1,200 yards apart, with the *Castor* and her destroyers almost due east of the three German cruisers. The senior German commander on the spot was Captain Hermann Bauer, the fleet's *Führer der Unterseeboote* (Commander of U-Boats). *Hamburg* was his flagship, but for the operation she was temporarily attached to von Reuter's Scouting Group. Essentially then, Bauer was an observer, but his quick thinking gave the Germans a slight edge. He suggested that Lieutenant-Commander Gerhard von Gaudecker, commanding the *Hamburg*, might use his signal lamp and flash the British recognition signal at the *Castor*. This was far more effective than he could have hoped. It allowed him to get a hundred yards closer to the British line. Then, on von Gaudecker's order, the three cruisers switched on their searchlights and opened fire. The poor *Castor* was bathed in light, and German shells began ripping into her hull and superstructure.

The *Castor* carried four 6-inch guns, and she returned fire as best she could, despite being heavily outgunned. After five minutes of this unequal contest she turned away to port, her superstructure on fire, three holes piercing her hull and her decks torn and splintered. She had been hit ten times in the brief exchange; twelve of her crew had been killed, and another 23 injured. Fortunately, though, after damage control teams worked their way onto her boat deck, they discovered most of the flames were coming from the ship's motor pinnace, which was blazing fiercely. This, of course, made the cruiser visible for miles. An officer on board the *Castor* described the situation; 'They fired only at us, being apparently unable to hit our destroyers, which were painted black.' He added; 'We fired a torpedo at the leading Hun, and the two after 6-inch guns – which were not being directly fired at – making very good practice at the enemy.'

Although the *Castor* was firing back, she was being pounded hard. The same officer wrote; 'We were hit direct four times. One shell hit the forecastle just under the bridge, and, bursting inside, made a hole about five feet in diameter . . . the splinters from it wounded a large number of men in the fore ammunition lobby. One shell went right through the fore mess deck . . . one hit the motor barge, bursting in her and setting her on fire. Another shell hit the disengaged side of the forebridge, and wiped out everyone in the way of signalmen, messengers etc. who had gathered there, with the exception of one man.' He described how the shell burst between the man's legs, but the blast blew a hole in the deck of the bridge, and the man fell through it to safety. Fortunately for this man and his shipmates, the German fire slackened and stopped as the *Castor* pulled away. As she turned, the German cruisers also broke off the action, for fear of being attacked by the British destroyers.

They needn't have worried. Most of them thought the German cruisers were friendly, and didn't open fire or launch torpedoes. Others complained that they couldn't see the enemy at all, having been blinded by the fire of *Castor*'s guns. In fact, only two destroyers took part in the action; both the *Marne* and the *Magic* fired off one torpedo each, as did *Castor*. Only one of them came close to hitting its target – it ran underneath the *Elbing*, but thanks to a faulty depth setting it didn't explode. Once again, this brief action highlighted the lack of training of the British crews in night fighting. If Hawksley's commanders had been willing to attack, then the outcome of the skirmish might have been very different. The Germans didn't emerge unscathed though; *Castor* managed to score at least three hits on *Hamburg* during the exchange, killing or injuring eleven of her crew, damaging her port engine and a deck gun mounting, and even knocking out her wireless.

After five minutes, the Germans switched off their searchlights and the guns fell silent. *Hamburg* and her consorts maintained their course, though, and watched as the burning *Castor* hauled away, her destroyers following her like ducklings behind their mother. The flames doused, Hawksley sent a brief report of the action to the *Iron Duke*, but decided not to chase after the Germans in the darkness. Instead, he resumed his station, off the starboard quarter of Jerram's squadron, forming a protective shield between it and the Germans. While the German Official History criticised his lack of initiative, Hawksley was quite correct to follow orders. At that moment, apart from Goodenough's light cruisers a few miles further south, he was all that lay between Jellicoe's dreadnoughts and the enemy. Scheer was also told of the action, but it didn't alter his plans. The German battle fleet kept on its heading, creeping ever closer to the British lines.

The Third Clash

Until now, these clashes had been minor affairs. If the skirmishes had taken place on land, they would have been deemed patrol encounters. Now, though, with the German battle fleet drawing closer to the British, the stakes were raised. Any clash now might draw in the larger ships of the two fleets, or even bring about the full-scale night action that neither admiral wanted. Scheer's dreadnoughts were now formed into a long line of sixteen ships led by *Westfalen*, with Scheer's flagship *Friedrich der Grosse* the ninth ship in the line. By 10.20 p.m., the line had been extended, as Mauve's six pre-dreadnoughts took up station astern of the last dreadnought, the *König*. The sixth pre-dreadnought was the *Hannover*, and behind her came the battlecruisers *Von der Tann* and the *Derfflinger*, followed by the light cruiser *Regensburg*. At 10.40 p.m., the whole line angled another half point (about 6°) to port, to close the gap between the fleets even faster than before.

Meanwhile, the *Moltke* and the *Seydlitz* had suddenly appeared off the starboard bow of the *Stettin*, which was leading the IV Scouting Group. To avoid a collision, von Reuter's flagship had to reduce speed hurriedly and turn. Behind her, the *München*, the *Frauenlob* and the *Stuttgart* were all forced to turn away to port to avoid running into the stern of the flagship. This near miss not only threw the light cruisers into disarray, but it also brought them into contact with the enemy. Less than a thousand yards away to the east, a line of British cruisers materialised out of the dark. The British were steering towards the south-west, and the Germans to the south-south-east, so unknowingly the two groups had been drawing closer to each other. The British ships were Commodore Goodenough's 2nd Light Cruiser Squadron, who were screening the western flank of the battle fleet. The German ships were not sure if the cruisers were friend or foe, so *München* flashed the German recognition signal.

Lieutenant Harold Burrough described the mood of doubt. He recalled that; 'It was a very tense moment while we were trying to make out in the dark whether they were friend or foes.' His colleague Lieutenant King-Hall was more specific. Commodore Goodenough was unsure about the identity of the five ships, but King-Hall said; 'They were evidently in as much doubt as us.' Then, as the *Southampton* was about to flash its recognition challenge; 'the Germans switched on coloured lights at their fore yardarms.' The British response was immediate; the leading two ships *Southampton* and *Dublin* opened fire. By now, the range was down to just 800 yards, so both sides were plainly visible. The two British cruisers also switched on their searchlights to illuminate the German ships, who did the same in return, pinning the two British cruisers in the glare of a dozen searchlights.

King-Hall described how the firing began. A second after the German recognition lights were lit; 'A solitary gun crashed forth from the *Dublin*, which was next astern of us. Simultaneously I saw the shell hit a ship just above the waterline, and about 800 yards away. As I caught a nightmare-like glimpse of her interior, which has remained photographed on my mind to this day, I said to myself "Dear God – they are alongside us!" At that moment, the Germans switched on their searchlights, and we switched on ours. Before I was blinded by the lights in my eyes, I caught sight of a line of light grey ships. Then the gun behind which I was standing answered my shout of "FIRE!".' Lieutenant Burroughs added; 'Apparently they made up their minds at the same time as ourselves, for at the same moment as the Commodore ordered us to open fire, they switched on their searchlights and opened fire at us.'

Within seconds, both sides were firing as fast as they could at the enemy ships – the four German cruisers targeting *Southampton* and *Dublin*, while the same two British ships shot at the *München*. Behind them, the *Nottingham* and *Birmingham* had not switched on their searchlights, so they escaped the hail of German fire. They targeted *Frauenlob* and *Stuttgart* without anyone firing back at them. An exchange of this ferocity was unsustainable. The leading ships of both sides instinctively turned away, although the *Southampton* had little choice, as after three minutes a blazing fire raged across her decks from bow to stern.

Southampton's searchlights had all been knocked out and their crews killed or wounded, as were many of the gunners serving her starboard 6-inch guns amidships. The fires had all been started by ammunition catching fire, and it would be some time before these flames could be extinguished. Visibly shaken by the damage to his ship, Commodore Goodenough had little option but to turn away, as his blazing flagship was now attracting the full weight of enemy fire. She suffered eighteen hits in three minutes. *Dublin* was hit eight times in the same few moments, and thirteen times overall, but the other two British cruisers were unscathed. King-Hall continued; 'The range was amazingly close . . . There could be no missing . . . there was a great deal of high explosive bursting all along HMS *Southampton's* upper deck . . . So, in a very few seconds my guns stopped firing, all through lack of flesh and blood. In fact, the Sergeant Major, with a burnt face, and myself seemed to be the only bits of flesh and blood left standing.'

The Germans suffered, too. The *Stettin* was trying to turn towards the British, so her bow underwater torpedo tubes could bear, but she was hit repeatedly, and the steam pipe supplying her foghorn was pierced. With the bridge enveloped in a cloud of steam and smoke, von Reuter abandoned the attempt to fire torpedoes. Instead, he turned back on course so his remaining guns could keep firing. *München* was hit twice, but at that moment two more German cruisers appeared out of the darkness, the *Hamburg* and the *Elbing*. The British turned their guns on these new targets. As the British turned away behind the *Southampton*, each of the newcomers was hit by a British 6-inch shell – presumably fired by *Nottingham* and *Birmingham*. The shell that hit *Hamburg* struck her foremost funnel, and exploded directly over her bridge, wounding Lieutenant Commander von Gaudecker and his navigating officer, as well as several others on the bridge. Ten of her crew were killed.

On the *Frauenlob*, Midshipman Stolzmann remembered the shells coming towards him just moments after the searchlights flicked on. He directed the beams at the cruiser opposite him. Then; 'The guns immediately opened fire. This was followed by such a furious rain of shell, which nearly all hit the after part of the ship, that it looked as if several enemy ships were concentrating their fire on us.' On both sides, men watched their shipmates die all around them in the storm of explosives, shrapnel and flying debris. *Elbing* was struck on her wireless room, destroying it and killing four of its occupants. Lieutenant Bassinge was dozing in the same wireless room, and counted himself lucky to have survived the brief but murderous explosion that blasted him awake, and ripped his metal world apart; 'I was awakened by a strong jet of flame, burning my face and hands, and I felt a terrific blast. I was thrown through the bulkhead, taking it with me onto the middle deck . . . I neither fainted nor died, but looked around and saw flames all around me. I quickly crawled out on my hands and knees. As I could not use my burned hands I used my elbows. A 15cm [5.9-inch] shell was standing in front of the wireless station. The ship was rolling, and this put the shell out.' As if this unexploded shell was not bad enough, Bassenge noted; 'As it rolled it landed on my hand, and crushed the tips of several of my fingers. I hardly noticed as I crawled desperately away . . .' The lieutenant managed to stagger to the sick bay, where the doctor was busy treating fourteen more men wounded in the blast. Bassenge was given a shot of morphine, cleaned, bandaged and left to rest as best he could.

This, though, was not the most spectacular British success of this brief and savage little action. Just seconds before she turned away, *Southampton*'s torpedo officer, Lieutenant John Williams, fired a single 21-inch Mark IV torpedo at the German cruisers. At that range, it took just forty-five seconds to reach the enemy line. Williams recalled the moment; 'On the bridge the full glare of the searchlights of the leading enemy ship was on us, and we could see nothing, but I had already received enough of the general direction of advance of the enemy for the purpose of torpedo fire, so I passed down an order to the torpedo flat and waited impatiently for a reply. When it came through – the report "ready" – I fired at a group of hostile searchlights, which were the only things visible.' Those searchlights were mounted beneath the funnels of the *Frauenlob*. The *Southampton*'s torpedo ran true, and struck the German cruiser amidships on her port side.

Midshipman Stolzmann recalled someone reported a fire in the after part of the ship, and then; 'Only a few seconds later a terrific crash there, with the characteristic tremor of a ship which has been hit by a torpedo.' The explosion was heard above the general din of battle, and a plume of water rose above her funnels. Immediately, the German cruiser began to heel over, and it was clear that the blow had been a mortal one. In the engine room, Machinist Max Müller remembered that as the torpedo struck; 'at the same moment both engines stopped, the lights went out, and there was a roar of water pouring in.' The ship was heeling over now, and the shells stacked beside her guns slid across the deck. Either they or a British shell set off another explosion, which added to the fire in the vessel's stern. Müller was lucky; he made it to the upper deck, but when the power supply failed, the sinking ship was plunged into darkness and most of her crew never made it to safety.

As Müller reached the deck, he saw the water was already pouring over the ship's port side. The *Frauenlob* was sinking fast. The Official

German history put a brave face on the tragedy, saying; 'Up to their waists in water, the crew of No. 4 gun, under Petty Officer Schmidt, continued to engage the enemy until fire and water put an end to the fighting.' She capsized and sank in just three minutes. Of *Frauenlob's* 321-strong crew, there were only five survivors, one of whom was Müller. Stolzmann strapped on a lifejacket and, as the ship rolled over, he threw himself off the after bridge and onto a raft; 'A few seconds later we saw the ship sink without any internal explosion.' He claimed that; 'Some of our guns continued firing when the gunlayers were already standing in the water, and the ship was sinking. As the last tremor ran through the vessel, three cheers for His Majesty the Kaiser rang out.' Whether this last comment was true or not, it was clear that the *Frauenlob* went down fighting.

As the *Frauenlob* began heeling over, the *Stuttgart* was just 400 yards astern of her. Commander Max Hagedorn ordered an emergency turn to starboard to avoid the wreckage, but this meant the ship lost contact with the rest of the squadron in the dark. Hagedorn kept searching for them for several minutes, until a line of German dreadnoughts was spotted off the cruiser's starboard bow. A relieved Hagedorn took up station astern of the battle fleet. The damaged *Hamburg* also became separated from the rest of the Scouting Group, and in the dark she was almost rammed by *Moltke*, which was now speeding back to the north-west. However, *Hamburg's* two consorts *Elbing* and *Rostock* managed to find von Reuter, and the cruiser force was reformed again, although it was now reduced to just five ships.

Hipper's Probe

Just before the fight, when Hipper's flagship almost collided with the *Stettin*, quick thinking by Captain von Egidy of the *Seydlitz* prevented another disaster. When he saw *Stettin* loom out of the dark off his port bow, von Egidy ordered an emergency turn to starboard, giving von Reuter's cruiser the room it needed to avoid the *Moltke*. When he resumed his old course, von Egidy found he could not see the shaded stern light of the *Moltke*. He was already having trouble keeping up with Hipper's flagship, as *Moltke* was steaming at 22 knots, and *Seydlitz*, with thousands of tons of water in her hull, was two knots slower. So the two German battlecruisers parted company in the dark. Von Egidy knew roughly where Scheer's battle fleet was, and von Reuter's squadron was still in sight, now lit up by gun flashes. Rather than careering on alone where he could easily blunder in to the British fleet, he turned the battered *Seydlitz* round to the north, hoping to find his own route home.

On the bridge of the *Seydlitz*, von Egidy described the problems he faced nursing his badly damaged battlecruiser back to port; 'At first we could continue to follow the battlecruiser SMS *Moltke*, but soon we had to slow down, for water began coming over the forecastle as our bows settled. Steering was difficult, as was finding the right course, for the main gyro compartment was flooded, and the after gyro unreliable. Its normal circuit had been destroyed, and the new connection short-circuited off and on. The shocks had made the magnetic compass entirely undependable. . . . Our charts were covered in blood, and the spare charts were inaccessible in a flooded compartment.' He then added with a singular degree of understatement; 'Under those circumstances it was not at all easy to make the correct course for the Horns Reef lightship.' Against all the odds, *Seydlitz* would make it safely back into port, although that evening her survival was far from assured.

It was now 10.40 p.m. *Moltke* was alone between the two battle fleets. That didn't deter Hipper, though. He wanted to discover exactly where the British battle fleet was and how far it extended. The only way he could find this out was by putting the *Moltke* in harm's way. So the battlecruiser reduced speed slightly to minimise her high bow wave, and Hipper grimly held his course towards the south-west. On her bridge, binoculars continually swept the darkness, looking for that greater black in the darkness that would reveal the presence of an enemy ship. Suddenly, the outlines of four large ships appeared off her port bow. Captain von Karpf issued the recognition challenge – a sequence of coloured lights – but there was no reply. Then he recognised the ships for what they were, dreadnoughts of the Orion class, followed by a light cruiser. That made them Rear-Admiral Leveson's division, part of the 2nd Battle Squadron.

The *Moltke* was no match for the British dreadnoughts, and Hipper ordered Captain von Karpf to turn away to starboard. The battlecruiser quietly turned back into the darkness, hoping to escape before the British could open fire. In fact, lookouts on the light cruiser *Boadicea* had spotted *Moltke* as soon as she appeared, although they reported sighting 'a large cruiser'. The cruiser reported the news to the *Thunderer*, the dreadnought immediately ahead of her, but her lookouts had seen the German ship too, and its recognition signal. Captain James Fergusson of the *Thunderer* later reported that though he had seen the mystery ship flash a German recognition signal, 'fire was not opened.' The reason he gave was that; 'it was considered inadvisable to show up [reveal presence of] battle fleet unless fleet action was intended.' As a result, the *Moltke* was able to slip away, when she could quite easily have been sent to the bottom before she could escape.

Fifteen minutes later, *Moltke* tried again. She spent those few minutes circling around to starboard, as Hipper was hoping to pass to the north of the British squadron. However, at 10.55 p.m., when *Moltke* headed west again, she came upon the same line of black shapes in the darkness. This time, Captain von Karpf managed to turn away without being seen. The battlecruiser was armed with G7 torpedoes, carried in a pair of tubes amidships. Von Karpf would have fired them had the British ships not disappeared from view before they could be readied. This time Hipper turned southwards, as he knew his own battle fleet was steering a south-westerly course, and he didn't want to lose contact with them. At 11.10 p.m., he altered course to the south-west himself, but ten minutes later he saw those same looming black shapes again, directly ahead. This time Hipper gave up the attempt, and ran south once more, hoping Scheer would find a way through for him.

For more than an hour, from 10 p.m. onwards, these German probes had tried to determine the extent of Jellicoe's fleet, and to find a way past it. Each time a probe was attempted, the British were there, blocking the way. All this while, the dreadnoughts of the High Seas Fleet were moving ever closer to the British battle line. Scheer, though, was largely kept in the dark. The clear sighting by Hipper at 10.40 p.m. would have helped him pin the location of the British dreadnoughts, but *Moltke*'s wireless equipment had been destroyed, so no sighting report was sent. At 10.38 p.m., the *Rostock* reported firing at enemy cruisers and destroyers in Square-012, a German map reference to a specific location. Unfortunately, Commander Otto Feldmann of the *Rostock* cited the wrong map square, one that Scheer was actually passing through at the time! So, without any further information, Scheer held his course, determined to force his way past Jellicoe, regardless of the consequences.

19

Death of a Flotilla

Until 11 p.m., Scheer was unsure where the enemy battle fleet was. All he knew with certainly was that it lay somewhere to the west of him. So far though, his probes hadn't managed to penetrate Jellicoe's screen of light forces – destroyers behind the battle fleet and cruisers on its flanks. During the past hour, a number of confusing reports had reached him, but none of them allowed him to work out where Jellicoe's dreadnoughts might be, what formation they were in or even their course and speed. In fact, since his last *Gefechtskehrtwendung* three-and-a-half hours earlier, he had had no real contact with Jellicoe's battle fleet. That was why, when the two fleets finally crossed paths, the clash took Scheer by surprise. Then, shortly after 11 p.m., or midnight on German clocks; 'The German battle fleet reached a point which the British had passed hardly a quarter of an hour earlier.' The two lines of ships – one British, the other German – were now about to cross.

A Crossing of Paths

The two fleets had been on slightly converging paths for some time now, their courses forming a 'V' shape. However, the British battle fleet was steaming at 17 knots, a knot faster than the Germans. Therefore, it was gradually drawing ahead at a rate of one nautical mile every hour. As visibility on that moonless night was often less than that – around a thousand yards – then this difference in speed became crucially important. So, too, did the way the two battle fleets were deployed. As Scheer put it; 'The battleship squadrons proceeded during the night

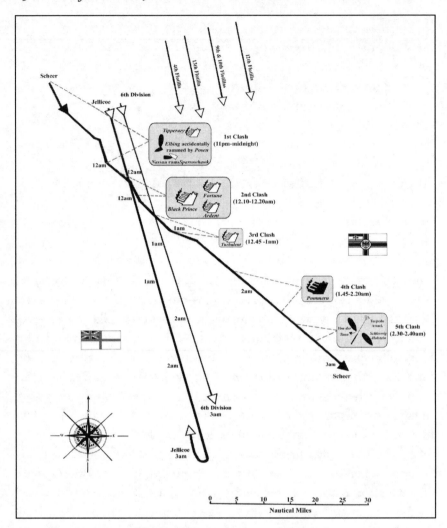

The Breakthrough, 11pm – 2.40am

in the following order: Squadron I, flagship of the fleet, Squadron III and Squadron II. Squadrons I and II were now in reversed positions; that is to say, the ships previously in the rear were now in the van.' That meant the whole battle fleet was deployed in a single long line, with the dreadnought *Westfalen* in the lead. Scheer, in *Friedrich der Grosse,* was the ninth ship in the German line.

In Gibson and Harper's *The Riddle of Jutland* (1934), this situation was summed up very neatly. 'Tiny factors, and no human plan, caused Jellicoe to arrive at the bottom of the "V" and pass through the junction point short minutes before the German ships arrived. The "V" became an "X" – the courses of the fleets crossed, neither side was conscious of what was happening, and from then onward, from the hour of midnight onward, they began to draw apart.' At 10 p.m., the German battle fleet was steering south-south-east by ¾ east (150°), and at 10.32 p.m. Scheer changed this to south-east by south (148°). Then, as if by intuition, at 11.02 p.m., Scheer altered course again, this time onto a heading of south-east by ¾ south (142°). Each change brought the line of ships angling a little more towards the east. So, when the two lines crossed, by luck rather than judgement, the *Westfalen* led the line of German ships precisely into a gap between the British battle fleet on one side and the British destroyers on the other.

At 11 p.m., as the German battle fleet was approaching them unseen from the north-west, the bulk of the British destroyer fleet was deployed in a series of columns, between two and five miles astern of the British dreadnoughts. Like the battle fleet itself, these destroyer flotillas were formed up into fairly compact formations. This made them easier to control them during the night. Most were well to the east of the approaching Germans, spread out over five miles of sea. Furthest to the west were three groups of destroyers, commanded by Captain James Farie, whose flagship was the light cruiser *Champion*. Following the *Champion* were two long columns of destroyers, in line astern. To port were the five boats of the combined 9th and 10th Flotillas, while the starboard column was made up of the seven boats of the 13th Flotilla. Astern of the port column was another larger group, the fourteen destroyers of the 12th Flotilla, led by Captain Anselan Stirling in the flotilla leader *Faulknor*.

This mass of 26 destroyers and a light cruiser were about two miles north of the 6th Division of dreadnoughts, part of Vice-Admiral Burney's 1st Battle Squadron. As the division was led by Burney's damaged flagship *Marlborough*, these dreadnoughts were lagging behind the rest of the battle fleet. After her torpedo hit, she tried to make the 17 knots ordered by Jellicoe, but was unable to maintain her speed and had dropped behind. Strangely, Burney kept his division together, which meant that the 6th Division had now lost contact with the other dreadnoughts. At 11 p.m., the *Iron Duke* was five miles ahead of the *Marlborough*, and south-south-west of her. Two miles to the west of

Burney's flagship was Rear-Admiral Evan-Thomas' 5th Battle Squadron. He had reduced speed slightly in order to support the *Marlborough*, and his three remaining fast battleships were now some way astern of the rest of the battle fleet. Neither admiral bothered to tell Jellicoe.

Three miles to the west of the other destroyers was Captain Wintour's 4th Flotilla – twelve boats steaming in line astern, with Wintour's flotilla leader *Tipperary* at their head. At 11 p.m., *Tipperary* was about three miles astern of the Evan-Thomas' 5th Battle Squadron. Unbeknown to either Evan-Thomas or Wintour, the *Westfalen* and the long line of German ships behind her were about to steam into that three-mile gap. When they did, the British destroyers would be on their port side and the fast battleships would be to starboard. At the time, the British ships were all steering towards the south-south-east, while the converging Germans were holding a south-easterly course. This meant that when they did appear, it would be off the starboard quarter of Wintour's flotilla leader. The unsuspecting *Tipperary* was about to be pitched into action against a whole battle fleet.

While Wintour in the *Tipperary* was commander of the whole 4th Flotilla, his force was divided into two divisions. Wintour commanded the first five-boat division himself. So, behind *Tipperary* came the destroyers *Spitfire*, *Sparrowhawk*, *Garland* and *Contest*. Behind *Conquest* was Commander William Allen in the *Broke*, commanding the second division. Behind her came the *Achates*, *Ambuscade*, *Ardent*, *Fortune*, *Porpoise* and *Unity*. *Tipperary* and *Broke* were large Faulknor class destroyers, carrying four 21-inch torpedoes in four single tubes amidships, as well as four 4-inch and 4.7-inch guns. The others were smaller Acasta class boats, with two torpedoes, and three 4-inch guns apiece. It was a powerful force, if used correctly. However, a contemporary American Vice-Admiral, William Sims, once said that; 'The destroyer is a projectile, the captain its fuse.' His point was that destroyer commanders needed to show aggression rather than just wait for orders.

Strangers in the Dark

At 11.03 p.m. when they first spotted the approaching ships, the crews of the British destroyers did nothing. Instead they waited for Captain Wintour to make the first move. On the destroyer *Garland*, Leading Torpedoman Maurice Cox was one of the first to spot the enemy; 'I sighted the blur of three ships on our starboard quarter, their bow waves showing faintly. They were apparently converging on our line of destroyers and were becoming more distinct.' Cox reported the sighting to the bridge, who in turn passed the news on to Wintour in the *Tipperary*. Then they waited for the order to fire. It was a frustrating time for Cox, as the torpedoman recalled that; 'at the time we had wonderful targets'. In fact, it was a torpedoman's dream; a line of ships approaching, at a range of a thousand yards and at a near-perfect angle of fire for the destroyers' torpedoes. It was a once-in-a-lifetime moment, and a flurry of torpedoes at this stage could have dramatically changed the course of the battle.

Few incidents betrayed the inexperience of the Royal Navy in night fighting than this hesitation to open fire. The destroyers were still unseen, and could have fired at the unsuspecting ships with clinical precision. A full spread of torpedoes – two or four from each boat – would almost certainly have caused carnage. The trouble was, initiative was discouraged in the British flotillas, and the flotilla commander was still unsure whether these dimly seen ships were British or German. So he held his course and held his fire. A little earlier, an erroneous report placed Commodore Hawksley's 11th Flotilla to the west of him. If these were really enemy ships, then he imagined that Hawksley would have engaged them. Finally, at 11.12 p.m., when the range had dropped to 600 yards, Wintour decided to do something. Rather than risk firing at a friendly target, he ordered his yeoman to flash a recognition signal at the leading ship. This would be the last command he would ever give.

Until the *Tipperary*'s signal light flashed, the lookouts on the *Westfalen* hadn't spotted the British destroyers off the port bow. The dreadnought's searchlights were ready, though, and within seconds the *Tipperary* was pinned in their beams. A few seconds after that, the *Westfalen*'s six port-side 15-cm. (6-inch) guns erupted, all aiming at the signalling lamp. The salvo of shells struck the destroyer, scything down most of her crew on the upper deck. One of the first casualties was Captain Wintour himself. A 15 cm shell hit the destroyer's open bridge, killing her captain and most of the bridge crew. In the destroyer's stern, Sub-Lieutenant Newton William-Powlett was in charge of the after guns. He watched with awe as the *Westfalen* opened fire; 'They were so close that I remember the guns seemed to be firing from some appreciable height above us.

At almost the same instant the *Tipperary* shook violently from the impact of being hit by shells.'

The destroyer began to settle in the water, her hull pierced below the waterline. Still, she was now fighting back. Only three shells had hit her behind her funnels, and back there all three of her main guns were still in action. William-Powlett explained; 'I opened fire with the after guns as soon as the enemy opened fire on us. Proper spotting was out of the question, but crouching behind the canvas screen of my control station (I felt much safer with this thin weather screen between me and the enemy guns, though it wouldn't have kept out a spent bullet) I yelled at the guns to open fire. I don't think they heard me, but they opened fire all right.' He recalled that the starboard torpedoes were launched, but the *Westfalen* was so close that they passed under her before their depth settings began to work. 'The enemy's second salvo hit and burst one of our main steam pipes, and the after part of the ship was enveloped in a cloud of steam, through which I could see nothing.'

Her engine rooms torn apart, the *Tipperary* was stopped dead in the water. As the white cloud of steam dissipated, it was replaced by a growing ball of fire and smoke as her fuel oil burned. From the *Spitfire*, Lieutenant Athelstan Bush recalled that the *Tipperary* was 'now a mass of burning wreckage, and looking very sad indeed. At a distance her bridge, wheelhouse and charthouse appeared to be one sheet of flame.' He noticed that the sea around her seemed on fire too, as the flames were reflected in the dark water. German shells were still pounding the blazing destroyer though; the gunner's attentions drawn by the blazing funeral pyre. In the *Spitfire*, Lieutenant Commander Clarence Trelawney was immediately astern of the flotilla leader when she was hit, and only his quick thinking prevented a collision. He turned the *Spitfire* hard to port to avoid the stricken *Tipperary*, then turned back on course again to let his torpedo tubes bear.

Bumps in the Night

The shock of this sudden hammer blow to the *Tipperary* took the crews of the other destroyers by surprise. Then their crews quickly gathered themselves and began firing their meagre 4-inch guns at the German ships steaming towards them. It wasn't just the dreadnoughts heading their way; on the port side of the *Westfalen* were four light cruisers, the

Rostock, Elbing, Stuttgart and *Hamburg*. When they saw the destroyers, the cruisers increased speed, to put themselves between the enemy boats and their own dreadnoughts. At that moment though, the first five boats – *Spitfire, Sparrowhawk, Garland, Contest* and *Broke* – all had an unobstructed torpedo shot, and each boat fired one or two torpedoes at the leading enemy ships. As soon as the torpedoes had gone, the boats all increased speed and made a hard turn to port, breaking contact with the enemy to reload their tubes, and to get away before the German gunners could retaliate.

On the *Spitfire*, Lieutenant Bush recalled the moment; 'We fired a torpedo, then waited until, with much joy and relief, it was seen to get the second enemy's ship between the after funnel and the mainmast, and she seemed to stop firing, heel over and all her lights went out.' In fact, the *Spitfire* fired two torpedoes, and her target was the *Elbing*, 800 yards away off her starboard beam. Behind her, the *Broke* fired at the cruiser too, an event remembered by Lieutenant Irvine Glennie; 'How we avoided their [search]lights I can't imagine. However, we did, and hauled out to port, firing a 'mouldy' [torpedo] at the after of the two cruisers as the bearing came on.' The crew of the *Broke*, as well as *Sparrowhawk* and *Garland*, all claimed a hit on the German cruiser.

This spread of six to eight torpedoes should have caused more damage. All of them but one either passed close to or beneath their targets. For some, the targets were too close for the torpedoes to run properly. In fact, there was only one probable hit – on the port quarter of the *Elbing*. Most, if not all, of the destroyers seem to have fired at the nearest enemy target – the light cruisers – rather than at the dreadnoughts behind them. The German ships replied with a hail of fire, but the small fast-moving boats made difficult targets. As well as firing torpedoes, the British destroyers popped away with their 4-inch guns, too. Many of them still could not see the dreadnoughts clearly, but they targeted the searchlights lighting up the *Tipperary*. *Westfalen, Nassau and Rheinland* all suffered 4-inch shell hits around their forward funnels, where the searchlights were clustered. There were casualties; Captain Johannes Redlich of the *Westfalen* was wounded when one shell hit his bridge.

Having swerved to avoid the blazing wreck of the *Tipperary*, the *Spitfire* shot past her, but then her captain ordered the wheel to be spun around and the boat began circling to starboard. His plan was to curve back around and come alongside the flotilla leader to rescue her crew. Her bridge crew were too engrossed in this task to notice that they were now within 500 yards of the German dreadnought *Nassau*. Captain Robert Kühne noticed it though, and ordered the dreadnought's wheel to be turned to port. He intended to cut the destroyer in two. Lieutenant Commander Trelawney had been half-blinded by his own ship's gun flashes, but at the last moment he spotted the dreadnought and spun his ship hard to starboard. It was almost enough – but not quite. The two ships met head on as the bows of the *Nassau* struck the port bow of the *Spitfire* with a grinding screech of metal.

The shock of the impact made the dreadnought heel over slightly, but the destroyer wasn't cut in two; instead she was pushed to the side, and the *Spitfire* screeched her way down the port side of the dreadnought. Lieutenant Bush watched with horror; 'I can recollect a fearful crash, then being hurled across the deck, and feeling the *Spitfire* rolling over to starboard as no sea ever made her roll. As we bumped, the enemy opened fire with their foc'sle guns.' The forward 11-inch guns of the *Nassau* were already trained to port and depressed to their lowest possible elevation. The 10-metre-long barrels almost touched the destroyer's masts as they fired. At 855 metres (2,800 feet) per second, the effect was instantaneous. Although the shells missed the destroyer, the blast from the guns was sufficient to wreck the bridge of the *Spitfire* and demolish her masts and funnels. Unlike most of his bridge crew, Trelawney survived, although he was blown off his bridge and onto the deck below.

Three men were killed in the blast and several wounded. Seconds later, the destroyer slipped astern of the dreadnought, a huge ninety-foot rip torn in her hull. She also had a twenty-foot length of the *Nassau*'s side plating lodged on her deck, after it had been ripped away during the collision. Amazingly, the destroyer would survive. Fires broke out in the area of her shattered bow and rose from the hole where her second funnel should have been. These, though, were soon extinguished, and the crippled destroyer limped away into the night. The *Nassau* had a hole torn in her bow by the destroyer, just above the waterline, and a piece of her plate armour ripped off and carried away by the *Spitfire*. On deck, the jar had wrecked the mounting of a 15 cm gun, but otherwise the dreadnought was unharmed. Thanks to that hole in her bow, though, her speed was now limited to just 15 knots. If it came to a running battle, this loss of speed might prove disastrous.

While this was taking place, the rest of the dreadnoughts of Vice-Admiral Schmidt's I Squadron were all beginning a simultaneous turn to starboard. Like the German cruisers off their port beam, they needed to turn away to avoid being hit by the British torpedoes. The two groups of German ships were now all turning in the same direction, and the cruisers were less than a mile off the dreadnoughts' port beam. It would take fast reactions and skilled ship-handling to evade the torpedoes, but now the crews of all these warships had to worry about collisions too. The best chance of avoiding contact was if the faster-moving cruisers could speed through the gaps between the dreadnoughts – a manoeuvre that required both skill and timing. This was a standard tactic, but the manoeuvre carried out at night, and with two lines of ships so close to each other, was a particularly dangerous undertaking.

If *Elbing* was hit by a torpedo, the blow was not a serious one. From the description of a thump without an explosion, it appears that the torpedo might have been a dud. However, her attempt to evade the torpedoes would cause mayhem in the German ranks. When the German cruisers saw the torpedoes heading towards them, the three leading ones all made emergency turns to starboard, to present as small a target as possible. Their way to safety, though, was barred by the column of German dreadnoughts. The only option was to try to weave through the German battle line, which was also beginning its emergency turn to starboard. Still, the cruisers were faster and more agile than the dreadnoughts, and with expert ship handling, the smaller vessels should be able to thread their way through the gaps in the dreadnought line.

Commodore Michelsen managed to steer *Rostock* through the 400-yard gap between *Nassau* and *Rheinland*, even though this second dreadnought had to make an emergency hard turn to starboard to avoid a glancing collision. The destroyer *S-32*, which was accompanying the cruisers, raced through the same gap. However, as she was making this crucial run she was hit by two 4-inch shells, one of which struck her bridge, the other severing her main steam pipe. She passed the dreadnoughts, steam escaping in a cloud, and there she lay, with most of her bridge crew dead and no power left in her engines. The next cruiser to make the run was the *Elbing*. She, though, had to avoid the *Stuttgart*, whose captain had decided not to make the attempt as no torpedoes were heading his way. Commander Rudolf Madlung decided to run the *Elbing* through the gap between the *Rheinland* and the next dreadnought astern, the *Posen*. This time the manoeuvre didn't work.

The delay caused by avoiding the *Stuttgart* meant that *Elbing* didn't have time to warn the *Posen* that she was making the attempt. On the *Posen's* bridge, Captain Richard Lange didn't see the cruiser turning towards him until it was too late. All he could do was to swing his wheel hard over to starboard, in a last-ditch attempt to minimise the force of the collision. The dreadnought struck *Elbing* on her starboard quarter, and the *Posen's* bows punched a great hole in the cruiser's waterline. Water poured into the *Elbing's* two engine rooms, drowning many of her stokers and putting the engines out of action. The blow also wrecked her steering gear and cut all electrical power to the ship. The cruiser was spun round and drifted down the starboard side of the *Posen*, as the dreadnought shoved her out of the way. The *Elbing* was now dead in the water, and utterly helpless. She drifted away from the action, watched by the rest of the German battle fleet as they steamed past her.

On board the stricken cruiser, Lieutenant Heinrich Bassenge had been lying in the sick bay, the victim of the wound inflicted just over half an hour before. He wrote; 'I was too weak to go and see what was happening. Soon everything around us was quiet, all engines stopped, the battle noise ceased. Doctors and attendants went to the upper deck to see to the badly injured. The lights went out, an uncanny silence after ten hours of battle made us feel very uneasy. I was worried that our dear *Elbing* was sinking, and looked continuously at the decks and bulkheads to see whether water was coming through.' The young lieutenant took solace from the idea that his shipmates wouldn't leave them there to drown; if the ship was sinking someone would come to rescue them. In fact, thanks to her watertight compartments, the flooding was contained, but the damage the ship had suffered meant that she was now incapable of moving or fighting.

A Pile of Destroyers

Following the spectacular death of Captain Wintour and the *Tipperary*, command of what remained of the 4th Flotilla fell to Commander Walter Allen, who led the flotilla's second division from the *Broke*. He decided to pull back, pull together the remnants of the flotilla, and either to launch another attack or, failing that, to head south and link up with the British battle fleet. He gathered six boats together and formed them up behind the *Broke* in line astern. He was heading south when, at 11.40 p.m., he spotted a large two-funnelled ship appear of his starboard bow. It was heading across his path, and he wasn't sure if it was friend or foe. Could it be a German dreadnought, or one of Evan-Thomas' squadron coming back to investigate all the firing? He decided to challenge her, and was about to flash a recognition signal at her when the mystery ship hoisted one herself – four green lights from her yardarm. That wasn't a signal used by British ships.

On the *Broke*, Telegraphist John Croad looked out of the open door of the wireless office and saw the outline of the large ship, just as she switched on a searchlight; 'She played her searchlight on a destroyer a little way from us, evidently not seeing us at first. But the searchlight, while taking a sweep, just caught sight of our ensign, which was flying at the foreyard arm. From there it was played right on us.' Seconds later, the large warship switched on more searchlights, gripped the *Broke* fully in their beams, and opened fire. She was the *Westfalen*, and with the range down to less than five cables – a thousand yards – almost every shell struck home. The cruiser *Rostock* opened up too, also from a thousand yards, as did the dreadnought *Rheinland*, from astern of the *Westfalen*. Allen had made the same mistake Captain Wintour had; in night actions of this kind it was always better for destroyers to fire first, whatever the risk. His hesitation would would have fatal consequences.

As the German fire swept over his ship, Allen reacted swiftly. As he put it; 'The order was given to fire the remaining starboard tube, full speed ahead both, and fire was opened.' According to Lieutenant Irving Glennie; 'We got off two or three rounds, and never fired the "mouldy" [torpedo].' The gun crews were among the first to be hit. Croad confirmed; 'The first shot swept our gun crews clean off the deck, the next cleared the forebridge.' With the boat pinned in the beam of German searchlights there was nowhere to run. As Lieutenant Glennie put it; 'It was perfectly damnable having their light right in our faces . . . and being properly biffed.' The range was dropping fast; within a minute the *Westfalen* was within a cable – 200 yards – and the German shells pounded the destroyer. Croad was amazed that he survived a devastating hit to the wireless office, and as men were killed; 'by shrapnel bullets or by the steam escaping from the broken steam pipes'.

Allen turned to the helmsman and gave the order to spin the wheel hard to starboard. However, before the boat began her turn, the helmsman was killed, and as he fell he was still gripping the wheel, and turned it hard to port. The destroyer slewed round, directly into the path of the destroyer *Sparrowhawk*, which was coming up astern of her. The *Sparrowhawk* had just begun to turn to fire her torpedoes, and her captain, Lieutenant Commander Sydney Hopkins, was unable to avoid the collision. Sub-Lieutenant Percy Wood was standing beside Hopkins on the *Sparrowhawk*'s bridge. As enemy gunfire began hitting the ship; 'We saw *Broke* coming straight for our bridge, absolutely end on, at 38 knots. I remember shouting a warning to everyone in hearing to hold on.' He found the spectacle strangely fascinating, but when the two boats collided, he remembered nothing; 'till I found myself lying on the foc'sle, not of our ship but of the *Broke*.'

Wood was not the only crewman to be thrown off his feet, or to land up on the deck of the other destroyer. On the *Broke*, Glennie recalled; 'We hit very hard, doing much damage ... I am afraid I was more rattled than I should have been, but my eyes were full of blood, and I thought I was much worse than I really was.' Steam clouds pouring out of the *Broke*'s damaged boiled rooms made it difficult to see, but it soon became clear the *Sparrowhawk* was in a bad way and probably sinking. The only good news for the crews was that the German fire was slackening, and their searchlights were no longer illuminating the *Broke*. Strangely, both captains thought their boats were sinking, and asked that their crew be taken aboard the other vessel. Just as Allen and Hopkins were sorting out the mess, another destroyer, the *Contest*, appeared astern of the *Sparrowhawk*. The already fraught situation was about to become much worse.

Five of the six destroyers following astern of the *Sparrowhawk* managed to turn hard to port and avoid the two intertwined boats. The *Contest* wasn't so lucky. Croad watched her approach; 'While we stood jammed into each other, HMS *Contest* ran into the *Sparrowhawk*, missing us by a hair's breadth, which was a marvellous piece of seamanship on the part of the man on the wheel.' However, the bows of the *Contest* rammed into *Sparrowhawk*'s port quarter, cutting the last six feet off her stern. She might have survived one ramming, but this second blow proved too much. The *Sparrowhawk* became a floating wreck, and while *Contest* and *Broke* managed to back away from her thirty minutes later, it was clear that the twice-rammed destroyer wasn't going to make it home. After some of his injured crew were taken on board the damaged *Broke*, Hopkins and what remained of his crew began the long nocturnal battle to keep the *Sparrowhawk* afloat.

The *Broke* was in a poor way too; her decks were wrecked by gunfire and streaked with blood, while the collision had shattered her bows. Still, she was able to manoeuvre – just – and so she and the *Contest* limped off, leaving Hopkins to do what he could to save his drifting ship. It came as a poignant relief when the *Tipperary* finally sank, as her flames had made the *Sparrowhawk* all too visible to the long column of German ships sliding past a few thousand yards to the south. Hopkins might also have been saved by Speer, who re-iterated his one-word message to the battle fleet: *Durchalten*, meaning 'to maintain course and speed, regardless of distractions'. A small crippled destroyer therefore became of little interest to the German ships, and Hopkins' men were left alone. Meanwhile, both the *Broke* and the *Contest* limped off to the north, keeping well away from the overwhelming firepower of the enemy dreadnoughts.

The Germans, though, had their own problems. As the *Broke* made her run, the light cruiser *Rostock* was trying to work her way between the *Westfalen* and the *Rheinland*. She had just lined up for the narrow gap between the two dreadnoughts when a torpedo struck her on her port side. The explosion ripped a hole in the side of her port boiler room, and the sea rushed into her machinery spaces. In less than a minute she had lost all propulsive power, her electrical systems had shut down, and her steering system had failed. She was lucky not to share the fate of the *Elbing*, but somehow she avoided a collision. Almost a thousand tons of water had flooded into her, and while her crew tried to contain this, the cruiser drifted off, listing to port, and the rest of the battle fleet steamed past her. The destroyer *S-54* was ordered to go to her aid; the two German warships would still be there at dawn, as Commodore Michelsen's engineers tried to restore power to their ship.

The Last Attack

Commander Reg Hutchinson of the *Achates* assumed command of what remained of the flotilla. Some two miles to the north-east of the reforming German battle line, he gathered together six destroyers, then led them in a final attack. The German battle line had just resumed its old course – south-east by ¾ south – and as Hutchinson's boats appeared they were formed in a line again, with the exception of the *Nassau*. After her encounter with the *Spitfire*, she was a little to port of the other ships, on the port beam of the *Helgoland*, the fifth ship in the German column. Ahead of the *Nassau* were the light cruisers *Rostock* and *Stuttgart*, which hadn't tried to weave through the battle line twenty minutes earlier. This time the Germans were ready for the clash and opened up as soon as the British destroyers appeared off their port beam. Hutchinson attacked in line astern, with *Achates* leading the way.

To give the boats the best possible chance of scoring hits with their torpedoes, they were approaching the Germans on a course which was almost parallel to them. Each of these Acasta class boats had two torpedoes apiece, and on each of them the two single tubes were trained round already, pointing off the starboard beam. This relatively shallow angle of approach also meant that they were easier targets. As the destroyers began their torpedo run they were met by a blaze of searchlights, and a curtain of German fire. The dreadnoughts were firing with their main guns as well as their secondary batteries; a single hit from an 11-inch or 12-inch shell could tear a destroyer apart. The first boat to suffer was the *Fortune*, the third destroyer in Hutchinson's line. Her bridge was swept clear by the first German salvo fired by *Westfalen*. Her mast was blown away and her gun crews scythed down. In less than thirty seconds, *Fortune* was turned into a blazing wreck.

On the *Oldenburg*, Warrant Officer Otto Busch, in charge of the after searchlight platform saw the whole thing; 'It was the most gallant fight I have ever seen. She [*Fortune*] was literally riddled with shell, but clear in the glare of our searchlights I could see a Petty Officer and two seamen loading and firing her after gun until she disappeared.' One of the sailors on the *Fortune* was Leading Seaman Thomas Clifford. During the attack he was manning a torpedo, and waited for orders to fire; 'I looked to the bridge and it was blown away . . . so I got my tube to bear and fired my torpedo. Waiting for the splash as she hit, I was blown off the tube by gunfire. We were that close I could see the searchlight crew on the big ship.' Although wounded, he was one of the few survivors of the *Fortune's* crew. He was rescued by the destroyer *Moresby* the following morning, after spending several hours in the water. The *Fortune* sank within minutes, taking most of her crew with her.

The firing was not all one way though. To avoid the British torpedoes, the leading six dreadnoughts – *Westfalen, Rheinland, Posen, Oldenburg* and *Thüringen* – all made simultaneous turns to starboard. Once again, the British gun crews aimed at the searchlights, and as the *Oldenburg* began her turn a 4-inch shell exploded on her forward searchlight platform beneath her forward funnel. Splinters showered the bridge, killing or wounding several officers and men. One of the casualties was Captain Wilhelm Höpfner, who was badly wounded by a flying splinter. Still dazed, he staggered to his feet to see the wheel unmanned; the helmsman had been cut down. Höpfner grabbed the wheel, and so prevented the *Oldenburg* from turning into the path of the *Helgoland*, which was making the same turn on her starboard side. Another German disaster was narrowly avoided.

The boats astern of the *Fortune* swerved round her to port, but this was enough to throw off their torpedo salvos. *Posen, Oldenburg* and *Helgoland* concentrated their fire at the leading destroyers *Achates* and *Ambuscade*, but these boats seemed to lead a charmed life. They tore through the wall of fire, fired their torpedoes – which missed – and raced off to the east. As they did they were fired on by two newcomers. A few minutes earlier the *Frankfurt* and the *Pillau* appeared from the north, exchanged recognition signals with the German dreadnoughts and took up station ahead of the line. Now the two cruisers opened up on the destroyers as they raced past them. The *Ardent* was the next casualty. She survived the attack, but lost her way in the dark. Ten minutes later she blundered into the main German battle line again, and was lit up by the searchlights of the *Westfalen*. The range was just 900 yards, and the destroyer was shattered by forty 3.5- and 5.9-inch shells.

Lieutenant Commander Arthur Marsden of the *Ardent* recounted his destroyer's last moments; 'I attacked at once, and from very close range our remaining torpedoes were fired.' Then, 'We opened fire and ran on at full speed. The next moments were perhaps the most thrilling that anyone could experience.' Having been gripped in the beam of searchlights, Marsden and his men knew the German shells would follow. 'There was perfect silence on the bridge, and not a word was spoken. It must have been only seconds, but it seemed like hours. At last it came . . . shell after shell hit us, and our speed diminished and then stopped. Then the dynamo stopped and all lights went out.' He watched the forecastle gun firing until her crew were killed, then the German searchlights were cut off. With his ship sinking under him, Marsden gave the order to abandon ship. Although badly wounded, he lived to tell the tale – in fact he went on to become a long-standing Conservative MP.

The British destroyer attack was over. The *Fortune* and the *Ardent* sank quickly, and the survivors were left to fend for themselves. Another casualty was the *Porpoise*, which took two direct hits from enemy shells. She would have suffered more if *Fortune* had not absorbed most of the punishment. One shell exploded beneath her bridge, the other hitting her torpedo deck. Steam sprayed out from severed pipes, her engines began losing power and her steering gear was wrecked. Surprisingly, only two men were killed and two wounded, a low butcher's bill for so much damage. It looked unlikely she would survive the night, but she did and eventually limped in to Tyneside late the following day. The crews of the *Fortune* and *Ardent* were less fortunate; of the 148 men crewing the two destroyers, there were only three survivors; Marsden from the *Ardent* and Clifford and a shipmate from the *Fortune*.

Effectively the 4th Destroyer Flotilla had ceased to exist. For an hour it had launched a series of gallant attacks against the German battle line. Despite all that bravery, though, they had only managed to damage two light cruisers; no dreadnoughts had been hit. The price for this had been high. Of the twelve boats available to Captain Wintour an hour earlier, only four were now left; the rest were either sunk or disabled. Even the four surviving boats were damaged in various degrees, and all of them had fired off their torpedoes. They were now scattered in the darkness, and it would be dawn before Commander Hutchinson would be able to regroup them. The flotilla had delayed the progress of the High Seas Fleet for about half an hour and forced it to deviate slightly from its course, but the sacrifice of its boats and crew hadn't really influenced the course of the battle. The main reason for that, apart from the lack of torpedo hits, was that nobody bothered to tell Jellicoe about their fight.

20

Breaking Through

At midnight the German battle fleet was still in line astern, with *Westfalen* in the lead, and it had brushed off the attacks of the British destroyer flotilla. Amazingly, the British battle fleet was still steaming southwards, even though the searchlights and gunfire from the night action could be seen beyond the stern of Evan-Thomas' fast battleships and Jerram's dreadnoughts. The problem was that nobody in the destroyer flotilla had thought of sending a wireless message to Jellicoe to tell him they were fighting Scheer's dreadnoughts. So Jellicoe remained blissfully unaware of Scheer's attempt to break through his line, and he continued on his original course. Others could have radioed the fleet flagship from the tail end of the battle fleet, but no captain wanted the responsibility of breaking radio silence. The presumption was that Jellicoe already knew about the fighting raging astern of them.

On the *Malaya*, Lieutenant Patrick Bird spotted the enemy dread-noughts behind him, and asked Captain Algernon Boyle for permission to open fire. Boyle said no, adding that the Admiral [Evan-Thomas] could see everything for himself. As late as 11.35 p.m., *Valiant* signalled Evan-Thomas' flagship *Barham*, reporting seeing enemy warships astern, but there was no reply. In the dreadnought *Benbow*, Midshipman Geoff Congreve was watching; 'About 11.45 p.m. there was a terrific burst of fire astern of us, fair going it, light cruisers and destroyers. It went on for about five minutes, and must have been a pretty hot show. One ship was badly hit and lit up the sky in a great red flame.' It was obvious that a battle was taking place, but nobody – not even Evan-Thomas or Burney

– thought of letting Jellicoe know. As a result, the Grand Fleet lost its last real chance to destroy the High Seas Fleet. If Jellicoe had turned the fleet to port, it could have intercepted Scheer before he reached Horns Reef. Instead, the fleet held its course, as its commander remained blissfully unaware of what was happening.

The *Black Prince*

As the 4th Flotilla destroyers *Achates* and *Ambuscade* escaped to the east, they saw what they took to be a lone German cruiser bearing down on them from the north. The destroyers kept out of her way. The mystery vessel held its course to the south, heading directly towards the German fleet. In fact, she was the British armoured cruiser *Black Prince*. She had formed part of Rear-Admiral Arbuthnot's 1st Cruiser Squadron, but after Arbuthnot's flagship *Defence* was sunk and the *Warrior* badly damaged, *Black Prince* lost contact with her one remaining consort, the *Duke of Edinburgh*. She kept to the north of Jellicoe's battle fleet after it deployed, and due to some unrecorded problem – probably an engine malfunction – she was unable to keep up with the fleet as it ran south. So she followed on behind, and by midnight she was still about five miles to the north of the *Agincourt*, the dreadnought at the rear of Vice-Admiral Burney's squadron.

Shortly after midnight Captain Thomas Bonham standing on *Black Prince*'s bridge would have seen a line of large ships materialise ahead of him. From his actions, the assumption was that Bonham thought the approaching ships were part of Jellicoe's battle fleet. Nobody really knows, as within a few minutes Captain Bonham and every member of his crew would be dead. At that moment, *Nassau* was still on the port side of the German battle line, and both she and the *Thüringen* spotted a large four-funnelled ship approaching, fine on their port bow. The dreadnoughts flashed a recognition signal, but the ship's only response was to alter course hard to port. That put the *Black Prince* on a parallel course to the German dreadnoughts. Almost at once they switched on their searchlights, then opened fire. The range was around 1,100 yards and so the armoured cruiser was clearly visible.

Before the *Black Prince* could train her own guns round, the *Thüringen*'s shells ploughed into her – four complete salvos of 5.9-inch shells in less than forty seconds. The dreadnought's 3.5-inch (8.8 cm) guns hit her another twenty-four times. So, within less than a minute the *Black Prince* was hit almost fifty times and was blazing fiercely. As if this was not enough, the *Ostfriesland* and the *Nassau* also joined in, until the *Black Prince* was little more than a blazing inferno of wreckage. Scheer witnessed her destruction, and wrote; 'Utterly mistaking the situation, a large enemy cruiser with four funnels came up at 2am [midnight], apparently one of the Cressy class, and was soon within 1,500 metres of Squadron I's battleships *Thüringen* and *Ostfriesland*. In a few seconds she was on fire, and sank with a terrible explosion four minutes after opening fire.' The sight of the blazing ship drifting past the German battle line was unforgettable, and produced feelings of pity for the poor men trapped inside.

Scheer, though, was more phlegmatic; 'The destruction of this vessel, which was so near that the crew could be seen rushing backwards and forwards on the burning deck, while the searchlights disclosed the flight of heavy projectiles till they fell and exploded, was a grand but terrible sight.' The German Official History added; 'She drifted down the line blazing furiously until, after several minor explosions she disappeared below the surface with the whole of her crew in one tremendous explosion.' Further astern, the crew of the crippled *Spitfire* saw her too. Lieutenant Bush claimed the cruiser missed them by a few feet, and then; 'She tore past us with a roar . . . and the very crackling and heat of the flames could be heard and felt. She was a mass of fire from foremast to mainmast, on deck and between decks. Flames were issuing out of her from every corner.' The end came for the *Black Prince* when the flames reached her magazines. There were no survivors.

A Second Chance

By 12.30 a.m., the head of the long column of German warships had passed to the east of the British battle fleet. The closest of these, the *Agincourt*, was five miles to the south, and was heading away from the Germans at a steady 17 knots, or 573 yards per minute. However, at least in theory, the German route to Horns Reef was still blocked by a mass of British destroyers; the twenty-six boats and a light cruiser that made up the 12th and 13th Flotillas, as well as the combined 9th and 10th Flotilla. These boats should have expected the Germans. After all, they had all seen the searchlights or heard the gunfire. Some might even have seen the explosions as the destroyers of the 4th Flotilla or the *Black Prince* were pounded to pieces. In fact, a few stray shots fired by the Germans during the running battle had overshot the scene of the fight and landed in the sea close to the light cruiser *Champion*, the flagship of the 13th Flotilla. Their effect would be dramatic.

In the *Champion*, Captain James Farie commanded not just his own flotilla, but the boats of the other two flotillas as well. His decision could make all the difference. As the German shells began to fall a little to the west of his flagship, Farie had two logical ways of interpret this. Either the Germans were shelling him but he couldn't see them yet, or the 4th Flotilla was in the midst of a grim battle and needed help. He decided that it was his own flotilla that was under attack and immediately called for full speed. The *Champion* turned to port and headed east, away from the falling shells. Unfortunately, only two destroyers, *Obdurate* and *Moresby*, followed him. The other eight boats of the flotilla never saw the change of course, as they were steaming in front of the cruiser. So they held course towards the south-south-east as the *Champion* and the two other destroyers disappeared into the night.

To the south of them were the five boats of the combined 9th and 10th Flotilla, led by Commander Malcolm Goldsmith, whose flagship was the destroyer *Lydiard*. His combined flotilla wasn't really part of the Grand Fleet at all; it was an element of Harwich Force, and was only temporarily attached to Beatty's Battlecruiser Fleet. Still, Goldsmith was an experienced destroyer commander – as was Captain Farie – and Jellicoe trusted them enough to make them his rearguard. The boats of the 13th Flotilla were steaming faster than Goldsmith's vessels, and they soon came up astern of the Harwich force. Without Farie to tell them otherwise, the eight boats attached themselves to the rear of Goldsmith's column, as did another stray, the *Unity*, a survivor of the 4th Flotilla.

All of these boats would have seen the fight raging a few miles to the west. The arrival of the *Unity* should have sent alarm bells ringing too, but it seems neither Lieutenant Commander Arthur Lecky who commanded her, nor Commander Goldsmith ahead of him, bothered to ask what had happened. The commander of the *Unity* could have warned Goldsmith the Germans were coming, but instead he was left in the dark. This was particularly unfortunate as Goldsmith had already ascribed the fighting to the west to 'friendly fire'. In his report he claimed that he thought the fast battleships of Evan-Thomas' 5th Battle Squadron had reversed course, a fracas had developed, and that the fast battleships were firing at the 4th Flotilla's destroyers. The real tragedy of this assumption was that he now half-expected a line of British capital ships to appear on his starboard beam. He never supposed that it was the High Seas Fleet that was bearing down on him.

Commander Goldsmith's assumption led him to plan a redeployment of his flotilla. He had originally been charged to follow astern of the British battle fleet, keeping about five miles behind the rear of Burney's squadron. He had done that, but this new development suggested there had been a change of plan, one he hadn't been told about. So he decided to place his flotilla on the starboard beam of Evan-Thomas' squadron, which he duly expected to turn and follow Burney's ships. He opted to increase speed to 30 knots, and then cut ahead of the approaching squadron to take up position to the west of the three fast battleships. The problem, of course, was that these ships were not British at all. Another slight problem was the length of Goldsmith's flotilla. It seems he didn't realise that he now led a force of fourteen boats, rather than just five. With the boats 250 yards apart, this meant his line of destroyers was not 1,500 yards long; it stretched for just over 4,000 yards – or two miles.

His manoeuvre would have worked to perfection if he had just had his own combined flotilla behind him. The boats passed well ahead of the approaching fast battleships, whose shapes could now be dimly made out to the west, approaching on a south-easterly heading. In fact, most of the destroyers passed the head of the approaching column safely; it was the rear four boats that were now in danger of colliding with the leading fast battleship, presumably the *Barham*. She sprang out of the darkness a few hundred yards away from the line of destroyers, and was now approaching it at right angles. Only it was not Evan-Thomas' flagship at all. Four boats from the rear of the column, Lieutenant-Commander Evan Ogilvie Thompson, who commanded the *Petard*, realised that the approaching ship was German rather than British. It was also increasing speed, and obviously trying to ram him.

Thompson recalled the moment when he identified the approaching ship; 'We sighted a dark mass about five or six points off our starboard bow, steering south-east about 600 yards away. On looking at her closely there could be no doubt at what she was, as at the angle we sighted her at, we could see clearly large crane derricks silhouetted against the sky – and only German ships have these fittings.' Thompson was already travelling at high speed, so he curved away to starboard to avoid the approaching dreadnought, passing across her bows, then ran past the side of the *Westfalen* close enough to make out her name. Thompson had no faith in the ability of his little 4-inch guns to harm the huge dreadnought, and he had already fired off all his torpedoes during the afternoon. So he decided to run. 'There was nothing we could do but get away, so we increased to full speed and altered course about a point to port to clear the enemy's stern.'

She almost made it too. The searchlights had trouble finding the fast-moving destroyer, but then they spotted her and *Petard* was caught in their beam. 'Immediately afterwards, we saw the flashes of the enemy's secondary armament being fired, and on the bridge we felt the ship tremble slightly, and guessed we had been hit.' The Germans kept firing, and then a second dreadnought, the *Rheinland*, joined in. *Petard* was hit six times before she escaped into the darkness, but at least her engines weren't hit, and she sped away to safety. Still, she lost fifteen men in those fraught moments – nine killed and six wounded. As they raced off, Thompson saw that; 'the foremost group of German searchlights were switched off, and trained round to port all together onto the *Turbulent* – my next astern.' *Turbulent* tried to follow *Petard* by crossing the bows of the German dreadnought, but the *Westfalen* was already turning to starboard, which meant that all of her port guns could now fire.

The *Westfalen*'s salvo was devastating. It hit the *Turbulent* square on and the destroyer was literally blown to pieces. One of the shells had pierced her boilers, which exploded, ripping the stern off the ship. Seconds earlier, the destroyer had altered course to starboard – she was less than 400 yards off the dreadnought's port side when she was hit. Observers on the *Westfalen* recall seeing a double explosion, first in her stern, then a split second later the rest of the ship was ripped apart. There were no survivors. In the great forge of battle, the spectacular loss of a destroyer and her crew might have been worth it if the rest of her flotilla could have launched an immediate attack – if they had avenged the loss by sinking the *Westfalen* with torpedoes. It was certainly a unique opportunity; a dozen British destroyers were there, and ready to act. Instead, Goldsmith kept on his original course, and led them away from the German fleet.

Once again no wireless message sent to Jellicoe. So, the Grand Fleet kept heading south, oblivious to the carnage taking place astern. The distance was increasing now; *Agincourt* was six miles away and Vice-Admiral Burney's flagship *Marlborough* almost two miles beyond her. The men on watch on these ships certainly knew that some form of battle was raging astern of them. Captain Percy Grant, Burney's flag captain on the *Marlborough*, stood on the bridge of his ship throughout the short night, and saw the signs of battle for himself; 'A terrific cannonade took place quite close. Flashes were clearly seen and every now and then a tremendous explosion was heard . . . this sort of thing went on all night until nearly dawn.' He added; 'It was fascinating to watch, in an awful sort of way.' However, neither Grant, Burney nor the captains of the other dreadnoughts at the tail of the battle fleet showed enough initiative to report these sightings to Jellicoe.

Stirling and the *Pommern*

The British 12th Flotilla was still between the Germans and Horns Reef. It had been on the eastern side of Jellicoe's belt of destroyers, and had fallen astern of the others. This was because its commander had used his own initiative to conduct a sweep towards the north of the other flotillas. The flotilla was now heading back to its station, running towards the south-south-east at high speed. It was about twenty-five miles astern of the *Agincourt*, while a few miles off its port beam were the light cruiser *Champion* and the destroyers *Obdurate* and *Moresby*, the remains of Captain Farie's 13th Flotilla. The 12th Flotilla was led by Captain Anselan Stirling in the flotilla leader *Faulknor*. His force was divided into three divisions; the first two divisions of four boats apiece were in two parallel columns 600 yards apart, deployed on the port and starboard quarters of the *Faulknor* to form a giant 'V' shape. The last five-boat division followed half a mile astern of the flotilla leader.

By 1.40 a.m. the darkness was on the wane, and the paling of the eastern sky heralded the coming of dawn. Still, conditions remained poor as a steady rain had begun to fall and, while it began to dissipate the lingering traces of mist, visibility was reduced to a thousand yards.

Three minutes later, lookouts on the *Obedient* leading Stirling's starboard column spotted a line of large ships off their starboard bow. This time there would be no recognition signal and the sacrifice of surprise. The destroyers waited and watched. Stirling soon identified the oncoming ships as German dreadnoughts. He was an experienced destroyer commander, and he didn't hesitate. He was pretty sure he hadn't been spotted yet, so he increased speed to 25 knots, swung his destroyers round onto a parallel course to the enemy, and then ordered Commander Bill Campbell in the *Obedient* to launch an attack. Unlike the other flotilla commanders, Stirling preferred attacking by divisions.

Campbell commanded the four boats of the flotilla's 1st Division – his own *Obedient*, then *Mindful*, *Marvel* and *Onslaught*. Campbell used a small signal lamp to flash the order to follow the *Obedient* into the attack, then turned sharply towards the enemy battle line. For once the Germans were slow to identify the threat, and didn't get a chance to fire their guns. However, the dreadnoughts in front of him – *Markgraf, Kronprinz, Grosser Kürfurst* and *König* – all made a simultaneous turn to starboard to avoid the spread of torpedoes they expected would be heading towards them. Campbell though, had lost sight of the dreadnoughts – the darkness was still lingering to the west, and Rear-Admiral Behncke's four dreadnoughts made full use of this. Denied a clear target, and having lost sight of the enemy, Campbell turned his boats away, and sped back to re-join the rest of the flotilla.

The sky was getting lighter by the minute, and when he saw Campbell return, Stirling decided he had to take advantage of what little remained of the pre-dawn darkness. First though, he ordered the *Faulknor's* wireless shack to send a message to Jellicoe. It read; 'Urgent Priority. Enemy battleships in sight. My position is ten miles astern of 1st Battle Squadron.' The signal was sent at 1.56 p.m., and repeated twelve minutes later, when there was no reply. Stirling might have been wrong about the distance between his flotilla and Burney's squadron – it was now about 20 miles away – but the gist of the signal was clear; Scheer's battle fleet was cutting past the stern of Jellicoe's dreadnoughts. In a third signal sent at 2.13 a.m., after he had drawn close enough to the enemy to confirm their course, he added that the German battle line was on a south-south-easterly heading. Unfortunately, these vital signals never reached the *Iron Duke*, just over 25 miles away to the south.

Stirling decided to lead the next attack himself. At 2 a.m., he ordered Campbell's division to fall in astern of the *Faulknor*, and then led these four boats off towards the south-east, so he could regain contact with the enemy. Six minutes later, he spotted the enemy ships ahead of him, and turned hard to starboard until he was heading towards the north-west, the reciprocal course to the one he had been on earlier. The leading German dreadnoughts were still turning back onto their original heading, and so were slightly further away from the British boats. This meant the closest enemy formation was Rear-Admiral Mauve's I Battle Squadron – the 'five-minute ships'. The line of destroyers and the line of pre-dreadnought battleships were on opposite headings, so in a few moments the pre-dreadnoughts would be directly on Stirling's beam. It was a textbook position from which to launch a torpedo attack. Now everything was down to skill, timing and luck.

Behind the *Faulknor* and Campbell's four boats the rest of the flotilla was struggling to keep up. Commander John Champion led the 2nd Division in the *Maenad*, and he managed to follow his flotilla leader, although he had fallen some distance behind Stirling, and so would only join the attack after the leading division had made its torpedo run. The bridge crew of the *Marksman*, the leading ship of the 3rd Division, hadn't noticed the flotilla's 180° turn, and so the boat maintained her south-easterly heading and missed the attack. The other four boats of the division managed to follow Champion though, and with his divisional leader absent, Commander Charles Sumner of the *Opal* assumed control of them. They would be the last group to attack.

So far the destroyers hadn't been shot at – Stirling assumed this was because they hadn't been seen. In fact, they had, but at the same moment the German V and IX Flotillas were approaching the German battle line from the port side, and so the German lookouts were unsure whether these dimly seen shapes were British or German. For once, it was the Germans who were hesitant. To make sure, the *Markgraf* flashed a recognition signal towards the line of boats that were dimly seen to the north. There was no reply. So, at 2.02 a.m. the *Grosser Kürfurst* turned away from the threat – a six point (67.5°) turn to starboard, and opened fire with her port secondary battery. She targeted the *Obedient*, the *Marvel* and the *Menace*, and within seconds 5.9-inch shells were falling around the frail destroyers. The wind, though, was hampering her gunnery, blowing the ship's funnel smoke in between the gunnery spotters and their target.

Further astern the *König* and *Deutschland* had the same problem when they began firing a few seconds later. They too followed Captain Ernst Goette's example and began turning their ships to starboard, a move repeated by the pre-dreadnoughts astern of their squadron flagship, and by the dreadnought *Nassau*, which was now tucked into the battle line between the *Hannover* and *Hessen*. It was at that moment that Stirling gave the order to launch torpedoes. The *Faulknor* launched first, followed a few moments later by *Obedient*, *Marvel* and *Onslaught*. The time was now 2.05 a.m., and at that range – a little over 1,000 yards the torpedoes took just under twenty seconds to reach their target. On the *Onslaught*, Able Seaman Fred Knight recalled the scene; 'We went straight in to attack. It was fast breaking daylight. We carried four 21" torpedoes which were all fired – one hitting the third ship in the line at a range of 1,000 yards.' *Onslaught* wasn't the only boat to claim a hit.

Unlike the older boats of Captain Wintour's command the M class destroyers of the 12th Flotilla carried four torpedo tubes, mounted in pairs on their centreline. In these modern boats, all four torpedoes could be launched simultaneously, and so a respectable spread of twelve torpedoes was launched at the German battle line. What saved most of the German ships was the fact that they were already turning to starboard. One passed within yards of the *Grosser Kürfurst*'s bow, while another hit the turbulence thrown up in *Kronprinz*'s wake and exploded a hundred yards astern of the dreadnought. Two more were seen heading straight for the *Markgraf*, and Captain Karl Seiferling must have willed his ship to turn faster as they sped towards him. He almost made it; one passed down her port bow as she turned, but the second headed straight towards the dreadnought's port quarter – and then passed underneath it.

Then, at 2.10 a.m., two torpedoes hit the pre-dreadnought *Pommern*, both striking her amidships on her port side. From the bridge of the *Hessen*, the next ship astern, onlookers reported that the initial detonations were followed a split second later by more explosions heard from inside her hull. Columns of smoke rose up over the pre-dreadnought's port side – white, black and pale yellow strands intermingling. Then angry red flames soared up from the battleship's side, and within seconds they engulfed the whole ship. The flames rose as high as her mastheads, and about thirty seconds later a huge explosion was heard, and *Pommern* broke in two. On the *Obedient*, Campbell saw; 'a dull red ball of fire amidships, which spread fore and aft and flared up the masts in big red tongues of flame, uniting in a black cloud of smoke and sparks'. Then they watched the ship explode and break in half.

On the *Onslaught*, Able Seaman George Wainford saw the *Pommern* explode; 'Cor, I said – we got her! And, the moment I said that either one shell or a salvo hit our bridge. There was a terrific bang, [and] a fire started [on] the port side of the foc'sle, where all the hammocks underneath the foc'scle deck were stowed.' Sub-Lieutenant Harry Kemmis had just been sent below to tell the engine room to make smoke to screen the boat when the shells hit the boat; 'I went back to the bridge, and finding everything wrecked, the Captain mortally wounded, and the First Lieutenant killed, I assumed command, and gave orders for the after steering position to be connected, which was done very smartly.' Quick thinking by Kemmis probably saved the ship, and *Onslaught* broke off the action, following her flotilla leader and the rest of her division run northwards, her departure covered by her own thick black smoke. Moments later, *Onslaught*'s captain died of his wounds.

When the *Pommern* was hit, Captain Wilhelm Heine of the *Hannover* jinked hard to starboard to avoid the wreckage. Turrets and chunks of superstructure were thrown into the air, which fell around the *Deutschland* and *Hannover*. As his ship steamed past, Heine saw *Pommern's* stern rise out of the water, exposing her propellers before sliding beneath the surface. It was impossible to stop – the German ships had to keep moving. The bow of the *Pommern* was still visible several minutes later as the last ships in the German line steamed past the spot. Almost certainly the torpedo detonations ignited the magazine of one of the *Pommern's* secondary 6.7-inch gun turrets on her port side. The resulting fireball then set off the magazines in other parts of the ship – a deadly chain reaction that ripped the battleship in two. None of *Pommern's* 844 officers and men survived the explosion.

After that the British attack fizzled out. The next division was led by Commander John Champion in the *Maenad*, who didn't follow Stirling's turn onto a reciprocal track to the Germans. While two of the other three boats in the division made the turn, the *Maenad* and the *Narwhal* kept on their old course. On *Maenad*, the crew frantically tried to swing their torpedo tubes around, as they were trained to starboard rather than port. Champion had pre-empted Stirling's orders, and so delayed making the turn until his torpedoes were ready. In the end, she made her own lone attack. *Maenad* made three torpedo runs at the enemy, but although she claimed a hit, all her torpedoes missed. Writing about it later, Champion added; 'Of course in these attacks we were fired at. Shots just short and just over, and certainly between the funnels and the bridge. We bore charmed lives – it is a miracle and nothing less.' Cutting her losses, *Maenad* then roared away towards the east.

Of the other boats in Champion's division, *Narwhal* left *Maenad* to it and turned after the rest of the division. She fired two torpedoes, scoring no hits, while Champion's other two destroyers *Nessus* and *Noble* don't seem to have fired at all. They may have been put off by the heavy fire coming their way. As Sub-Lieutenant Eric Lees of the *Nessus* described it; 'I saw a line of enemy battleships on the port bow. They opened fire and almost at once we were hit by a 5.9-inch shell, which struck the base of the foremast, cutting it in two.' The blast killed seven men and wounded eight more. As casualties were brought aft – the ship's medic had been killed – Lees patched them up as best he could. He recalled, 'Our two worst cases were a young Ordinary Seaman who had a piece of shell in his head . . . and an Able Seaman with one shoulder completely shattered.'

The 12th Flotilla's last division never got into action at all. After the division leader *Marksman* had headed off in the wrong direction, Commander Charles Sumner in the *Opal* took control of the four remaining boats, but before he saw the enemy battle line he came upon a pair of German light cruisers – probably the *Frankfurt* and *Pillau*. One of the boats in the division was Lieutenant-Commander Charles Poignand's *Menace*, and he described what happened after the rest of the flotilla reversed course to launch their attack; 'Before we had got to the turning point, they [Stirling's boats] were discovered and scattered, coming back at full speed in our direction, and in turn were being heavily shelled. . . . the boat ahead of us and all the others following had to turn the other way to avoid [a] collision, so none of us got a shot in.'

Effectively, only half of the destroyers in the flotilla had launched their torpedoes – if the boats' commanders had been a little more enterprising then more than just one pre-dreadnought battleship might have been hit. For instance, astern of the pre-dreadnoughts were the battlecruisers *Von der Tann* and *Derfflinger*. A hit on either of them – particularly the heavily damaged *Derfflinger* – would have sunk her. There was one mystery casualty, though. At 2.15 a.m., just a few minutes after *Pommern* exploded, the German destroyer *V-4* blew up. She wasn't under fire, and it came without warning. She and some other boats of the V Flotilla had formed up beside the front of the battle line, and the sudden explosion ripped off the boat's bow. She sank in minutes, but most of her surviving crew were rescued by the other destroyers. Although the cause isn't known, the likelihood is that one of her own torpedoes had accidentally detonated.

The Last Attack

Only one more small British force lay between the High Seas Fleet and safety. That was the rump of the 13th Destroyer Flotilla, formed by Captain John Farie in the light cruiser *Champion*, and the destroyers *Moresby* and *Obdurate*. After becoming separated from the rest of his flotilla, Farie had led his trio of ships east and then south, and by the time the 12th Flotilla was carrying out its attack he was about three miles further to the east. That put him due north of the *Westfalen* and the head of the German battle line. He was hoping to run south at high speed until he made contact with Jellicoe's battle fleet again, not knowing that in between lay Scheer's dreadnoughts. At 2.20 a.m. lookouts on board the *Champion* sighted a destroyer approaching them from their starboard beam. It turned out to be the *Marksman*, the 12th Flotilla boat that had become separated from the rest of its division while Stirling was manoeuvring into position.

Farie flashed a signal to the *Marksman*, asking; 'Where are enemy's ships?' Commander Norton Sulivan of the *Marksman* hadn't even made contact with the enemy battle fleet, so he replied 'Suspicious ships south'. Next, Farie asked 'Where is our battlefleet?' Sulivan sent a similar reply; 'Bearing South'. So a few minutes later, when the *Champion*'s lookouts spotted the shapes of large ships to the south, Farie didn't really know whether they were friend or foe. He ordered *Marksman* to join his force, as well as the *Maenad*, which had just made an appearance from the west. Farie led his enlarged force off towards the south to investigate. Visibility was still poor thanks to the light rain. At 2.30 a.m., Sulivan signalled the *Champion*, asking, 'What are ships bearing south?' Farie peered at them through his binoculars, then replied, 'Germans I think.' Farie decided to get a little closer.

The mysterious ships were about two miles away to the south-west, and as the destroyers drew closer they could see they were German pre-dreadnought battleships. In these circumstances the light cruiser *Champion* would be a liability as she lacked the firepower to take on the pre-dreadnoughts. So Farie ordered *Champion* to turn away towards the east-north-east. In fact, Sub-Lieutenant Harry Oram on the *Obdurate* painted a slightly different picture when he wrote; 'At 2.30 a.m. we caught a glimpse of four large shadowy shapes looming against the western horizon. *Champion*, thinking we had overtaken the rear ships of the Grand Fleet, turned away to avoid confusion. Whatever the reason, *Champion* left *Moresby*, *Obdurate* and *Marksman* to fend for themselves. They had teeth though; all of them apart from the *Maenad* had all their torpedoes left, and the light was still poor enough to give the boats a fighting chance of surviving a torpedo run.

In the end, only Commander Roger Alison of the *Moresby* was either brave or rash enough to launch an attack. As he wrote; 'I considered action imperative, hoisted compass west, hauled out to port, firing an AS [anti-shipping] torpedo at 2.37 a.m.' In other words, at about 2.34 a.m., Alison pulled out of the column of destroyers following the *Champion*, which was now running towards the east. He circled to port, passing astern of the last destroyer – the *Maenad* – and then headed directly towards the enemy. After three minutes he spun the wheel to port and fired a single torpedo out of one of his two pairs of torpedo tubes, which had already been trained on the enemy line. The boat then turned away to follow the *Maenad*. Alison had selected the 21-inch Mark I torpedo's fastest setting, which meant that it set off towards the enemy at an impressive 44 ½ knots. At that speed the torpedo only had a range of 4,500 yards, but the enemy was still just within range.

Two minutes later, the torpedo was spotted by lookouts on the battlecruiser *Von der Tann*, which was the second ship from the end of the long German line. Captain Johannes von Karpf ordered an immediate emergency turn to starboard, and as the torpedo drew closer the battlecruiser slowly began to turn. Just before 2.40 a.m. the torpedo shot close under the bow of the *Von der Tann*; if von Karpf hadn't ordered the turn, then she would have been hit amidships. It was a very fortunate escape, but then the battlecruiser seemed to have had luck on her side throughout the battle. As the *Moresby* re-joined her companions though, her crew were certain they'd scored a hit. Strangely, Farie's other destroyers never tried to carry out an attack of their own, but seemed content to follow the light cruiser in the opposite direction. Nobody knew it – in fact few knew about the torpedo run – but this torpedo launch by the *Moresby* was the last hostile action of the battle.

The High Seas Fleet had done it; they had passed behind the Grand Fleet, and now nothing stood in their way. Thanks to a lack of training, the British destroyers had proved largely ineffectual, and their attacks had been brushed aside with relatively minor losses. However, the destroyers' greatest failure was that they didn't tell Jellicoe that the German fleet was behind him. Only one flotilla commander tried, and his message never got through. The captains of the dreadnoughts and fast battleships forming Jellicoe's rearguard were just as guilty. As a result, thanks to Scheer's grim determination to break through Jellicoe's fleet whatever the cost, his High Seas Fleet was now just 25 miles – or eighty minutes – from Horns Reef. Dawn was breaking. With Jellicoe more than 35 miles away, and Beatty further still, it was now physically impossible to bring the Germans to battle. So, as dawn broke the British chance had passed. Against all the odds, Scheer had pulled it off.

Part IV

The Elusive Victory

21

An Empty Horizon

As dawn broke on 1 June, lookouts on the *Iron Duke* scanned the horizon, but there was no enemy in sight. Jellicoe had expected to see Scheer's battle fleet to the west of him, but the sea was empty. Visibility was still poor though – the sea was shrouded in mist – so Jellicoe was reasonably confident that the Germans were out there, and that the battle would be renewed as soon as the enemy were spotted. The British battle fleet was in a compact formation, although part of Vice-Admiral Burney's squadron and the fast battleships had fallen behind the other dreadnoughts during the night. So Jellicoe busied himself recalling his light forces – his cruisers and destroyers – ready for the fleet action he thought was imminent. His ships were ready for the fight, and morale was high; everyone wanted to finish the job started the previous afternoon. As the minutes ticked by, though, and the seas remained empty, this certainty began to evaporate

A Victory Denied

As dawn broke, Jellicoe returned to the *Iron Duke*'s bridge. He genuinely believed that Scheer was still trapped, as he had been when he retired to his cabin for a few hours of rest. His first action was to check the signal log. No important signals had come in during the short night. Anyway, his staff had orders to wake him if anything untoward occurred, and his brief sleep was uninterrupted. None of the few messages sent to the fleet flagship during the night had actually reached him, and so he fully expected he would be able to reap the reward of his advantageous position.

Given the odds, victory was almost assured. A midshipman on the fleet flagship recalled the mood of the ship early that morning; 'The promise of a better day. We had plenty of ammunition left and felt that, given the chance, we would make short work of what remained of the enemy. The guns had been left loaded and we were ready to start again.'

Visibility was little more than 2½ miles (5,000 yards), but Jellicoe could make out the columns of dreadnoughts steaming on either beam. Looking more closely, he noticed that only half of Burney's squadron was in its proper station. This was soon explained. A signal came in from Burney, reporting that the *Marlborough* had been unable to contain the flooding from her torpedo hit the previous afternoon. Her speed had now dropped to 12 knots and Burney's division had lagged behind the rest of the battle fleet. He had just released the other three dreadnoughts in his division, which were now heading south to rejoin the rest of the battle fleet. At that moment Jellicoe was expecting to fight a battle and so concentrating his battle fleet was his top priority. The absence of *Marlborough* was unfortunate, but that was less important to Jellicoe than the return of Burney's three other dreadnoughts, *Revenge, Hercules* and *Agincourt*.

Jellicoe also needed his lighter forces; his cruisers which should be on his flanks, and the destroyers following astern of him. So, at 2.12 a.m., he gave orders for the fleet to 'conform and close' around the flagship. Once his light forces had re-joined him, then he could begin the search for Scheer, either to the west or further to the north. Jellicoe's letters reveal that he planned to head towards Horns Reef if he couldn't find Scheer at sunrise. At the time, though, he didn't know that Scheer's fleet was almost there already. His wireless message to the fleet also said that at 2.30 a.m. his intention was to alter course to the north. To make this as easy as possible, he gave the flagship's estimated position for that time – 55° 7' North, 6° 21' West. He sent the message to Beatty too, whose forces were probably somewhere through the mist to the south-west. In fact, the battlecruisers were 15 miles away, with the 1st and 3rd Light Cruiser Squadrons off their starboard beam, between Beatty and Scheer – or rather where he thought Scheer should be.

Instead, at 2.15 a.m., Scheer was fifteen miles to the north-east of Jellicoe, and ten miles to the north-east of Burney in the *Marlborough*. However, the High Seas Fleet was heading almost directly towards

Horns Reef, which lay to the south-west, while the Grand Fleet was still heading south. Each passing minute brought the Germans closer to safety, and the two fleets further apart. The last action of the battle – the torpedo attack by the destroyer *Moresby* – took place at 2.40 a.m., by which time the gap between the *Friedrich der Grosse* and the *Iron Duke* had widened to 27 miles. With such poor visibility, the gap might as well have been ten times that. Jellicoe might have decided to head north to look for Scheer, but by then it was too late. He had already missed his chance.

The turn was delayed by a few minutes while Jellicoe waited for more news. It never came, so at 2.39 a.m., the 'execute' signal was given and the turn began. With the Germans probably just out of sight through the mist, Jellicoe decided to play it safe. The fleet would turn by divisions, but then it would reform into a single line. That way he would be ready for anything. The manoeuvre began with Vice-Admiral Jerram's 2nd Battle Squadron, led by the *King George V.* Vice-Admiral Doveton Sturdee's 4th Battle Squadron took up position astern of Jerram's rearmost ship, the *Thunderer.* Behind Doveton Sturdee came the four dreadnoughts of the 5th Division; the rest of the 1st Battle Squadron was still somewhere to the north. Finally, the three fast battleships of Rear-Admiral Evan-Thomas took up station ahead of Jerram, with *Barham* in the lead. So, by 3 a.m., Jellicoe's battle was heading north again, with 23 dreadnoughts under his command. All he needed now was Scheer.

That night, Captain Peter Strasser commanding the Naval Airship Division, sent up five zeppelins with orders to try and locate the Grand Fleet. The poor visibility really hindered the air crews, but a little after 3.10 a.m., Lieutenant Commander Viktor Schütze in the *L-11* spotted British warships through a gap in the clouds. Schütze described the sighting; 'At 4.15 a.m. [3.15 a.m.], after encountering the first battleship squadron, the enemy opened fire with all ships and weapons, with anti-aircraft and other guns of all calibres; the main turrets fired broadsides. . . . Although the firing was without result, the passage of the big shells and the bursting of shrapnel nearby caused such heavy vibrations to the framework that it seemed advisable to increase the distance. The gunfire lasted till 5.20 a.m. [4.20 a.m.]. At this time the battlecruisers, pushing up from the south-west to within close range of the *L-11*, forced her off to the north-east to avoid their heavy fire.

As soon as he spotted the dreadnoughts Schütze radioed the news to his air base at Nordholz near Cuxhaven, and to Scheer, who read Schütze's message at 3.30 a.m. Schütze followed it with more information, and a position. So Scheer should have known that Jellicoe was safely out of range. Instead, though, he wrote this; 'In our opinion the ships in a south-westerly direction could only have come from the Channel to try, on hearing the news of the battle, to join up with their main fleet and advance against us.' Scheer wrote more, claiming to have considered attacking this new force, but to have decided against it. As he put it; 'I therefore abandoned the idea of further operations and ordered the return to port.' This was as disingenuous as most of Scheer's post-battle 'analysis' of his own actions. By his reckoning then, both Jellicoe and Beatty were somewhere closer to him, and possibly waiting for him off Horns Reef. That morning, he had no option but to run for home.

So the British fleet continued its sweep to the north, and all the while the lookouts peered into the mist, hoping to be the first to spot the elusive enemy. The minutes ticked by, but there was no dramatic sighting, only the empty sea. The only enemy in sight was the *L-11*, which explained why it attracted the attention of the whole battle fleet. On the *Agincourt*, Lieutenant Angus Graham fired the ship's only anti-aircraft gun, a high-angle 12-pounder; 'We cheerfully engaged the airship which was probably eight or nine miles away, but it gave us something to do – and something to laugh at.' Then, he told how; 'The *Revenge* opened fire with her 15-inch guns at maximum elevation.' The shells didn't hit the zeppelin, but they landed close to the *Malaya*. Captain Algernon Boyle was perplexed, and according to Sub-Lieutenant Clifford Caslon he thought the salvo was fired by an enemy ship, shouting 'Where are they? Where are they?' Caslon added; 'We learned much later that it was the *Revenge*, who, some fifteen miles away, was firing at a zeppelin!'

Jellicoe's hopes were finally dashed at 4.10 a.m. That was when a telegram from the Admiralty was handed to him as he stood on the bridge of the *Iron Duke*. It had actually been sent forty-one minutes earlier, but decoding it had taken longer than it should have, as the senior coding officer had to be roused from his bunk. The signal read; 'Urgent. At 2.30 German main battle fleet at Lat. 55° 33' N, Long. 6° 50' E. Course SE by S, 16 knots.' The news came from a Room 40 wireless intercept. Jellicoe's heart must have sunk as he read it. He didn't need to glance at the chart to confirm that an hour and forty minutes before Scheer had been just ten or twelve miles to the north-east of the *Iron Duke*. Now, if the German battle fleet had maintained the course and speed given in the signal, then Scheer would be forty miles away, and already well past the Horns Reef lightship. There would be no decisive battle that morning.

A wretchedly disappointed Jellicoe summed up the situation; 'This signal made it evident that by no possibility could I catch the enemy before he reached port, even if I disregarded the danger of following him through the minefields.' That, though, was not a viable option. Jellicoe was too sensible a commander to risk his fleet in the minefields, whether British or German. The enemy had swept channels through them, and only they knew where these safe channels lay. To continue on was to invite disaster. So, with a heavy heart, Jellicoe had to resign himself to the fact that Scheer had slipped through his fingers. All that was left was to reform the fleet into its normal cruising formation – a column of divisions – link up with Burney's four dreadnoughts, including the damaged *Marlborough*, and then send his light forces to sweep the battlefield, to look for German stragglers and to rescue any survivors.

Some fifteen miles to the south-west, Beatty had had no contact with the enemy since early the previous evening. He was still hoping to intercept the Germans, and at 4.04 a.m., he sent a signal to Jellicoe, which read; 'When last seen enemy was to the W, steering SW and proceeding slowly. Zeppelin has past astern of me, heading west. Submit I may sweep SW to locate the enemy.' Jellicoe didn't respond immediately; he was still digesting the unpalatable signal from the Admiralty. So, at 4.30 a.m., Beatty signalled the ships in his Battlecruiser Fleet, saying this; 'Damage yesterday was heavy on both sides, but we hope today to cut off and annihilate the whole German fleet. Every man must do his utmost. *Lützow* is sinking, and another German battlecruiser expected to have sunk.' This signal deliberately mimicked Nelson's signal before Trafalgar, showing that Beatty still fully expected a climactic battle that morning.

At 4.40 a.m., Jellicoe crushed that dream with a nine-word signal. It read; 'Enemy has returned to harbour. Try to locate *Lützow*.' According to his Flag Lieutenant, William Chalmers, Beatty took the news badly. During the forenoon watch a burial service was held for the ninety-nine crewmen of the *Lion* who were killed the previous day. As the ship's chaplain the Rev. Cecil Lydall was among the dead, the service was taken by the Flag Captain, Ernle Chatfield. As Chalmers recalled; 'Beatty, deeply moved, stood on the poop behind Chatfield.' Chalmers continues; 'In the afternoon, Beatty came into the *Lion*'s charthouse. Tired and depressed, he sat down on the settee, and settling himself in a corner he closed his eyes. Unable to hide his disappointment at the result of the battle, he repeated in a weary voice "There is something wrong with our ships". Then, opening his eyes and looking at the writer, he added "and something wrong with our system". Having thus unburdened himself he fell asleep.'

German Stragglers

Scheer was certainly well on his way home. At 2.30 a.m. he reported his position to the Admiralstab in Berlin, claiming he was at the right of Square 101, course south-east-by-south, speed 16 knots. This was the message that was passed on to Jellicoe over an hour-and-a-half later, when it was too late to intercept the enemy battle fleet. With Horns Reef Lightship just seventeen miles away, Scheer was fairly sure he was home and dry. Inevitably, his thoughts turned to the damaged or stricken warships he had left behind, or which were struggling to make it home independently. The most important of these were the heavily damaged battlecruisers *Lützow* and *Seydlitz*. *Derfflinger* and *Von der Tann* were in poor shape – at 2.55 a.m. Hipper reported they had two working guns left between them – but they were still keeping up with the battle fleet. *Moltke* was returning home on her own, but there were also three crippled light cruisers out there; the *Wiesbaden*, *Elbing* and *Rostock*.

At 3 a.m. a message from the British Admiralty – another wireless intercept – reported that at 10 p.m. the *Lützow* was at 56° 26' North, 5° 41' East, steering south at 7 knots. That meant that if the ships held that course, at 4 a.m. it would be around the latitude of 55° 30' North, due west of Horns Reef. Jellicoe ordered his commanders to look out for her, not knowing that the battlecruiser had already lost her battle to stay afloat. After sending the intercepted message, Captain Harder turned the *Lützow* towards Horns Reef, following in the wake of the battle fleet as best she could. Her escorting destroyers were still clustered round her, and the hope was that she could still make it home. However, at midnight the pumps could no longer cope, as water reached the dynamo rooms, then the forward boiler room. Harder tried to steer his ship stern-first, but the bows were so far under that her stern was raised up, lifting her propellers clear of the water. There was now no hope for her.

At 1.20 a.m. Harder gave the order to abandon ship. As the Official German History records, 'The ship's company fell in on the quarterdeck, and the destroyers G-37, G-38, G-40 and V-45 . . . came alongside. After three cheers for the Kaiser and for the Lützow were given, the ship's company – the wounded first – left the sinking vessel, quietly and in good order. By 2.45 a.m. [1.45 a.m.] she was submerged as far as the bridge. Two torpedoes fired by the G-37 then gave the Lützow the coup de grâce, and two minutes later she disappeared below the waves. The overcrowded destroyers then set a course for home.

At 2.20 a.m. the four destroyers spotted two British destroyers to the south of them. They were the Garland and Conquest, searching for the rest of their 4th Flotilla. Lieutenant Richard Beitzen of the G-40 decided to attack, even though his destroyers were impossibly overcrowded. They were carrying a thousand extra men between them – the crew of the Lützow. The two sides fired at each other for a few minutes, then the two British boats turned away into the mist. The V-45 launched a torpedo and claimed a torpedo hit, but in fact neither of the British boats were damaged during the brief skirmish. This took place just minutes before the last torpedo attack of the battle, the launch of a torpedo by the Moresby at the Von der Tann. Beitzen and his men then resumed their old course and sped on after the rest of the fleet.

The Wiesbaden finally sank at about 1.45 a.m. The handful of her crew who were still alive took to the water. We don't know how many men abandoned ship that night, but only one survived. Stoker Hugo Zenne wrote; 'I ran to the quarterdeck, undid the mooring of a float, climbed onboard and shoved . . . Kneeling on it, I frantically used my hands to paddle towards the stern, to avoid the suction when the ship sank. Everything was quite quiet. My companions who stood on the deck jumped off the stern and swam towards my raft.' Zenne described the ship sinking, battle ensign still flying. Then he looked around; 'We floated between dead comrades, dead fishes, hammocks and lifejackets . . . All the feeling of confidence had disappeared from me. You can hope as long as you have a ship beneath you, but when you're afloat in a raft in the sea, the cold slowly spreads up from the toes, and then slowly the limbs grow stiff.'

Another straggler, the *Elbing,* had been drifting ever since her collision with the *Posen* late the previous evening. With her engine rooms flooded, there was no chance of getting her moving again. Undeterred, Captain Madlung tried to rig a makeshift sail from the foremast, but it did little other than keep her turned in the right direction. At 1 a.m. he transferred most of his crew to the escorting destroyer *S-53* and sent her away, but he remained on board the cruiser, together with a skeleton crew. Then, at around 2 a.m. Madlung spotted British destroyers a mile-and-a-half to the south. He decided to scuttle the *Elbing* using explosive charges rather than risk letting her be captured. Ironically, the destroyer he spotted was the *Sparrowhawk,* which was sinking herself. On the crippled British boat, Sub-Lieutenant Percy Wood thought they were doomed. Then he noticed something strange about the enemy cruiser; 'I had some spotting glasses . . . I thought she started to heel over to one side slightly . . . Then everyone else noticed it . . . She settled down forward, very slowly, and then quietly stood on her head and sank.'

The majority of the *Elbing*'s crew were heading home in the dangerously overcrowded *S-53,* but her captain and his skeleton crew had nothing to escape in but the ship's launch. As they headed away towards the east they spotted a man in the water, a survivor from the British destroyer *Tipperary.* No sooner was he hauled on board than they came upon more of the destroyer's crew, clinging to a raft. Madlung couldn't fit them on board his own craft, but he fired off a blue flare to attract attention, apologised, and continued on his way. Later that morning Madlung and his men were rescued by the neutral Dutch trawler *Ijmuiden.* The men of the *Tipperary* were less fortunate; most drowned in the freezing water. Only a dozen men survived, and of those eight – including the man rescued by Madlung – did so as prisoners of war.

Commodore Michelsen tried to save the *Rostock* after she was hit by a torpedo during the night, but damage to her engines meant she could barely make steam. She was finally taken in tow by the destroyer *S-54,* and they headed west at ten knots, accompanied by two other destroyers. Shortly before 4 a.m. a British cruiser appeared. The two warships exchanged recognition signals, and seemingly convinced the *Rostock* was friendly, the cruiser *Dublin* headed away on a reciprocal course to the west. What sealed the *Rostock*'s fate though, was the report from a patrolling zeppelin that a division of British dreadnoughts was heading her way. To save his crew, Michelsen ordered them taken on board the *S-54*, and at 4.25 a.m., he watched as the *Rostock* was sunk by torpedoes launched from the *V-71* and *V-73*. After that, the trio of destroyers made it safely to Horns Reef without incident.

That left the *Moltke* and the *Seydlitz*. Even though she was on her own, the *Moltke* made it past the British fleet at about 1.30 a.m., about twenty miles to the south of Scheer and the battle fleet. Vice-Admiral Hipper and Captain von Karpf were lucky to find a gap in the British line, the result of Burney's squadron falling behind the rest of the battle fleet. The battlecruiser was damaged, and carrying a thousand tons of seawater inside her hull. Still, she actually reached the passage south of Horns Reef before the rest of the battle fleet, and accompanied it as it steamed south through the channels in the German minefields. Captain von Egidy in the *Seydlitz* was less fortunate. He passed the British a little over ten miles to the north of the battle fleet, but thanks to the flooding, progress was agonisingly slow. By 2.30 a.m. the *Seydlitz* was off the north-west of the Horns Reef Lightship. That was when disaster struck, just when her crew thought they had made it to safety.

Captain von Egidy explained the situation they were in. They were barely able to contain the flooding in the battlecruiser's bow, and the damage was too severe to repair. Just as seriously; 'The navigation apparatus had suffered severely during the action, the charts were partially obliterated by the blood of the men who had been killed in the control tower, and the reserve charts were below, in a flooded compartment. As the gyro compass was out of action, we had to steer with the magnetic compass on the upper bridge. Only the hand-steering gear was available for steering.' This made it difficult to steer and navigate the wallowing sluggish ship, which was already riding dozens of feet lower in the water than normal. So, at 2.40 a.m., the *Seydlitz* ran squarely on to Horns Reef. It took two attempts, three hours and a rising tide to refloat her, von Egidy gunning her propellers until she finally edged astern into deeper water.

Then the *Seydlitz* limped south through the Amrum Channel, making seven knots, with all available hands working her pumps. The men had to; 'stand for hours up to their thighs in water, and suffered horribly from the steam formed by the moisture when evaporating on the steam pipes'. Each passing hour brought the water a little further aft, as flooded compartments had to be abandoned. Von Egidy used a chain of messengers to relay his commands – more sophisticated methods were impossible – but at 9 a.m. they ran aground again, this time off the southern end of Sylt island. It took half an hour to refloat the ship, and she pressed on, settling further in the water as she went. It was hardly surprising; it was calculated the battlecruiser had 5,300 tons of sea water inside her. It was noon on 2 June when tugs finally hauled the half-submerged *Seydlitz* over the bar into the Jade Roads. There, divers did what they could to keep her afloat, while a fleet of tenders landed her dead and wounded.

The rest of the High Seas Fleet headed south from the Horns Reef in greater style, at least until they reached the Amrum Channel. Then, at 5.20 a.m., and without warning, the dreadnought *Ostfriesland* struck a mine. Seven other dreadnoughts had passed the same spot ahead of her, preceded by the cruisers of Von Reuter's IV Scouting Group. It was almost as if the mine was sentient, and had singled her out. It exploded against her starboard side, hurling debris and bits of mine casing onto her deck. Still, the blow was not a mortal one. It flooded several coal bunkers, killed one man and wounded ten more, but her internal torpedo bulkhead absorbed the blast and the flooding was contained. She pulled out of line to port, and while the rest of the fleet steamed on, *Ostfriesland* was left to make it home under her own steam. She did too, escorted by two destroyers, and at 1.40 p.m. she finally limped into the Jade Estuary and dropped anchor.

In a way, the Germans were lucky. The mine was probably one that had been laid by the British minelayer *Abdiel* three weeks before, but the fleet missed the rest of the minefield the *Abdiel* had sown during that mission. In fact, the *Abdiel* had just finished laying a fresh field of 80 mines early in the morning of 1 June. She had been sent there by Jellicoe the evening before, and she completed her minelaying just before 3 a.m. The minelayer narrowly missed running into the High Seas Fleet as she made her escape back into open water. This time though, Scheer's fleet didn't pass through the new field, so her efforts went unrewarded. The British also missed an even greater opportunity that morning. Three British submarines were lying on the bottom near the Amrum Bank, with orders to remain submerged until 2 June. The German fleet passed right over them, and their crews knew nothing of this – or of the great sea battle – until they returned to Harwich on 3 June.

By early afternoon the rest of the battle fleet were lying safely at anchor off Wilhelmshaven and the grim task of ferrying the dead and wounded ashore began. Tugs, pumping barges, diving teams and medical help were all on hand though, and the most seriously damaged ships were taken straight to the quayside. Priority was given to the battle-cruisers, some of which could barely float. Pumps on the quayside kept *Derfflinger* above water while temporary patches could be fitted to her many waterline holes. Days later, the poor *Seydlitz* reached the dock stern first, her bows completely submerged. Scheer knew perfectly well he had had a lucky escape, and when he called his captains to his flagship for champagne, the gathering was less a celebration of victory than of deliverance. Against the odds, and largely thanks to his own deter-mination during the night, the High Seas Fleet had survived. It remained a 'fleet in being' and, at least in theory, it lived to fight another day.

The Unhappy Return

By 5.30 a.m., just as the crew of the *Ostfriesland* were dealing with their encounter with a mine, the Grand Fleet was approaching the previous day's battlefield. An hour before, Jellicoe had spread his dreadnoughts out into six columns, and the cruisers and destroyers fanned out ahead of the fleet, with everyone looking for German stragglers. From the dreadnought *Monarch*, Able Seamen Myers described the battlefield; 'We steamed over the scene of the action. We passed masses of floating wreckage: spars, ditty boxes, fragments of lifeboats and many bodies.' On the battlecruiser *New Zealand*, Midshipman Eady viewed the same forlorn spectacle; 'The sea was strewn with wreckage for miles, and we steamed for half an hour through large numbers of dead bodies, mostly German, floating in a mass of blood, oil, dead fish, seagulls, cartridge cases. etc.; This was what the aftermath of a modern sea battle looked like.

They found pitifully few survivors, though. The main reason was exposure. When Lieutenant Commander Marsden, captain of the *Ardent* was pulled out of the water, he said of his dead crew: 'None appeared to suffer at all. They just seemed to lie back and go to sleep.' On the destroyer *Maenad*, Commander Champion described rescuing other British sailors; 'I came across a raft full of men from the [destroyer] *Fortune*, and picked up eleven of them, not without excitement, because just as I dropped a boat a submarine was sighted close to.' He got under way, and claimed that a torpedo was fired, but German records show no submarine was operating in the area. *Champion* returned and picked up the boat, and all but one of the men he rescued lived to tell the tale. This imagined U-Boat sighting was pretty common that morning; *Iron Duke* even opened fire on an imagined submarine, wasting her ammunition as she shot at an empty patch of sea.

The sweep continued. Bubbles occasionally broke the surface, pockets of air rising from the compartment of a sunken warship, but apart from the occasional survivor and the wheeling seabirds, there was little sign of life amid the flotsam. The Grand Fleet steamed through the debris in an almost reverential silence, broken only by the occasional order from the officer of the watch or a response from the helmsman. The only flurry of noise came when a lookout thought he had spotted the periscope of a U-Boat, and the passing ships opened fire, only to find there was nothing there. The crew of the ships remained at action stations throughout the day, but as the morning wore on it became apparent that there was not going to be any more fighting that day. For all their desire to finish the job, most of the dog-tired crew would have been relieved that their ordeal was over.

Visibility was now about three to four miles, so while Jellicoe had given up all hope of meeting Scheer's battle fleet, he still hoped to make contact with a German straggler. In fact, the Admiralty had already passed on wireless intercepts which suggested that the *Lützow* and the *Elbing* were still in the area. The cruiser *Dublin* had sighted an enemy cruiser and accompanying destroyers – the *Rostock* – but the position Captain Albert Scott of the *Dublin* gave was highly suspect, so the fleet kept searching. At 6 a.m. another signal mistakenly suggested that the *Elbing* was still afloat and so three minutes later Jellicoe altered course towards the south-east in an attempt to investigate. He gave up the search ninety minutes later and ordered the fleet to resume its northerly heading. It was now pretty clear that no German ships were still still at large. The reason, of course, is that by the time the Grand Fleet arrived, these German stragglers had all sunk.

Shortly after 10 a.m. Jellicoe received news that must have shocked him to the core. A little earlier, he had signalled Beatty, asking him if all his cruisers and destroyers were accounted for. He also asked; 'Where are *New Zealand* and *Indefatigable*?' Beatty replied at 10.01 a.m., and a few minutes later a no doubt ashen-faced signals officer handed Jellicoe the decoded message. It didn't answer Jellicoe's question. Instead it gave the positions for the wrecks of the *Queen Mary*, the *Invincible* and the *Indefatigable*. Jellicoe already knew about the sinking of Hood's flagship; he had steamed past the wreck the previous evening. This, though, was the first time Beatty had told him about the other two battlecruisers. There was a long pause as Jellicoe absorbed the grim news. At 11.04 a.m. he asked Beatty; 'When did *Queen Mary* and *Indefatigable* go down?' Beatty was forced to admit that they had sunk the previous afternoon. It had taken him more than six hours to tell Jellicoe what happened. Even then, he had to be asked by his fleet commander.

Finally, at 11 a.m., a downcast Jellicoe called it a day. The first indication that the sweep was at an end came fifteen minutes before. At 3 a.m. that morning, the Admiralty had ordered the Harwich Force to sea to reinforce the Grand Fleet. At 10.44 a.m., before Commodore Tyrwhitt's reinforcements reached him, he ordered them to the north to form a protective screen around the *Marlborough*. Jellicoe had detached her from the fleet earlier that morning, and she was now heading towards the shipyards of Tyneside. At 11.08 a.m. Jellicoe sent a signal to the Admiralty, saying nothing more could be achieved in the area, and that he was returning to Scapa Flow. The battle was over, as was the sweep of the battlefield. All that remained was to head home. It would be a melancholy afternoon, as the crews scraped together what remained of some of their shipmates and prepared to bury their remains.

It was the custom in the Royal Navy to bury the dead at sea. Bodies were identified, if at all possible, and then sewn into their hammocks, after a weight was placed at their feet. On the *Barham*, teenage Boy Seaman Henry Hawkins was shocked by the spectacle; 'The biggest fright at my age was to see the bodies, the canvas bags being made and the old-fashioned cannon balls being used for the burial at sea.' In some cases it was impossible to identify the remains; the crew had to gather scraps of body together in bags. Then, accompanied by a marine bugler and the serried ranks of the living, the ship's chaplain performed a committal service on the side of the ship.

On the *Malaya*, Surgeon Lieutenant Duncan Lorimer left his wounded for a few minutes, and came on deck to watch the service; 'The ship had slowed down, and there was a burial going on of the poor unrecognisable scraps of humanity from the explosion. . . . It was a gloomy scene, the grey sky, the grey sea, the stitched up hammocks, the padre with his gown blowing in the breeze. The *Last Post* was sounded by the marine buglers, and our shipmates plunged into the sullen waters.' The same grim scene was repeated on other vessels in the fleet, and as the Grand Fleet steamed home, bodies bobbed in its wake. As Signalman John Handley of the *Barham* observed; 'Many didn't sink immediately, but kind of floated in a horizontal position for a time until the weights took effect, when they gradually righted themselves . . . before finally disappearing beneath the waves.'

Having dealt with the dead, and with the wounded already being tended to, the next problem was to nurse home the ships that had been badly damaged during the battle. The armoured cruiser *Warrior* was being towed by the small seaplane carrier *Engadine*, a ship a tenth of her size. The *Engadine* could barely cope, and during the night they made little more than three knots. During the early morning the wind rose, making towing increasingly difficult as the two ships pitched and yawed. Finally, at 7 a.m., when they were still 160 miles east of Aberdeen, Captain Vincent Molteno of the *Warrior* was forced to concede defeat. It was clear his ship was sinking; his priority now was to save the crew. It was too rough to use small boats, so in a rare display of seamanship Lieutenant Commander Charles Robertson brought the *Engadine*, a former car ferry, alongside the cruiser. It took two attempts, and all the time the *Warrior* was settling lower in the water.

The wounded went over first, then the rest of the crew were mustered on the upper deck. When the order came, each group of messmates jumped across the gap between the two ships. Signalman Reuben Poole was one of the jumpers; 'When my turn came to abandon ship my goods and relics were thrown onto the deck of the rescue ship. Then, as the sea rose with the waves, I grabbed at the *Engadine*'s taffrails, and rolled inboard.' At least one man was not so lucky. One stretcher case was dropped between the two ships, and 'Rutland of Jutland' jumped in after him, tied a rope around him and the pair were hauled aboard. By 8.52 a.m., the transfer was complete and the tethers were cut. As the *Warriors* watched, their battle-scarred ship gave a convulsive heave and then vanished, her white ensign still flying from the masthead.

Two other badly damaged but infinitely more valuable ships were the *Warspite* and the *Marlborough*. It was a long way to Rosyth, and the *Warspite* steamed on alone through the night. While she had been badly clawed about during her antics near the *Warrior*, her engines were still in good shape, even though her steering was still proving erratic. She was still a hundred miles from home and labouring through a heavy sea when a torpedo bobbed to the surface next to the ship. Clearly *Warspite* was under attack, so Captain Phillpotts turned away. Two hours later, lookouts spotted another periscope a hundred yards ahead of them. This time Phillpotts tried to ram the U-Boat, but the boat – the *U-63* – managed to crash dive in the nick of time. *Warspite* kept going, and by 3 p.m. she was entering the Firth of Forth. Two hours later, she was being towed into dry dock, as her exhausted crew prepared to land their wounded shipmates.

The first torpedo attack on *Warspite* took place at 9.35 a.m. At about the same moment, around a hundred miles to the east, Lieutenant Leo Hillebrand of the *U-46* spotted a cruiser and a dreadnought heading towards him. They were the *Fearless* and the *Marlborough*, on their way to the Tyne. The flooding had increased during the night, so *Marlborough* was moving slowly, at less than ten knots. When the range dropped to a little over one-and-a-half miles, Hillebrand fired a single torpedo, but the *Marlborough* was zig-zagging, and it missed her, running past her port side. *Marlborough* turned away, and in the heavy sea Hillebrand was unable to give chase. A few hours later, *Marlborough* was joined by the Harwich Force, who formed an anti-submarine cordon around her. Together, the force continued on to the west, and eventually reached the River Humber on the morning of 2 June.

Another battle-scarred British warship to limp home under her own steam was the destroyer *Spitfire*. She refused the help of a neutral merchant ship, and struggled on at ten knots. Lieutenant Bush was on watch for much of the voyage, trying to make a landfall with only a single scrap of damaged chart left; 'As the morning drew on we met a patrol drifter, which informed us we were 22 miles north-east of the Tyne.' They eventually reached the safety of the River Tyne, still carrying that twenty-foot section of the *Nassau*'s armoured plating on their upper deck.

At 8.30 a.m. on the morning of 2 June, the Battlecruiser Fleet – what remained of it – steamed into the Firth of Forth. Hospital ships were ready to come alongside and take the seriously wounded as soon as the ships moored, and a small cluster of drifters waited to embark the walking wounded, to ferry them to the hospital in Rosyth. Three hours later, the rest of the Grand Fleet passed the Hoxa Head battery and entered Scapa Flow. As the ships filed past, the gunners may well not have noticed, but the naval lookouts on duty would have spotted that the *Marlborough* was not among the other dreadnoughts. Even more noticeably, of the four ships of the 1st Cruiser Squadron, only the *Duke of Edinburgh* was left. One army gunner, though, wrote; 'I was on duty when the fleet came in from the Battle of Jutland . . . It was a sad sight – no flags flying, no bands playing, but with some dreadnoughts with their 12-inch guns cocked in the air. Some of them had covers over the places where they had been hit.'

To an untrained army gunner, it might have been a forlorn sight, but a more experienced naval eye would have noticed that of the dreadnoughts, very few bore any signs of damage. The cruisers and destroyers might have been knocked around, but the core of the battle fleet was still in full fighting trim. In Rosyth and Scapa Flow, as the wounded went ashore, fresh drafts of seamen came aboard to replace them. During the afternoon and early evening, the ships took on coal, fuel oil, ammunition and stores. So, at 9.45 p.m. on 2 June, Jellicoe was able to report to the Admiralty that the Grand Fleet was ready for action again, and was at four hours' notice to put to sea. In Wilhelmshaven, while the German newspapers crowed about a victory, Scheer knew his fleet was in no condition to make another sortie that summer. That, ultimately, was the reality behind the propaganda war that was about to ensue.

22

The Propaganda Battle

On the evening of Tuesday 30 May, when Vice-Admiral Beatty's battle-cruisers steamed under the Forth Rail Bridge, railwaymen cheered the warships as they passed beneath them. A little after noon on Friday 2 June when the battlecruisers passed under the bridge again, the railway-men stood in stony silence. As the other ships picked up their moorings off Rosyth, the railwaymen watched while Beatty's flagship *Lion* turned to berth alongside the quay. It was clear she had been roughly handled. Her amidships turret had been ripped apart, other guns were damaged and her decks still bore the scars of her savage twelve-hour battle. As she pulled alongside her berth, dockyard workers jeered at her bemused crew. Once she had docked, and the wounded were taken down the gangplank to a fleet of waiting ambulances, the workers booed them too. It was hardly a homecoming worthy of heroes. The reason for both the silence and the jeers was that, as far as the British public were concerned, they had been betrayed. They expected their navy to win a glorious victory; instead it suffered an ignominious defeat. It was true; after all, they had read about it in their morning newspaper.

The German Coup

Thanks to a major propaganda coup, the British public first heard about Jutland from the Germans. While the Grand Fleet had been combing the battlefield for German stragglers, the High Seas Fleet was arriving back in Wilhelmshaven. Effectively, it had a day's head start. By Thursday evening the German Admiralty had already published its official

299

communiqué. This was the first that the world knew of the sea battle, and it was a heavily doctored German version of what had happened off Jutland. The communiqué proclaimed the battle fought off Skagerrak the previous day had been a great German victory. British losses – while heavy enough – were inflated, and German ones were reduced. The following morning German newspaper headlines claimed 'Great Victory at Sea', 'Many English Battleships Destroyed and Damaged', and even 'Trafalgar is Wiped Out!' By then, the international news agencies had already picked up on the story, and the next day the same headlines were trumpeted around the world. Starved of their own official news, on Friday morning the British press printed a translation of the German communiqué.

On 2 June, as the Grand Fleet was nearing its wartime Scottish bases, the headlines circulating around the world proclaimed that Jellicoe had suffered a major defeat. In Britain, the rumours had already been spreading, encouraged by hospitals being warned to expect casualties and dockyards told that repairs were urgently needed. For a crucial twenty-four hours, while the German propaganda machine had been spinning its own story, Jellicoe had been at sea, maintaining radio silence and keeping his country in the dark. With no official word from the Admiralty, the British press simply ran the German story. Soon the newspapers were proclaiming 'Five British Battleships Lost!' or 'Great Naval Disaster'. For more than a century, the British public had expected nothing short of victory from the Royal Navy. Now it seemed that the hugely expensive and much-vaunted Grand Fleet had let them down. It was hardly surprising the sailors were booed as they came ashore.

When it finally came, the British Admiralty's own press release was bald, unadorned and unsparing. It was drafted by Arthur Balfour, the First Lord of the Admiralty during the afternoon of 2 June and was issued at 7 p.m. that evening. It said; 'On the afternoon of Wednesday 31 May, a naval engagement took place off the coast of Jutland. The British ships on which the brunt of the fighting fell were the Battlecruiser Fleet, and some cruisers and light cruisers, supported by four fast battleships. Among these the losses were heavy.' It continued; 'The battlecruisers *Queen Mary*, *Indefatigable* and *Invincible* and the cruisers *Defence* and *Black Prince* were sunk.' It added that the *Warrior* was badly damaged, and had to be abandoned. To counter this, it declared; 'The enemy's losses were serious. At least one battlecruiser was destroyed, one battleship was reported sunk . . . two cruisers were disabled and probably sunk.'

It was clear that Lord Balfour was no expert in public relations. He had no interest in mollycoddling the British public.' Instead, as he put it, 'I desired to let the people know the best and worst that I knew.' Even a line about the German fleet running for home, or that the German fleet had come within a hair's-breadth of annihilation would have sweetened the bitter pill. Balfour didn't even think of it. The public read the communiqué in their newspapers the following morning, accompanied by editorials demanding more information. It all fuelled the impression that the Grand Fleet had been defeated and that the Navy had failed the nation. Even the hidebound *Daily Telegraph* admitted, 'The result could not be viewed with satisfaction.' At a time when newspaper headlines around the world were proclaiming 'British Fleet Almost Annihilated', the official British response did nothing but confirm these rumours. It also stoked the fire of public anger, fuelled by the newspaper editorials demanding action.

Instead it was the Germans who were guilty of a cover-up. On 2 June, the *Frankfurt Zeitung* admitted *Pommern* and *Wiesbaden* had been sunk, and that *Frauenlob* and some destroyers were missing, but it also claimed; 'Many English battleships destroyed and damaged.' It was 7 June before the German Admiralty announced that the *Lützow* had been sunk, and they proved equally reticent about the *Rostock* and *Elbing*. Throughout this period, they remained silent about the extensive repairs being carried out on other major German warships. By then, the damage had been done, though, and the whole world – including the British public – believed the Germans had won a great victory. The British had clearly lost the propaganda battle. For once, British stiff upper-lipped reserve was not the answer.

The British Riposte

Jellicoe was furious with Balfour, and wrote to protest. He rightly felt the official communiqué had magnified the British losses, minimised the German ones, and painted a completely misleading picture of the battle. A second Admiralty communiqué, issued on Saturday evening, was based on better information, after Balfour had read the reports submitted by Jellicoe and Beatty. He also invited Winston Churchill to help him draft it. It presented a more balanced view, although it still did nothing to counter German claims to have won the battle. While in Germany, children were given the day off, the Kaiser visited the fleet and declared, 'The English were beaten' and flags were flown everywhere, in Britain, the British Admiralty were still unwilling to tell Britain's side of the story.

Meanwhile, sailors returning home on leave had to run the gauntlet of public anger, while both politicians and the press hounded the Admiralty, demanding answers. Finally, on Sunday evening, the Admiralty issued a third communiqué, which at last declared – thanks to Churchill – that the battle had been a British victory. It said that Jellicoe; 'Having driven the enemy into port, returned to the main scene and scoured the sea in search of disabled vessels.' This was printed in the Monday morning papers, together with excerpts of a telegram from King George V – once a naval officer himself – to Jellicoe. The King commented on the gallantry shown by the fleet, and then wrote; 'I regret that the German High Seas Fleet, in spite of its heavy losses, was enabled by the misty weather to evade the full consequences of the encounter they have always professed to desire, but for which, when the opportunity arrived, they showed no inclination.' This finally turned the tide, at least in Britain.

One reason for the Admiralty's earlier reticence was its desire to keep the activities of Room 40 a secret. In a message to Jellicoe, sent on 1 June while the Grand Fleet was still at sea, the First Sea Lord, Admiral Sir Henry Jackson reported that wireless intercepts had revealed that *Lützow* and *Elbing* had been sunk, and that other ships were damaged or missing. He added; 'Wilhelmshaven has a good docking programme ordered. *Derfflinger, Moltke, Ostfriesland, Oldenburg, Seydlitz, Nassau, König* . . . I think they were completely surprised.' To say as much, though, was to invite the suspicion of the Germans. To Jackson, a brief public relations problem was less important than the protection of his vital strategic asset, the ability to read German naval signals. So, until the Germans came clean about their losses, the Admiralty held its tongue.

Still, it was clear that Jellicoe disliked the bad publicity. After the third communiqué, Lord Balfour wrote to Jellicoe to say; 'If the Grand Fleet had some reason to feel disappointed over the public attitude on Friday night and Saturday morning, they certainly have no reason to be dissatisfied now. Opinion has undergone a revolution, both rapid and complete.' He added; 'You were robbed by physical conditions of a victory, which, with a little good fortune, would have been complete and crushing, and I feel deeply for your disappointment . . . You have gained a victory, which is of the utmost value to the Allied cause.' Jellicoe might have been a saint if he had not wished Balfour had expressed these sentiments in public, four days before. Jellicoe was still bridling at the Grand Fleet's rough handling in the press. On the same day he wrote to Jackson to see if the press could somehow be taken to task, or even censored; 'The enemy and neutral press only quote what suits them, and amongst their quotations we read quite untrue articles from the British press. It disgusts us all completely.'

This highlighted another problem. The British newspapers still printed German claims of winning a victory, culled from Press Association wires. Most printed these stories verbatim, uncensored by the British authorities. One of the worst offenders, the *Weekly Despatch*, continued to claim the Admiralty were hiding the full facts until the Department of Public Prosecution threatened to intervene – an act that could have led to the newspaper being shut down. Other newspapers, though, while no longer claiming Jutland was a defeat, demanded to know why it was not a crushing victory. This, really, was what it was all about. The British expectation of victory had been high. They had great confidence in the Royal Navy – in its ships, its men and above all in the institution itself, imbued with its long tradition of success. Now this confidence was shattered. Driving the enemy back into port was not good enough. The British people wanted nothing less than a second Trafalgar. Anything else was unacceptable. Afterwards, claims of a strategic victory appeared hollow, at best a consolation prize for a team expected to win every trophy.

There was no such thing as a spin doctor in 1916. Even if there had been, one suspects that the practical, professional and temperate Admiral Jellicoe would have had little truck with them. That was more the style of Beatty, his more mercurial deputy. Jellicoe could have countered German claims far more effectively. Had he signalled the Admiralty on the afternoon of 1 June, listing the likely losses of both sides, but adding that the Germans had fled back to port, then much of the public relations disaster of the following few days might have been averted. If Churchill or even Jackson had drafted that first communiqué and sent it earlier, then that would have helped even more. Above all, someone should have assured the public that the Germans had been defeated, and that the Grand Fleet was still in complete control of the North Sea. That would have countered any amount of German bluster.

It was the following week that the press, both in Britain and around the world, began to adopt a more balanced tone. It also began to question German claims to have won. Even in Germany, a sense of reality was beginning to set in, as it was realised just how much the High Seas Fleet had been battered. This was summed up by a *Punch* cartoon, which showed German civilians at the gates of the Wilhelmshaven naval base. 'Can we see our victorious ships,' they asked? 'Nein!' came the stern guard's reply! In Britain the populist John Saxon Mills published a poem in the *Pall Mall Gazette* entitled *The Paradox*:

> *The Germans cry loudly we've won!*
> *But surely, 'tis a curious view,*
> *That those are conquerors who run,*
> *And those the vanquished who pursue*

In mid-June, a New York newspaper editorial summed up the situation perfectly. It declared; 'The German fleet has assaulted the jailor, but is still in jail.' So it was. The Grand Fleet would remain the undisputed ruler of the North Sea. Just as importantly, the blockade would remain in place. Scheer had tried and failed to counter British seapower and so, as a consequence, his country was inevitably destined to lose the war.

23

Who Won?

The argument over who won the Battle of Jutland has rumbled on ever since the first German press release was written. A century later the debate continues, mainly because there is no easy way of answering the question. The German claim – the one first trumpeted in the German newspapers on the morning of 2 June – relied on numbers. The British claim involved numbers too, but not the same lists of ships, tonnage and casualties. Its numbers were related to two other factors; status quo and seapower. The two claims were both valid, but both sides preferred to ignore the solid case put forward by their opponent.

In the early 1980s, the author – then a young naval officer – listened to equally young German naval officers re-hash the old arguments, claiming that statistically Jutland (known as the *Skaggerakschlacht* in Germany) had been a German victory. The obvious riposte was to pose the question. 'If you won, then how come your fleet spent the rest of the war hiding in port?'. At that time, I didn't know that the High Seas Fleet had sortied again, but coming from Orkney I was well aware of the German fleet's ultimate fate. After all, I had dived on the wrecks. The trouble with all circular arguments is that they never really get resolved. Now, a century after the battle, it might be time to take a more dispassionate look at the two arguments, and try to answer the question – Who won the Battle of Jutland?

Behind the Statistics

If you look at the battle simply in terms of ships sunk and casualties suffered, then the Germans clearly come out on top.

Ship type	British	German
Capital Ships	*Indefatigable* *Invincible* *Queen Mary*	*Lützow* *Pommern*
Cruisers	*Black Prince* *Defence* *Warrior*	*Elbing* *Frauenlob* *Rostock* *Wiesbaden*
Destroyers	*Ardent* *Fortune* *Nestor* *Nomad* *Shark* *Sparrowhawk* *Tipperary* *Turbulent*	*S-35* *V-4* *V-27* *V-29* *V-48*

While the losses do not look especially uneven – fourteen British losses as opposed to eleven German ones, or six ships each if we leave out the destroyers – the tonnage of these sunken ships is far more disproportionate; the British lost 115,025 tons, to the German loss of 61,180 tons. Based on tonnage, the Germans were the clear-cut winners. The same balance in favour of the Germans is seen in the casualty list. The British suffered 6,945 casualties at Jutland, of which 6,094 were men killed in battle, or who died of their wounds. The German total was less than half that – 3,058 men, of whom 2,551 were killed. This decidedly one-sided total reflects the fact that of the six battlecruisers and cruisers the British lost at Jutland, five of them blew up, taking almost all of their crew up with them. By contrast, with the exception of the *Frauenlob* and the *Wiesbaden*, the Germans were able to rescue most of the crew of the ships they lost, thereby sparing the lives of more than two thousand sailors.

Not all of these twenty-five warships were of equal value. The destroyers were fairly well matched, although the British boats were larger, better armed but not necessarily better designed than their

German counterparts. The Germans evidently got the better of the battle in terms of destroyers – hardly surprising when in the night battle the British boats were engaged by dreadnoughts. The three British armoured cruisers were obsolete, even more so than the German *Blücher* which was sunk at Dogger Bank. These were ships which were not really designed to fight in a major fleet action, but they were still substantial warships, displacing more than 12,000 tons and with crews of 700 to 800 men apiece. They had all been rendered obsolete with the coming of the *Dreadnought*; in naval terms they were no great loss to Jellicoe, but their crews were irreplaceable.

With the exception of the *Frauenlob*, which was also obsolete – an older generation of cruiser – all the German cruisers lost at Jutland were modern ships, displacing between 4,300 and 5,200 tons, with crews of between 350 and 500 men each. These were the real 'eyes of the fleet', and their demise was a real blow to Scheer, whose fleet was already woefully short of light cruisers after his losses earlier in the war. In a modern naval war, they were certainly more important than the old pre-dreadnought battleship *Pommern*, which was torpedoed by the destroyer *Onslaught* during the night battle. She displaced a little over 13,000 tons – roughly the same as the British armoured cruisers – and while she carried four powerful 11-inch guns, her military value was minimal. Like the three British cruisers, her real value lay in the 845 seamen who crewed her, all but one of whom were lost when she sank. The speed with which these older ships – the British armoured cruisers, the pre-dreadnought and the old protected cruiser – went down all highlighted the vulnerability of these obsolete vessels to modern guns and torpedoes.

The most significant losses on both sides were the battlecruisers. Of these the *Lützow* and the *Queen Mary* were first-line warships, and highly valuable naval assets. Hipper's flagship had only entered service in late March – her first operation was the bombardment of Yarmouth and Lowestoft – and her loss was a major blow to the 1st Scouting Group. Similarly, the *Queen Mary* was one of Beatty's quartet of 'Splendid Cats', and when she blew up, taking over 1,200 of her crew with her, she dramatically reduced the fighting potential of Beatty's premier battlecruiser squadron. Of only slightly less significance were the losses of the older battlecruisers *Indefatigable* and *Invincible*. Although their guns were of a smaller calibre than the 'Splendid Cats', they were still useful members of the Battlecruiser Fleet – certainly only slightly inferior to the German *Von der Tann*.

While it could be argued that as 'first-generation' ships of their kind they were 'second-class' battlecruisers, they still had the fighting potential to hurt the enemy, and so they remained 'first-class' naval assets. Just as importantly, between them they carried more than a thousand men each, almost all of whom were blown to atoms when their ship exploded. Statistically, if you set aside the 3,309 men who were killed in the three British battlecruisers, the British and German casualties from the battle would have been roughly the same. It just shows how easily things could have turned out differently if better magazine protection had been available, or more rigorous anti-flash procedures had been in place. While some with, more than a little justification, have laid the blame for the latter at Beatty's feet, the Vice-Admiral wasn't responsible for his ships' lack of armour, nor for the inherent flaws in their design. After all, these ships were 'Fisher's Follies'.

Two other things are noticeable in the casualty lists. First is the large discrepancy between the number of men killed or wounded. This is only partly due to the spectacular and almost immediate way all of the capital ships sank, with the exception of the *Lützow*. In many of the British destroyers and in the German cruiser *Wiesbaden*, substantial numbers of men, many of them wounded, managed to abandon ship. The lucky ones made it onto rafts, or into lifeboats. Most had nothing to cling to but wreckage. The average temperature in the North Sea in May is 11.1°C (52°F). Since the development of the North Sea oil industry, a lot of research has gone into survival times. Obviously, a number of factors are involved here, including clothing, physiology, activity, sea state, wind, air temperature, mental determination and the presence of buoyancy aids and contaminants such as oil. However, even in a modern survival suit, scientists estimate that within half an hour some uninjured survivors will begin to succumb to exposure.

None of the sailors at Jutland had survival suits, and very few had lifejackets. Many were wounded, some shockingly so. All they had going for them was that for the most part they were young and fit. For most young men in their situation, exhaustion sets in within one to two hours – less if the survivors are wounded or dispirited. Some men would begin dying within an hour, while others could be expected to survive for up to six hours. In most cases at Jutland, the men in the water weren't rescued until long after dawn. By then, very few of the original survivors were still alive. Hugo Zenne, the sole survivor of the *Wiesbaden*, described the way his shipmates died; 'Gradually, strength gave out – one after another the others let go. Finally, there were only three men left. Then we sat on top of the float. Suddenly it tipped over, and one man didn't surface after that.' By mid-morning, only Zenne was left alive, and he clambered onto the float. He was eventually rescued after twenty hours in the water.

The second fact hidden by the casualty lists is the egalitarian nature of naval warfare. When a ship blows up it takes its whole crew with it, from the admiral or captain down to the ship's boys. On the horrific battlefields of 1916 – Verdun, the Somme, Galicia or the Italian Alps – generals, and even colonels, rarely featured in the list of casualties. At Jutland, almost ten thousand men became casualties, roughly one sailor in ten of the men who took part. This total included three admirals and eighteen ship's captains. War at sea can be a great leveller, and Jutland was no exception to this.

Repairing the Damage

The list of ships which were lost doesn't tell the full story either. During the battle, the German battle fleet was more roughly handled than its British counterpart. Similarly, while *Lion* and *Tiger* were badly damaged, all of the German battlecruisers were effectively put out of action, and most were lucky to make it home. It is worth taking a quick look at how long it took to repair these damaged ships, and how many warships were available for fresh operations. We can ignore the pre-dreadnoughts; after Jutland, Scheer wisely relegated them to training or coastal defence duties. The Germans had sixteen dreadnoughts at Jutland, and five battlecruisers. One with more dreadnought, the *König Albert*, was in refit when the battle was fought. Including their fast battleships, twenty-eight British dreadnoughts took part in the battle, as well as nine battlecruisers. On the evening of 2 June, a total of twenty-three British dreadnoughts and the fast battleship *Valiant* were available for duty, as well as three battlecruisers. In the High Seas Fleet, only nine dreadnoughts and none of the battlecruisers were battle-ready at that time.

Five other British capital ships – the dreadnoughts *Dreadnought, Empress of India, Royal Sovereign,* the battlecruiser *Australia* and the fast battleship *Queen Elizabeth* – were in refit at the time of Jutland, undergoing minor repairs and modifications. All of them were returned to service in the days after the battle, thereby allowing their dry docks to be used by more deserving battle-damaged warships. All of these, apart from *Dreadnought,* were sent to Scapa Flow to join the Grand Fleet, which gave Jellicoe a battle fleet which was unquestionably more powerful than anything the Germans could muster. On both sides of the North Sea, shipyard workers swarmed over the damaged warships, cutting away damaged turrets and armour plates, and removing the scars of battle. On 1 July, a month after the battle, *Malaya* and *Tiger* had rejoined the British fleet, while repairs on the three lightly damaged German dreadnoughts *Rheinland, Helgoland* and *Westfalen* had also been completed. Jellicoe, though, now overwhelmingly outnumbered Scheer in available capital ships.

A little over three weeks later, on 26 July, and almost two months after the battle, the *Ostfriesland* re-joined the High Seas Fleet. Together with the repair of the *König, Grosser Kurfürst,* and *Markgraf* and the return of the *König Albert,* this brought Scheer's battle fleet back up to full strength of seventeen dreadnoughts. However, all of Hipper's four surviving German battlecruisers were still in dry dock. In Rosyth the two 'Splendid Cats' *Lion* and the *Princess Royal* had re-joined Beatty's force, bringing him up to a full post-Jutland complement of seven battlecruisers. *Lion,* though, was still missing 'Q' turret; the barbette was plated over until September, when the replacement turret was fitted in Tyneside. In addition, two brand-new extra-fast battlecruisers – *Repulse* and *Renown* – were due to join the Battlecruiser Fleet within a few weeks. With new safety measures in place, Beatty was confident that his ships would have little trouble overwhelming Hipper's battlecruisers if they ever returned to sea.

In Scapa Flow, *Marlborough* rejoined the fleet on 2 August, bringing Jellicoe's Grand Fleet up to full strength. He now had twenty-six dreadnoughts in his battle fleet. With the return of *Warspite* on 20 July, he also had five fast battleships at his disposal, and two more 15-inch gun dreadnoughts would join the fleet before the end of the year. This meant that the British battle fleet was even stronger than it had been at Jutland,

and was almost double the size of its German counterpart. The 2 August was an important day in Wilhelmshaven too; it was when the repairs were completed on the *Von der Tann*, the second of Hipper's battlecruisers to re-join the fleet. The newly repaired *Moltke* had become Hipper's new flagship three days earlier. However, for the next six weeks these two battlecruisers were all that he could muster. It would be mid-September before the *Seydlitz* was ready for service again, and it was not until mid-October that *Derfflinger* re-joined the fleet. From this it is clear that, while it took the Germans three months to recover from Jutland, for all practical purposes the fighting potential of the British fleet was undiminished.

Although the records for some of the German dreadnoughts have not survived, repairing the battle damage suffered by the High Seas Feet took about 644 days in dry dock – over twice the British total of 297 days. Effectively, Scheer's battle fleet was not ready for active service again until the middle of August. Even then, it had to make do without two of its most powerful battlecruisers. By contrast, Jellicoe was ready to resume operations within hours of his fleet's return to Scapa Flow, with all but one of the dreadnoughts that made up his battle fleet. Even this was offset by the temporary addition of the fast battleship *Valiant*. So, for almost three months, the Germans were unable to stage any significant naval operations, while the British enjoyed unchallenged control of the North Sea. While the German newspapers were busy proclaiming their fleet's great victory, that same fleet was stuck in port, licking its wounds.

Before Jutland, Scheer's whole strategy centred around *Kräfteausgleich* ('The equalisation of forces'). That was the policy of trying to trap part of the British fleet – Beatty's forces being the most likely candidate – and overwhelm them. A few successful operations of this kind would tip the balance of ships in Germany's favour. Then, the High Seas Fleet would be ideally placed to wrest control of the North Sea from the British. If victory at Jutland was measured by *Kräfteausgleich*, then the battle was an abject defeat. While three British battlecruisers were lost compared to one German one, the strength of the two rival fleets – even the battlecruiser forces – remained resolutely in Britain's favour. Instead, Scheer came within an ace of losing a substantial portion of his battle fleet. So, measured by Scheer's own objective for the fighting of a fleet battle, Jutland was a sad disappointment. It also highlighted the fact that his policy of *Kräfteausgleich* was not working.

Still, in terms of statistics, the claim that the High Seas Fleet won the battle had some validity. The Germans sank more ships than the British and killed more men. They sank more tonnage too, and after the war they even claimed to have scored a greater percentage of hits compared to the number of shells fired. Even that statistic was not straightforward, as it turned out that many of the British armour-piercing shells were faulty, and burst on impact rather than inside the enemy ship. Expert analysis after the war suggested that Scheer could have lost several more ships – certainly two more battlecruisers – if the British ammunition had been better. While the gunnery debate would rumble on in tandem with the 'who won?' argument, the fact remains that victory in naval battles or campaigns is rarely judged merely by ships sunk, or casualties inflicted. Nobody suggested that the hunt for the *Bismarck* in 1941 was a draw because both sides lost a capital ship, or that the Battle for the Mediterranean in 1940–43 was an Italian victory because more British ships were lost than Italian ones. No; the outcome of a battle involves looking at the bigger picture too.

One British commentator on Jutland, Major A.C.B Alexander, likened the battle to a boxing match. A veteran heavyweight was pitted against an unknown middleweight, but failed to deliver a knockout blow. Instead it became a contest for a 'win on points'. Let us follow Alexander's analogy further. If Jutland was a boxing match where victory was determined solely by counting the number of telling blows struck, then the middleweight Scheer would have won it handsomely. However, boxing doesn't work that way. In a fight where nobody throws a knock-out punch, the boxers have to 'go the distance' and fight all dozen rounds, or else concede by 'throwing in the towel'. The British would argue that this towel-throwing is exactly what Scheer did. He got out of the ring before the fight was over. Under the Marquis of Queensberry rules that makes him the unequivocal loser. Also, the British would be keen to point out, after Jutland, apart from a couple of lacklustre and abortive attempts, Scheer never got back into the ring again.

24

The Big Picture

The real problem with Jutland, at least for the British, was that it wasn't Trafalgar. Nelson's great victory had established Britain's naval supremacy, and for more than a century the Royal Navy's position had never really been challenged. Jutland was the first sea battle since 1805 where Britain's naval reputation was put on the line. The Navy's failure to inflict a decisive defeat – the boxer's knock-out blow – meant that this reputation never fully recovered. For a decade, the British taxpayer had invested in a fleet of dreadnoughts of unparalleled fighting power. The Grand Fleet's failure to deliver a clear victory undermined the British public's faith in its navy, and made it question the value of this great investment. While British claims that Jutland was a victory might have been justifiable in terms of naval balance, grand strategy and long-term objectives, they still had an unpalatably hollow ring to them.

Seapower

While the German claim to victory centred on statistics, the British adopted a more pragmatic argument. Their case centred on the fact that they effectively controlled the North Sea before Jutland, and they did so afterwards. In a land battle, 'control of the field' usually meant that after a battle one side withdrew, leaving the other protagonist holding the battlefield. This allowed the field-holder to claim a tactical victory if the fight was indecisive, or at least a moral one, by right of holding the ground. This made sense. Usually, the side still on the field went on to lay claim to nearby towns or the surrounding province. Warfare on land was usually about territory, and so 'control of the field' was a tangible result. Territory though, doesn't have the same meaning in naval engagements, where the battlefield itself was nothing more than a patch of sea. Here, it was all about the projection of seapower.

The notion of seapower was first proposed by the American naval historian Alfred Mahan in the 1890s. However, he was merely putting a name to a naval maxim which had been around for centuries. Essentially, a strong naval and mercantile power was bound to triumph over a weaker one, thanks to a combination of naval muscle and maritime trade. In a war it could strangle the weaker naval power by economic blockade, and so, in time, that smaller power would wither through lack of supplies, however big and powerful its army might be.

Mahan's ideal model for this was the period of the French Revolutionary and Napoleonic Wars. Between 1792–1802 and then 1803–14, the British instituted a close blockade of French ports, and the harbours of their continental allies. This blockade, and the embargo of trade with France helped to cripple the French war effort, and allowed Britain to establish complete naval supremacy over her adversary. This is exactly what happened during the First World War. So, unless Scheer could defeat Jellicoe and lift the blockade, then seapower would take its course. Scheer tried and failed to win that victory. Simply by avoiding defeat at Jutland, Jellicoe achieved a strategic victory in terms of seapower.

Before the battle, Britain effectively controlled the North Sea. Its economic blockade was becoming increasingly effective, and by the early summer of 1916, shortages of food and supplies in Germany were really beginning to bite. That year the author's German-born father – an eight-year-old schoolboy from Königstein-am-Taunus near Frankfurt – was sent with his schoolmates to gather grass from the roadsides to feed to the underfed German horses on the Western Front. Belts were already tightening, and the German war machine was suffering. Four days after the battle, the British evening paper *The Globe* posed an important rhetorical question; 'Will a shouting, flag-waving people get any more of the copper, rubber and cotton their government so sorely needs? Not a pound. Will meat and butter be cheaper in Berlin? Not by a pfennig. There is one test, and one only of victory. Who held the battle at the end of the fight?'

The trouble was, there was no glory in this – no newspaper headlines proclaiming a second Trafalgar, and certainly no quick result where victory was achieved in a matter of hours. Instead, the strategy of economic blockade was one that took years to reach fruition, a Fabian approach to warfare in which there was no real victory short of an ultimate one, the collapse of the enemy's ability to fight. When Jellicoe was appointed to command the Grand Fleet in August 1914, he not only accepted the command, but also the strategy that came with it. The idea of waging a naval war by instituting an economic blockade was not new; it was a policy that had served Britain well throughout the Age of Fighting Sail. Then, though, the French or Spanish occasionally broke out of port, and the resulting sea battle invariably ended in a clear-cut British victory. Now, in the modern form of naval blockage proposed by Fisher and implemented by Jellicoe, victory in a sea battle had almost become an irrelevance.

Certainly a Trafalgar-like victory would have been wonderful – and Jellicoe almost pulled that off. It remained his biggest regret that he came within an ace of crushing the High Seas Fleet, but for a number of reasons that wasn't destined to happen. Inflicting a decisive defeat on Scheer might have allowed Britain to redirect its resources elsewhere to bring about a breakthrough on the Western Front, or to better counter the growing threat of German U-Boats. It might, conceivably, have shortened the war by allowing the Allies to expand the naval blockade into the Baltic Sea. That though is mere speculation, just as meaningless to a historian as wondering what might have occurred if Scheer had won a decisive victory himself – something that was probably never going to happen. So, while the British press and public might clamour for a new Trafalgar in the age of steam, steel and torpedoes, Jellicoe had to play the long game.

For him, maintaining the naval status quo would ensure a victory every bit as decisive as Trafalgar, and one that might be achieved without the bloodshed. The instructions given to him by the Admiralty urged caution; strategic objectives should not be jeopardised by unnecessary risk in battle. Jellicoe's own *Fleet Battle Orders* – thirty close-typed pages of them – emphasised defensive measures, and the avoidance of needless danger. So it is hardly surprising that Jellicoe fought a largely defensive battle. Throughout the fight, his battle fleet was never in any real danger, while twice within the space of an hour he outmanoeuvred Scheer, so that the High Seas Fleet faced annihilation. Given he was 'the man who could lose the war in an afternoon', Jellicoe fought a near-perfect battle, then threw this away by letting a decisive conclusion slip through his fingers. Jutland might have been a flawed victory for Jellicoe, but it was certainly no defeat.

If it had not been for those three exploding battlecruisers, Jellicoe would have been hailed as a new national hero. If British shells had been better, the casualty lists would have favoured the British rather than the Germans. If Scheer had not managed to find a way through the Grand Fleet at night, or if Jellicoe's subordinates had kept him better informed, the British commander would almost certainly have won his modern Trafalgar, and history would have viewed him very differently. None of this was to be, though. Instead, Jellicoe was left with one consolation prize, albeit a major one. He had successfully maintained the naval status quo, and Scheer's final determined attempt to alter the naval balance of power had come to naught. So Jutland can be seen as a victory for Jellicoe and for the Royal Navy, albeit a Fabian one. It was also one that, thanks to the continuation of the blockade, would unequivocally guarantee that Germany would lose the war.

The Long Game

By the time he returned to Wilhelmshaven, Scheer had realised that his *Kräfteausgleich* policy was doomed to failure. Germany had entered the war without any real war aim for its High Seas Fleet, a force dubbed a 'luxury fleet' by its critics. The High Seas Fleet was outnumbered in August 1914, and by May 1916 the naval imbalance had increased. *Kräfteausgleich*, the equalisation of forces by ambushing detachments of the enemy fleet was the solution. That would help even the odds, and would eventually permit a decisive battle when the naval balance was more favourable. If Germany won a decisive victory, then the strategic consequences could be immense. Great Britain was nothing without its fleet, and a large-scale British defeat could well have led to a humiliating armistice, followed by a withdrawal from the Allied camp. That would have meant a lifting of the Allied blockade, and a redoubling of Germany's military effort.

At Jutland, Scheer tried to trap Beatty's Battlecruiser Fleet, but instead found himself drawn into a fleet engagement with the whole Grand

Fleet. With sixteen German dreadnoughts pitted against twenty-four British ones – twenty-eight including the fast battleships – this full-scale encounter was a battle Scheer couldn't win. Indeed, he counted himself fortunate to have escaped with most of his fleet intact. It was also clear that by then the naval balance had shifted too much in Jellicoe's favour for *Kräfteausgleich* to work. The chances of achieving decisive results against such a large British battle fleet were minimal, and the presence of those fast battleships also reduced the chances of luring Beatty into battle on favourable terms. Above all, the aftermath of Jutland demonstrated that the British could repair their warships faster than the Germans could, and they also had more capital ships under construction than were being built in Germany. *Kräfteausgleich* had to be abandoned.

On 4 July, Scheer sent a report to the Kaiser, saying that he was planning 'further strikes against the enemy' He began with an optimistic tone; 'Should these future operations take a favourable course, we should be able to inflict serious damage upon the enemy.' This was clearly a reference to *Kräfteausgleich*, a policy he had already all but abandoned. He then added; 'Nevertheless, there can be no doubt that even the most successful outcome of a fleet action in this war will not force England to make peace . . . the enemy's great material superiority, cannot be compensated by our fleet to the extent where we shall be able to overcome the blockade of the British Isles themselves ...' In other words, he could lead sorties if the Kaiser demanded it, but it wouldn't alter the naval balance of power, and it certainly wouldn't lift the blockade. That was why Scheer then advocated a change of policy.

Scheer declared; 'A victorious end to the war within a reasonable time can only be achieved through the defeat of British economic life – that is, by using U-Boats against British trade. In this connection, I feel it my duty again to strongly advise Your Majesty against the adoption of any half measures.' Effectively, this meant unrestricted U-Boat warfare, a policy Germany had tried before, but had veered away from for fear of bringing the United States into the war on the Allied side. Scheer counselled an unfettered U-Boat offensive because half measures didn't lend themselves to U-boat warfare, but also because he saw incidents involving American ships as inevitable. Scheer's solution was to brazen it out, adding; 'Unless we can act with full determination, such incidents involve us in the humiliation of having to give way.' Effectively, he planned to counter the Allied economic blockade with a counter-blockade of his own, regardless of the inevitable international consequences.

This change of naval strategy had the full approval of the German Naval Staff, who saw the high-risk policy as the only one with even a slight chance of bringing the Allied economic blockade to an end. It was also one that relegated the High Seas Fleet to a supporting role. From now on it served to pin down British naval resources – destroyers and other light forces that might otherwise be used to hunt down U-Boats. This sidelining of the High Seas Fleet though, couldn't happen immediately. For the sake of public face-saving as much as anything else, Scheer had to lead it on another sortie, the one he'd told the Kaiser he was planning for mid-August. Some British historians have claimed that after Jutland, the High Seas Fleet never put to sea again. This is not true, although for all practicable purposes it could be.

The Endgame

On the evening of 18 August Scheer began what was effectively a re-hash of the Sunderland plan he had abandoned in May. Hipper, with his two serviceable battlecruisers and three dreadnoughts set a course towards Sunderland, followed at some distance by the battle fleet. Scheer made up for his lack of cruisers by using U-Boats and zeppelins, which patrolled well ahead of the fleet. Jellicoe was forewarned by Room 40 and put to sea in good time. He rendezvoused with Beatty off the Firth of Forth, then headed south to intercept Scheer. Tyrwhitt's Harwich Force also advanced from the south, and was duly spotted by zeppelin *L-13*. Scheer moved to intercept Tyrwhitt, but the British kept their distance. When Jellicoe's Grand Fleet was spotted by U-Boats, Scheer withdrew to Wilhelmshaven. As Scheer was determined to avoid Jellicoe, it was unlikely this sortie would have led to a second Jutland. However, at least it demonstrated a willingness to put to sea.

In October, a limited sweep as far as the Dogger Bank was abandoned when the light cruiser *München* was torpedoed by a British submarine. The cruiser was towed back to Wilhelmshaven, but she never re-joined the fleet; instead she was turned into a floating naval barracks. Scheer claimed he abandoned the operation due to bad weather, but from his correspondence it seems he was more concerned that the submarine was part of a larger British force, lying in wait for him through the mist. In fact, the Grand Fleet never bothered putting to sea, as Jellicoe felt Scheer would simply flee before he made contact. He was absolutely right. During the winter of 1916–17, the fleet remained in port, as Scheer had to deal with a growing unrest among his men. That summer a few ships moved into the Baltic to conduct operations in Riga Sound, but apart from occasional forays by light forces, the rest of the fleet stayed in port.

Meanwhile, the U-Boat campaign got underway. By 1 February 1917, when the offensive began, just over one-hundred U-Boats were at sea, and in its first two months half a million tons of Allied shipping were sunk. Britain alone lost over 250 merchantmen during that opening period of the offensive. Then Britain gained an ally. The entry of the United States into the war in April brought an influx of much-needed Allied merchant ships and escorts. Britain certainly needed them; in April alone 860,000 tons of shipping were sunk by German U-Boats. After that, a combination of better-organised convoys and more escorts turned the tide, and while losses continued, the U-Boats began suffering too, with losses running at eight to ten boats a month by the middle of the year. Meanwhile, the bulk of the High Seas Fleet remained in port, or limited itself to training operations inside the defensive minefields. Meanwhile, the morale of the German sailors in Wilhelmshaven fell steadily, as shortages caused by the blockade continued to bite.

In the summer of 1917, the Grand Fleet was reinforced by a squadron of American dreadnoughts, but it too remained on the defensive. By then Beatty was in charge, as Jellicoe had been transferred to the Admiralty the previous December. So it was Beatty rather than Jellicoe who led the fleet out to sea to counter the High Seas Fleet's final operational sortie. In late April 1918, Scheer emerged from behind his minefields to launch an attack on Allied convoys operating between Britain and Norway. Faulty intelligence meant that the German fleet never made contact, and Scheer retreated before Beatty could intercept him. On 25 April, the *Moltke* was torpedoed by a British submarine off Helgoland, but she managed to limp back into Wilhelmshaven. It was a miserable end to Scheer's last operation.

He planned one more sortie in late October – a *Götterdämmerung* action, where the fleet would be sacrificed in order to inflict as much damage as possible on the Grand Fleet. An armistice was already being negotiated, and Scheer knew that the British would insist on the dismemberment of his fleet. So he planned to go down fighting. However, his men thought otherwise. The evening before the fleet sailed, the sailors mutinied and Scheer was forced to cancel the operation. Effectively this meant the end of the High Seas Fleet as a fighting force. It would make one more sortie, and meet the Grand Fleet one more time, but by then the fighting would be over, and the great guns would remain silent.

Fisher's Blockade

During those long months after Jutland, much had changed. Russia had been knocked out of the war, and on the Western Front the Allies were driving the German army back towards the German frontier. Throughout all this, though, and despite the activity of German U-Boats, the economic blockade of Germany continued. Historians still disagree over the role the blockade played in the collapse of Germany, but there is a wide consensus that its impact was severe. German munitions factories were deprived of the phosphates they needed to make explosives, or rubber for wheels. Farmers ran out of fertiliser, and even coal stocks dwindled, despite Germany's having its own mines in Silesia. A lack of access to imported drugs and medicines led to a growing inability to treat the sick or wounded, while oil and petrol became increasingly scarce. However, it was the shortage of food that really hurt the most.

Rationing was introduced in early 1915, but food shortages increased as agricultural production declined. In the months after Jutland, the shortage of meat, poultry, eggs, potatoes, cereals and dairy products had become widespread, even in rural areas. The situation was much worse in German cities, or at the front, although at least here the highly efficient military commissariat did what it could to ensure supplies reached the troops. By early 1917, there were growing reports of widespread hunger, while the reduced diet had a detrimental effect on health and on resistance to disease. As a result, epidemics became more common, and by the end of the year people were beginning to starve.

By 1918, starvation was commonplace, and by the war's end it has been estimated that as many as half a million Germans died from it or from disease. These were all deaths which were directly attributed to the blockade. The German authorities did what they could to alleviate the suffering, or to increase production, but they were unable to reverse the cycle of starvation and death. This led to an almost irresistible pressure to end the war, and so stop the misery. Food riots broke out in several German cities, and there was a consequent breakdown in civil order. The loss of the Balkans that autumn – Germany's largest source of food – proved the final straw. By October, the Kaiser and his ministers had no option but to sue for peace. German troops were still fighting, but the country's will to continue had been eroded, not by bombs and bullets, but by a humble line of patrol boats strung out across the North Sea.

The U-Boat offensive was a chimera. It was never designed to counter the economic blockade, only to exert a similar pressure on Britain. If the United States had not entered the war, it may have succeeded; by the early summer of 1917, Britain was losing merchantmen far faster than it could replace them, and wheat reserves – usually imported in bulk from Canada – had become dangerously low. By midsummer, Britain would have run out of bread. This, fascinating though it was, didn't have any impact on the blockade of Germany. Germany's only real chance to break the blockade was to wrest control of the North Sea from Britain. The only realistic way this could happen was through *Kräfteausgleich*. When the last hopes of success for that policy died at Jutland, the hope of Germany died with it.

Jutland's Legacy

Over the past century several historians have described Jutland as an 'indecisive' battle. That suggests it didn't decide anything, or was inconclusive, or that its result was undecided. This isn't really true at all. Quite the contrary, the battle had a major impact on the naval war and on the eventual outcome of the conflict. In the short term, it led directly to a dramatic change in German naval strategy – an abandonment of surface operations in favour of unrestricted U-Boat warfare. Over a longer period, it ensured that the blockade would completely undermine German morale and bring about the collapse of Germany's will to fight. Jutland, therefore, did more to bring about an Allied victory than any amount of fighting in Flanders, the Somme or Verdun. These battles reduced the fighting ability of the German army; they didn't bring about the end of the war. That happened at Jutland; not through a great victory, but because one side maintained its control of the sea.

A century later, Jutland remains an enigmatic battle, particularly for the British. It isn't just the long-running debate over who won. In Britain, the public never quite got over the shock of the initial German claims of victory, and while they understood the solid British counter-argument, the notion of seapower seemed less tangible than the hard evidence of tonnage and casualties. They saw it as unseemly when, afterwards, Beatty and his supporters attempted to pillory Jellicoe, and then tried to rewrite the history books to show the vice-admiral in a better light. That smacked of a cover-up, or at best a lack of transparency by someone; either the Admiralty, the commanders or the politicians. Claims of victory, however valid they might be, still had a slightly bitter taste. While seapower achieved its ends, it was not the great patriotic victory the British expected from their navy.

Above all though, most people in Britain, whether they admitted it or not, sensed that Jutland marked the end of an era. When the Grand Fleet steamed into action that afternoon, it was the greatest, most expensive fighting force the country had ever created. It was a fleet to be proud of. For a decade the British public saw it as the touchstone of British power and greatness. The Royal Navy's failure to win – or rather to win decisively – was a profound disappointment. It was a psychological blow that not only effected the British public, but it had major global repercussions.

For a century or more, British naval supremacy had been unquestioned. It carried with it a certain moral and geopolitical ascendency. A decisive victory that afternoon would have guaranteed Britain would retain this for decades to come. Without a clear British victory, the moral foundation of Britain's maritime power was undermined. Arguments about seapower and maintaining the status quo were all very well, but at Jutland the Navy lost that unquestioned global ascendancy. The modern decline of the Royal Navy, and possibly of Great Britain too, began that afternoon off the coast of Jutland.

Postscript

Sixty feet below the surface of Scapa Flow lies the crumbling upturned hull of a great dreadnought. A century ago, the SMS *König* was the flagship of Rear-Admiral Paul Behncke, commander of the III Battle Squadron of the High Seas Fleet. Completed in August 1914, this 25,000-ton leviathan was the namesake of the most powerful class of dreadnoughts in the German fleet, and the most modern. Twice at Jutland, at 6.30 p.m. and again at 7.15 p.m., she was the closest German dreadnought to the British fleet, and she paid a heavy price for it. She was hit ten times during the battle, and nine of these hits came during these two brief encounters. A total of forty-five of her crew were killed at Jutland, and another twenty-seven were wounded. Behncke himself was one of these, wounded by fragments from a shell fired by Jellicoe's flagship *Iron Duke*, shortly after 6.35 p.m., as he stood on *König*'s open bridge.

Today that bridge rests on the seabed of Scapa Flow, pinned beneath the upturned hull of the dreadnought. For divers, her remains are confusing, not just because there's a sixty-foot drop from her upturned hull to the seabed, but because, thanks to the attentions of salvors, much of her hull has been torn apart. Still, the remains of her rudders and her propeller shafts can still be seen. Once these sped the ship through the water at 21 knots. Now they're little more than curiosities to entertain the hundreds of sports divers who visit the wreck every year, and the thousands of fish who call the wreck their home. Close by lie the remains of two of *König*'s sister ships, the *Markgraf* and the *Kronprinz*. Together, these three dreadnoughts are all that remains of Scheer's battle fleet –the force that a century ago fought the dreadnoughts of the Grand Fleet off Jutland.

How these three great dreadnoughts came to be lying on the seabed of Scapa Flow is an interesting story. The Armistice of 11 November 1918 came with one major proviso. The High Seas Fleet would have to be surrendered to the Allies and sent to Scapa Flow for internment while the peace negotiations ran their course. Three months before, Scheer had become Chief of the Naval Staff, and Hipper now commanded the fleet. However, he was so reluctant to see its surrender that command was devolved to Vice-Admiral von Reuter, who had commanded the IV Scouting Group at Jutland. So at noon on 19 November, the High Seas Fleet left Wilhelmshaven for the last time. With the 1st Scouting Group in the lead, it crossed the North Sea, and at 8 a.m. on 21 November it rendezvoused with Beatty's Grand Fleet to the east of the Firth of Forth. It was a supremely humiliating moment for the German navy, and Beatty made sure that the newsreel cameras were there to record their discomfiture.

The tension mounted as the two fleets approached each other. As Major Rendell of the Marines commented; 'It just needs a shot from either side to start the whole show again!' He needn't have worried; according to the terms of the armistice the Germans had removed the breech blocks of their guns. As the two fleets drew abreast Beatty, ever the showman, carried out a neat 180° turn – his own *Gefechtskehrtwendung* – and he led the whole procession of ships off towards the Firth of Forth. Admiral Rodman of the US Navy likened it to a scene from his childhood in rural Kentucky, where he had seen a small child leading a herd of bullocks by the nose. For many of the British seamen, this was the closest they'd got to the enemy – the one they had last seen at Jutland. Then, one batch of ships at a time, the High Seas Fleet were led off to internment in Scapa Flow.

There the fleet remained, seventy-four ships anchored between the island of Hoy and the Orkney mainland. The peace talks dragged on, and while most of the German sailors returned home, skeleton crews remained, unable to go ashore, or even visit their comrades in other ships. Effectively, they were in a floating prison, and seeing their provisions were shipped from Germany, their fare was both meagre and of poor quality. The men augmented their rations by fishing, but as weeks turned into months, boredom and indiscipline took their toll. Then, in May 1919, von Reuter read in an old copy of *The Times* that the interned ships would be distributed between the Allied powers, and the German navy would be reduced to a token force. Von Reuter was determined that his ships wouldn't fall into enemy hands. So he decided to scuttle the whole fleet.

On midsummer day a party of Orkney schoolchildren boarded the small steamer *Flying Kestrel*, and embarked on an outing to view the interned fleet. They had a ringside seat for the spectacle of a lifetime. A little after 12.16 p.m. a bell began tolling on the *Friedrich der Grosse*. As the children watched, she rolled over and sank. Soon the water was filled with small boats full of German sailors, as the rest of the fleet began sinking too. Many of the younger children were terrified, but the older ones found it all fascinating. On the dreadnought *Royal Sovereign*, the ship's chaplain George Bourdillon missed the start of the scuttling, as his ship was just entering Scapa Flow, but he clambered into the foretop for a better view; 'One dreadnought had her quarterdeck awash, and as we watched through glasses, we saw her gradually lift her bows out of the water, roll over and disappear beneath the surface, leaving nothing but a vast patch of bubbling foam. It was one of the most thrilling sights I have witnessed!'

Nine German sailors were killed – either drowned or shot by zealous British guards – and the rest were shipped south as prisoners of war. In a way they did the Allies a favour; dividing the High Seas Fleet up among the victorious powers would have been something of a diplomatic nightmare. During the 1920s, the salvage firm of Cox & Danks bought the wrecks from the Admiralty and set about raising them. This was a major undertaking, but in an unprecedented feat of salvage the bulk of the fleet was raised, then towed away for scrap. The collapse of the scrap metal market in the early 1930s made the enterprise unprofitable, and the pace of salvage slowed. The last to be brought up was the *Derfflinger*, which in 1939 was towed keel-up into shallow water off Hoy. There she remained throughout the Second World War. Ironically, she was moored near Jellicoe's old flagship *Iron Duke*, which had been relegated to the role of a floating administrative centre and post office. After the war, the two were both towed down to the Clyde to be scrapped.

By then, only the three König class dreadnoughts remained in Scapa Flow, accompanied by the wrecks of three post-Jutland light cruisers. There they remained undisturbed, save for the occasional visit by small salvage teams, who came seeking steel plate. The wrecks still form one of the world's greatest sources of non-radiated (or low-background) steel, as the waters of Scapa Flow shielded the hulls from the low-level radiation emitted by nuclear explosions from 1945 onwards. Today, they attract a new generation of visitors. Together, the wrecks constitute one of the world's great diving attractions, and every year hundreds of sports divers explore their remains. More than three decades later, I still remember my first glimpse of these great ships, and how I was profoundly impressed by their scale. On the *Kronprinz*, her stern 12-inch turrets can still be seen, proof that these sunken ships once had a very deadly purpose.

It's strange to think that these powerful and well-armed dreadnoughts, ships which had fought for their very survival at Jutland, should be meekly surrendered to the Grand Fleet, and then, just over half a year later, their crews would scuttle them rather than let them fall into the hands of their old enemies. The reason they did was seapower. The British Admiralty summed up their situation very succinctly at the time; 'The surrender of the German fleet, accomplished without shock of battle, will remain for all time the example of wonderful silence and sureness with which seapower attains its ends.' This was very true, but still, this impressive demonstration of seapower was poor consolation for the modern Trafalgar that could have been, but never was. I find it hard not to wish, a century on, that rather than being in Scapa Flow, these three dreadnoughts were lying on the seabed of the North Sea, seventy-five miles off the coast of Jutland.

Appendix

The Grand Fleet at Jutland

Battle Fleet (Admiral Jellicoe)

Dreadnoughts
(Listed in order from van to rear)

2nd Battle Squadron (Vice-Admiral Jerram)

1st Division	*King George V*	(flagship, V.-Adml. Jerram)
	Ajax	
	Centurion	
	Erin	
2nd Division	*Orion*	(flagship, R.-Adml. Leveson)
	Monarch	
	Conqueror	
	Thunderer	

4th Battle Squadron (Vice Admiral Sturdee)

3rd Division	*Iron Duke*	(fleet flagship, Adml. Jellicoe)
	Royal Oak	
	Superb	(flagship, R.-Adml. Duff)
	Canada	
4th Division	*Benbow*	(flagship, V.-Adml. Sturdee)
	Bellerophon	
	Temeraire	
	Vanguard	

1st Battle Squadron (Vice Admiral Burney)

3rd Division	*Colossus*	(flagship, R.-Adml. Gaunt)
	Collingwood	
	Neptune	
	St. Vincent	
4th Division	*Marlborough*	(flagship, V.-Adml. Burney)
	Revenge	
	Hercules	
	Agincourt	

Battlecruisers

3rd Battlecruiser Squadron

Invincible	(flagship, R.-Adml. Hood)
Inflexible	
Indomitable	

Armoured Cruisers

1st Cruiser Squadron

Defence	(flagship, R.-Adml. Arbuthnot)
Warrior	
Duke of Edinburgh	
Black Prince	

2nd Cruiser Squadron

Minotaur	(flagship, R.-Adml. Heath)
Hampshire	
Cochrane	
Shannon	

Light Cruisers

4th Light Cruiser Squadron

Calliope	(flagship, Comm. Le Mesurier)
Constance	
Caroline	
Royalist	
Comus	

Light cruisers attached to Battle Fleet: *Active, Bellona, Blanche, Boadicea*
Light cruisers attached to 3rd Battlecruiser Squadron: *Chester, Canterbury*

Destroyers

4th Destroyer Flotilla (eighteen boats)
Tipperary (Capt. Wintour), *Acasta, Achates, Ambuscade, Ardent, Broke, Christopher, Contest, Fortune, Garland, Hardy, Midge, Ophelia, Owl, Porpoise, Shark, Sparrowhawk, Spitfire, Unity*

11th Destroyer Flotilla (fifteen boats)
Castor (light cruiser – Comm. Hawksley),
Kempenfelt, Magic, Mandate, Manners, Marne, Martial, Michael, Millbrook, Minion, Mons, Moon, Morning Star, Mounsey, Mystic, Ossory

12th Destroyer Flotilla (sixteen boats)
Faulknor (Capt. Stirling), *Maenad, Marksman, Marvel, Mary Rose, Menace, Mindful, Mischief, Munster, Narwhal, Nessus, Noble, Nonsuch, Obedient, Onslaught, Opal*

Attached to Fleet Flagship: *Oak*

Battlecruiser Fleet (Vice Admiral Beatty)

Battlecruisers

1st Battlecruiser Squadron
Lion	(flagship, V.-Adml. Beatty)
Princess Royal	
Queen Mary	
Tiger	

2nd Battlecruiser Squadron
New Zealand	(flagship, R.-Adml. Pakenham)
Indefatigable	

Fast Battleships

5th Battle Squadron
Barham	(flagship, R.-Adml. Evan-Thomas)
Valiant	
Warspite	
Malaya	

Light Cruisers

1st Light Cruiser Squadron

       Galatea   (flagship, Comm. Alexander-Sinclair)

       Phaeton

       Inconstant

       Cordelia

2nd Light Cruiser Squadron

       Southampton   (flagship, Comm. Goodenough)

       Birmingham

       Nottingham

       Dublin

3rd Light Cruiser Squadron

       Falmouth   (flagship, R.-Adml. Napier)

       Yarmouth

       Birkenhead

       Gloucester

Attached: *Engadine* (Seaplane Carrier)

Destroyers

1st Destroyer Flotilla (nine boats)

Fearless (light cruiser – Capt. Roper),

Acheron, Ariel, Attack, Badger, Defender, Goshawk, Hydra, Lapwing, Lizard

9th & 10th Destroyer Flotillas (eight boats)

Lydiard (Cdr. Goldsmith), *Landrail, Laurel, Liberty, Moorsom, Morris, Termagant, Turbulent*

13th Destroyer Flotilla (ten boats)

Champion (light cruiser - Comm. Hawksley),

Moresby, Narborough, Nerissa, Nestor, Nicator, Nomad, Obdurate, Onslow, Pelican, Petard

The High Seas Fleet at Jutland

Battle Fleet (Vice-Admiral Scheer)
Dreadnoughts
(Listed in order from van to rear)
III Battle Squadron (Rear-Admiral Behncke)

V Division	*König*	(flagship, R.-Adml. Behnke)
	Kronprinz	
	Markgraf	
	Grosser Kurfürst	
VI Division	*Kaiser*	(flagship, R.-Adml. Nordmann)
	Kaiserin	
	Prinzregent Luitpold	
	Friedrich der Grosse	(fleet flagship, V.-Adml. Scheer)

I Battle Squadron (Vice-Admiral Schmidt)

I Division	*Ostfriesland*	(flagship, V.-Adml. Schmidt)
	Thuringen	
	Helgoland	
	Oldenburg	
II Division	*Posen*	(flagship, R.-Adml. Engelhardt)
	Rheinland	
	Nassau	
	Westfalen	

Pre-Dreadnought Battleships

II Battle Squadron (Rear-Admiral Mauve)

III Division	*Deutschland*	(flagship, R.-Adml. Mauve)
	Hessen	
	Pommern	
IV Division	*Hannover*	(flagship, R.-Adml. von Dalwigk zu Lichtenfels)
	Schlesien	
	Schleswig-Holstein	

Light Cruisers

IV Scouting Group

Stettin	(flagship, Comm. von Reuter)
München	
Hamburg	
Frauenlob	
Stuttgart	
Moltke	

Destroyer Flotillas

Rostock   (light cruiser – flagship. Comm. Michelson)

I Torpedo Boat (Destroyer) Flotilla (four boats)
    I Half Flotilla: *G-39* (flag), *G-40*, *G-38*, *S-32*

III Torpedo Boat (Destroyer) Flotilla (seven boats)
    S-53 (flag)
    V Half Flotilla: *V-71*, *V-73*, *G-88*
    VI Half Flotilla: *S-54*, *V-48*, *G-42*

VII Torpedo Boat (Destroyer) Flotilla (eight boats)
    S-24 (flag)
    XIII Half Flotilla: S-15, S-17, S-20, S-16, S-18
    XIV Half Flotilla: S-19, S-23, V-189

Scouting Force (Vice-Admiral Hipper)

Battlecruisers

I Scouting Group

Lützow	(Flaqship, Vice-Admiral Hipper)
Derfflinger	

Seydlitz
Moltke
Von der Tann

Light Cruisers

II Scouting Group

Frankfurt   (R.-Adml. Bödicker)
Wiesbaden
Pillau
Elbing

Destroyer Flotillas

Regensburg   (light cruiser – flagship, Comm.
                                                  Heinrich)

II Torpedo Boat (Destroyer) Flotilla (ten boats)
B-98 (flag)
III Half Flotilla: G-101, *G-102, B-112*, G-86
IV Half Flotilla: *B-109, B-110, B-111*, G-103, *G-104*

VI Torpedo Boat (Destroyer) Flotilla (nine boats)
G-41 (flag)
XI Half Flotilla: *V-44, G-87*, G-86
XII Half Flotilla: *V-69, V-45, V-46, S-50, G-37*

IX Torpedo Boat (Destroyer) Flotilla (eleven boats)
V-28 (flag)
XVII Half Flotilla: *V-37, V-26, S-36, S-51, S-52*
XVIII Half Flotilla: *V-30, S-34, S-33, V-29, S-35*

Bibliography

Admiralty Manual of Navigation, Vol. 1 (London, 1964) HMSO

Admiralty Manual of Seamanship, Vol. 1 (London, 1979) HMSO

Archibald, E.H.H.; *The Fighting Ship in the Royal Navy, AD897–1984* (Poole, 1984) Blandford Press Ltd.

Archibald, E.H.H. (ed.); *Concise Catalogue of Oil Paintings in the National Maritime Museum* (Woodbridge, 1988) Antique Collectors' Club

Bachrach, Harriet; *Jutland Letters, June–October 1916* (Salisbury, 2006) Wessex Books

Bacon, Reginald; *The Jutland Scandal* (London, 1925) Hutchinson & Co

Barnett, Corelli; *The Swordbearers* (London, 1963) Eyre & Spottiswode

Banks, Arthur; *A Military Atlas of the First World War* (London, 1975) Leo Cooper

Bennett, Geoffrey; *Coronel and the Falklands* (London, 1962) Batsford Ltd.

The Battle of Jutland (London, 1964) Batsford Ltd

Naval Battles of the First World War (London, 1968) Batsford Ltd

Bonney, George; *The Battle of Jutland, 1916* (Stroud, 2002) The History Press

Brooks, John; *Dreadnought Gunnery and the Battle of Jutland: The Question of Fire Control* (Abingdon, 2005) Routledge

Brown, David K.; *Warrior to Dreadnought: Warship Development, 1860–1905* (Rochester, 1997) Chatham Publishing

The Grand Fleet: Warship Design and Development, 1906–1922 (Barnsley, 2010) Seaforth Publishing

Burr, Lawrence; *British Battlecruisers, 1914–18* (Oxford, 2006) Osprey Publishing

Burt, R.A.; *British Battleships of World War One* (Barnsley, 2012) Pen & Sword

Busch, Fritz Otto; *Die Schlacht am Skagerrak* (Leipzig, 1933) Schneider

Butler, Daniel Allen; *Distant Victory: The Battle of Jutland and the Allied Triumph in the First World War* (Westport, Ct, 2006) Praeger

Campbell, John; *Naval Weapons of World War Two* (London, 2002) Conway Maritime Press

Jutland: An Analysis of the Fighting (London, 1986) Conway Maritime Press

Chalmers, W.S; *The Life and Letters of David Beatty, Admiral of the Fleet* (London, 1951) Hodder & Stoughton

Chickering, Roger; *Imperial Germany and the Great War, 1914–18* (Cambridge, 1998) Cambridge University Press

Churchill, W.S.; *The World Crisis* (London, 1923–31) Thornton Butterworth Ltd. (6 vols.)

Colledge, J.J. & Warlow, Ben; *Ships of the Royal Navy: The Complete Record of all Fighting Ships from the 15th Century to the Present* (Havertown, PA, 2010) Casemate

Corbett, Julian S.; *History of the Great War: Naval Operations* (London, 1920–31) Longmans, Green and Co. (5 vols.)

Epkenhans, Michael, Hillmann, Jörg & Nägler, Frank; *Skagerrakschlacht: Vorgeschichte, Ereignis, Verabeitung* (München, 2009) Oldenbourg

Epkenhans, Michael (ed).; *Jutland: World War I's Greatest Naval Battle* (Lexington, KY, 2015) University Press of Kentucky

Fawcett, H.W. & Hooper, G.W.W.; *The Fighting at Jutland: The Personal Experiences of Sixty Officers and Men of the British Fleet* (Rochester, 2001) Chatham Publishing

Ferguson, David M.; *Shipwrecks of Orkney, Shetlands and Pentland Firth* (Newton Abbot, 1988) David & Charles Inc.

Friedman, Norman; *Naval Firepower: Battleship Guns and Gunnery in the Dreadnought Era* (Barnsley, 2008) Seaforth Publishing

British Cruisers: Two World Wars and After (Barnsley, 2010) Seaforth Publishing

Naval Weapons of World War One: An Illustrated Directory (Barnsley, 2011) Seaforth Publishing

Fighting the Great War at Sea: Strategy, Tactics and Technology (Barnsley, 2014) Seaforth Publishing

Frost, Holloway H.; *The Battle of Jutland* (London, 1936) B.F. Stevens & Brown Ltd.

Gardiner, Robert (ed.); *Conway's All the World's Fighting Ships, 1860–1905* (London, 1979) Conway Maritime Press

Conway's All the World's Fighting Ships, 1906–1921 (London, 1986) Conway Maritime Press

The Eclipse of the Big Gun: The Warship, 1906–45 (London, 1992) Conway Maritime Press [Conway's History of the Ship Series]

George, S.C; *Jutland to Junkyard: The Raising of the Scuttled German High Seas Fleet from Scapa Flow* (Cambridge, 1972) Patrick Stevens Ltd

Gibson, Langhorne & Harper, J.E.T; *The Riddle of Jutland: An Authentic History* (London, 1934) Cassell

Gibson, W.M.; *Old Orkney Sea Yarns* (Kirkwall, 1986) Kirkwall Press Ltd

Gottschall, Terrell D.; *By Order of the Kaiser: Otto von Diederichs and the Rise of the Imperial German Navy, 1865–1902* (Annapolis, MD, 2003) Naval Institute Press

Gregory, Adrian; *The Last Great War: British Society and the First World War* (Cambridge, 2008) Cambridge University Press

Grimes, Shawn T.; *Strategy and War Planning in the British Navy, 1887–1918* (Woodbridge, 2012) Boydell Press

Gröner, Erich; *Die Deutschen Kriegsschiffe, 1815–1945.* (Coblenz, 1989) Bernard & Graefe (8 vols.)

Groos, Otto; Der Krieg zur See, 1914-18. Nordsee (Vol. 5) (Berlin, 1925) Mittler & Sohn [Herausgegeben von Marine-Archiv]

Goldbrick, James; *Before Jutland: The Naval War in North European Waters, August 1914 – February 1915* (Annapolis, MD, 2015) Naval Institute Press

Gordon, Andrew; *The Rules of the Game: Jutland and British Naval Command* (London, 1996) John Murray

Halpern, Paul G.; *A Naval History of World War 1* (Annapolis, MD, 1994) Naval Institute Press

Harper, J.E.P. *The Record of the Battle of Jutland* (London, 1927) HMSO

Herwig, Holger H.; *Luxury Fleet: The Imperial German Navy 1888–1919* (London, 1980) George Allen & Unwin Ltd.

Hansen, Clas Broder; *Deutschland wird Seemacht: Der Aufblau der Kaiserlichen Marine, 1867–1880* (München, 1991) Urbes

Hase, George von; Kiel & Jutland: *The Famous Naval Battle of the First World War from the German Perspective* (London, 2011) Leonaur

Hewison, W.S.; *Scapa Flow in War and Peace* (Kirkwall, 1995) The Orcadian Ltd.

This Great Harbour Scapa Flow (Edinburgh, 2005) Birlinn

Hewson, J.B.; *A History of the Practice of Navigation* (Glasgow, 1983) Brown, Son & Ferguson Ltd

Hodges, Peter; *The Big Gun: Battleship Main Armament, 1860–1945* (London, 1981) Conway Maritime Press

Howarth, David (ed.); *The Dreadnoughts* (Alexandria, VA, 1981) Time-Life Books

Jane, Fred T.; *Jane's Fighting Ships, 1914* (Newton Abbot, 1968) David & Charles (reprint)

Kelly, Patrick J.; *Tirpitz and the Imperial German Navy* (Bloomington, IN, 2011) Indiana University Press

Kemp, Peter (ed.); *The Oxford Companion of Ships and the Sea* (Oxford, 1977) Oxford University Press

King-Hall, Stephen ('Etienne'); *A Naval Lieutenant, 1914–18* (London, 1919) Methuen & Co. Ltd.

Konstam, Angus; *Scapa Flow: The Defences of Britain's Great Fleet Anchorage, 1914–45* (Oxford, 2009) Osprey Publishing

British Battleships, 1914–18 (1) The Early Dreadnoughts (Oxford, 2013) Osprey Publishing

British Battleships (2) The Super Dreadnoughts (Oxford, 2013) Osprey Publishing

Lambert, Andrew; *Admirals: The Naval Commanders who made Britain Great* (London, 2008) Faber & Faber

Lambert, Nicholas A.; *Sir John Fisher's Naval Revolution* (Columbia, SC, 1999) University of South Carolina Press

Lavery, Brian; *Maritime Scotland* (London, 2001) B.T. Batsford Ltd./ Historic Scotland

Shield of Empire: The Royal Navy and Scotland (Edinburgh, 2007) Birlinn

Le Fleming, H.M.; *Warships of World War 1* (London, 1961) Ian Allen (4 vols.)

London, Charles; Jutland 1916: Clash of the Dreadnoughts (Oxford, 2000) Osprey Publishing

Macintyre, Donald; *Jutland* (London, 1957) Evans Brothers Ltd

McNally, Michael; *Coronel and Falklands, 1914: Duel in the South Atlantic* (Oxford, 2012) Osprey Publishing

Mackay, Ruddock; *Fisher of Kilverstone* (Oxford, 1973) Oxford University Press

Marder, Arthur J; *From the Dreadnought to Scapa Flow* (Barnsley, 2014) Seaforth Publishing (3 vols.)

Marshall, Ian H.; *Armored Ships* (London, 1980) Conway Maritime Press

Massie, Robert K.; *Dreadnought: Britain, Germany and the Coming of the Great War* (London, 1992) Jonathan Cape

Castles of Steel: Britain, Germany and the Winning of the Great War at Sea (London, 2003) Jonathan Cape

Mehl, Hans; *Naval Guns: 500 Years of Ship and Coastal Artillery* (Rochester, 2002) Chatham Publishing

Miller, James; *Scapa* (Edinburgh, 2000) Birlinn

Moore, John (ed.) *Jane's Fighting Ships of World War I* (London, 1990) Studio Editions

Newbolt, Henry; *Naval Operations* (History of the Great War) vols. IV–V (London, 1928–31) Longmans, Green & Co.

Offer, Avner; *The First World War: An Agrarian Interpretation* (Oxford, 1989) Clarendon Press

Osborne, Eric W.; *Britain's Economic Blockade of Germany, 1914–19* (London, 2004) Frank Cass

The Battle of Heligoland Bight (Bloomington, IN, 2006) Indiana University Press

Palmer, Alan; *The Kaiser* (London, 1978) Weidenfeld & Nicolson

Parkes, Oscar; *British Battleships, 1860–1950: A History of Design, Construction and Armament* (London, 1966) Seeley Service & Co

Padfield, Peter; *Guns at Sea* (London, 1973) Hugh Evelyn Ltd.

Patterson, A. Temple; *The Jellicoe Papers: Selections from the private and official correspondence of Admiral of the Fleet Earl Jellicoe* (London, 1968) Spottiswoode, Ballantyne & Co. Ltd/Naval Records Society (2 vols.)

Pears, Randolph; *British Battleships, 1892–1957* (London, 1957) Putnam & Co. Ltd.

Pemsel, Helmut; *Atlas of Naval Warfare* (London, 1977) Arms and Armour Press

Perrett, Bryan; *North Sea Battleground: The War at Sea, 1914–18* (Barnsley, 2001) Pen & Sword

Philipp, O.; *Englands Flotte im Kampfe mit der deutschenFlotte im Weltkriege, 1914–18 bis nach der Schlacht vor dem Skagerrak* (Leipzig, 1920) Hillmann

Pollen, Anthony; *The Great Gunnery Scandal: The Mystery of Jutland* (London, 1980) Collins

Ranft, B. McL. (ed.); *The Beatty Papers: Selections from the Private and Official Correspondence of Admiral of the Fleet Earl Beatty* (London, 1993) Scolar Press/Naval Records Society (3 vols.)

Robbins, Guy; *The Aircraft Carrier Story, 1908–1945* (London, 2001) Cassell

Roberts, John; *Battlecruisers* (London, 1997) Chatham Publishing

Robinson, Douglas H.; *The Zeppelin in Combat: History of the German Naval Airship Division, 1912–18* (Atglen, PA, 1994) Schiffer Publishing Ltd

Roskill, Stephen; Admiral of the Fleet Earl Beatty (London, 1980) Collins

Scheer, Reinhard; *Germany's High Sea Fleet in the First World War* (Barnsley, 2014) Frontline Books

Scheibe, Albert; *Die Seeschlacht vor dem Skagerrak am Mai 31–Juni 1916: auf Grand Amtlieben Materials* (Berlin, 1916) Mittler

Schmalenbach, Paul; *Die Geschichte der deutschen Schiffsartillerie* (Herford, 1968) Koehlers Verlagsgesellschaft

Sondhaus, Lawrence; *The Great War at Sea: A Naval History of the First World War* (Cambridge, 2014) Cambridge University Press

Staff, Gary; *German Battlecruisers, 1914–18* (Oxford, 2006) Osprey Publishing

German Battleships, 1914–18 (1) Deutschland, Nassau and Helgoland classes (Oxford, 2009) Osprey Publishing

German Battleships, 1914–18 (2) Kaiser, König and Bayern classes (Oxford, 2010) Osprey Publishing

German Battlecruisers of World War One: Their Design, Construction and Operations (Barnsley, 2014) Seaforth Publishing

Steel, Nigel & Hart, Peter; *Jutland 1916: Death in the Grey Wastes* (London, 2003) Cassel

Stille, Mark; *British Dreadnought versus German Dreadnought: Jutland 1916* (Oxford, 2010) Osprey Publishing

Sumida, Jon Tetsuro; *The Pollen Papers: The Privately Circulated Printed Works of*

Arthur Hungerford Pollen, 1901–1916 (London, 1984) George Allen & Unwin/
    Naval Records Society

Tarrant, V.E.; *Battleship Warspite* (London, 1990) Arms and Armour Press

Jutland: The German Perspective (London, 1999) Brockhampton Press

Thomas, Roger D. & Patterson, Brian; *Dreadnoughts in Camera, 1905–1920*
    (Stroud, 1998) Sutton Publishing

Van der Vat, Dan; *The Grand Scuttle: The Sinking of the German Fleet at Scapa
    Flow in 1919* (Edinburgh, 2007) Birlinn

Waldeyer-Hartz, Hugo von; *Admiral von Hipper* (London, 1933)
    Rich & Cowan

Watton, Ross; *The Battleship Warspite* (London, 2002) Conway Maritime Press
    (Anatomy of the Ship Series)

Wells, John; *The Royal Navy: An Illustrated Social History* (Stroud, 1994) Sutton
    Publishing Ltd.

Winton, John; *Jellicoe* (London, 1981) Michael Joseph

Wolz, Nicolas; *From Imperial Splendour to Internment: The German Navy in the
    First World War* (Barnsley, 2015) Seaforth Publishing

Woodward, David; *The Collapse of Power: Mutiny in the High Seas Fleet* (London,
    1973) Arthur Barker Ltd.

Yates, Keith; *Flawed Victory: Jutland, 1916* (Annapolis, MD, 2000)
    Naval Institute Press

Young, Filson; *With the Battlecruisers* (London, 1921) Cassell & Co

Notes

Throughout the book, ships are often described as being ahead, astern, on the quarter or on the beam etc. This nautical terminology may appear confusing, but it follows a simple logic, and is best explained by a diagram.

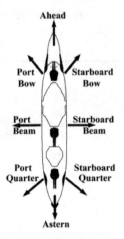

Preface / Prologue

p.4 'A battlecruiser was a new kind of warship . . .' Roberts, John; *Battlecruisers* (1997) and Staff, Gary; *German Battlecruisers of World War One* (Barnsley, 2014) both provide a detailed study of the strengths and weaknesses of the battlecruiser, and explore the concept behind its design in considerable detail.

p.5 'Five minutes before, at 3.55 p.m., . . .' The timing of hits given in this prologue are based on those detailed in Campbell, John; *Jutland: An Analysis of the Fighting* (1986), p.60–95. Campbell provides an exhaustive analysis of the damage inflicted and suffered by the capital ships of both sides.

p.6 'We were altering course at the time . . .' Narrative by the Navigating Officer of HMS New Zealand, in Fawcett, H.W. & Hooper, G.W.W.; *The Fighting at Jutland: The Personal Experiences of Sixty Officers and Men of the British Fleet* (2001), p.38

p.6 'Two or three shells falling together . . .' National Maritime Museum (NMM), Pakenham Papers PAC 16–01/12. Pakenham's view of the disaster is also described in Campbell (1986) p.60

p.6 'There was a terrific explosion . . .' Imperial War Museums (IWM) sound recording, AC 4096/Reel 1 C. Falmer, cited in Steel, Nigel & Hart, Peter; *Jutland 1916: Death in the Grey Wastes* (2003), p.95–96

p.6 'The main explosion . . .' Fawcett & Hooper (2001), p.38

PART 1 – THE INEVITABLE SHOWDOWN
Chapter 1: The First Dreadnought

p.11 'To his contemporaries . . .' Massie, Robert K.; *Dreadnought* (1992), p.401–407

p.13 'The day I joined . . .' *Ibid*, p.410

p.13 'I never smelled such a horrid smell ..' *Ibid*, p.412

p.13 'Fisher later described . . .' *Ibid*, p.412

p.14 'As a sailor . . .' *Ibid*, p.413

p.16 'It is difficult for anyone . . .' Mackay, Ruddock; *Fisher of Kilverstone* (1973), p.255. Also quoted in Massie (op cit) p.p.438

p.17 'There was no doubt . . .' Archibald E.H.H. (1984), p.152–155. Archibald was a great admirer of the aesthetic qualities of White's designs, which he once described to the author as 'the most aesthetically perfect design of battleship you could ever wish for.'

p18 '*Fisher and Watts* . . .' This description of the design of Dreadnought is drawn largely from Brown, David K; *Warrior to Dreadnought* (1997), augmented by Massie; *op. cit.*, p.467–478.

p.20 'Everything about Dreadnought was impressive.' Archibald, op cit, p.160–161, and Brown. K.; *The Grand Fleet* (1997) p.36–37. For her particulars, see Gardiner, Robert (ed.); *Conway's All the World's Fighting Ships, 1906–21* (1986) p.21–22.

Chapter 2: Racing towards Armageddon

p.22 'While Dreadnought was still being completed . . .' Gardiner; *op. cit.*, p.22

p.23 'His detailed report . . .' Massie, *op. cit.*, p.485

p.24 'A *Punch* cartoon of the time ..' Illustrated in Bonney; *The Battle of Jutland 1916* (2002), p.12. The same book contains a useful précis of Anglo-German naval rivalry during the period.

p.25 'Germany already had a navy of sorts.' Hansen; *Deutschland wird Seemacht* (1991) contains a useful description of the foundation of the German Navy. Also see Herwig; *Luxury Fleet* (1980) p.9–16.

p.25 'Within months of his coronation . . .' Gardiner (ed.); *Conway's All the World's Fighting Ships, 1860–1905* (1979), p.242, 246. Also Holger, *op. cit.*, p.24

p.25 'The first of them . . .' Burt (2012) *Ibid*, p.149–171

p.26 'Alfred Tirpitz has been called . . .' Massie, *op. cit.* p.165. Also see Herwig, *op. cit.*, p.33–39.

p.27 'In 1895 Tirpitz . . .' Massie, *op. cit.*, p.169–170.

p.29 'Meanwhile, German shipyards . . .' Gardiner (ed.), *op. cit.*, p.248–249, Heerwig, *op. cit.*, p.43–45

p.30 'This was verified . . .' Massie, *op. cit.*, p.165

p.31 'This would be the SMS *Nassau* . . .' Gardiner (ed.); (1986), p.144–145. Also Heerwig, *op. cit*, p.55–60.

p.32 'Still, minor improvements were made . . .' Gardiner , *op. cit*, p.22–23, 25–26. Also Archibald, *op. cit*, p.161–163, Brown, *op. cit*, p.37–41 and Burt; *British Battleships of World War One* (2012), p.122–148.

p.34 'These four super-dreadnoughts ... ' *Ibid*, 191–207

p.35 **Table** compiled using information provided in Gardiner, op cit, p.21–38, 145–148

Chapter 3: Fisher's Follies

p.37 'Fisher's new armoured cruiser . . .' Massie, op cit, p.492–493

p.38 'The first big-gun armoured cruiser . . .' Massie, p.495. Also Burt, op cit, p.42–60

p.38 'The Germans had already been building . . .' Gardiner, op cit. p.150–152

p.39 'The one-off *Seydlitz* . . .' Staff, op cit, p.137–200

p.39 'The cost of these ships . . .' Heerwig, op cit., p.71–72

p.41 'Admiral Sir John Fisher . . .', Massie, op cit, p.541

p.42 'Fisher called for fast, well-armed . . .' Gardiner (1979), p.86–87, Gardiner (1985), p.72

p.43 'Fisher also did what his successors . . .' This strategic plan is discussed in Massie, op cit, 745–745, and the blockade of Germany examined at length in Osborne; *Britain's Economic Blockade of Germany, 1914–19* (2004).

Chapter 4: The First Clashes

p.47 'The Kaiser set sail . . .' Massie (2003), p.12–13.

p.48 'On 1 August, the British Home Fleet . . .' Hewison; *This Great Harbour Scapa Flow* (2005), p.56

p.49 'When Jellicoe arrived . . .' *Ibid*, p.57–58

p.49 'So, his plan was to . . .' Wolz; *From Imperial Splendour to Internment* (2013), p.24. The German strategy during this period is also laid out in detail in Tarrant; *'Jutland: The German Perspective* (1999), p.22

p.50 'I am quite homeless.' Bennett; *Naval Battles of the First World War* (1968), p.55

p.51 'Still, he decided to fight.' This account of the Battle of Coronel drawn heavily on Bennett, Geoffrey; *Coronel and the Falklands* (1962), as well as Bennett (1968), p.71–80., as well as Massie, op cit. 225–235

p.51 'An officer from the *Glasgow* . . .' Bennett, Op Cit, p.77–78

p.52 'Sturdee described the last moments . . .' *Ibid*, p.104

p.52 'Many men sought shelter . . .' *Ibid*, p.108

p.53 'Rear-Admiral Wilhelm Souchon . . .' *Ibid*, p.14–16 and Massie, *op. cit.* 27–29

p.54 'Six days later . . .' Massie, op cit., p.49

p.55 'During these heady weeks . . .' Hewison, op cit., p.68

p.56 'At 7 a.m. on 28 August the cruiser *Arethusa* . . .' The following account of the Battle of Helgoland Bight is primarily drawn from Osborne; *The Battle of Helgoland Bight* (2006), p.47–77

p.57 'An officer on the *Ariadne* . . .' Bennett, op cit, p.132

p.57 'In fact, as Tirpitz put it . . .' Massie, op cit, p.120

Chapter 5: Baiting the British

p.59 'At dawn the next day they arrived off the port' This operation is described in detail in Goldrick *Before Jutland* (2015), p.171–177, as well as in Bennett (1968), p.37–39, and Tarrant, op cit, p.27–28.

p.60 'In late August the German light cruiser *Magdeburg* . . .' The importance of this intelligence breakthrough, and those which followed it were vital to the British naval war effort. While a full study of the work undertaken by the staff of the Admiralty's Room 40 still needs to be undertaken, the gist of these events are recounted in Massie, *op cit*, p.316–318.

p.62 'At 8 a.m. the southern group opened fire . . .' Goldrick, op cit. p.208, Tarrant, *op. cit.*, p.30.

p.65 'On 24 January 1915 . . .' This account of the Battle of Dogger Bank is drawn from Goldrick, *op. cit*, p.256–281, Tarrant, op cit, p.33–39, Bennett, op cit., 141–145 and Marder; *From the Dreadnought to Scapa Flow* (2013) Vol II, p.158–164

p.67 'Hipper must have sensed he was heading into danger.' Hipper's after-action report is cited in Tarrant, op cit., p.35.

p.67 'This was something of a milestone . . .' While warships were perfectly capable of firing at these longer ranges, their fire control systems were – for the most part – calibrated for ranges of less than 16,000 yards. A full explanation of gunnery fire control during this period is provided in Friedman, Norman; *Naval Firepower* (2008), p.16–39

p.68 'On board *Lion*, Lieutenant Young . . .' Massie, *op. cit.*, p.390

p.68 ' A young British officer was watching . . .' Bennett, *op. cit.* p.142–143

p.69 'It ignited a powder charge . . .' The German naval report into the loss of the turret on *Seydlitz* is cited at length in Bennett, op cit., 146.

p.70 'A German survivor recalled . . .' Tarrant, *op. cit.* p.37

p.70 'You can imagine how distressing it was . . .' Bennett, *op. cit.* p.144–145. Robinson; *The Zeppelin in Combat* (1994), p.99–100 provides a useful account of zeppelin operations in support of the High Seas Fleet during the battle.

p.71 'Captain von Egidy of the *Seydlitz* . . .' Yates; *Flawed Victory*, (2000), p.98

PART II – CLASH OF TITANS
Chapter 6: The Spring Sorties

p.76 'After the Dogger Bank battle . . .' This debate on German naval strategy is covered in Herwig, p.152–53, Massie, p.421–423 and above all in Goldrick, op cit, p.285–290. Halpern; *A Naval History of World War 1* (1994) p.290 cites the Tirpitz memorandum.

p.77 'The sortie began . . .' See Tarrant, op cit. p.45–46, Yates, *op. cit.*, p.112

p.78 'The German battlecruisers slipped out of Wilhelmshaven . . .' This account of the Lowestoft operation based on Massie, *op cit.*, p.557–560, Tarrant, *op cit.*, p.46–49, Marder, *op.ci.* p.424–427 and Halpern, *op. cit.*, p.313.

p.79 'At 5.11am . . .' Captain Zenker quoted in Tarrant, op cit. p.48

p.81 'I hope you do not think . . .' Temple Patterson (ed.); The Jellicoe Papers (1966) Vol. I, p.207

p.81 'The term fast battleship . . .' A detailed discussion of the notion of the 'fast battleship' is provided in Burt, op cit., p.277–287.

p.82 'By dawn on 4 May . . .' Friedman; *British Carrier Operation* (Barnsley, 1988) p.365–367 provided a detail account of this operation from the British perspective. Robinson, *op. cit.*, p.161 provided a German viewpoint. Also Massie, *op. cit.*, p.556.

p.85 'Three other boats would lay mines off Orkney . . .' On the evening of 5 June one of these mines lain by *U-75* would sink the armoured cruiser HMS *Hampshire*,, as she steamed up the west coast of Orkney, bound for Russia. Only 12 men of her 655 man crew survived. The dead included seven passengers – the military delegation led by Field Marshal Lord Kitchener, who was on his way to Russia to discuss war plans. His body was never recovered.

Chapter 7: Enemy in Sight!

p.89 'The eve of Jutland I always remember . . .' F.F. Clark, quoted in Brown & Meehan; *Scapa Flow* (1968) p.95

p.89 'But, after all these alarms . . .' *Ibid*, p.24

p.91 'For me, therefore, every cruise . . .' Hase, Georg von; *Kiel and Jutland* (2001), p.69

p.92 'The morning breaks fine and clear . . .' IWM Archives, Misc 1010, R. Church Colln., letter

p.92 ' That the entire English fleet was already at sea . . .' von Hase, op cit, p.70

p.94 'Madlung had just sent B-110 to investigate . . .' et seq; IWM Archive, Misc. 1010, R. Church Colln., Bassenge, response to questionnaire (trans.)

p.95 'They put a shell through our ship's side . . .' IWM Archive, Farquhar, diary, 1916

p.97 '*Lion* had been signalling to *Barham* . . .' Bacon; *The Jutland Scandal*, p.178, also quoted in Massie, *op. cit.*, p.585

p.98 'Clouds were at 1,000 to 1,200 feet . . .' F. Rutland, quoted in Fawcett, H.W. & Hooper, G.W.W.; *The Fighting at Jutland* (1921, p.8

p.99 'A little enemy seaplane came up . . .' IWM Archive, Misc. 1010, R. Church Colln., Bassenge, response to questionnaire (trans.)

p.99 'At 4.28pm [3.28pm in British ships] . . .' von Hase, op cit, p.75

p.100 'As there was a 12-inch magazine . . .' IWM Archive, Misc. 1010, R. Church Colln., Eady, response to questionnaire

p.100 'The British cruisers came in view . . .' Von Egidy, *Jutland: A German View* Published in *History of the First World War* (London, 1975) Purnell Partworks, vol. 4: 3, p, 1417

Chapter 8: Our Bloody Ships

p.101 'Imagine then ... a room eighteen feet square . . .' IWM Archive, Misc. 1010, R. Church Colln., Hayler, letter

p.104 'Estimated Speed: 26 knots, Course 110° . . .' Pashen, Günther; *SMS Lützow at Jutland*, in *Journal of the Royal United Service Institution* (RUSI), vol. lxxii, p.33

p.105 'The range was 16,000 yards . . .' Lord Chatfield, *The Navy & Defence* (London, 1942), p.140–141, cited in Steel & Hart, op cit., p.81

p.105 'Almost immediately after the enemy had opened fire . . .' IWM Archive, Combe, manuscript: *Account of the Action on May 31st 1916*,

p.105 ' A blinding flash through our gun port . . .' IWM Archive, Hayward, manuscript: *HMS Tiger*

p.105 'By some mistake we were being left out . . .' Von Hase, *op. cit.*, p.82

p.106 'The sixth salvo . . .' *Ibid*, p.81

p.107 'The cries of the wounded and burnt men . . .' IWM Archive, Bradley, diary, 1916

p.108 'The poor fellow was wounded in several places . . .' *Ibid*, same diary entry

p.109 'The Gunnery Central Station . . .' Von Egidy, *op. cit.*, p.1417

p.110 'The enemy's shooting at *Lion* . . .' Mackenzie-Grieve, Alan; *Battle of Jutland, 31st May 1916*, published in *Cinque Ports Gazette*, December 1934, p.60

p.113 'Out of the blue came a heavy barrage of fire . . .' IWM Archive, Misc. 1010, R. Church Colln., Bassenge, response to questionnaire (trans.)

p.115 'At 4.26 p.m. Midshipman Jocelyn Storey . . .' Account drawn from Brotherton Library, Leeds University, Peter Liddle Colln., McWilliam Papers, Storey, manuscript, cited in Steel & Hart, op cit.,

p.115 'Immediately after that came what I call the big smash . . .' IWM Archive, Field Colln., Francis, manuscript: *Impressions of a Gunner's Mate at Jutland*

p.116 'She was broken amidships . . .' IWM Archive, Owen, manuscript

p.117 'Beatty turned to me and said . . .' Chatfield, *op. cit.*, p.143

p.117 'The two signallers present remember a different version . . .' IWM Archive, Misc. 1010, R. Church Colln., Lewis, response to questionnaire, and Tempest, ditto.

Chapter 9: The Run to the North

p.119 'It was a wild scene . . .' Corbett; *History of the Great War: Naval Operations* (1922) Vol. III, p.345 –346.

p.120 'Our misfortune lay in getting a shell . . .' National Register of Archives, London (NRA), ADM 137/4808, Whitfield, letter

p.121 'If you are going to make that signal . . .' Yates, *op. cit.*, p.140

p.122 'However, my throat was so dry . . .' IWM Archive, Misc. 1010, R. Church Colln., King-Hall, manuscript

p.126 ' Very soon after the turn . . .' IWM Archive, Walwyn, manuscript: *HMS Warspite*, also cited in Tarrant; *Battleship Warspite* (1990), p.27

p.127 'I saw all four rounds ...' IWM Archive, Misc. 1010, R. Church Colln., Tillard, response to questionnaire

p.129 'One of the 38cm [15-inch] shells ...' et. seq. Foerster, Richard; *The Sea Battle off the Skagerrak on 31 May 1916* (London, 1924) published pamphlet (trans.)

p.130 'On the *Derfflinger* ...' von Hase, *op. cit.*, p.96

p.130 'The *Warspite* received one hit ...' IWM Archive, Bickmore, manuscript

p.130 'I remember seeing *Nicator* making an attack ...' IWM Archive, Misc. 1010, R. Church Colln., Owen, response to questionnaire

p.131 'Their course necessarily led them past ...' Bingham, B.; *Falklands, Jutland and the Bight* (London, 1919) p.143

p.131 'The ship was sinking fast ...' NRA, ADM 137/4808, Whitfield, letter

p.131 'Very soon we were enveloped ...' Bingham, *op. cit.*, p.143–144

Chapter 10: Jellicoe enters the fray

p.134 'Exposed cordite was exploded ...' IWM Archive, Misc. 1010, R. Church Colln., Rudall, response to questionnaire

p.134 'One of his assistants ...' IWM Archive, Misc. 1010, R. Church Colln., Gulliver, response to questionnaire

p.134 'The Chester came close across our bows ...' *Narrative from HMS Castor*, in Fawcett. & Hooper, *op. cit.*, p.202

p.135 'We sighted gun flashes ...' *HMS Inflexible*, in Fawcett. & Hooper, *op. cit.*, p.226–227

p.135 'Am under fire ...' Signal cited in Tarrant (1999), p.281

p.136 'I reported steering gear gone ...' NRA, ADM 116/1485, Griffin, manuscript

p.136 'The gun crew lying dead ...' IWM Archive, Misc. 1010, R. Church Colln., Clement-Ford, response to questionnaire

p.136 'The [German] destroyers were supported ...' et seq., *The Adventures of HMS Acasta*, in Fawcett. & Hooper, *op. cit.*, p.235–236

p.139 'It was Scheer who summed up the uncertainty ...' Massie, *op. cit.* p.605 given an excellent description of Scheer's situation at that moment.

p.140 'This consisted of clearing away guard rails ...' Graham, A. Cunninghame; *Random Naval Recollections, 1905–1951* (Gartocharn, 1979) p.50

p.142 'The only man on either side ...' This much-quoted line was originally penned by Churchill in his history of the war; *The World Crisis*, 1911–19 (London, 1927) Vol. 1.

p.143 'I must confess it was a magnificent sight ...' IWM Archive, James Colln., Norman, copy of letter

p.144 'The enemy could not be seen without glasses ...' IWM Archive, Misc. 1010, R. Church Colln., Lawder, response to questionnaire

p.144 'With the Grand Fleet in sight ...' Yates, *op. cit.*, p.153

Chapter 11: Dreadnoughts in action

p.146 'I heard at once the sharp distinctive step ...' et seq., Dreyer, Sir Frederic; *The Sea Heritage* (London, 1955) p.146–147, quoted in Massie, *op. cit.* p.612–613

p.148 'When I first saw them ...' IWM Archive, Lorrimer Colln., Brind, manuscript

p.149 'At first glance I recognised ...' Paschen, *op. cit.*, p.36

p.149 'The *Defence* suddenly disappeared ...' et seq., IWM Archive, Lorrimer Colln., Brind, manuscript

p.149 'The secondary armament was trained ...' Von Hase, *op. cit.* p.100

p.151 'The steering gear episode ...' IWM Archive, Walwyn, manuscript: *HMS Warspite*

p.151 'We knew that the gun crew must be burnt ...' IWM Archive, Bostock, microfilm account, cited in Steel & Hart, op.cot., p.208–209.

p.152 'The upper deck and superstructure . . .' IWM Archive, Walwyn, manuscript: *HMS Warspite*, cited in Tarrant, *op. cit.*, p.36

p.152 'It is my opinion that our light grey colour . . .' Von Hase, *op. cit.* p.101

p.153 'Two columns of smoke appeared . . .' IWM Archive, Misc. 1010, R. Church Colln., Webber, response to questionnaire

p.153 'At 8.24 p.m. [6.24p.m.] I began to engage . . .' Von Hase, *op. cit.* p.101

p.153 'There began a phase . . .' Paschen, *op. cit.*, p.37

p.154 'On the starboard bow we had the German fleet . . .' IWM Archive, Misc. 1010, R. Church Colln., Webber, response to questionnaire

p.154 'Hood used the voicepipe . . .' IWM Archive, Misc. 1010, R. Church Colln., Dannreuther, letter

p.155 'There was a terrific flash from the *Invincible* . . .' IWM Archive, Croome, manuscript

p.155 'The flashes passed down to both amidships magazines . . .' IWM Archive, Misc. 1010, R. Church Colln., Gasson, response to questionnaire

p.156 'She went down with a crash . . .' IWM Archive, Misc. 1010, R. Church Colln., Dannreuther, letter

p.156 'Right aft she was crowded with men . . .' IWM Archive, Myers, manuscript

p.159 'According to statements of prisoners . . .' Signal cited in Tarrant (1999), p.281

p.160 'Admiral Scheer had stood freely . . .' Cited in Steel & Hart, *op. cit.*, p.216

p.160 'It was now quite obvious . . .' Scheer, Reinhardt; Germany's *High Seas Fleet in the First World War* (1920, reprinted 2014), p.151–152

Chapter 12: *Gefechtsskehrtwendung*

p.163 'At 6.47 p.m. the track of a torpedo . . .' *Narrative of HMS Duke of Edinburgh*, in Fawcett. & Hooper, *op. cit.*, p.177

p.163 'At this time . . .' Cited in Massie, *op. cit*, p.622

p.165 'While the battle is progressing . . .' *Ibid*, p.622.

p.165 'The exceptional training . . .' Groos, Otto; *Der Krieg zur See, 1914–18* (1920) Vol. 5 Nordsee, p.300

p.166 'Rather pompously, the official history . . .' *Ibid*, p.301

p.168 '*Lützow* sheers out of the line . . .' Paschen, *op. cit.*, p.38

p.168 'The Captain gave the order . . .' Von Hase, *op. cit.*, p.107

p.170 'Lieutenant Commander John Tovey . . .' NRA, ADM 116/1485, Tovey, report

p.171 'For a second there was a tense silence . . .' IWM Archive, Nichol, manuscript: *The Battle of Jutland*

p.171 'Simply lifted the ship like a ball . . .' IWM Archive, AC 751, Reel 7, Fox, audio recording, cited in Steel & Hart, *op. cit.*, p.245.

p.172 'I have often wondered . . .' IWM Archive, Howell, letter

Chapter 13: A Second Chance

p.175 'Enemy's van bears East by South . . .' Signal cited in Tarrant, *op. cit.*, p.282

p.175 'Turn together 16 points . . .' *Ibid*, p.282

p.177 'The enemy could have compelled us . . .' et seq., Scheer; *Immediatbericht*, 4 July 1916, German Ministry of Marine, manuscript. Translation provided in Tarrant, *Ibid.*, p.151

p.177 'Scheer now advanced . . .' Groos, *op. cit.*, p.305

p.179 'The *Wiesbaden*, and the boats making for her . . .' Scheer (1920, reprinted 2014), p.156

p.179 'Our secondary armament opened fire . . .' *Narrative of a midshipman stationed in the fore-top of* HMS Neptune, in Fawcett. & Hooper, *op. cit.*, p.212

p.179 'The enemy ships were again at the extreme limit . . .' Von Hase, *op. cit.*, p.110

p.180 'We observed German destroyers . . .' et. seq., *Narrative of an officer in 'A' turret, HMS Conqueror*, in Fawcett. & Hooper, *op. cit.*, p.198–199

p.180 ' Suddenly we were practically surrounded . . .' NRA, ADM 137/4809, Blessman, letter

p.181 ' The English fleet knew this . . .' IWM Archive, Misc. 1010, R. Church Colln., von Gymnich, response to questionnaire(trans.)

p.181 'One was able to distinguish the difference . . .' IWM Archive, Misc. 1010, R. Church Colln., Wright, response to questionnaire

p.181 'The Commander in Chief realised . . .' Von Hase, *op. cit.*, p.110

Chapter 14: Hartog's 'Death Ride'

p.184 'Battlecruisers - turn towards the enemy . . .' Signal cited in Tarrant, *op. cit.*, p.283

p.184 'At about 9.12 a.m. [7.12 p.m.] . . .' Von Hase, *op. cit.*, p.110–111

p.185 'The battlecruisers, temporarily under the command . . .' *Ibid*, p.111

p.185 'Followed by the *Seydlitz* . . .' *Ibid*, p.111

p.186 'Visibility decreased . . .' Von Egidy, *op. cit.*, p.1420

p.186 'Salvo after salvo fell around us . . .' et seq., Von Hase, *op. cit.*,p.111–114

p.189 'Our men called these exercises . . .' et. seq., Von Egidy, *op. cit.*, p.1420–1421

p.190 'There was a huge blow . . .' Foerster; *op. cit.*, pamphlet.

p.191 ' Our ship was in great danger . . .' IWM Archive, Misc. 1010, R. Church Colln., Melms, response to questionnaire(trans.)

p.191 ' The range-taker, who was standing next to me . . .' IWM Archive, Misc. 1010, R. Church Colln., Foot, letter

p.192 'A minute later, at 7.13 p.m. . . .' Signal cited in Tarrant, *op. cit.*, p.283

p.195 'After we had fired about four salvos . . .' IWM Archive, Misc. 1010, R. Church Colln., Congreve, letter

p.196 'As they approached to within torpedo range . . .' IWM Archive, Misc. 1010, R. Church Colln., Brister, response to questionnaire

p.196 'Only one destroyer got to within close range . . .' et seq., IWM Archive, Caslon Colln., Caslon, manuscript: *Recollections of the Battle of Jutland*

p.198 'We should certainly have been hit . . .' Ross, George P., *Jutland* (1926) Transcript of talk given at Royal Scots Club, Edinburgh, pamphlet

p.199 ' A little later another torpedo . . .' IWM Archive, Misc. 1010, R. Church Colln., Phipp, response to questionnaire

p.199 'The torpedo was following exactly in our course . . .' Massie, *op. cit.*, p.630

PART III – SCHEER'S ESCAPE
Chapter 15: Fading Light, Fading Hope

p.205 'Enemy bears from me NW by W . . .' Signal cited in Admiralty; *Battle of Jutland – Official Despatches*, p.464

p.206 'Urgent. Submit van of battleships . . .' Signal cited in Admiralty *Official Despatches*, p.466. Massie, op cit., p.633, follows with a subsequent quote by Jellicoe; 'To tell the truth, I thought it was rather subordinate.' This signal lay at the centre of the later controversy between supporters of Jellicoe and Beatty, and is discussed at length in Marder (reprinted 2014), Vol, III, p.142–146. Today, it is hard to view the subsequent claims by Beatty and his supporters in a favourable light.

p.209 'We, half the squadron . . .' IWM Archive, Servaes, letter

p.209 'We were in sight of the German battleships . . .' et seq., *Narrative from HMS Calliope, Flagship of the 4th L.C.S.* in Fawcett. & Hooper, *op. cit.*, p.269

p.210 'Our second little excursion . . .' Le Mesurier, letter to wife, reprinted in Bachrach, Harriet; *Jutland Letters* (2006), p.14

p.211 'At 8pm we were ordered to sweep . . .' *Narrative from HMS Falmouth, Flagship of the 3rd L.C.S.* in Fawcett. & Hooper, *op. cit.*, p.273–274

p.212 'Four enemy light cruisers . . .' Signal cited in Tarrant, *op. cit.*, p.284

p.213 'Clear for action! sounded once more . . .' Von Hase, *op. cit.*, p.119–120

p.214 'When we were engaged on the starboard side . . .' IWM Archive, AC 9260, Reel 2, Fox, audio recording, cited in Steel & Hart, *op. cit.*, p.277–278

Chapter 16: Duelling in the Dusk

p.219 'Owing to interference from smoke . . .' Groos, *op. cit.*, p.345–348.

p.219 'Many of our squadron's salvos hit . . .' Narrative from HMS *Indomitable*, in Fawcett. & Hooper, *op. cit.*, p.243

p.219 ' Help came from the quarter . . .' et seq., Von Hase, *op. cit.*, p.121

p.221 'At 10.31 pm [8.31pm] . . .' *Ibid*, p.121

p.223 'The shells screamed over our heads . . .' Cited in Steel & Hart, *op. cit.*, p.279–280

p.223 'It was not dark enough to make an attack . . .' Cited in Frost, Holloway; *The Battle of Jutland* (1936), p.308

p.224 'On her bridge the same scene was repeated . . .' Yates, *op. cit.*, p.185

Chapter 17: The Cover of Night

p.225 'Everything that had happened . . .' Dreyer, *op. cit*, p.151

p.226 'When we switched off our searchlights . . .' IWM Archive, Misc. 1010, R. Church Colln., Bennett, response to questionnaire

p.226 ' At approximately 9.45 p.m. . . .' IWM Archive, Misc. 1010, R. Church Colln., King-Hall, manuscript

p.227 'We showed them the English recognition signals . . .' IWM Archive, Misc. 1010, R. Church Colln., Bassenge, response to questionnaire (trans.)

p.227 'It may be necessary to force . . .' Temple-Paterson, *op. cit.*, p.248. This section of the Grand Fleet Battle Orders is entitled: XIII. *Orders for the Conduct of the Fleet after Action*

p.227 'At 9 p.m., light being very bad . . .' Quoted in Jellicoe, Sir John; *The Grand Fleet, 1914–1916* (1919) p.374. Also see . . .' Temple-Paterson, *op. cit.*, p.267

p.229 'No night intentions . . .' Bennett, *op. cit.* p.128

p.231 'If we could succeed . . .' Scheer, *op. cit.*, p.159

p.231 'The gun firing had ceased . . .' Von Hase, *op. cit.*, p.116

p.231 'At 9.14pm, Scheer ordered his battle fleet . . .' Signal cited in Tarrant, *op. cit.*, p.285

p.231 'Next, Scheer angled his battle line . . .' Signal cited in Tarrant, *op. cit.*, p.286

Chapter 18: Probing the Line

p.236 'The next [dreadnought] ahead . . .' Cited Steel & Hart, *op. cit.*, p.289

p.238 'At about 9.50pm a very violent explosion . . .' *Narrative of the Navigating Officer of HMS Broke*, in Fawcett. & Hooper, *op. cit.*, p.307

p.240 ' They fired only at us . . .' *Narrative from HMS Castor*, in Fawcett. & Hooper, *op. cit.*, p.351

p.242 'It was a very tense moment . . .' IWM Archive, Misc. 1010, R. Church Colln., Burroughs, manuscript

p.243 'A solitary gun crashed forth . . .' King-Hall, *op. cit.*, p.148–149

p.243 'Apparently they made up their minds . . .' IWM Archive, Misc. 1010, R. Church Colln., Burroughs, manuscript

P.244 'The range was amazingly close . . .' King-Hall, *op. cit.*, p.149

p.244 'The guns immediately opened fire . . .' NRA, ADM 137/4808. Stolzmann, Interview in *Norddeutsche Allgemeine Zeitung*, 25 June 1916 (trans.)

p.244 'I was awakened by a strong jet of flame . . .' IWM Archive, Misc. 1010, R. Church Colln., Bassenge, response to questionnaire (trans.)

p.245 'On the bridge the full glare of the searchlights . . .' *Narrative of the Torpedo Lieutenant of HMS Southampton*, in Fawcett. & Hooper, *op. cit.*, p.290

p.245 'Only a few seconds later . . .' NRA, ADM 137/4808. Stolzmann, Interview in *Norddeutsche Allgemeine Zeitung*, 25 June 1916 (trans.)

p.245 'At the same moment both engines stopped . . .' NRA, ADM 137/4808. Müller, Interview in *Norddeutsche Allgemeine Zeitung*, 25 June 1916 (trans.)

p.246 'Up to their waists in water . . .' Groos, *op. cit.*, p.366

p.246 'A few seconds later we saw the ship sink . . .' NRA, ADM 137/4808. Stolzmann, Interview in *Norddeutsche Allgemeine Zeitung*, 25 June 1916 (trans.)

p.247 'At first we could continue to follow the battlecruiser . . .' Von Egidy, *op. cit.*, p.1420

p.248 'Captain James Fergusson of the *Thunderer* . . .' Yates, *op. cit.*, p.192

Chapter 19: Death of a Flotilla

p.250 'Tiny factors, and no human plan . . .' Gibson, & Harper, *The Riddle of Jutland* (1934), p.219–210

p.251 'At 10 p.m., the German battle fleet . . .' Signal cited in Tarrant, p.286–287

p.252 ' The destroyer is a projectile . . .' Quoted in Frost, *op. cit.*, p.346

p.252 'I sighted the blur of three ships . . .' IWM Archive, Misc. 1010, R. Church Colln., Cox, response to questionnaire

p.253 'They were so close that I remember . . .' *Narrative of a survivor of HMS Tipperary*, in Fawcett. & Hooper, *op. cit.*, p.339–340

p.254 'I opened fire with the after guns . . .' *Narrative of a survivor of HMS Tipperary*, in Fawcett. & Hooper, *op. cit.*, p.340

P.255 'We fired a torpedo, then waited . . .' *HMS Spitfire and the night action of Jutland*, in Fawcett. & Hooper, *op. cit.*, p.321

p.255 'How we avoided their [search]lights . . .' IWM Archive, Milford Haven Colln., Glennie, letter (microfilm), cited in Steel & Hart, *op. cit.*, p.311–312

p.256 'I can recollect a fearful crash . . .' *HMS Spitfire and the night action of Jutland*, in Fawcett. & Hooper, *op. cit.*, p.322

p.258 'I was too weak to go and see . . .' IWM Archive, Misc. 1010, R. Church Colln., Bassenge, response to questionnaire (trans.)

p.259 'She played her searchlight on a destroyer . . .' IWM Archive, Croad, manuscript, cited in Steel & Hart, *op. cit.*, p.316

p.259 'We got off two or three rounds . . .' IWM Archive, Milford Haven Colln., Glennie, letter (microfilm), cited in Steel & Hart, *op. cit.*, p.318

p.259 'The first shot swept our gun crews . . .' IWM Archive, Croad, manuscript, cited in Steel & Hart, *op. cit.*, p.318

p.259 'It was perfectly damnable . . .' IWM Archive, Milford Haven Colln., Glennie, letter (microfilm), cited in Steel & Hart, *op. cit.*, p.318

p.260 'We saw Broke coming straight for our bridge . . .' *The Adventures of HMS Sparrowhawk*, in Fawcett. & Hooper, *op. cit.*, p.332

p.260 'We hit very hard, doing much damage . . .' IWM Archive, Milford Haven Colln., Glennie, letter (microfilm), cited in Steel & Hart, *op. cit.*, p.319

p.260 'While we stood jammed into each other . . .' IWM Archive, Croad, manuscript, cited in Steel & Hart, *op. cit.*, p.320

p.260 'It was the most gallant fight . . .' Busch quoted in Dorling, T.; *Endless Story* (1932), p.207

p.262 'I looked to the bridge and it was blown away . . .' IWM Archive, Misc. 1010, R. Church Colln., Clifford, response to questionnaire

p.263 'I attacked at once . . .' National Maritime Museum, Greenwich (NMM), Archive, Marsden, manuscript: *HMS Ardent and Jutland Action*

Chapter 20: Breaking Through

p.265 'On the *Malaya*, Lieutenant Patrick Bird . . .' Massie, *op. cit.* p.645–646. Also see Yates, *op. cit.*, p.198

p.265 'About 11.45pm there was a terrific burst of fire . . .' IWM Archive, Misc. 1010, R. Church Colln., Congreve, letter

p.267 'Utterly mistaking the situation . . .' et. seq., Scheer, *op. cit.*, p.161–162

p.267 'She drifted down the line blazing furiously . . .' Groos, *op. cit.*, p.377

p.267 'She tore past us with a roar . . .' *HMS Spitfire and the night action of Jutland*, in Fawcett. & Hooper, *op. cit.*, p.326

p.269 'We sighted a dark mass . . .'*Loss of HMS Turbulent*, in Fawcett. & Hooper, *op. cit.*, p.354

p.271 'A terrific cannonade took place . . .' IWM Archive, Grant, letter

P.272 'Urgent Priority. Enemy battleships in sight . . .' Yates, *op. cit.*, p.200

p.274 'We went straight in to attack . . .' IWM Archive, Misc. 1010, R. Church Colln., Knight, response to questionnaire

p.275 'A dull red ball of fire . . .' *Narrative of HMS Obedient*, in Fawcett. & Hooper, *op. cit.*, p.360–362

p.275 'Cor, I said – we got her! . . .' IWM Archive, AC9953. audio recording, cited in Steel & Hart, *op. cit.*, p.357

p.276 'Of course in these attacks we were fired at . . .' IWM Archive, Misc. 1010, R. Church Colln., Champion, letter

p.276 'I saw a line of enemy battleships . . .' IWM Archive, Misc. 1010, R. Church Colln., Lees, response to questionnaire

p.276 'Before we had got to the turning point . . .' IWM Archive, Poignand, diary, 1916

p.277 'Farie flashed a signal to the *Marksman* . . .' Frost, *op. cit.*, p.376

p.278 'At 2.30 p.m. we caught a glimpse . . .' Oram, H.K.; *Ready for Sea* (London 1975) p.172

p.278 'I considered action imperative . . .' *A destroyer of the 12th Flotilla in the Day and Night Actions*, in Fawcett. & Hooper, *op. cit.*, p.420–421

PART IV – THE ELUSIVE VICTORY
Chapter 21: An Empty Horizon

p.284 'The promise of a better day . . .' Quoted in Yates, op[cit., p.203

p.285 'At 4.15 a.m. [3.15 a.m.] . . .' Robinson, *op. cit.*, p.168–169. Also see Scheer, *op. cit.*, p.165

p.286 'In our opinion the ships in a south-westerly direction . . .' Scheer; *Ibid*, p.165–166. Also *Immediatbericht*, 4 July 1916, German Ministry of Marine, manuscript. Translation provided in Yates, op cit., p201.

p.286 'We cheerfully engaged the airship . . .' Graham, A. Cunninghame; *Random Naval Recollections, 1905–1951* (Gartocharn, 1979) p.54

p.286 'We learned much later . . .' IWM Archive, Caslon, manuscript: *Recollections of the Battle of Jutland*

p.287 'This signal made it evident . . .' Quoted in Yates, *op. cit.*, p.204

P.287 'When last seen enemy was to the W . . .' Temple Patterson, *op. cit.*, p.261

p.288 'Beatty, deeply moved, stood on the poop . . .' Chalmers, W.S. *The Life and Letters of David Earl Beatty* (1951), p.262

p.289 'I ran to the quarterdeck . . .' Wrakmuseum, Cuxhaven, Zenne, copy of magazine interview: Oberheizer Zenne : Der letzte Mann der Wiesbaden 1917 (trans.)

p.290 'I had some spotting glasses . . .' *The Adventures of HMS Sparrowhawk*, in Fawcett. & Hooper, *op. cit.*, p.335–336

p.291 'The navigation apparatus had suffered severely . . .' Von Egidy, *op. cit.* p.1420

p.293 'We steamed over the scene of the action . . .' IWM Archive, Myers, manuscript

p.293 'None appeared to suffer at all . . .' *Narrative of the Commanding Officer of HMS Ardent*, in Fawcett. & Hooper, *op. cit.*, p.347

p.293 'I came across a raft full of men . . .' IWM Archive, Misc. 1010, R. Church Colln., Champion, letter

p.294 'Where are *New Zealand* and *Indefatigable*? . . .' Temple Patterson, *op. cit.*, p.261

p.295 'The biggest fright at my age . . .' IWM Archive, Misc. 1010, R. Church Colln., Hawkins, reply to questionnaire

p.295 'The ship had slowed down . . .' IWM Archive, Lorimer, manuscript

p.296 'Many did not sink immediately . . .' IWM Archive, Misc. 1010, R. Church Colln., Handley, reply to questionnaire

p.296 'When my turn came to abandon ship . . .' IWM Archive, Misc. 1010, R. Church Colln., Poole, manuscript

p.297 'As the morning drew on . . .' Quoted in Fawcett. & Hooper, *op. cit.*, p.376

p.298 'I was on duty when the fleet came in . . .' Brown & Meehan, *op. cit.*, p.101

Chapter 22: The Propaganda Battle

p.300 'This was the first that the world knew . . .' Massie, *op. cit.* p.658

p.300 'For a crucial 24 hours . . .' *Ibid*, p.659–660

p.300 'On the afternoon of Wednesday 31 May . . .' Quoted in full in Massie, *op. cit.*, p.661

p.301 'on 2 June the *Frankfurt Zeitung* . . .' Yates, *op. cit.*, p.208

p.302 'Having driven the enemy into port . . .' *Ibid*, p.211. Yates also cites the message from King George V to Jellicoe

p.302 'In a message to Jellicoe . . .' Temple Patterson, *op. cit.*, p.268

P.304 'The Germans cry loudly we've won! . . .' Quoted in Yates, *op. cit.*, p.212

Chapter 23: Who Won?

p.306 'While the losses don't look particularly uneven . . .' While all sources agree on the tally of warships sunk at Jutland, there is some discrepancy between the figures given for tonnage lost, and the number of casualties. This is in part due to confusion between standard and fully-laden displacements, and in the inclusion of badly wounded men who died after the battle, in the number of missing, and in prisoners of war. The figures given here are based on the most recent study of these losses, as outlined in Epkenhans; *Jutland* (2015)

p.306 'With the exception of the *Frauenlob* . . .' et seq., Gardiner, Robert (ed) *Conway's All the World's Fighting Ships, 1906–1921* (, 1986) p.155–162

p.308 'The average temperature . . .' Information cited here derived from interviews with Oil Industry emergency survival specialists, Aberdeen, 2014, and Staff in the Royal Naval Hospital, Haslar, 2015

p.311 'Before Jutland, Scheer's whole strategy . . .' See Wolz, *op. cit.*, p.119 and Herwig, *op. cit.*, p.143–149

p.312 'One British commentator on Jutland . . .' National Library of Scotland, Alexander, A.C.B., pamphlet, 1916: *Jutland*

Chapter 24: The Big Picture

p.314 'Four days after the battle . . .' Massie, *op. cit.*, p.662

p.317 'On 4 July, Scheer sent a report to the Kaiser . . .' et seq., cheer; *Immediatbericht*, 4 July 1916, German Ministry of Marine, manuscript.

p.318 'On the evening of 18 August . . .' Frost, *op. cit.*, p.396

p.319 'Meanwhile the U-Boat campaign . . .' Halpern, *op. cit.*, 335–369 contains a valuable account of the crisis of the U-Boat campaign in 1917, and a reliable summary of losses.

p.319 'He planned one more sortie . . .' *Ibid*, p.444–447

p.320 'Historians still disagree . . .' The effects of the economic blockade still cause controversy, largely due to the significant loss of life attributed to its effect. Accounts of the number of German casualties and indeed the impact of the blockade vary depending on the raw statistics used, and the attribution to deaths through disease and other possibly related causes, as well as to starvation. For the most part i have been guided by Osborne, Eric; *Britain's Economic Blockade of Germany, 1914–19* (2004).

Postscript

p.323 'A century ago, the SMS *König* . . .' Staff, Gary, *German Battleships 1914–18 (2): Kaiser, König and Bayern classes* (2010), p.23–38.

p.324 'It just needs a shot from either side . . .' Quoted in Brown and Meehan, *op. cit.*, p.127

p.325 'On midsummer day . . .' This account of the scuttling of the High Seas Fleet in Scapa Flow is drawn largely from Van der Vat, Dan; *The Grand Scuttle* (2007), George, S.C.; *Jutland to Junkyard* (1973) and material held in the Orkney Library and Archive, Kirkwall.

p.325 'One dreadnought had her quarterdeck awash . . .' Quoted in Brown and Meehan, *op. cit.*, p.134

A note on distance, direction and time

Throughout this book, when the term 'mile' is used, I mean a 'sea mile'. Practically, a 'sea mile' and a 'nautical mile' are the same – the first being a simplified version of the second. Historically, the nautical mile traditionally represents a minute of arc of the earth's circumference at a meridian- its 360° being divided into 60 minutes.

At the time of Jutland, a nautical mile was established as being 6,080 feet, but for all practical purposes – like navigation and gunnery – it was far more convenient to divide distances at sea up into miles which were 2,000 yards long. That was the distance known as a 'sea mile'. This in turn was divided into ten cables, each of 200 yards, or a hundred fathoms, each of six feet, or two yards. After 1925, the 'international nautical mile' was defined as being 1,852 metres long, and today that's the system everybody uses. We though, we'll stick to the 'sea mile' used at Jutland.

For more than two millennia, seafarers have used a compass to work out their direction. Everyone is familiar with its compass rose, divided into its 16 points – North, North-North-East, North-East, East-North-East, East and so on. Mariners though, preferred a compass rose with 32 points. That means inserting extra points, with a 'by' appended to them. So, between North and North-North East was North-by-East, and between South-West and South-South-West was South-West-by-South. Each of these 32 points spanned 11¼°, so a turn of three points was a 33¾° turn, and a four point one was 45°. Today, we give a ship»s direction by its compass bearing, measured in degrees (for instance 145°). In 1916 they'd call that South-East-by-South. This sounds confusing to modern ears, but for the helmsman of a Great War dreadnought, it was a terminology that had been in place for generations.

For the purposes of simplicity, in this book we're the minor difference between true and magnetic north off Jutland. Then there's the way the crewmen at Jutland told the time. Although Britain and Germany had both adopted Daylight Savings Time (DST) by late May of 1916, the German clocks were one hour ahead of British ones. I've stuck to British timekeeping throughout the book, except when the time is mentioned in a quote from a German source. In those cases the British equivalent is added in parenthesis afterwards. I have also used the 12-hour clock, as while the Royal Navy had officially embraced the 24-hour clock, the Imperial German Navy hadn't. Besides, most of those who wrote about their experiences at Jutland did so using the 12-hour clock.

Finally, ranges and distances are mentioned throughout the book. Most of these came from gunnery rangefinders, but some are merely the estimates of the men who recorded them. Some may be wrong. So too might every map in the book. There was no Satnav in those days, and navigation relied on dead reckoning. During the battle, navigators might have got it wrong.

This is summed up beautifully in the following quote from a Sub Lieutenant on a British destroyer; 'I, with sandwich and dividers in hand, pored over the chart in a vain endeavour to work out our position. It was a case of making bricks without straw, because the Captain had been far too preoccupied to jot down our many changes of course and speed. The pages of the navigator's notebook, which I had hopefully left on the chart table, were virginally blank. However, navigation was not at the forefront of our problems at the moment, and drawing an optimistic circle on the chart , I marked it 20.30 (approx).'

Index